Ripley's Believe It or Not! 2012

Executive VP Norm Deska
VP, Exhibits & Archives Edward Meyer

Publisher Anne Marshall

Editorial Director Rebecca Miles
Senior Researcher & Picture Manager James Proud
Researcher Lucas Stram
Assistant Editor Charlotte Howell
Additional Research Rosie Alexander
Text Geoff Tibballs
Additional Text James Proud
Editors Judy Barratt, Sally McFall
Factchecker Alex Bazlinton
Indexer Hilary Bird

Art Director Sam South
Design Dynamo Design
Reprographics Juice Creative

The Random House Group Limited supports The
Forest Stewardship Council (FSC), the leading
international forest certification organisation.
All our titles that are printed on Greenpeace
approved FSC certified paper carry the FSC logo.
Our paper procurement policy can be found at
www.randomhouse.co.uk/environment

No part of this publication may be reproduced in
whole or in part, or stored in a retrieval system,
or transmitted in any form or by any means,
electronic, mechanical, photocopying, recording,
or otherwise, without written permission from the
publisher. For information regarding permission,
write to VP Intellectual Property, Ripley
Entertainment Inc., Suite 188, 7576 Kingspointe
Parkway, Orlando, Florida 32819
e-mail: publishing@ripleys.com

A CIP catalogue record for this book
is available from the British Library

Printed in China

PUBLISHER'S NOTE
While every effort has been made to verify
the accuracy of the entries in this book, the
Publishers cannot be held responsible for any
errors contained in the work. They would be
glad to receive any information from readers.

WARNING
Some of the stunts and activities in this book
are undertaken by experts and should not
be attempted by anyone without adequate
training and supervision.

Ripley's Believe It or Not!®

2012

STRIKINGLY TRUE

PUBLISHING

a Jim Pattison Company

contents

Ripley's World 6

Featuring New Museum in South Korea 6, Crazy Contributors 7, Making the Lizardman 8, Ripley's Top 12 Purchases of the Year 9

Believe It! 10

Featuring Diving Horses 14, Sky-high Dining 17, Beard full of Birds 21, Mind-blowing Mummies 22, Tattooed Ladies 26, The Amazing Jumbo 30

page 15

World 34

page 35

Featuring March of the Lava 36, Starling Patterns 41, Serious Sandstorm 48, Weeping Glacier 50, Dried-up Niagara Falls 52, Ice Lighthouse 53, River Runs Red 54

Animals 56

page 241

Featuring Plant Potty 62, Exploding Ants 63, Muscle Hound 67, Spot the Caterpillar 70, Tale of Ripley the Dog 76, Lightning Cow 81, Two-legged Pig 84

Sports 86

Featuring Olympic Oddities 88, Mighty Mouth 92, Airbed Race 94, Climbing Frozen Waterfalls 95, Skiing on Sand 96, Survival Stories 98

Body 102

Featuring Presidential Portraits on a Hair 104, Magnetic Fingers 107, Belly-button Fluff Bears 108, Too Many Toes 109, Major Mite 116, Heavenly Strike 118

Transport 130

Featuring Lost Squadron 132, GatorBike 134, Parking Problem 135, Sparkling Blades 136, Monster Limo 140, Fake Porsche 142, Inflatable Tanks 143

page 136

page 161

Feats 144

Featuring Balloon Ride 149, Wall of Death 150, Human Sparkler 152, Serpent Queen 156, Ripley's Odditorium— Chicago World's Fair 161, Tightrope Terror 169

Ripley's Odditorium Special Feature

Mysteries 172

Featuring Real Fairies? 175, Extreme Ectoplasm 176, Pod People 178, Bizarre Beach Monster 180, Alien Autopsy 181

page 173

Food 182

Featuring Larvae Soup 187, Squeaky Loaf 189, Chocolate Skulls 190, Cutlery for Dinner 191, Squirrel Beer Bottles 193, Volcano Barbecue 194

Arts 196

Featuring Inflated Animals 198, Tape Jellyfish 202, Carved Pencil Tips 208, Gum Dog 210, Tabletop Landscapes 216, Plastic Penguins 218, Man-made Monsters 220

Science 224

Featuring Self-appendectomy 226, Snake Digestion 228, Hand Grafted onto Foot 229, Invisibility Coat 230

Beyond Belief 232

Featuring Hanged Elephant 234, Headstand on Glass 236, Roadside Angel 237, Dried Shark 240, King of Cobras 241, Car Coffins 242, Saved by Ears 244, Weird Airports 245

Index 246

Smallest Man

Born on June 18, 1993, Junrey Balawing of the Philippines stands just 22 in (56 cm) tall.

Believe it or Not!

RIPLEY'S WORLD

Ripley's operates with the energy of its founder, Robert Ripley, who, in 1918, began his quest to uncover the world's most unbelievable true stories.

At the time, he was working as a cartoonist at the *New York Globe*. At first, his column pinpointed unusual achievements in athletics, but he soon broadened his search into every aspect of life. Traveling endlessly to collect material, he covered more than 464,000 mi (747,000 km) in his lifetime, and his enthusiasm for the bizarre was matched only by that of his readership—the mailbags dumped on his desk contained as many as 170,000 letters a week from fans with a curious tale to tell.

The world of Ripley's is a vast, elaborate machine. There are researchers, curators, archivists and model-makers, as well as editors and correspondents who compile articles and write for the Ripley's Believe It or Not! books. Dedicated and passionate about what they do, these people never tire in their mission to uncover and preserve the unbelievable side of life.

Across the world, 31 museums showcase the Ripley's collection. On display are unforgettable exhibits supplied by the huge central archive that is kept in the vast storage warehouse at Ripley's headquarters in Orlando, Florida. This is also where all of the wax-work sculptures of extraordinary people, past and present, are conceived and lovingly brought to life (see page 8).

RIPLEY'S SOUTH KOREA

The world of Ripley's continued to expand in 2010 when a new Ripley's museum opened on Jeju Island, South Korea. Among the 600 exhibits inside the robot-shaped building is Buzz Aldrin's space suit, a meteorite from Mars, a big piece of the Berlin Wall and a collection of Ripley's South American shrunken heads.

▲ Ripley's gives special certificates to its contributors to recognize their particular achievements. Here, Gary Duschl is presented with a certificate in recognition of his 12-mi-long (19-km) gum-wrapper chain by Ripley's President, Jim Pattison, Jr.

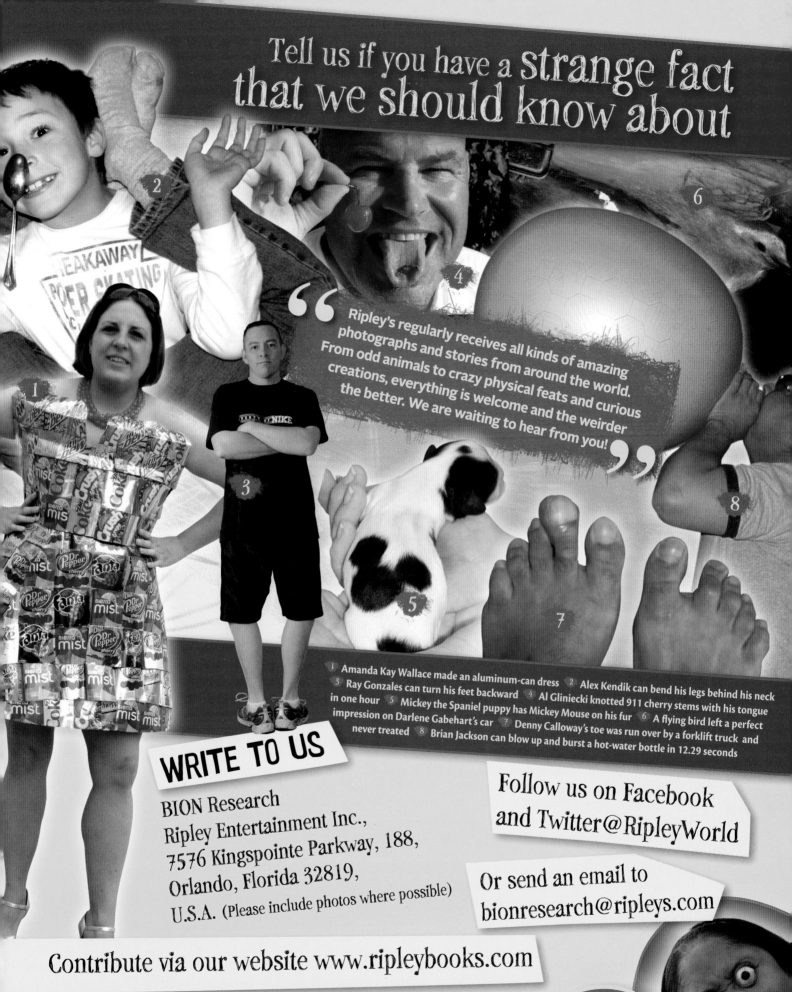

Tell us if you have a **strange fact** that we should know about

> **Ripley's regularly receives all kinds of amazing photographs and stories from around the world. From odd animals to crazy physical feats and curious creations, everything is welcome and the weirder the better. We are waiting to hear from you!**

1 Amanda Kay Wallace made an aluminum-can dress   2 Alex Kendik can bend his legs behind his neck   3 Ray Gonzales can turn his feet backward   4 Al Gliniecki knotted 911 cherry stems with his tongue in one hour   5 Mickey the Spaniel puppy has Mickey Mouse on his fur   6 A flying bird left a perfect impression on Darlene Gabehart's car   7 Denny Calloway's toe was run over by a forklift truck and never treated   8 Brian Jackson can blow up and burst a hot-water bottle in 12.29 seconds

WRITE TO US

BION Research
Ripley Entertainment Inc.,
7576 Kingspointe Parkway, 188,
Orlando, Florida 32819,
U.S.A. (Please include photos where possible)

Follow us on Facebook
and Twitter@RipleyWorld

Or send an email to
bionresearch@ripleys.com

Contribute via our website www.ripleybooks.com

Go to your phone's APP store for our eye-popping APPS!

Ripley's Believe It or Not!®

Ripley's world

1 Being immortalized for Ripley's is a messy process!

2 Erik spent two days having the casts made

3 Covering Erik's entire body makes an exact replica for the model

4 Applying finishing touches to Erik's head mold

MAKING THE LIZARDMAN

The Lizardman, also known as Erik Sprague from Austin, Texas, is one of the most iconic individuals featured in *Ripley's Believe It or Not!* A performance artist who has spent years transforming himself into a reptile-man hybrid, Erik's entire body is covered in scaly tattoos, his teeth are filed to a point, he has implants in his forehead and a forked tongue.

Ripley's wanted to immortalize the Lizardman by creating a life-size model to display in the Ripley's museums. Erik was invited to a session with the art team at Ripley's headquarters in Orlando, Florida, where his entire head, and then his body, was covered in silicone and plaster to make a mold. The final figure was formed from a hardwearing resin and has an incredible resemblance to human—or lizard—skin and flesh.

chocolate wedding favor from Michael Jackson
and Lisa-Marie Presley's wedding

Edward's Choice

Ripley's archivist, Edward Meyer, chooses his favorite acquisitions of the year—many of which are featured in this book—and lists the strangest items he bought in 2011.

Top 12 items bought by Ripley's this year

1. Two driftwood sculptures—*A Matter of Time* and *Ocean's 11th Hour*
2. Elephant armor, with replica elephant
3. Imperial jade burial suit from the Han Dynasty of ancient China
4. *Lucy in the Sky with Diamonds*, a Beatles themed art car
5. Series of portraits made from carved telephone books
6. Crucifixion portrait made from toast
7. Giant portraits of Bill and Hillary Clinton painted with hamburger grease
8. Collection of celebrity portraits made from cassette tape
9. Picture of *The Last Supper* made from laundry lint
10. Miniature writings of complete movie scripts making up pictures of scenes or characters from famous movies
11. *Cathedrals of the Sea*, a matchstick oil rig
12. Optimus Prime, a robot-transformer made from car parts

Top 12 strangest things Ripley's bought at auctions in 2011

1. Small piece of the burnt skin of an elephant from the P.T. Barnum museum fire of July 13, 1865, New York City
2. Autographed leather Michael Jackson "Bad" outfit custom-made for his chimpanzee "Bubbles"
3. Marilyn Monroe's handprint from Grauman's Chinese Theater stone slab
4. Handmade 1932 tri-plane prototype aero-car
5. Autographed metal funnel worn as a hat by the Tin Man in the 1939 movie *The Wizard of Oz*
6. Sleeping mask worn by actress Rita Hayworth in the 1940s
7. Inscribed chocolate bar that was a wedding reception favor at Michael Jackson and Lisa-Marie Presley's wedding
8. Series of five flags flown on the Moon during *Apollo* space missions and a vial of Moon dust
9. Dean Cain's *Superman* costume
10. *Apollo* space mission decontamination bootie worn by an astronaut on return to Earth
11. Michael Jackson's plaster werewolf fangs from the original *Thriller* video
12. Elvis Presley's black eyeliner make-up kit

All in a day's work...

The tragic but fascinating story of Mary, the hanged elephant, is featured in this book on page 234. How Ripley's acquired photographic evidence of this terrible event is another story in itself. Edward Meyer, Ripley's archivist, explains...

"As for the photo... The story was featured in a Ripley cartoon in the 1930s, so I knew it well and, in fact, considered it one of the strangest BION stories of all time. Just south of Orlando is where all the circuses "winter," and at least once a year Tampa has a big circus garage sale-auction. I was there to buy a 100-year-old miniature carousel, the kind used by salesmen at the turn of the century to sell actual carousels to different towns. The guy who was selling it tried to get my interest by wooing me with a box of old postcards and photos—he literally gave them to me in exchange for a good lunch. Well, the Mary photo was in this old shoebox! Also in the box was a collection of amazing Major Mite photos [see pages 116–17]."

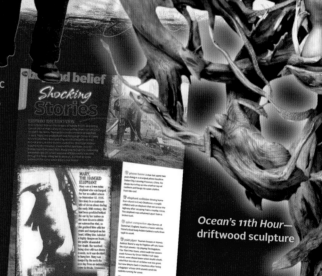

Ripley's
EXHIBITS

Ocean's 11th Hour—driftwood sculpture

food

arts

science

beyond belief

believe it!

world

animals

sports

body

transport

feats

mysteries

Burger Bill

Ripley's recently bought large portraits of Bill and Hillary Clinton made entirely from burger grease. Created by Washington artist Phil Hansen, the artworks are intended to show just how greasy fast food burgers are. Bill measures 8 x 4 ft (2.4 x 1.2 m) and was made with grease from more than 50 burgers.

Ripley's **EXHIBITS**

Ripley's Believe It or Not!

Body of Work

Ripley's Ask

A closer look at these images reveals that they are all created using the human body. By painting directly onto skin, artist Craig Tracy of New Orleans, Louisiana, manipulates the natural shape of his models against a meticulously designed background, creating mind-blowing illusions without the use of computer trickery.

Craig uses photographs to plan the image and then models often sit for hours at a time as he applies the paint, with each painting taking on average one day to complete.

How did you start painting on people? I had been a conventional professional artist for 20 years, but I never felt satisfied with what I was creating. I kept searching for a style or a technique that would not only fulfill and push me, but that would also contribute to the evolution of contemporary art. I was in my mid-thirties before I considered bodypainting as the solution to my creative dilemma. I had painted on several bodies before and the idea of taking bodypainting seriously as fine art made the difference. Only a handful of artists had approached bodypainting as fine art before me, and this allowed for plenty of room to contribute.

How long can a bodypainting take to complete? The amount of time that my work takes to produce can vary greatly. Some of my pieces incorporate custom-painted backdrops and these can easily take a full day of work or more to create and complete. Other, simpler images require only a few hours to achieve. My average bodypainting takes about eight hours to complete and about 40 minutes to photograph.

What do you like about body art as opposed to more conventional painting? In the past 30 years, I've painted on almost every surface known to man and I can unequivocally state that nothing even comes close to the beauty and complexity of working on the human body. We are the most interesting and sophisticated entity in our known universe. I've chosen to not just artistically represent the human figure, I've purposefully decided to create directly on and with the beauty and soulfulness of the human being.

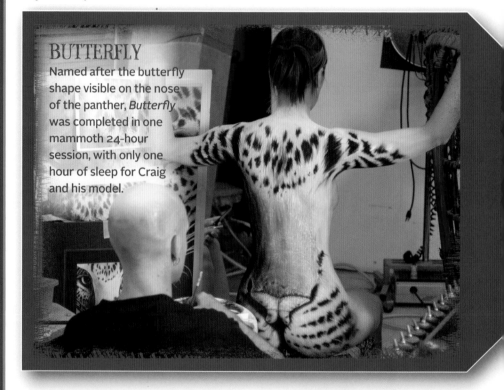

BUTTERFLY

Named after the butterfly shape visible on the nose of the panther, *Butterfly* was completed in one mammoth 24-hour session, with only one hour of sleep for Craig and his model.

IMMACULATE ▲

Immaculate features a hand-painted and airbrushed background. Once the models are in position, Craig adds the final paint to their body.

Ripley's Believe It or Not!®

High Horse

From the 1880s through to the 1970s, one of the most popular shows on the Steel Pier in Atlantic City, New Jersey, was the horse high dive. Highly trained horses, usually ridden by girls, would leap from heights of up to 60 ft (18 m) into a pool 10 ft (3 m) deep. Riders asserted at the time that the horses enjoyed diving, were excellent swimmers and were never forced to jump. However, owing to public pressure, diving horse shows died out in the 1970s and only one show remains—in a scaled-down form—in New York, where a riderless horse named Lightning will jump 10 ft (3 m) into water for a bucket of oats.

roar deal A thief in Germany stole a circus trailer in November 2009, unaware that there was a five-year-old lion in the back. The vehicle was later abandoned with its engine running after crashing into a road sign. Police believe the driver may have panicked on hearing the lion—named Caesar—let out a hungry roar.

double take When Helen MacGregor was sent a 21-year-old postcard of the town in Yorkshire, England, where she grew up, she was amazed to see herself in the center of the photo as a toddler. A friend had sent her the postcard of Otley, unaware that the child pictured in the street scene was Miss MacGregor, then aged three.

mistaken identity The dead body of a 75-year-old man slumped over a chair on the balcony of his third-floor Los Angeles, California, apartment was left undisturbed for several days in October 2009 as neighbors thought it was a Halloween dummy.

money to burn A German snowboarder stranded in the Austrian Alps for six hours in February 2010 was rescued after attracting attention by setting fire to his money. Stuck 33 ft (10 m) above ground after the ski lift was switched off at dusk, Dominik Podolsky was finally spotted by cleaners as he burned the last of his euros.

incriminating evidence An 18-year-old from Philadelphia, Pennsylvania, turned himself in to police in December 2009 for stealing a cell phone—after he took a photo of himself with it and it automatically sent a copy to the owner's e-mail!

close relatives Adopted by different families at a young age, biological brothers Stephen Goosney and Tommy Larkin finally found each other nearly 30 years later—and discovered that for the past seven months they had been living almost directly across the street from each other in Corner Brook, Newfoundland, Canada.

unexpected mourner Brazilian bricklayer Ademir Jorge Goncalves gave friends and family a surprise in November 2009 by turning up at his own funeral. Relatives had identified him as the disfigured victim of a car crash in Parana state, but actually he had been out on a drinking spree and did not hear about his funeral until it was already underway.

lottery luck Since 1993, Joan Ginther of Las Vegas, Nevada, has won the Texas Lottery four times, each time scooping at least $1 million, with total prize money of more than $20 million. She bought two of her winning tickets at the same store in Bishop, Texas, while visiting her father. Her chances of winning four lottery jackpots were put at more than 200-million-to-one.

classroom relic In June 2010, while cleaning up her classroom before a move, schoolteacher Michelle Eugenio of Peabody, Massachusetts, discovered a colonial-era document dating back to April 1792 among a pile of old books and scraps of paper.

dump dig Sanitation workers in Parsippany, New Jersey, dug through 10 tons of trash at a city dump to successfully recover a wedding ring that had been accidentally thrown away by a couple. Bridget Pericolo had placed the ring in a cup, but her husband of 55 years, Angelo, mistakenly threw it out with the garbage before leaving for work.

spelling mistake The general manager of the Chilean mint was fired after the country's name was spelt incorrectly on thousands of coins. The 2008 batch of 50-peso coins bore the stamp CHIIE, but amazingly the spelling mistake was not spotted until late 2009.

BUOYANCY CASTLE

Three men from London, England, invented a bizarre new water sport when they fulfilled an ambition to ride a full-size bouncy castle across Lake Garda in Italy in May 2010. After drifting into the path of a sailing regatta and being redirected by a police launch, adventurers Jack Watkins, Chris Hayes and Dave Sibley completed the 5-mi (8-km) voyage in two hours.

secret stash Calin Tarescu of Alba Iulia, Romania, discovered that his wife had thrown away a pair of his old shoes in which he had stashed $64,000. Police helped him to recover the majority of the money.

hand stolen The mummified hand of a cheating gambler was stolen from a locked cabinet at a pub in Wiltshire, England, in March 2010. The hand, said to have been cut off a gambler caught cheating at the card game whist, was clutching a pack of 18th-century playing cards and is rumored to be cursed.

late appointment Reynolds Smith Jr. was appointed by the Alabama Democratic Party to sit on a party panel in October 2009—even though he had died 11 months earlier!

buried alive After spending hours digging a 10-ft-deep (3-m) tunnel at a beach on Tenerife in Spain's Canary Islands, a 23-year-old German tourist had to be rescued when the sand collapsed and buried him up to his head. He was trapped on the beach for nearly two hours before 15 firefighters were able to free him.

Ripley's REVISITED

FACE PAINT

Lucky Diamond Rich is almost 100 percent covered with tattoos. Every inch of his skin is inked, including his eyelids and the insides of his ears. Lucky's incredibly dense face tattoos have developed over the last few years: He was last featured in *Ripley's Believe It or Not! Expect the Unexpected*, and his amazing transformation can clearly be seen. An international circus and street performer from Adelaide, Australia, Lucky has alloy-capped teeth with which he can perform extreme feats of strength.

Ripley's Believe It or Not!®

FAITHFUL FEET

Hua Chi, a monk at a monastery near Tongren, China, has been coming to exactly the same spot to kowtow at the temple for so many years that perfect footprints have been worn into the wooden floor. For nearly 20 years he has carefully placed his feet to bend down, and lie prostrate, two- to three-thousand times a day, although now that he's over 70 years old, he can manage only a thousand!

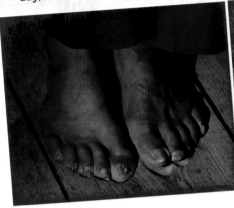

four babies Four sisters from one family each gave birth within four days in 2010. The same obstetrician delivered the babies of Lilian Sepulveda, Saby Pazos and Leslie Pazos at the same Chicago, Illinois, hospital on August 6 and 7, and a fourth sister, Heidi Lopez, gave birth in California on August 9.

200 grandkids During her life, Yitta Schwartz (1917–2010) of Kiryas Joel, New York, had 15 children, more than 200 grandchildren and a staggering total of more than 2,000 living descendants.

WORKING FLAT OUT

Hurrying to impose new parking restrictions ahead of the 2010 Tall Ships sailing races, council workers in Hartlepool, England, painted yellow lines right over a squashed, dead hedgehog in the road rather than move the animal.

cash bonfire Infamous Colombian drug baron Pablo Escobar once burned more than $1.5 million in cash to keep his daughter Manuela warm during a single night on the run. When he realized she was suffering from hypothermia at his mountain hideout, he lit a bonfire using wads of U.S. dollars.

extra time A Thai man spent three extra years behind bars in an Indonesian prison because of a typo in his paperwork. Kamjai Khong Thavorn should have been released in 2007 after serving a 20-year sentence for possessing heroin, but a clerical error wrongly stated his first year in prison as 1997 instead of 1987. The error was not spotted until 2010.

fake workers After adding biometric scanning to record employee attendance in 2009, the city of Delhi, India, discovered 22,853 fake workers on its payroll.

croc monsieur After receiving reports of a 12-ft-long (3.6-m) crocodile circling boats in the English Channel, French authorities banned swimming near Boulogne and broadcast warnings to vacationers in both French and English—only to discover that the reptile was nothing more dangerous than a floating piece of wood.

satan image A family in Budapest, Hungary, abandoned their new-look bathroom after an image of Satan appeared overnight in a tile. Emerging from her first shower in the freshly decorated room, Andrea Csrefko fled in horror when she noticed the horned head of the devil in one of the tiles. The spooky image had not been there when husband Laszlo had put the tiles up and no cleaning detergent was able to remove it.

what fire? A man in Pittsburgh, Pennsylvania, slept while his house caught fire and part of the roof collapsed. It was not until fire crews did a walk-through of the house more than two hours later that he woke up.

document leak A 2,400-page restricted document from Britain's Ministry of Defence giving advice on how to stop documents leaking onto the Internet was itself leaked onto the Internet in 2009.

unique stamp The one-of-a-kind Treskilling Yellow postage stamp is worth about $7.4 million. First issued in Sweden in 1855, it owes its value to the fact that it was printed in yellow by mistake, when the rest of the batch was green. It survives today thanks only to a 14-year-old Swedish schoolboy who rescued it from his grandmother's garbage bin in 1885 and sold it to a dealer for about $1.

end of war Although fighting in World War I finished in 1918, the war did not officially end until October 3, 2010— 92 years later—when Germany finally settled its war debt by paying $90 million, which was the last instalment of the reparations imposed on it by the Allies. Germany was forced to pay compensation toward the cost of the war by the 1919 Treaty of Versailles— the bill would have been settled much earlier but Adolf Hitler reneged on the agreement.

High Tea

Waiters serve lunch to two steel workers perched on a girder high above New York City in 1930. The men were working on the construction of the 47-story, 625-ft-high (190-m) Waldorf-Astoria Hotel on Park Avenue.

delayed delivery Gill Smeathers of Northamptonshire, England, received a package in February 2010 that was postmarked November 4, 1982.

inflated numbers During World War II, the 1,100 men of the U.S. Army's 23rd Headquarters Special Troops used inflatable vehicles, sound recordings and fake radio broadcasts to deceive the enemy into thinking they were an army of 30,000 soldiers.

mattress mishap After accidentally throwing away a mattress that her mother had stuffed with $1 million, a Tel Aviv woman searched in vain through Israeli landfill sites containing thousands of tons of garbage. She had bought her mother a new mattress as a surprise.

battle dead In 2010, Brian Freeman, a former Australian army captain, uncovered the forgotten site of a World-War-II battle in Papua New Guinea, with the bodies of three Japanese soldiers still lying where they fell in 1942. Local villagers led him to Eora Creek—the biggest single battle of the Kokoda campaign—where he found the remains of the soldiers, along with their weapons and equipment.

lucky numbers Beating astronomical odds, Ernest Pullen of Bonne Terre, Missouri, won $3 million in two separate lotteries in the space of three months. After picking up $1 million in June 2010, he won another $2 million in September, combining his lucky numbers with numbers he had dreamed about six years earlier when foreseeing that he would one day win a lot of money.

own phone After his cell phone was stolen, a Californian man bought a new one on classifieds website Craigslist, choosing it because it looked just like his old phone. When it arrived, it actually was his old phone and still had his numbers stored. Luckily for the police, the thief had put his return address on the package.

balloon daredevils Early balloonists used highly flammable hydrogen gas instead of hot air or helium. In 1785, the French inventor Jean-Pierre Blanchard and American John Jeffries used an early hydrogen gas balloon to fly across the English Channel between England and France. When Jean-François Pilâtre de Rozier attempted to do the same, his balloon exploded and he became the first to die in an air accident.

Tim on chewing molten lead:

"Fire-eaters have been doing this stunt for over 200 years, and the technique is still a closely guarded secret. Just like fire-eating, it takes years of practice before you can be ready to perform, and even then it is still highly dangerous. First, the metal is melted in a small furnace, and then a small amount (about a tablespoon) is transferred to a spoon. I then take this into my mouth and keep it there until it solidifies completely. After about 30 seconds I spit the nugget out onto a tray or catch it with a pair of thick gloves."

Tim Cockerill, aka The Great Inferno, happily gargles hot molten lead until it cools and hardens into solid metal in his mouth. During the day, Tim is a zoologist at Cambridge University in the U.K.

When he is not working in the lab, or trekking through a jungle to study insects, Tim wows audiences with such stunts as heating his tongue with a blowtorch, swallowing fire, and hammering nails into his head. The Great Inferno has been amazing audiences for 15 years with his extremely painful-looking acts.

The Great Inferno

Tim on the blowtorch stunt:

"The blowtorch stunt is one of the most difficult of the fire-eater's stunts to perform. With a flame that burns at around 1600°C [2,900°F], there is no margin for error—any hesitation would result in a serious burn. There is no real secret here, but the trick is to come at the flame with confidence and respect. This is one stunt that is just as intimidating no matter how many times you perform it!"

Tim on the blockhead stunt:

"The Human Blockhead was invented in the 1930s by sideshow performer Melvin Burkhart, 'The Anatomical Wonder.' What you see is what you get with this stunt—a solid steel nail is hammered all the way into the face. This is not something to be tried by anyone—get the angle wrong and the nail would go straight through the skull and into the brain!"

Ripley's Believe It or Not!®

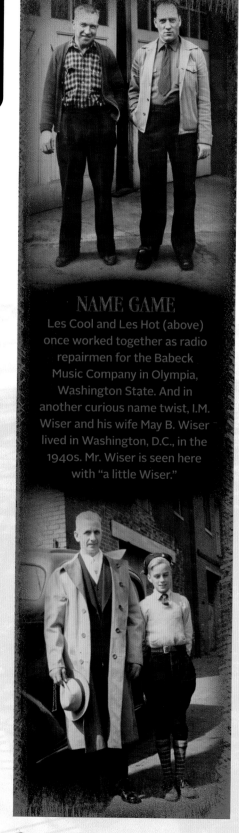

NAME GAME

Les Cool and Les Hot (above) once worked together as radio repairmen for the Babeck Music Company in Olympia, Washington State. And in another curious name twist, I.M. Wiser and his wife May B. Wiser lived in Washington, D.C., in the 1940s. Mr. Wiser is seen here with "a little Wiser."

small world In 1980, when Alex and Donna Voutsinas lived in different countries and long before they met and married, they were captured in the same photo at Walt Disney World, Orlando, Florida. Five-year-old Donna was photographed at the same moment as three-year-old Alex, who then lived in Montréal, Canada, was being pushed down Main Street in a stroller by his father.

same name In 2009, 77-year-old retired policeman Geraint Woolford was admitted to Abergele Hospital in North Wales and placed in a bed next to a 52-year-old Geraint Woolford, unrelated and also a retired policeman! The two men had never met before and checks showed they are the only two people in the whole of Great Britain named Geraint Woolford.

short journey Six-year-old Heidi Kay Werstler tossed a message in a bottle into the sea at Ocean City, New Jersey, in 1985 and it washed ashore 24 years later at Duck, North Carolina—less than 300 mi (480 km) away.

spoon dig A female convict used a spoon to dig her way out of a prison in Breda in the Netherlands, in February 2010. Using the spoon, she dug a tunnel under the cellar of the prison's kitchen to the outside world.

treasure trove A Scottish game warden who bought a metal detector for a new hobby struck gold on his very first treasure hunt, discovering a $1.5 million hoard of Iron-Age jewelry. Five days after taking delivery of the detector and just seven steps into his first hunt, David Booth unearthed four 2,300-year-old items made of pure gold—the most significant discovery ever of Iron-Age metalwork in Scotland.

force farce The entire police force in a Hungarian town quit after winning more than $15 million on the lottery in 2009. The 15-strong squad in Budaörs resigned immediately after scooping the jackpot.

shoe thief A second-hand shoe store owner stole more than 1,200 pairs of designer shoes by posing as a mourner at hospitals and funeral homes in South Korea. His victims were genuine friends and relatives of the deceased, who had slipped off their shoes in a traditional demonstration of respect. The thief would remove his own footwear, pay his respects, then put on a more expensive pair and walk off.

last post A postcard bringing holiday news to a couple in West Yorkshire, England, was delivered in 2009—40 years after it was posted.

family graduation Chao Muhe, 96, and his grandson Zhao Shuangzhan, 32, both graduated from university in June 2009. Retired lecturer Chao, who enrolled to set an example to his grandson, earned a master's degree in philosophy from the University of South China in Taiwan, while Zhao graduated from Chung Hua University. During the six-year course, Chao never missed a class despite needing to get up at 5 a.m. every day to catch several buses to the university.

vader raider In July 2010, a man robbed a bank in Setauket, New York State, dressed in the mask and cape of Darth Vader, the villain from the *Star Wars* movies.

bad timing At Lowestoft, Suffolk, England in 2010, an unlucky 13-year-old boy was struck by lightning at 13.13 on Friday, August 13. Thankfully, he suffered only minor burns and made a full recovery.

winner winner A store in Winner, South Dakota, sold the winning ticket, worth $232 million, in the drawing of the Powerball Lottery on May 27, 2009.

thumb find When fisherman Blake Robinson caught a 6½-lb (2.9-kg) lake trout at Flaming Gorge Reservoir, Wyoming, he discovered a human thumb inside it.

crushed crustacean A lobster became one of the last casualties of World War II when it was blown up inside an unexploded mine in 2009. The crustacean had made its home inside the 600-lb (272-kg) mine that had lay dormant on the seabed off the coast of Dorset, England, for more than 60 years—but when the Royal Navy's bomb disposal unit tried to coax it out before detonating the device, it refused to move and instead delivered a nasty nip to the divers.

watch returned A pocket watch was returned to the family of Welsh sailor Richard Prichard in 2009—128 years after his death. In 2000, diver Rich Hughes had been exploring the wreck of Prichard's ship—the *Barbara*—that sank in 1881, when he found the watch. After nine years of painstaking research, he was finally able to identify the owner's family and give the watch back.

Singing Bar With Venezuela suffering from serious water and energy shortages in 2009, the country's President Hugo Chavez ordered his citizens to stop singing in the shower. He hoped the ban would limit the amount of time people spent using water in the bathroom.

SWING THE LIZARD

As a change from roaming the grassland at India's Corbett National Park, an Indian elephant named Madhuri picked up a passing monitor lizard and played with it for several days. With the lizard's tail firmly grasped in her trunk, she carried it with her wherever she went, swinging it around in the air over and over again, sometimes tossing it high and even dropping it before finally letting the dazed reptile go.

Watch the Beardie

Charles Earnshaw of Anchorage, Alaska, displays his "Beards of a Feather" facial hair sculpture at the 2010 U.S. National Beard and Mustache Championships in Bend, Oregon. There were over 200 entrants, and this creation earned him a prize in the freestyle section.

BUDDHIST MONK

Thai Buddhist monk Loung Pordaeng died in 1973, but to this day remains sitting in the Lotus position, the very position in which he died—naturally mummified in a temple on the Thai island of Koh Samui. Two months before he died at the age of 79, Loung believed his death to be imminent and asked that if his body did not decompose could it stay on display in the temple to inspire future generations to follow Buddhism. He meditated in silence for the final week of his life, eating and drinking nothing, and when he died his wishes were carried out. Local monks added a pair of sunglasses when his eyes eventually fell into his head.

ANCIENT TATTOOS

In 2006, a 1,500-year-old, heavily tattooed and very well-preserved female mummy was discovered in a mud-brick pyramid in northern Peru. She was buried with many weapons, leading experts to believe that she could have been a rare warrior queen of the warlike Moche people.

BABY MUMMY

This incredibly well-preserved, mummified body of a young Peruvian child, who died some 6,500 years ago, is one of the oldest mummies ever found, and is hundreds of years older than the earliest known Egyptian mummies. It formed part of the largest collection of mummies ever assembled, which went on display at the California Science Center in Los Angeles in 2010.

® RIPLEY RESEARCH

Mummification—where skin, soft flesh and hair remain on the bones—can preserve the human body for thousands of years. It can be achieved intentionally, such as with the elaborate Egyptian embalming ritual where the organs are removed from the body, or it can occur completely naturally. Natural mummification generally requires a dry atmosphere and a lack of oxygen to keep the natural process of decay at bay.

EGYPTIAN CAT

[Th]e ancient Egyptians, who practiced mummification on [roy]al personages, also [m]ummified animals. These underwent the same elaborate [t]reatment as human corpses, with cloth [wr]aps, a large amount [o]f salt and resin. This [E]gyptian cat is more [t]han 2,000 years old.

THE ICE MAIDEN OF AMPATO

The frozen, mummified body of a teenage Incan girl was discovered near the 20,700-ft (6,310-m) summit of Mount Ampato, Peru, in 1995. It is thought that she was ritually sacrificed more than 500 years ago. Other mummified children have also been found on the mountain. The "Ice Maiden," as she is known, was removed from the site and is kept under controlled conditions in a Peruvian museum.

Mummies

ANCIENT BEAUTY

[In 1]934, a Swedish archeologist discovered hundreds of ancient [m]ummies buried under boats in a mysterious cemetery in a remote [d]esert in the Xinjiang region of China. The location, which featured [ri]vers and lakes thousands of years ago, was lost until 2000, [an]d researchers began to excavate the area in 2003. [Th]ey found the body of a woman thought to have [di]ed almost 4,000 years ago, who has become [kn]own as the most beautiful mummy [in] the world, owing to incredibly [w]ell-preserved features that [e]ven include her eyelashes.

Ripley's Believe It or Not!®

gold rush A huge 220-lb (100-kg) Canadian gold coin was sold at auction to a Spanish company for $4 million in 2010. One of only five $1 million Maple Leaf coins ever produced by the Royal Canadian Mint, it measures 21 in (53 cm) in diameter and is 1¼ in (3 cm) thick.

changing fortunes Brothers Zsolt and Geza Peladi were homeless and living in a cave outside Budapest, Hungary, when they discovered in December 2009 that they were due to inherit part of their grandmother's multi-billion euro fortune.

dummy guard In July 2010, two prisoners escaped from a jail in Argentina that, because of a lack of resources, was using a dummy to man one of its guard towers. Staff had put a prison officer's cap on a football to try to fool the convicts into thinking they were being watched from the tower by a real person.

blood match Eight years after breaking into a house in rural Tasmania, Australia, Peter Cannon was convicted of armed robbery because his DNA matched that of blood found inside a leech at the scene of the crime.

PIGLET BANK

An Internet site is selling a piggy bank made from a real piglet! The brainchild of designer Colin Hart from Belfast, Northern Ireland, the taxidermied pig with a slot in its back costs $4,000 and must be ordered 12 months in advance.

picture perfect When Royal Dutch Navy sergeant Dick de Bruin lost his camera while scuba diving off the Caribbean island of Aruba, he thought he would never see it again. However, seven months later the camera was found 1,130 mi (1,800 km) away by a coastguard at Key West, Florida—and although it was covered in crusty sea growth, it still worked.

remote patrol Burglars who broke into a man's apartment in Midwest City, Oklahoma, were caught via webcam by the man's wife more than 8,000 mi (12,875 km) away in the Philippines. Jim and Maribel Chouinard used the webcam to communicate face-to-face when they were apart.

old student A woman in China became an elementary school pupil at age 102. Ma Xiuxian from Jinan, Shandong Province, started work in a cotton mill at age 13 but had always longed for a proper education. So in 2010—89 years after leaving school—the grandmother went back, joining the grade one class at Weishan Road Elementary School. She uses hearing aids to make sure she can hear the teacher and a magnifying glass to help read text books.

frozen assets In May 2010, the Iowa Court of Appeals ordered the family of Orville Richardson, who died in February 2009 at age 81, to exhume his body so that his head could be cut off and frozen. In 2004, he had signed a contract with an Arizona company and paid $53,500 to have his head placed in cryogenic suspension after his death, but his siblings had buried him instead.

GO SLOW

Road safety campaigners in Canada encouraged motorists to reduce their speed by painting a large 3-D image of a child on to the road outside an elementary school in West Vancouver, British Columbia. The picture of a girl chasing after a ball appeared to come alive when drivers were 100 ft (30 m) away, giving them time to slow down.

ant arsonists A 2009 house fire in Daytona Beach, Florida, was started by ants. Dozens of carpenter ants had built their nest around an electrical box and, when the insects came in contact with the live wiring, they ignited. The resulting flames burst out of the box, set fire to an adjacent desk and then spread to the rest of the house.

dead candidate Carl Robin Geary Sr. was elected mayor of Tracy City, Tennessee, on April 13, 2010, several weeks after he had died.

parallel lives Identical twins Jim Lewis and Jim Springer from Ohio were separated a month after birth, then reunited at age 39. Both had divorced a Linda, married a Betty, had sons named James, driven blue Chevrolets and owned dogs named Toy.

lennon's toilet A toilet once owned by Beatle John Lennon was sold for the grand sum of $14,740 in 2010. The builder who had removed the lavatory from Lennon's Berkshire, England, home in 1971 kept it in his shed for almost 40 years.

granny auction Ten-year-old Zoe Pemberton of Essex, England, put her grandmother Marion Goodall up for sale on eBay in 2009, describing her as "cuddly" but "'annoying." Although the listing was meant as a joke, bidding for the granny reached $30,000 before the auction website took it down.

soap drama A wife from Pune, Maharashtra, India, divorced her husband in August 2009 on the grounds that his refusal to allow her to watch her favorite soap operas on TV amounted to a form of domestic cruelty.

Long Hair

▶ When Tran Van Hay from Vietnam died in February 2010 his hair measured 22 ft (6.7 m) in length and weighed more than 23 lb (10.5 kg). He had not cut his hair for 50 years.

▶ Sardar Pishora Singh from India spent eight years cultivating a 3½-in-long (9-cm) eyebrow hair.

▶ When measured in 2004, Chinese Xie Quiping's hair measured 18 ft (5.5 m) in length. It had been growing for over 30 years without a trim.

▶ Justin Shaw from Miami has hair on his arms that measures 5¾ in (14.6 cm) in length.

▶ Brian Peterkin-Vertanesian from Washington, D.C., has a bizarre single eyebrow hair that has grown to more than 6 in (15 cm) in length.

▶ When Wesley Pemberton of Texas measured his leg hair in 2007, one of them was 6½ in (16.5 cm) long.

▶ Badamsinh Juwansinh Gurjar grew his mustache for 22 years, until it reached a length of 12½ ft (3.8 m).

▶ Norway's Hans Langseth died in 1927 with a beard that measured 17½ ft (5.3 m).

Ear Wig

Radhakant Bajpai has a striking claim to fame: magnificent ear tufts that are longer than the hair on most men's heads, and probably the longest ear hair in the world. When Radhakant's hair was officially measured last, it stretched 5.2 in (13.2 cm), but since then it has more than doubled to a reported 11 in (28 cm). Although some think that his extreme ear hair is odd, Radhakant is very proud of his achievement.

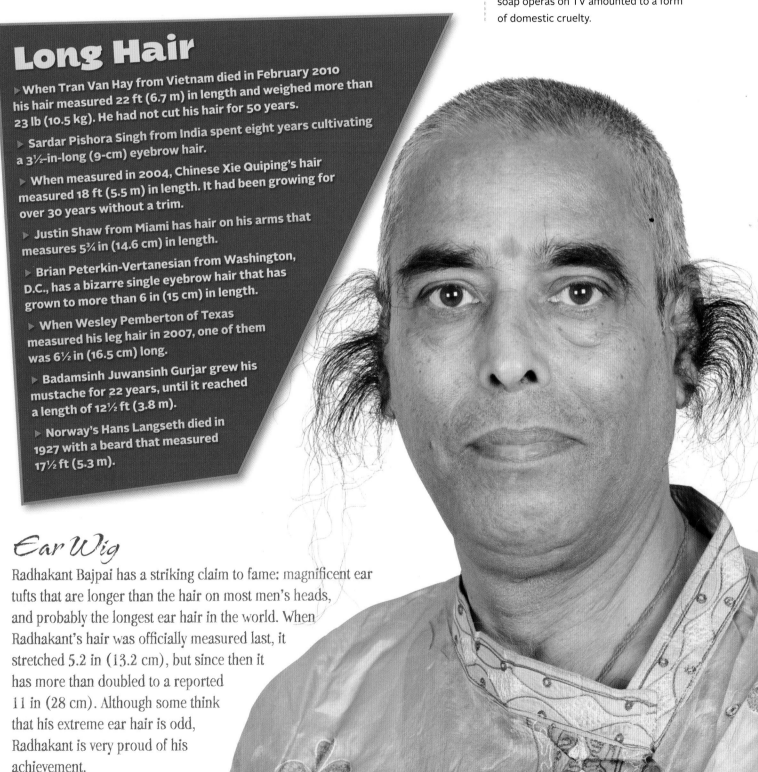

Tattooed Ladies

The tattooed lady was an astonishing and beautiful addition to the circus sideshows, dime museums and carnivals that were found in North America and Europe in the late 19th century. They featured in such shows until the late 20th century, when the last tattooed lady retired, aged 80, in 1995.

TRIBAL CUSTOM

The outlandish stories of Nora Hildebrandt and Irene Woodward (see far right) were perhaps based on the true tale of Olive Oatman. In 1850, as she traveled with her family in a wagon train, they were attacked by Yavapai Indians. She and her sister were the only ones to survive and were sold to the Mojave tribe, who treated Olive kindly but tattooed her chin in keeping with tribal custom. Olive was content with her captors and was reluctant to leave the Mojave tribe when she was "rescued" two years later.

Olive Oatman

Betty Broadbent

TATTOO BARGAIN

As a young girl, Lady Viola had made an agreement with her family that if she trained as a nurse she could do anything she liked afterward. Once qualified, she kept them to their word and got her first tattoo. Often billed as "The Most Beautiful Tattooed Woman in the World," Lady Viola's tattoos included the portraits of six U.S. presidents across her chest. The Capitol decorated her back, the Statue of Liberty and Rock of Ages her legs. During the outdoor season in the 1930s, she worked with the Ringling Brothers Circus, while winter months found her in dime museums, such as Gorman's in Philadelphia. She was still working at the age of 73.

Lady Viola

DISOWNED

Betty was born in 1909. During a girls' weekend in Atlantic City, New Jersey, she got a small tattoo and, as a result, her family disowned her. She claimed she had no other choice but to get more tattoos and make a career out of them. Betty worked with many circuses and was an attraction at the 1939 New York World's Fair with the "John Hix Strange as it Seems" sideshow.

INK REPELLANT

One of the first Western women to be significantly tattooed was Irene Woodward. On her debut in 1882, she scandalized the public with her tattoos, which had previously only been seen on sailors. Inked by her father, Irene maintained (probably not truthfully) that he did it to protect her from being captured by American Indians. Described on one show billboard as "A pretty picturesque specimen of punctured purity," she was a shy and dignified performer.

Irene Woodward

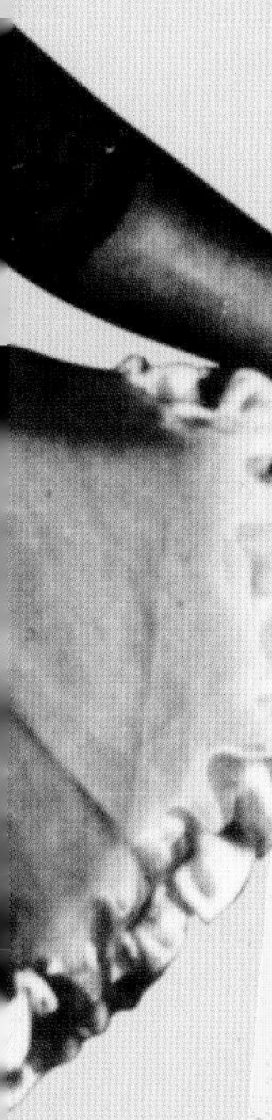

SHOCKING STORY

Every great tattooed lady had a sensational story, and Nora Hildebrandt dramatically claimed that she'd been forcibly tattooed by American Indians while tied to a tree for a year. She even said that Sitting Bull was involved in the murky affair. The truth was a little less scandalous— Nora's father tattooed soldiers fighting in the Civil War and used to practice his designs on his daughter. By the time she began to exhibit herself in 1882, she had 365 tattoos.

Nora Hildebrandt

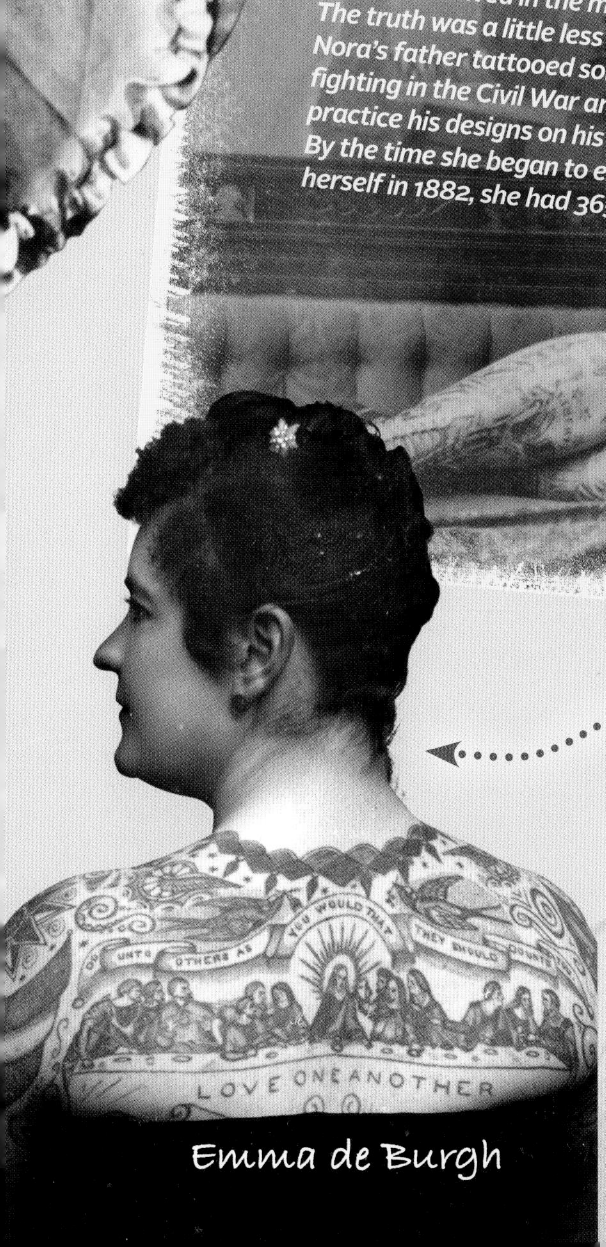

MARRIAGE OF EQUALS

One night in July 1885, the audience at the Sells Brothers Circus in Burlington, Iowa, got a surprise. During the performance, tattooed Frank de Burgh came into the ring bare-chested to marry Emma Kohl, who wore a revealing costume that showed off her own wonderful designs.

Emma de Burgh

SNAKE CHARMER

In the late 19th and early 20th century, it was fashionable for aristocrats, including women, to be tattooed. Lady Randolph Churchill, Winston Churchill's mother, had a snake tattooed on her wrist. Tattoos then were very expensive. Later, as costs came down, tattooing was adopted by the lower classes and the practice fell out of favor with the social élite.

Ripley's Believe It or Not!®

Nose for Trouble

An anti-landmine organization based in Belgium uses African giant pouched rats to sniff out deadly landmines in Mozambique and Tanzania. The rats' relatively light weight means they are unlikely to explode the mines, even when scratching at the ground to indicate their whereabouts. These super rats, trained with food rewards, can also smell the life-threatening disease tuberculosis, analyzing samples more than 50 times quicker than a laboratory scientist.

surprise visit After nine-year-old Beatrice Delap wrote to Captain Jack Sparrow—Johnny Depp's character in the *Pirates of the Caribbean* movies—asking for help with an uprising against teachers at her school in Greenwich, London, Depp responded by turning up at the school in full pirate costume. The Hollywood star was in the area filming the fourth movie in the series in October 2010 and gave the school 10 minutes' notice that he was on his way.

deadly shock A 70-year-old Indian man was so shocked to receive a bogus receipt for his own cremation service that he suffered a fatal heart attack. Horrified to read that he had supposedly been cremated the week before, dairy farmer Frail Than Singh collapsed with chest pains—and his body was subsequently delivered to the same crematorium in Ghaziabad and given the same serial number, 89, as listed on the fake letter.

unlucky number Superstitious phone company bosses in Bulgaria suspended a jinxed cell phone number—0888 888 888—in 2010 after all three customers to whom it had been assigned over the previous ten years suffered untimely deaths.

identical couples Identical twin brothers married identical twin sisters in a joint wedding ceremony in China. Grooms Yang Kang and Yang Jian sported different haircuts for the ceremony so that people could tell them apart, while brides Zhang Lanxiang and Jiang Juxiang wore differently colored dresses.

ghostly sale Two vials said to contain the spirits of ghosts exorcised from a house in Christchurch, New Zealand, were sold on an online auction site for more than $1,500 in March 2010. The sales pitch claimed that the "holy water" in the vials had dulled the spirits' energy and put them to sleep. To revive them, the buyer would need to pour the contents into a dish and let them "evaporate into your house." The seller, Avie Woodbury, said that once an exorcist's fee had been deducted, the proceeds of the spirit sale would go to an animal welfare group.

sold soul More than 7,000 online shoppers unwittingly agreed to sell their souls in 2010, thanks to a clause in the terms and conditions of a British computer-game retailer. As an April Fool's Day joke to highlight the fact that online shoppers do not read the small print, GameStation added a clause to its contract granting it a "non transferable option to claim, for now and for ever more, your immortal soul."

lucky seven On March 31, 2010, the four-number state lottery in Pennsylvania came up 7-7-7-7 and had a $7.77 million payout!

DEAD RINGER

Biker David Morales Colón of San Juan, Puerto Rico, became a dead ringer for his idol Meat Loaf by attending his own funeral in 2010 on the back of his beloved Honda motorcycle. So that friends could pay their respects at his wake, undertakers mounted his embalmed body carefully on the machine, hiding a series of body braces beneath his clothes and covering his eyes with wraparound sunglasses.

ruff justice In Athens, Georgia, a woman scared off a would-be burglar by acting like a dog. Police said she got on the floor and began scratching at the door and acting like a large dog when the intruder tried turning the door knob—he then ran away.

kept corpses Jean Stevens of Bradford County, Pennsylvania, lived with the corpse of her dead husband for ten years and with the body of her dead twin sister for almost a year. After they died, she had their embalmed bodies dug up and stored at her house. She maintained the immaculately dressed corpses as best she could, spraying sister June with expensive perfume and keeping her on a couch in a spare room while husband James rested on a couch in the garage.

frustrated caller A woman from Clarksville, Tennessee, was arrested in 2009 after she kept calling 911 to complain that a man refused to marry her.

OFF ROAD
Lin Su from China drove his brand new Subaru SUV 100 ft (30 m) into the sea from Sanya beach, Hainan Province, in 2010, before getting out and leaving his vehicle in the waves. He announced that the car was no longer needed, and that he had abandoned it as an offering to the Chinese dragon water god, to ask for respite for recent severe flooding. The Subaru was eventually salvaged from the sea by the police.

confused clergy Two female clerics at the same church in Cambridgeshire, England, share the same three names—Rhiannon Elizabeth Jones. Both are also graduates of the same college.

antique gown When three-month-old George Parfitt was baptized in Devon, England, in 2009, he wore the same antique christening gown that had been used by 20 members of his family since it was made by his great-great-great-grandmother in 1884.

lung stolen Organizers offered $2,000 for the return of a left lung that was stolen from a traveling exhibition of human cadavers in Peru in 2009.

BEARDED MOTHER
Richard Lorenc of Kansas finally tracked down his birth mother in 2010—and discovered that she is a famous bearded lady who as a young girl worked in a circus sideshow. Vivian Wheeler boasts an 11-in-long (28-cm) beard, as a result of inheriting the condition hypertrichosis, also known as werewolf syndrome, which causes the growth of excessive facial hair from an early age.

prize catch Barbara and Dennis Gregory of Johannesburg, South Africa, lost their camera when it dropped into the sea from the *Queen Mary 2* cruise ship en route from New York to Southampton in 2008. Sixteen months later, Spanish fisherman Benito Estevez found the camera in his nets and traced the couple after posting the photographs online.

cash stash Four children aged between 10 and 13 who found $20,000 stuffed in a brown envelope on their way to school in Frankfurt, Germany, shared it out among their friends in the playground. After teachers were alerted, police managed to recoup most of the cash.

grim find A Dutch riverboat captain who dropped anchor in the River Danube in Austria had a surprise when he raised it. He hauled up a BMW car—with the dead driver still behind the steering wheel.

prison landing A driver escaping from police officers in Cleveland, Ohio, abandoned his car after a 90-mph (145-km/h) chase and jumped a fence—only to land in the yard of the state women's prison where he was quickly arrested.

all the nines Henry Michael Berendes of Wisconsin was born at 9.09 a.m. on 9-9-09 and weighed 9 lb 9 oz (4.3 kg).

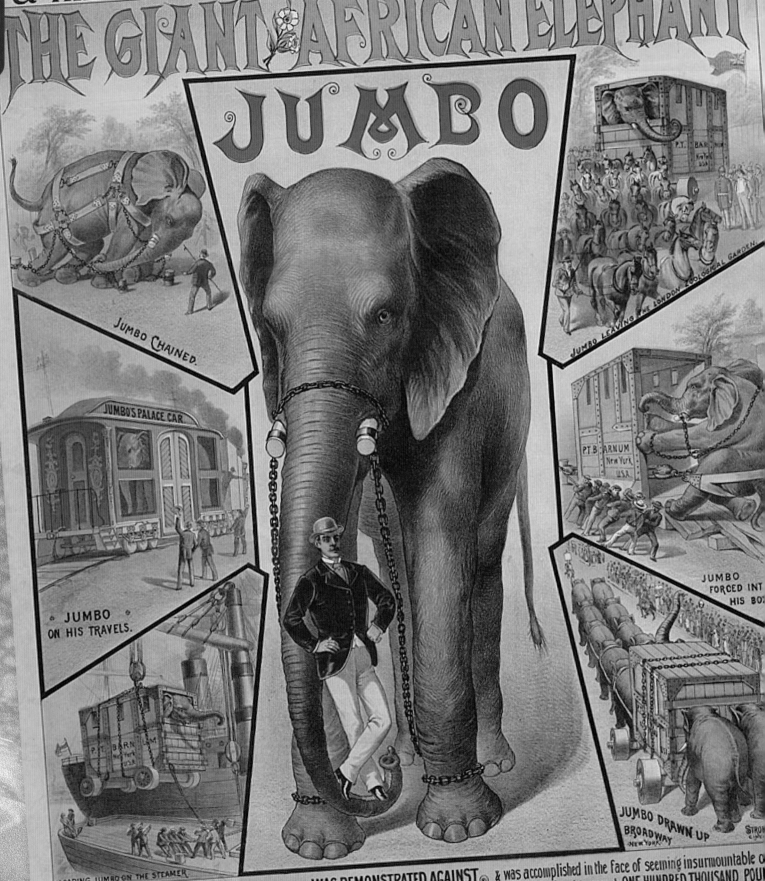

Jumbo was an African elephant of monumental proportions, and he enjoyed fame on both sides of the Atlantic every bit as huge as his stature. At the end of the 19th century, he drew crowds in the same way that a baseball team would today, won the heart of a queen, and became an advertising superstar, before dying a hero's death.

Jumbomania, as it was called, began in 1861 when the elephant was captured in the French Sudan and then exported to the Jardins des Plantes Zoo in Paris, France. He then moved on to London Zoo, where he became famous for giving rides to visitors. Placed under such unnatural restraints, Jumbo's patience wore thin. The elephant, whose name was based on jumbe, the Swahili word for "chief," became too hot to handle and he was sold to "The Greatest Show on Earth"—the Barnum & Bailey Circus based in the U.S.A. The whole British nation rose up to protest. Crowds converged on the zoo, legal proceedings against the decision began, and Queen Victoria, herself a huge fan, received 100,000 letters appealing for her to intervene. American P.T. Barnum was offered £100,000 in exchange for the precious elephant, but in a moment of huge showbiz drama, the offer was refused. Jumbo was to be shipped out of London for good.

▲ ON LEAVING LONDON ZOO, ALL MANNER OF JUMBO MEMORABILIA APPEARED, EVEN A SPOOF MEMORIAL CARD FROM JUMBO'S "WIFE," ANOTHER ELEPHANT AT THE ZOO.

WHAT HAPPENED TO JUMBO?▼

After his death, the *New York Times* reported that taxidermists had removed Jumbo's hide—which weighed 1,600 lb (726 kg) and needed 100 tons of salt and 100 lb (45 kg) of elm bark to cure it—and bones. His skeleton was given to New York's Museum of Natural History, and his heart was bought by Cornell University. The rest of his body was cremated. His stuffed hide traveled with the circus until Barnum donated it to Tufts University, near Boston (see left), where Jumbo became the official mascot. He was displayed there until destroyed by a fire in 1975.

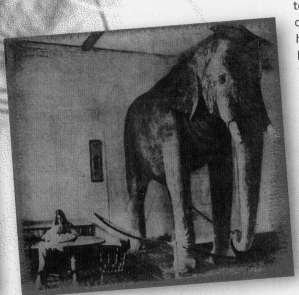

A HEROIC END ▲

On the night of September 15, 1885, the circus was showing in St. Thomas, Ontario. Its 29 elephants had finished their routines and were being led from the big top to their railway cars. Only Jumbo and the smallest elephant, Tom Thumb, remained to take a final bow. Afterward, as they walked back to their carriages, reports say that Jumbo saw Tom Thumb wander onto the railtrack and rushed toward him to lead him to safety. Before he could get there, an unscheduled express train hit Tom. The train derailed, and Jumbo was crushed by the flying wreckage, his skull broken in 100 places. His devoted keeper, Matthew Scott, who had come with Jumbo to the U.S.A. in 1882, stayed with him until he died on the sidings.

Fun
FUNERALS

● Although Ozella McHargue of St. John, Indiana, died in September 2004, her family gave her a Christmas-themed funeral—with holly, mistletoe and "Rudolph the Red-Nosed Reindeer"—because she loved Christmas so much.

● Ice-cream salesman Derek Greenwood of Rochdale, England, had a funeral cortege of 12 ice-cream vans all playing their jingles on the way to the cemetery.

● For the 2004 funeral of Maine tractor enthusiast Harold Peabody, his son led a procession of antique tractors to the cemetery.

● Arne Shield always wanted a Viking-themed funeral—so his ashes were put on a papier-maché Viking ship, set ablaze, and cast adrift on Lake Michigan.

● A Queensland, Australia, funeral firm offers the deceased the opportunity to be transported to the cemetery on a Fat Boy Harley-Davidson motorbike hearse.

KICKING THE BUCKET

Gaetano Di Furia's coffin was carried to his funeral in Lincolnshire, England, in the bucket of a JCB digger. His family chose it instead of a traditional hearse because he had always enjoyed driving JCBs at work.

same name Even though he had no connection with the town, Eric Gordon Douglas, of Edinburgh, Scotland, left over $17,000 in his will to Douglas, Isle of Man, simply because it shared his surname.

family church When Daryl McClure married Dean Sutcliffe at St. Michael's and All Angels' Church in Ashton-under-Lyne, Greater Manchester, England, in August 2010, she became the seventh generation of her family to marry at that church. At least 11 members of her family have been married there since 1825, but the connection could date back as far as the 17th century.

long dead Tokyo officials trying to update their list of centenarians in preparation for Japan's Respect for the Elderly Day in September 2010 discovered that the city's "oldest man" had actually died more than 30 years earlier. Police said Sogen Kato, who was born in July 1899 and would therefore have been 111, was discovered lying in his bed in a mummified state, wearing pajamas and covered with a blanket.

you can't hurry love A couple with a combined age of 184 married in England in July 2010. After a four-year courtship, Henry Kerr, 97, tied the knot with 87-year-old Valerie Berkowitz in North London.

body snatchers The New York Police Department towed away an illegally parked funeral van in March 2010—with a corpse inside. Funeral director Paul DeNigris had parked his 2002 Dodge minivan outside the funeral home while he went inside on business, but he returned to find the vehicle—and the body in the back—had been towed to the city pound. He had to rush there to reclaim the corpse and put it on a flight to Miami, where it was headed for cremation.

faint pulse Pronounced dead three hours after suffering a suspected heart attack, Jozef Guzy of Katowice, Poland, was about to be sealed up in a coffin when a funeral director detected a faint pulse. Mr Guzy, 76, was taken to hospital where mystified doctors could find nothing wrong with him, and a few days later he was sent home.

MODEL FATHER

When Paul Challis of Cheshire, England, died aged 38, his widow Maria wanted to keep his memory alive for their two children by creating a life-size cardboard cutout of her late husband to live in the family home. The 6-ft-1-in (1.8-m) 2-D father was a guest at his own funeral and a few weeks later even attended a friend's wedding.

video girlfriend In 2009, a man in Tokyo, Japan, married his animated video-game girlfriend—who exists only in a Nintendo DS game—in a public ceremony complete with a priest, a DJ, and speeches from friends and family.

macabre marriage To mark the end of his bachelor days bridegroom Pat Vincent arrived for his wedding in London, England, in 2009 in a coffin. After marrying Jacqueline Brick, he climbed back into the wooden box and was carried by train to the reception.

age gap A couple who married in Guriceel, Somalia, in 2009 had an age difference of 95 years. Ahmed Muhamed Dore, who claimed to be 112, wed 17-year-old Safia Abdulleh, making him old enough to be her great-great-great grandfather.

ASH MAN

Artist Daniel Roberto Ortega from San Diego, California, turns the ashes of dead people and pets into cherished works of art. His first human cremation piece included the ashes of his late father. Bereaved relatives or pet owners send the former mortician's assistant ashes and bone fragments, together with a photograph and biography. He mixes the cremated remains into a paste, adds artifacts representing aspects of the subject's life, and then paints the resulting pattern before drying it and applying an acrylic finish.

arts

science

beyond belief

believe it!

world

animals

sports

body

transport

feats

mysteries

food

Driftwood Sculpture

Floridian artist Paul Baliker carved this magnificent sculpture from driftwood found at Cedar Key, Florida. *Ocean's 11th Hour* is 8 ft (2.4 m) wide and features 22 endangered ocean creatures encircling Father Time at its center.

Ripley's
EXHIBITS

Ripley's
Believe It or Not!®

March of the Lava

The active volcano of Kilauea in Hawaii has been constantly erupting since 1983, and its unstoppable flow of burning lava has devastated hundreds of homes and businesses in its vicinity. Incredibly, it has also gradually extended Hawaii's coastline by an area the size of Washington, D.C.

In 1990, the entire town of Kaimū and part of the town of Kalapana were buried under 50 ft (15 m) of slow-moving lava from Kilauea. Despite the constant threat from the volcano, there are a few Kalapana residents who still choose to live alongside the lava.

Run! These scientists got a little too close when the eruption began in 1983.

sun block When Tambora, a volcano on the island of Sumbawa, Indonesia, erupted in 1815, the 200 million tons of sulfur dioxide gas that were ejected into the atmosphere reduced the amount of sunlight reaching the ground. This caused temperatures to drop dramatically all over the world, resulting in crop failures throughout Europe, and, in 1816, North America's "year without a summer," snow fell in June and New England experienced severe frosts in August.

rapid growth Just a week after it first appeared in a Mexican cornfield in 1943, the volcano Parícutin had reached a height of five stories, and a year later it stood 1,102 ft (336 m) tall.

lava flow Volcanic lava can reach a temperature of 2,300°F (1,250°C) and flow at speeds of up to 62 mph (100 km/h)— that's nearly three times as fast as an Olympic sprinter.

constant eruption Known as the "Lighthouse of the Mediterranean," 3,038-ft-high (926-m) Stromboli, off the coast of Italy, has been erupting almost continuously for over 20,000 years, emitting smoke and lava fragments about every 20 to 40 minutes.

sole survivor The city of St. Pierre (population 30,000) on the French-Caribbean island of Martinique was flattened in 1902 by the eruption of Mount Pelée, leaving just one survivor in the direct path of the volcano— Louis Auguste Cyparis. This man owed his life to the fact that he was being held in a poorly ventilated prison cell. After the disaster he was pardoned and joined the circus, until his death in 1929, as the "Prisoner of St. Pierre," earning a living by locking himself in an exact replica of his cell.

deadly river The 1783 Laki eruption in Iceland sent enough lava spewing from a 15-mi-long (25-km) crack to fill two deep river valleys and cover an area of more than 190 sq mi (500 sq km). The lava river, which was 100 ft (30 m) deep, engulfed villages and released poisonous gases that killed many of those who managed to escape its flow.

nuclear noise The 1883 eruption of Krakatoa, near Java, unleashed the power of 15,000 nuclear bombs with a noise so loud it could be heard nearly 3,100 mi (5,000 km) away. Before the eruption, the island of Krakatoa stood 1,476 ft (450 m) above sea level, but the blast leveled most of the island to 820 ft (250 m) below sea level.

As the lava builds in height, it tears road signs out of the ground before cooling to solid rock.

undersea blast There are at least 1,500 active volcanoes on the surface of the Earth and an estimated 10,000 volcanoes beneath the ocean. When an underwater volcano off the coast of Iceland erupted in 1963, it did so with such force that it punched through the sea and formed the 1-sq-mi (2.7-sq-km) Surtsey Island.

volcano threat Some 500 million people live close to active volcanoes—that's about one in 13 of the world's population. Popocatépetl, nicknamed El Popo, is just 33 mi (53 km) from Mexico City and every year it sends thousands of tons of gas and volcanic ash into the air.

Molten lava oozes toward the house.

The building finally succumbs to the heat.

Ripley's **Believe It or Not!**®

SPIDER CITY

A gigantic 600-ft-long (183-m) web appeared over the course of two weeks along the banks of a lake in a Texas state park. The unnerving sight at Lake Tawakoni drew more than 3,000 curious visitors on one weekend. Experts believe that the giant web was spun by thousands of spiders from several different species working together to trap as many insects as possible.

king carbone Former flower grower Giorgio Carbone spent nearly 50 years championing the independence of the Italian village of Seborga, which he claimed should be recognized as a separate nation because it had never been formally included in the 19th-century unification of Italy. Proclaiming himself His Tremendousness Giorgio I, he ruled over 360 subjects until his death in 2009. He gave the principality its own currency, stamps, flag and even a Latin motto—*Sub Umbra Sede* ("Sit in the Shade").

sewer fat In a huge underground cleanup of central London in 2010, more than 1,000 tons of putrid fat were removed from sewers—enough fat to fill nine double-decker buses.

DOWN THE DRAIN

This giant chasm in Lake Berryessa, California, is the biggest drain hole in the world, at 30 ft (9 m) in diameter. When the lake reaches capacity, water tips over the lip of the drain and surges down a 700-ft-long (213-m) concrete pipe to exit through the Monticello Dam some 300 ft (91 m) below. Swimming or even boating near the hole is strongly discouraged; in 1997, a swimmer strayed too close and was sucked into the powerful drain. Water gushes through the "glory hole," as locals have named it, at a rate of 362,057 gallons every second—that's enough to fill 15,000 bathtubs. When the lake's level is low, local skateboarders and BMX bikers ride the giant exit pipe.

inaccessible inn Built in the middle of the 17th century, the Old Forge pub on the Knoydart peninsula in Northern Scotland can be reached only by boat or by walking 18 mi (29 km) from the nearest road over hills that rise to 3,500 ft (1,067 m).

moon lake The 39,000-sq-mi (101,000-sq-km) lake on the north pole of Saturn's moon Titan is bigger than Lake Superior and most likely filled with liquid methane and ethane.

limestone forest Water erosion has turned parts of Madagascar's Tsingy de Bemaraha National Park into forests of giant limestone spikes made of fossils and shellfish that died in the sea 200 million years ago.

acid drip Snottites are colonies of bacteria that hang from the ceilings of caves and are similar to stalactites. The bacteria derive their energy from volcanic sulfur compounds and drip sulfuric acid that is as corrosive as battery acid.

dam cops Nevada's Hoover Dam has its own police department whose duties include protecting the dam and safeguarding the lives of visitors and employees.

haunted house Josh Bond of Cuchillo, New Mexico, put his 130-year-old haunted house up for sale on the Internet auction site eBay. The listing offered 1,250 sq ft (115 sq m) of space spread over three bedrooms, an antique wood-burning stove and the spirits of the restless dead.

new ocean A 2005 volcanic eruption caused a 35-mi-long (56-km) rift, 20 ft (6 m) wide in places, to open up in the Ethiopian desert in just days. In 2010, geologists predicted that the rift would slowly become a new ocean, as Africa begins to split in two.

cursing festival Every February, youngsters in the neighboring South Nepalese villages of Parsawa and Laxmipur hurl insults at each other and passersby in a ten-day cursing festival. On the final day of the festival, they set heaps of straw ablaze and celebrate the Hindu festival of Holi, which is marked by raucous "play" fights using powdered colored paints and water.

more singapore Thanks to numerous land reclamation projects, the island city-state of Singapore has 20 percent more land than it did four decades ago.

cargo cult For more than 60 years, villagers on the island of Tanna, Vanuatu, have worshiped "John Frum," an American they believe will one day return with a bounty of cargo. Clan leaders first saw the mysterious figure in the late 1930s and he is said to have appeared before them again during World War II, dressed in white like a Navy seaman. In his honor, the islanders celebrate John Frum Day every February 15.

crystal clouds Noctilucent clouds are formed by ice crystals 50 mi (80 km) above the Earth, on the very edge of space. They reflect sunlight at night, so that they glow.

passion play The village of Oberammergau, Bavaria, Germany, has held a Passion play, depicting the Crucifixion of Jesus, every ten years with few exceptions since 1633, when villagers swore an oath to perform the play every decade after their town was spared from the plague.

tree dwellers Members of the Korowai tribe of Papua New Guinea live in tree houses that are built as high as 150 ft (46 m) off the ground. They reach them by climbing vines or stairs carved into the trunks.

Festival of the Skulls

Every year worshipers in the Bolivian city of La Paz offer gifts of flowers, food and alcohol to the "snub noses"—decorated skulls of their relatives—to thank the dead for protecting the homes of the living. The "Day of the Skulls" festival is part of wider "Day of the Dead" rituals across Latin America, and traditionally entire skeletons were honored in this way.

TAKING A LIBERTY

At 8.45 p.m. on the night of September 22, 2010, New York City photographer Jay Fine took this incredible photo of lightning striking the Statue of Liberty. He spent two hours braving the storm and took more than 80 shots before finally striking lucky. The iconic statue attracts over 600 bolts of lightning each year.

mail boat Since 1916, a boat has been delivering mail to dozens of homes on Lake Geneva, Wisconsin—and because it never stops, teenage carriers are hired to jump off the moving boat, put the mail in mailboxes on the dock, then scurry back on board, hopefully without falling into the lake.

huge hailstone A giant hailstone that fell in Vivian, South Dakota, on the night of July 23, 2010, measured 8 in (20 cm) in diameter, 18½ in (47 cm) in circumference and weighed 1 lb 15 oz (900 g)! This and other ice missiles were so large that some punched holes into roofs big enough for householders to put their arms through, while other hailstones gouged holes in the ground more than an inch deep.

watery grave As drought conditions dried up a pond in Aligarh, Uttar Pradesh, India, in May 2009, 98 human skulls were found at the bottom.

sparsely populated The state of Nevada covers an area about the size of Britain and Ireland combined, but has only 70 towns, whereas the British Isles has more than 40,000.

last speaker An ancient dialect called Bo, thought to date back 65,000 years, became extinct in 2010 after Boa Sr., the last person to speak it, died on a remote Indian island. At 85, Boa Sr. was the oldest member of the Great Andamanese Bo tribe before her death in Port Blair, the capital of Andaman and Nicobar Islands.

dual rule The U.S. city of Bristol straddles the borders of Virginia and Tennessee and has two governments, one for each half.

burning river The Cuyahoga River in Ohio was so polluted in the 20th century that it caught fire more than half a dozen times.

volcano video In May 2009, U.S. scientists videotaped an undersea volcanic eruption off the coast of Samoa, 4,000 ft (1,220 m) beneath the surface—the first time a sea floor eruption had been filmed.

rabbit island It cost more than one million dollars to rid the tiny Scottish island of Canna of rats in 2006, and now, less than four years later, it has been overrun with thousands of rabbits—because there are no rats to keep their numbers down! The island's only restaurant has responded by adding a number of rabbit dishes to its menu.

shifting city The Chilean earthquake of February 27, 2010, moved the city of Concepción about 10 ft (3 m) to the west. The quake was so powerful that it shortened the length of the day by 1.26 microseconds, and even Buenos Aires—840 mi (1,350 km) from Concepción—shifted by 1.5 in (3.8 cm).

Pink Lake

Lake Retba (the Rose Lake), situated 25 mi (40 km) north of Dakar in Senegal, has pink water, which can even turn purple in strong sunshine. The 1-sq-mi (3-sq-km) lake gets its unusual color from unique cyan bacteria in the water and also from its very high salt content.

buried lake At 155 mi (250 km) long and 31 mi (50 km) wide, Lake Vostok is about the same size as Lake Ontario—but lies beneath 2.5 mi (4 km) of Antarctic ice.

ginkgo stink The ginkgo tree species, native to Asia, is so resilient that several survived the atomic bomb blast in Hiroshima, Japan—but its smell is proving its downfall in Iowa City, U.S.A. When the tree drops its seed shells, it produces a sticky mess that smells of rotten eggs, creating a sanitation problem for the city.

floating stump The Old Man of the Lake, a 30-ft-tall (9-m) tree stump, has floated around Crater Lake, Oregon, for more than 100 years. During that time, high winds and waves have caused it to move great distances—in one three-month period of observation in 1938 it traveled more than 62 mi (100 km).

hot water At the bottom of shallow bodies of very salty water, temperatures can reach 176°F (80°C) and stay that way 24 hours a day.

river logjam Over several centuries, a natural logjam in North America's Red River grew to a length of more than 160 mi (256 km). When people began clearing it in the early 1800s, it took 40 years to complete the task.

lightning storm In just one hour on September 9, 2010, Hong Kong was hit by 13,102 lightning strikes. The violent electrical storm contained wind gusts of 62 mph (100 km/h) and caused power cuts that left people trapped in elevators.

widespread snow On February 12, 2010, all of the states in the U.S.A. except Hawaii received some snow.

fog nets Communities in Chile's Atacama Desert use nets to catch the morning fog—the only accessible fresh water in the region. One of the driest places on Earth, it only gets significant rainfall two to four times a century, and in some parts of the desert no rain has ever been recorded.

asteroid blast A 33-ft-wide (10-m) asteroid exploded with the energy of three Hiroshima atom bombs in the atmosphere above Indonesia on October 8, 2009. The asteroid hit the atmosphere at about 45,000 mph (72,000 km/h), causing a blast that was estimated by NASA to be equivalent to 55,000 tons of TNT, and which was heard by monitoring stations 10,000 mi (16,000 km) away. There was no damage on the ground, however, because it occurred at least 9.3 mi (15 km) above the Earth's surface.

life on mars? Huge plumes of methane—a gas that can indicate the presence of living organisms—have been found on the northern side of Mars. The methane may come from live organisms or from the decomposing remains of dead ones.

RIPLEY RESEARCH

In winter, starlings flock in groups of anything from a few thousand to 20 million birds—huge numbers that turn the sky black. Flying at speeds of more than 20 mph (32 km/h) while they search for somewhere safe to roost for the night, they group together to avoid predators such as sparrowhawks and peregrine falcons. In flight, each starling is able to track seven other birds irrespective of distance—and this is what enables them to maintain such a cohesive overall shape.

STARLING FLOCK

Thousands of starlings in the sky above Taunton in Somerset, England, formed the shape of one giant starling! These acrobatic birds have created many different patterns in the sky, including a rabbit, a rubber duck and a turtle.

®️ **leaning skyscraper** The 530-ft-high (160-m) Capital Gate building in Abu Dhabi leans at an angle of 18 degrees—four times more than Italy's famous Leaning Tower of Pisa. The new 35-story building achieves this angle by using staggered floor plates from the 12th floor up.

®️ **towering tent** A giant tent 490 ft (150 m) high opened in Astana, Kazakhstan, in 2010. Designed to withstand the nation's extreme variations in temperature, the Khan Shatyr Entertainment Center took four years to build. Made from three layers of transparent plastic, it stands on a 650-ft (200-m) concrete base and houses shops, restaurants, cinemas and even an artificial beach and running track.

®️ **security cage** After being burgled eight times in six months, 80-year-old Chinese grandmother Ling Wan turned her apartment in Changsha into a giant birdcage. She sealed up the stairs and built an iron cage around the apartment so that the only way in and out is via a ladder that is securely locked on her balcony.

®️ **capsule hotels** Japan's capsule hotels have rooms that measure roughly 7 x 4 x 3 ft (2.1 x 1.2 x 0.9 m)—not much bigger than a coffin! They are stacked side by side on two levels, with steps providing access to the upper capsule. Some hotels have more than 700 capsules.

®️ **light tower** The Eiffel Tower in Paris, France, weighs less than a cylinder of air occupying the same dimensions. The force of the wind causes the top of the lightweight metal tower to sway up to 3 in (7.6 cm).

®️ **sole occupant** Owing to the recession, for three years Les Harrington was the only resident of a 2.4-acre (1-ha) luxury village in Essex, England, that boasted 58 cottages and apartments.

®️ **007 tribute** For a 2009 New Year's Eve party, James Bond fanatics Simon and Angie Mullane spent four months and $4,500 transforming their Dorset, England, home into a 007 movie set. Guests were greeted at a homemade checkpoint manned by dummies dressed in authentic East German border guard uniforms bought on the Internet, while a Sean Connery mannequin dangled from a real hang glider in the garden.

®️ **luxury igloo** In January 2010, Jimmy Grey built a luxury, four-room igloo in the yard of his home in Aquilla, Ohio. The igloo had 6-ft-high (1.8-m) ceilings and an entertainment room, complete with cable TV (plugged into an outlet in his garage) and surround-sound stereo.

Container Store

Shoppers visiting the flagship Freitag bag store in Zurich, Switzerland, certainly need a head for heights, as the building is made from a dizzying stack of used steel shipping containers. It consists of 17 containers of which nine form the 85-ft-high (26-m) tower. The recycling theme of the building mirrors the bags sold inside, which are made from such items as old truck tarpaulins, bicycle inner tubes and car seat belts.

TUNNEL VISION

Over a period of four weeks, sculptors Dan Havel and Dean Ruck from Houston, Texas, transformed two connected properties to create a large, tunnel-like vortex, making it look as if the interior of the buildings had exploded. The outer skin of the two houses—made from planks of pine—was peeled off and used to create a 60-ft-long (18-m) spiral, which narrowed to a width of about 2 ft (60 cm) at the far end.

poop light In 2010, a park in Cambridge, Massachusetts, had a street light that was powered by dog poop. Created by artist Matthew Mazzotta, the "Park Spark" project encouraged dog walkers to dump their pets' poop in biodegradable bags and drop it into one of two 500-gal (1,900-l) steel tanks. Microbes in the waste gave off methane gas, which was fed through a second tank to the lamp and burned off.

mecca clock The Royal Mecca Clock, located on a skyscraper in Mecca, Saudi Arabia, has four amazing faces each measuring 151 ft (46 m) in diameter—that's more than six times larger than the faces of London's Big Ben clock. More than 90 million pieces of colored glass mosaic decorate the sides of the clock, which is visible from every part of the city. On special occasions, 16 bands of vertical lights shoot from the clock 6 mi (10 km) into the sky.

lost language The writing on the back of a letter discovered in 2008 by archeologists at a 17th-century dig site reveals a previously unknown language spoken by indigenous peoples in northern Peru. The letter, found under a pile of clay bricks in a collapsed church near Trujillo, shows a column of numbers written in Spanish and translated into a mysterious language that has been extinct for at least 400 years.

home wrecker In February 2010, a man bulldozed his $350,000 Moscow, Ohio, home when a bank claimed it as collateral for outstanding debt.

whistle blowers Officials in Alor Setar, Malaysia, blow whistles loudly at litterbugs in the hope of shaming them into never littering again.

rotating house A rotating house north of Sydney, Australia, guarantees Luke Everingham and his family a different view every time they wake up. The octagonal-shaped house sits on a turntable powered by a small electric motor and controlled by a computer, which allows it to move on demand, completing a full rotation in half an hour.

vast collection The British Museum in London has 80,000 objects on display—but that is only one per cent of its total collection.

railroad room The Washington Hotel in Tokyo, Japan, has created a special room for model railway enthusiasts to sleep in. It includes a grand model of the local area, complete with working railroads. Train lovers can bring their own models or, alternatively, the hotel will happily provide some.

school mascot The mascot of Yuma Union High School in Yuma, Arizona, is a criminal dressed in a prison uniform. It was adopted nearly a century ago after classes were held in a prison building when the original school burned down.

CIGARETTE HOUSE

A house in Hangzhou, Zhejiang Province, China, is brightly decorated throughout with more than 30,000 empty cigarette packets. The occupant collected them over a period of six years and has even created seats and tables from the empty packs.

44
world
Believe It or Not!®

FLAMING FESTIVAL

Each year the city of Toyohashi in Japan hosts an extreme fire festival. Fearless volunteers launch enormous homemade bamboo fireworks, known as *tezutsu hanabi*, which explode inches from their faces. The 300-year-old festival sets off 12,000 fireworks and can draw more than 350 homemade cannons that spew fire up to 65 ft (20 m) into the sky.

luminous beams A mysterious "rain" of vertical luminous beams appeared for nearly an hour in the night sky above Xiamen, China, in July 2010. At first there were just five beams, hanging low in the sky, but soon the number increased to 50. A local observatory confirmed that it was definitely not a meteor shower.

glass elephant Built on top of an old coalminer's washroom, the Glass Elephant in the Maximillianpark, Hamm, Germany—designed in 1984 by artist and architect Horst Rellecke—stands an amazing 115 ft (35 m) tall.

mud volcano A mud volcano in Sidoarjo, East Java, Indonesia, spews enough scalding mud daily to fill 50 Olympic-size swimming pools. Since its first eruption in 2006, it has buried 12 villages.

royal shrine Mehrangarh Fort in Jodhpur, Rajasthan, India, has a shrine bearing carvings of the handprints of royal widows that committed *suttee*—a ceremony in which women were burned alive upon the funeral pyre of their husbands.

falling ice In 2008, a 6-lb (2.7-kg) chunk of ice fell from the sky, crashed through the roof of a home in York Township, Pennsylvania, and hit Mary Ann Foster, who was sleeping, on the head. It turned out to be atmospheric ice, formed when moisture in the atmosphere freezes into small ice balls, which then bump into each other and sometimes attach themselves together to create larger chunks.

underground home Unable to afford a bigger house, retired Chinese miner Chen Xinnian tunneled out a one-bedroom apartment measuring 540-sq-ft (50-sq-m) beneath his existing home in Zhengzhou, Henan Province. The apartment is 20 ft (6 m) underground and is so cool that food does not need to be kept in a refrigerator.

hard wood Ironwood trees—including the black ironwood species that is native to the U.S.A.—have wood so dense that it won't float in water. It sinks instead.

river ritual More than ten million devotees from across the country came to Haridwar, India, in February 2010 for the Kumbh Mela Festival, held here once every 12 years, to bathe in the River Ganges.

desert snow China's largest desert, the Taklamakan, covers approximately 125,000 sq mi (325,000 sq km) and, in January 2008, snow blanketed the entire area for the first time ever.

violent quake On February 7, 1812, a massive earthquake struck near New Madrid, Missouri, and shook so violently that the Mississippi River flowed backward for several hours.

lunar pit Photographs of the Moon taken from the Japanese Kaguya spacecraft revealed a giant pit about 427 ft (130 m) in diameter on the lunar surface—that's large enough to swallow an entire football field.

hanging coffins The Bo people, an ethnic group from China's Sichuan Province that disappeared hundreds of years ago, hung the coffins of their dead on the sides of cliffs. The coffins were lowered on ropes from above to rest on precipices or wooden stakes. Some were hung as high as 425 ft (130 m) above ground, as the belief was that the higher the coffin was placed, the more propitious it was for the dead. The earliest hanging coffins found in the region date back 2,500 years.

CRACKERS

During the Chinese Lantern Festival celebrations in Taiwan, it's customary for onlookers to launch firecrackers at a shirtless man who represents the god of wealth. The more fireworks that hit their intended target, the more successful the firework thrower will become. This dangerous-looking ritual has been performed in the area for over 50 years.

Fire in the Hole

In the middle of a remote desert in Turkmenistan, the Darvaza crater is continually ablaze. The 200-ft-wide (60-m) chasm was created when a sinkhole collapsed under a gas-mining rig in 1971. The miners started a fire to burn off the gas, but it just kept coming and the crater has been burning ever since. If you can stand the heat, it is possible to walk right to the edge of the hole, which is 65 ft (20 m) deep.

Ripley's Believe It or Not!®

▶ The building is designed to minimize twisting in high winds, but it still sways 5 ft (1.5 m) at its highest point. The 656-ft-high (200-m) spire was made from 4,000 tons of steel.

▶ The overall floor area of the building is 3,331,100 sq ft (309,469 sq m), the size of more than 700 basketball courts.

▶ The building is so large that it can take four months for a 30-strong team to clean the surface.

▶ Double-decker elevators ascend at an incredible 40 mph (64 km/h) to the 160th floor. Alternatively, there are 2,909 stairs from the bottom to the top.

▶ The glass on the Burj Khalifa would cover more than 30 football fields.

▶ The tower weighs 551,000 tons when empty. That's about the equivalent of 8,000 U.S. homes piled up on top of each other.

▶ At peak periods the tower uses enough electricity to power almost 20 passenger trains.

▶ Floors 77–108: Over 1,000 apartments. The tower is expected to hold 35,000 people at once—the equivalent of the population of a small town in one building.

▶ The building uses the weight of 26,000 family sedans in reinforced steel, and the exterior stainless-steel cladding weighs as much as 75 Statues of Liberty.

Burj Khalifa

The Burj Khalifa, which opened in January 2010, is the tallest structure ever built. At 2,717 ft (828 m) tall, it is more than twice the height of the Empire State Building—the equivalent of 180 giraffes standing on each other's heads. Each of the 160 floors took just three days to build, with the complete tower taking 5½ years to finish, at a cost of $1.5 billion.

▶ In January 2010, two base jumpers made the highest ever free-fall leap from the 160th floor of the towers, free-falling for 10 seconds before opening their parachutes.

▶ 11,653,840 cubic ft (330,000 cubic m) of concrete were used in the construction of the tower. This is enough to have laid a sidewalk from London to Madrid—a distance of 785 mi (1,263 km).

▶ From the outdoor observation deck on the 124th floor, 1,483 ft (452 m) up, you can see Iran, 50 mi (80 km) away.

▶ Owing to Dubai's desert location, the Burj Khalifa is built to withstand sandstorms and temperatures of up to 118°F (48°C). The building moves up to 3 ft (1 m) as the metal expands in the heat. A water system collects enough condensation from the air conditioning every year to fill 20 Olympic swimming pools.

▶ There is an outside swimming pool on the 76th floor.

The Burj Khalifa is built on desert sand, so the tower's foundations are an incredible 165 ft (50 m) deep, filled with 110,000 tons of concrete. However, by the time of the official opening, the building had already sunk 2.5 in (6.3 cm) into the ground.

tower highway

The 16-story Gate Tower Building in Osaka, Japan, has a highway running through its middle between the fifth and seventh floors. An exit of the Hanshin Expressway passes through as a bridge, held up by supports next to the building. The office block's elevator moves through the vacant floors without stopping between floor four and floor eight.

time for change

A giant astronomical clock at Wells Cathedral in Somerset, England, was painstakingly wound by hand for more than 600 years—and from 1919 to 2010 it was operated by five generations of the Fisher family. From 1987, Paul Fisher spent an hour, three times a week, turning the three 550-lb (250-kg) weights about 800 times. The weights were winched up on a pulley system and powered the clock as they descended over the next two days.

gladiator school

The University of Regensburg, Germany, has a summer camp in which students live and train like Roman gladiators.

happy harry

Harry Hallowes, an Irish tramp who squatted for more than 20 years in one of London's most expensive suburbs, was awarded a plot of land that could be worth up to $6 million. He was given squatters' rights to a patch of land 120 x 60 ft (36 x 18 m) on Hampstead Heath, where he has lived in a tiny shack since 1986.

4,200 clocks

The Pentagon, headquarters for the U.S. Department of Defense, has 4,200 wall clocks. Over 200,000 telephone calls are made from the Pentagon every day through phones connected by 100,000 mi (160,000 km) of cable, and although there are 17½ mi (28 km) of corridors, it takes only seven minutes to walk between any two points in the building.

pub crawl

Rather than demolish the 124-year-old Birdcage Tavern to make way for a new road tunnel in Auckland, New Zealand, the country's transport authority decided to move the landmark hostelry 130 ft (40 m) up a hill. After the walls were reinforced by inserting carbon-fiber rods, the three-story building was jacked onto concrete rails lubricated with Teflon and liquid silicon, then painstakingly pushed up the hill by hydraulic ramps. The move took two days.

gold machine

The Emirates Palace Hotel in Abu Dhabi, U.A.E., has a vending machine that dispenses gold bars—with prices updated to correspond to the world markets every 10 minutes.

rat free

A Japanese shipwreck in 1780 inadvertently introduced rats to Rat Island, Alaska, and the island was heavily infested until 2009, when it finally became free of rats again—229 years later.

BEER CRATE HOUSE

Architect Jörn Bihain used 43,000 plastic beer crates to create what he named the "Pavilion of Temporary Happiness," in the grounds of the Atomium building in Brussels, Belgium, in 2008. The vast temporary structure commemorated 50 years since the Atomium was erected at the 1958 Brussels World Fair.

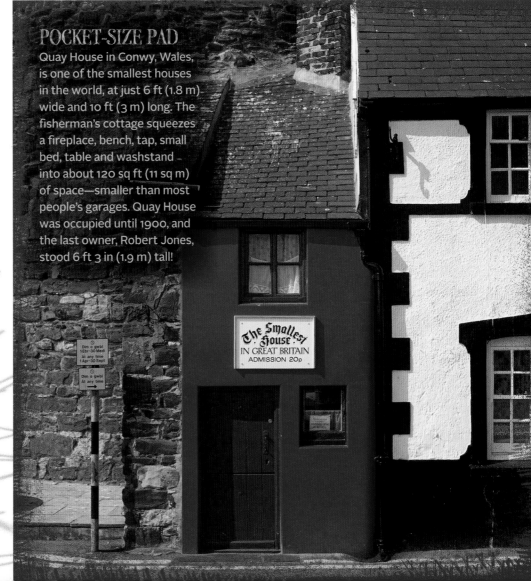

POCKET-SIZE PAD

Quay House in Conwy, Wales, is one of the smallest houses in the world, at just 6 ft (1.8 m) wide and 10 ft (3 m) long. The fisherman's cottage squeezes a fireplace, bench, tap, small bed, table and washstand into about 120 sq ft (11 sq m) of space—smaller than most people's garages. Quay House was occupied until 1900, and the last owner, Robert Jones, stood 6 ft 3 in (1.9 m) tall!

Ripley's Believe It or Not!®

🙋 RIPLEY RESEARCH

The Gobi Desert is expanding into China very rapidly, claiming an area of 3,860 sq mi (10,000 sq km) each year—that's almost four times the size of the state of Rhode Island. The desert is now less than 50 mi (80 km) from Beijing, China, where the largest sandstorms can dump hundreds of thousands of tons of sand on the city.

monster star Scientists from the University of Sheffield, England, have discovered a new star that weighs 265 times the mass of our Sun and is almost 10 million times brighter. The monster star—named R136a1—is believed to be around a million years old and is so bright that if it were located where our Sun is, it would completely fry the Earth within minutes.

disappearing island An island that was at the center of a 30-year dispute between India and Bangladesh disappeared beneath rising seas in 2010. Measuring 2.2 mi (3.5 km) long and 1.9 mi (3 km) wide, uninhabited New Moore Island in the Bay of Bengal had been claimed by both countries—however, environmental experts said that global warming had finally resolved the matter of ownership.

Snow Patrol To prevent bad weather spoiling important Moscow holidays, such as Victory Day and City Day, the Russian Air Force blasts snow clouds from the sky before they can reach the capital. When heavy snow is forecast for a Moscow celebration, airplanes spray liquid nitrogen, silver or cement particles into the cloud mass, forcing the snow to fall on other parts of Russia instead.

painted peak Using water jugs to splash an eco-friendly whitewash onto the rocks, a team of workers in Peru have painted the 15,600-ft-high (4,756-m) Chalon Sombrero mountain white. The peak in the Andes was once home to a sprawling glacier and it is hoped that the newly painted mountain will reflect away sunlight and help cool down the slopes to trigger a re-growth of its ice.

meteorite attack The same house in Gornji Lajici, Bosnia, was hit by meteorites six times in three years between 2007 and 2010. The repeated bombardment of white-hot rocks forced owner Radivoje Lajic to reinforce the roof with a steel girder. He says the chances of being hit by a meteorite once are so small that to be hit six times must mean that he is being targeted by aliens.

windy planet Wind speeds of 4,350 mph (7,000 km/h) were measured in 2010 in the atmosphere of planet HD209458b, which orbits a star in the constellation Pegasus, some 150 light years from Earth. The planet has a temperature of about 1,800°F (1,000°C) on its hot side.

toxic island Owing to the risk of toxic volcanic gases on Miyakejima Island, Japan, residents carry gas masks with them at all times—and sometimes even sleep with them.

fish rain For two days in February 2010, the remote desert town of Lajamanu in Australia's Northern Territory was bombarded with hundreds of small fish falling from rain clouds in the sky—even though it is 326 mi (525 km) from the nearest river.

in the dark A power outage in 2009 left the town of Quipeio, Angola (population 1,000), in the dark for more than two months.

black gold Beverly Hills High School in California has oil wells beneath its grounds, which earn the school hundreds of thousands of dollars in revenue every year.

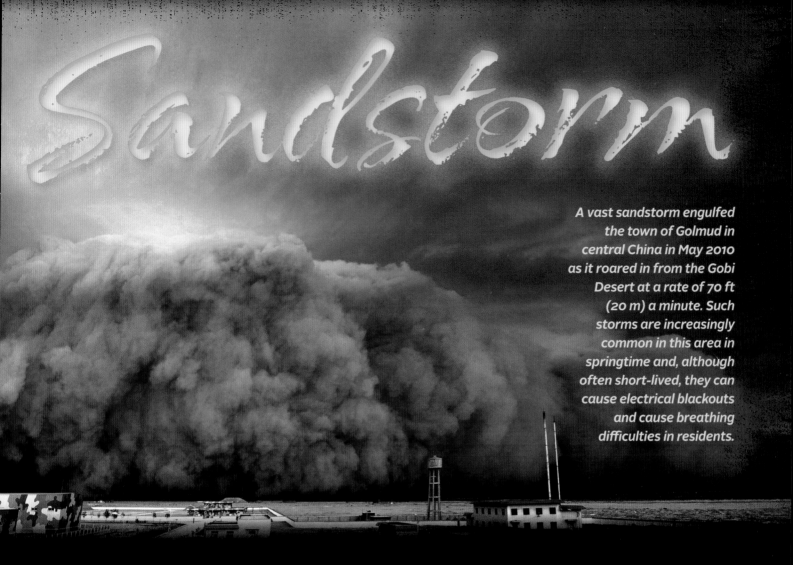

Sandstorm

A vast sandstorm engulfed the town of Golmud in central China in May 2010 as it roared in from the Gobi Desert at a rate of 70 ft (20 m) a minute. Such storms are increasingly common in this area in springtime and, although often short-lived, they can cause electrical blackouts and cause breathing difficulties in residents.

glowing urine A glowing trail spotted in the night sky above North America in September 2009 was caused by a falling block of astronaut urine. It came from the Space Shuttle *Discovery* which, unable to unload human waste while it was docked to the International Space Station, had then been forced to dump nearly two weeks' worth of waste in one drop.

lightning hotspot An area near the village of Kifuka, in the Democratic Republic of the Congo, has the greatest number of lightning strikes per square kilometer in the world—about 158 a year.

deadly icicles In the winter of 2009 to 2010, Russia's coldest in 30 years, five people were killed and over 150 injured by icicles falling from the rooftops of buildings in St. Petersburg.

space smash A 4.6-billion-year-old meteorite smashed through the windshield of a truck in Grimsby, Ontario, Canada, in September 2009. Minutes beforehand, local astronomers had witnessed a "brilliant fireball," 100 times brighter than a full moon, streaking across the night sky.

starfish graveyard More than 10,000 starfish died on a beach in Norfolk, England, in December 2009 after being washed ashore during a storm. The creatures had gathered in the shallows to feed on mussels, but were swept on to the beach during high tide and quickly perished once they were out of water.

shrinking storm Jupiter's giant storm, the Great Red Spot, shrank by more than 0.6 mi (1 km) per day between 1996 and 2006.

high cloud Morning Glory clouds, which appear regularly over Northern Australia each spring, stand one mile (1.6 km) high and can stretch for hundreds of miles. The clouds are often accompanied by sudden wind squalls and can move at speeds of up to 37 mph (60 km/h).

rocky rain On the distant planet COROT-7b, which is nearly twice the size of Earth, it rains rocks! Scientists from Washington University in St. Louis, Missouri, found that the planet's atmosphere is made up of vaporized rock, and when a weather front moves in, pebbles condense out of the air and rain down on the surface.

bio blitz On a single day in August 2009, a team of 125 scientists and volunteers found more than 1,100 species of life—plants, lichens, mushrooms, bees, bugs, butterflies, worms and bats—in just 2 sq mi (5 sq km) of Yellowstone National Park, including several species not previously known to exist there.

unconquered peak Gangkhar Puensum, a mountain in Bhutan standing 24,836 ft (7,570 m) tall, is the highest unclimbed mountain on the planet.

blown away When Cyclone Olivia hit Australia's Barrow Island in 1996, it created a wind gust of 253 mph (407 km/h).

changing places The moons Janus and Epimetheus are in the same orbit around Saturn, with one a little farther out and slower than the other. The faster moon catches its neighbor every four years and the two moons swap places and the cycle begins again.

single bloom The *Tahina spectabilis* palm tree of Madagascar grows for decades up to a height of more than 50 ft (15 m) before it finally flowers for a single time, then dies.

hamster hotel In 2009, a hotel in Nantes, France, offered guests the chance to live like a hamster for a day. Architects Frederic Tabary and Yann Falquerho designed the room to resemble the inside of a hamster's cage, and for $130 a night visitors could feast on hamster grain, get a workout by running in a giant hamster wheel and sleep in piles of hay.

toilet tour German guide Anna Haase runs a different kind of sightseeing tour— instead of showing visitors the traditional sights of Berlin, she takes them on a tour of the city's famous toilets. These range from a historic 19th-century toilet block to a Japanese automatic toilet that costs as much as a small car.

tar lake Covering an area of 100 acres (40 ha) and delving to about 250 ft (80 m) deep at the center, Pitch Lake on the island of Trinidad is filled with liquid asphalt, the result of oil being forced up through the faults on which the lake sits. Despite the highly toxic chemicals, the lake is home to bacterial life.

tunnel network During the Vietnam War (1955–75), Viet Cong soldiers using only hand tools dug a single tunnel network all the way from Saigon to the Cambodian border—a distance of over 150 mi (240 km). They created an underground city with living areas, kitchens, weapons factories and field hospitals, installing large air vents (which were disguised as anthills or termite mounds), baffled vents to dissipate cooking smells, and lethal booby traps. Up to 10,000 people lived underground for years, getting married, giving birth, and only coming out at night to tend to their crops under cover of darkness.

jesus image While looking for holiday destinations on the mapping website Google Earth, Zach Evans from Southampton, England, spotted an outline of the face of Jesus Christ in satellite pictures of a field near Puspokladany, Hungary.

sewage symphony A sewage plant near Berlin, Germany, is breaking down sludge more quickly by playing the music of Mozart to its microbes. The composer's classics are piped in to the plant around the clock via a series of speakers because the sonic patterns of the music help stimulate activity among the tiny organisms, speeding up the breakdown of waste.

bone décor The Sedlec Ossuary in Sedlec, Czech Republic, is a Roman Catholic chapel containing more than 40,000 human skeletons, the bones of which have been arranged to form the chapel's decorations and furnishings.

cave man After living in a 7-ft-wide (2.1-m) cave for 16 years, officials evicted Hilaire Purbrick of Brighton, England, in 2009 because his underground home lacked a second fire exit.

no flow When astronauts cry in space, their tears stay in a ball against their eyes until they are wiped away, because there is no gravity to make them fall naturally.

tough tree A Sabal palm tree with a 6-in-wide (15-cm) hole through its trunk has survived several hurricanes in Estero, Florida.

great hedge The Great Hedge of India was planted across the country by the British in the mid-19th century to prevent salt smuggling. It was a 2,000-mi-long (3,200-km) barrier of living impenetrable thorny hedge that was patrolled by up to 14,000 attendants.

snowball payment For hundreds of years, Scotland's Clan MacIntyre delivered a single snowball in the summer to Clan Campbell as part of a long-standing debt.

WEEPING GLACIER
A human face, appearing to cry, appeared in a glacier in Svalbard, Norway, in 2009. As the ice cap melted, the water poured into the sea, eroding the ice and creating the mysterious shape.

Away from the more organized areas of the catacombs, bones lie scattered in forgotten tunnels.

Secret City

Believe it or not, hidden directly below the busy streets of Paris, France, there are countless secret tunnels and caverns, and millions of human bones.

The city expanded so quickly in the 18th century that cemeteries and mass graves were soon literally overflowing—it is said that the cellar walls of adjoining buildings would ooze with human remains, and disease was rife. To solve the problem, bodies were removed each night and buried in caves adjoining the Parisian sewers. These catacombs—or underground cemeteries—and the tunnels between them were recycled Roman stone quarries that stretched for 500 mi (805 km). It is thought that the bones of six million Parisians are piled up in the catacombs—over half the current live population. It is still possible to wander through the maze of passages that run 65 ft (20 m) below the city streets.

IN THE MEMORY OF PHILIBERT ASPAIRT LOST IN THIS QUARRY ON NOVEMBER 3RD 1793 FOUND ELEVEN YEARS LATER AND BURIED AT THE SAME PLACE ON APRIL 30TH 1804

BURIED ALIVE

In 1793, Philibert Aspairt descended into the catacombs under the hospital where he worked, hoping to steal wine from cellars belonging to monks. His body was found 11 years later, only yards from an exit.

• French resistance troops used the catacombs as a base during World War II, as did occupying German forces. The tunnels also served as air-raid shelters for Parisians seeking refuge from enemy bombing.

• In 1787, the future King Charles X of France held a party in a large cavern deep in the catacombs.

• A gang of thieves was arrested in the catacombs in 1905 after attempting to steal skulls and bones to sell to medical students.

• A team of experts constantly surveys hundreds of miles of the catacombs to prevent any of the caves collapsing, which would potentially cause parts of the city, lying directly above them, to fall into the ground.

• An escaped orangutan perished in the Paris underground tunnels over 200 years ago. Its skeleton is still kept on public display.

• In 1871, 100 rebel soldiers escaped into the catacombs. They got lost in the dark tunnels and were never seen again.

OSSEMENTS DU CIMETIÈRE DES INNOCENTS DÉPOSÉS LE 2 JUILLET 1809

THE GATEWAY TO THE CATACOMBS STATES *"ARRÊTE! C'EST ICI L'EMPIRE DE LA MORT"* ("STOP! HERE IS THE EMPIRE OF DEATH.")

CRAZY KINK

A 7.1-magnitude earthquake near Canterbury, New Zealand, in September 2010 caused rail tracks in the region to buckle alarmingly. A train engineer managed to stop his two engines just 100 ft (30 m) short of this crazy kink. Repairs involved removing the crippled rails and replacing them with new rails that measured about 6½ ft (2 m) shorter than the originals.

ring of fire Three-quarters of the world's active and dormant volcanoes exist within the 25,000-mi (40,000-km) Ring of Fire, situated along the edges of the Pacific Ocean. Among them is Alaska's Mount Redoubt, which erupted in March 2009, sending a plume of smoke nearly 10 mi (16 km) into the air.

shooting spores *Pilobolis* fungi live in animal dung and are less than 0.4 in (1 cm) tall, but they shoot packets of spores up to 6 ft (1.8 m) in the air to reproduce.

meteorite crater Max Rocca, an amateur geologist from Buenos Aires, Argentina, found an ancient meteorite crater 31 mi (50 km) across in the Colombian rainforest—by examining satellite pictures. His interest was aroused after he detected a near-perfect semicircular curve in the Vichada River.

young star On November 7, 2008, 14-year-old amateur astronomer Caroline Moore of Warwick, New York, discovered a supernova—and the exploding star she found (dubbed SN 2008ha) was about 1,000 times dimmer than a typical supernova.

multiple eclipse Solar eclipses are a major phenomenon here on Earth, but the planet Jupiter, because it has 50 confirmed moons, can have multiple eclipses happening simultaneously.

nuclear reactions The Sun's core has enough hydrogen to continue fueling its nuclear reactions for another five billion years.

new cloud Meteorologists believe they have discovered a new type of cloud. The Cloud Appreciation Society has named it *asperatus*, after the Latin word for "rough," on account of its rough and choppy underside. If it becomes officially recognized, it will be the first new cloud type since 1951.

black hole NASA has found a gigantic black hole 100 million times the mass of the Sun, feeding off gas, dust and stars at the center of a galaxy, 50 million light-years away.

toxic lake Argentina's Lake Diamante is filled with thriving bacteria despite being oxygen depleted, hyper-saline, spectacularly toxic and bombarded with ultraviolet radiation.

school climb Erping Village Elementary School in Sichuan Province, China, is built on a platform nearly 10,000 ft (3,050 m) up a remote mountainside. Until 2010, when a new steel stairway was built on the cliff, students could get to school only by climbing a series of rickety, homemade wooden ladders. The school's two teachers had to escort the children up and down the ladders because the journey was so dangerous and exhausting.

DRY RUN

The U.S. side of the mighty Niagara Falls was nearly as dry as a desert for five months in 1969. Engineers stopped the waterfall for the first time in 12,000 years by building a temporary 600-ft-wide (180-m) dam from 27,800 tons of rock and diverting the flow of the Niagara River over the larger Horseshoe Falls on the Canadian side. The work was carried out to remove a large quantity of loose rock from the base of the U.S. side of the Falls, which, if left in place, might eventually prevent the waterfall from flowing at all. To delay the gradual erosion of the U.S. side, faults were also mechanically strengthened. When the task was finished and the dam was blown up, 60,000 gal (227,000 l) of water once again thundered over the U.S. side of the Falls every second.

Ice House

The Cleveland Harbor West Pierhead Lighthouse on the shores of Lake Erie, Ohio, looked more like a fairy-tale castle in December 2010 when it became completely covered in layers of ice. High winds caused waves to crash over the lighthouse, where the water then froze in the bitterly cold temperatures.

phone access Only about one-third of India's population has access to modern sanitation—but nearly half of the population has a cell phone!

narrow house A three-story house in Brighton, East Sussex, England, is just 6 ft (1.8 m) wide. Owners Iain and Rachel Boyle bought the former donkey-cart shed for just $12,000 in 1998, but have turned it into such a stylish home—complete with a mezzanine bedroom—that they now rent it out.

one-way traffic Between 2004 and 2009, nearly 10,000 North Koreans defected to South Korea—while only two people went in the other direction!

hot ash Volcanic avalanches of hot ash, rock fragments and gas—known as pyroclastic flows—can move at 150 mph (240 km/h) and are capable of knocking down and burning everything in their path.

judge numbers India has 11 judges for every million people, while the U.S.A. has 110 per million—ten times as many.

reduced alphabet Rotokas, a language spoken on the island of Bougainville, Papua New Guinea, has only 12 letters in its entire alphabet—they are A, E, G, I, K, O, P, R, S, T, U and V.

boy power China has 32 million more boys under the age of 20 than it has girls.

lonely lighthouse The Stannard Rock lighthouse, Michigan, is the only structure on a large rock 23 mi (37 km) off the coast of Lake Superior. It was staffed for eight decades, until it was finally automated in 1962.

ooh-la-law! In 2010, French politicians finally sought to repeal a 1799 law that banned women in Paris from wearing pants except when riding horses or bicycles.

new ring In 2009, U.S. astronomers discovered a new ring around Saturn that is so large it could hold a billion Earths. The ring is made up of debris from Saturn's distant moon Phoebe.

flood terror In January 2011, torrential rain in the state of Victoria, Australia, killed over 22,000 sheep and 300,000 poultry and led to the formation of an inland lake of floodwater more than 50 mi (80 km) long. Further north in Queensland, the floods submerged an area of land the size of France and Germany combined.

the twitchhiker Paul Smith traveled around the world for free in 30 days relying solely on the goodwill of people using the social networking site Twitter. By accepting free accommodation and transport from his fellow tweeters, he managed to travel from his home in Newcastle upon Tyne, England, to Stewart Island, New Zealand, via Amsterdam, Paris, Frankfurt, New York, Washington, D.C., Chicago, San Francisco, Los Angeles and Auckland.

deadly storm On April 30, 1888, a violent hailstorm dropped ice balls the size of oranges on the city of Moradabad in India, killing 230 people.

RIVER RUNS RED

The water rushing over Cameron Falls, Alberta, Canada, turned pinky red following a heavy storm. The phenomenon was caused by high levels of rain that washed a red sediment called argolite from 1,500-million-year-old rocks into the river.

underwater meeting In October 2009, the government of the low-lying islands of the Maldives in the Indian Ocean held an underwater meeting to highlight the dangers of global warming. Dressed in full scuba gear, President Nasheed and ten colleagues took part in the 30-minute meeting at a depth of 20 ft (6 m) off the coast, near the country's capital Malé. Most of the Maldives is barely 3 ft (1 m) above sea level, and scientists fear it could be uninhabitable in fewer than 100 years.

time tunnel Ramchandra Das of Bihar, India, spent 14 years digging a tunnel 33 ft (10 m) long and 13 ft (4 m) wide through a mountain with only a hammer and chisel so that his neighbors could avoid an arduous 4½-mi (7-km) trek around the mountain to work and so that he could park his truck closer to home.

hidden home Sharon Simpson created a luxurious tent home—complete with solar shower and satellite TV—on a busy traffic circle in the center of Derby, England. She lived there unnoticed for five months and moved out only when leaves falling off nearby bushes took away her privacy.

souvenir snowball For more than 30 years, Prena Thomas of Lakeland, Florida, has kept a snowball in her freezer—the souvenir of a rare Florida snowfall. When 2 in (5 cm) of snow fell on the normally balmy state on January 19, 1977, she was so surprised that she collected some of the snow and put it in her freezer.

piping hot The sidewalks of Klamath Falls, Oregon, are kept free from snow and ice—and therefore safe for pedestrians—by hot-water pipes that run underneath them.

new castle Since 1997, some 50 workers in central France have been building a new medieval castle using only the tools and materials that were available in the 13th century. The brainchild of local landowner Michel Guyot, the Château de Guédelon is being built from sandstone, and when it's finished in around 2022 will boast a main tower more than 90 ft (27 m) tall.

BROCKEN SPECTER

Local climbers in the Polish Tatra Mountains believe that if they witness a Brocken Specter—their own giant shadow projected on thick cloud below them—then they are doomed to die on the mountain. The phenomenon is named after the Brocken Mountain in Germany.

jet power The Dubai Fountain, located beside the Burj Khalifa skyscraper in Dubai, is almost 900 ft (275 m) long and can fire jets of water 500 ft (150 m) into the air.

ice man Nicknamed the "Ice man of Ladakh," retired Indian engineer Chewang Norphel has tackled environmental problems by building more than a dozen new glaciers in the Himalayas. He constructs his own glaciers by diverting meltwater through pipes into artificial lakes. Shaded by the mountains and kept in place by dams, the water in the lakes remains frozen until springtime when it melts and feeds the rivers below, which in turn irrigate surrounding farmland. He decided to act after melting glaciers caused floods that destroyed homes and crops.

time travel Russia has no fewer than nine different time zones—and the eastern region of Chukotka (just across the Bering Strait from Alaska) is nine hours ahead of Kaliningrad in the extreme west of the country. There were 11 time zones in Russia until two were scrapped in 2010.

storm hole A Guatemala City clothing factory and an entire traffic intersection were swallowed by a cavernous sinkhole, which suddenly opened up during a tropical storm in 2010. The sinkhole was almost perfectly round and measured 65 ft (20 m) wide and 100 ft (30 m) deep.

purple snow In March 2010, purple snow fell in Stavropol, southern Russia. The unusual coloration was the result of dust from Africa rising in a massive cyclone to layers of the upper atmosphere and then mixing with regular snow clouds over Russia.

Freeze that Fire!

When water was used to put out a burning building in Montreal, Quebec, Canada, in the late 19th century, the air temperature was so cold that the water quickly turned to ice.

St. James Street Fire, Montreal.

science

beyond belief

believe it!

world

animals

sports

body

transport

feats

mysteries

food

arts

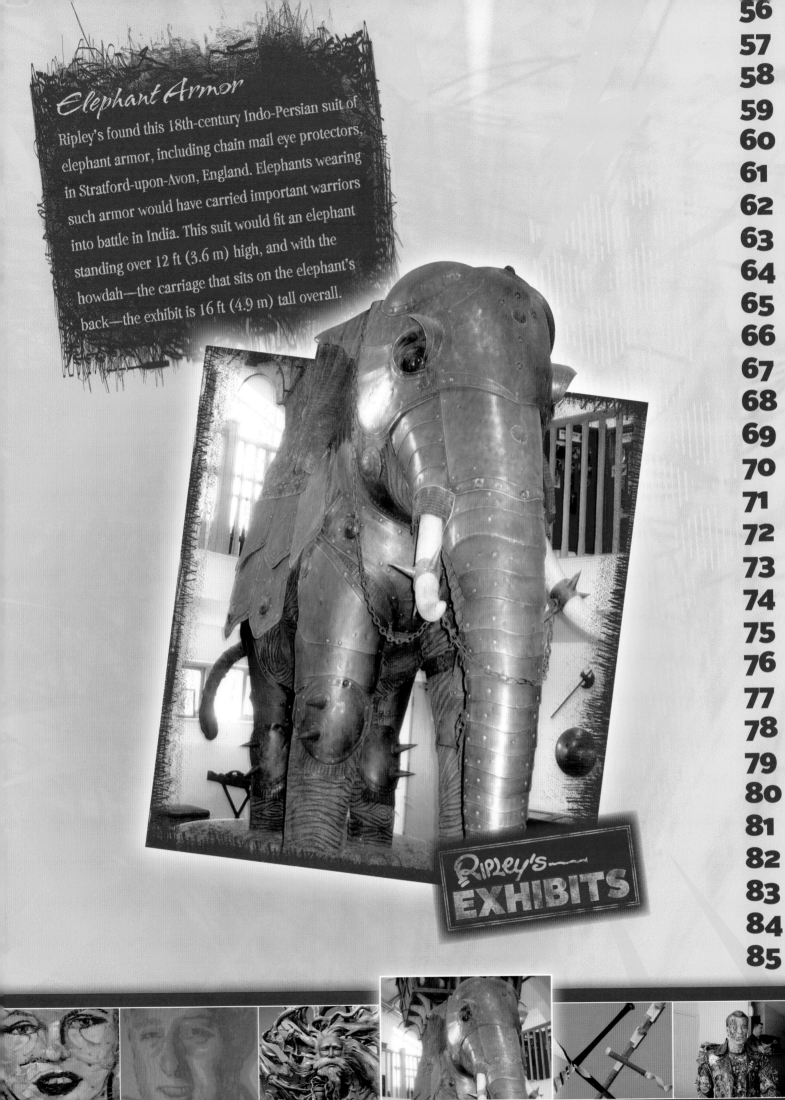

Elephant Armor

Ripley's found this 18th-century Indo-Persian suit of elephant armor, including chain mail eye protectors, in Stratford-upon-Avon, England. Elephants wearing such armor would have carried important warriors into battle in India. This suit would fit an elephant standing over 12 ft (3.6 m) high, and with the howdah—the carriage that sits on the elephant's back—the exhibit is 16 ft (4.9 m) tall overall.

Ripley's EXHIBITS

animals

Ripley's
Believe It or Not!®

A Bug's Life

Artist Chris Trueman of Claremont, California, came up with an unusual way to make this portrait of his younger brother dressed up as a cowboy look like an old, yellowed photograph—he used 200,000 dead ants. At first Chris tried to catch the harvester ants himself, but he soon realized that it would take him years to catch enough for the painting. So, he bought the ants live over the Internet and, after killing them, incorporated their bodies into the painting with tweezers and a resin called Galkyd, which has a yellowish color. It took him about two weeks to apply each batch of 40,000 ants to the portrait. The painting was first exhibited at the Alexander Salazar gallery in San Diego, but is now owned by Ripley's and will soon be on display in one of Ripley's 32 museums worldwide.

Ripley's Ask

What is the story behind the original photograph?
I staged and photographed my youngest brother Bryce when he was 6 or 7. I had him dress up in my old cowboy outfit and hold my father's unloaded rifle. He was in my parents' suburban backyard. It was a menacing image, as he pretended to be a cowboy, but was holding a real gun.

Why did you decide to use ants for the image? I was revisiting a specific experience from my childhood. When I was five years old, my younger brother and I attacked an anthill and were bitten by red ants. That was the first time I intentionally tried to harm intelligent life and, more than 25 years later, I decided to return to that experience. Ants ride the line of what we consider intelligent life—if we see them in the kitchen, many of us think little of killing them all. But if we take the time to look at them closely, they are remarkable creatures.

How long did it take to complete? It took several years, not because of the actual labor, but because at one point I started to feel bad about killing all of the ants and I stopped the project for over a year. Then I decided that because I was most of the way done, the first ants would have died in vain if I didn't finish the work, so I decided to continue. It was also quite an expensive work to produce as each shipment of ants would cost $500.

Can you explain how you work the ants into the painting? In the detailed areas I worked with tweezers and would put down a layer of Galkyd resin and then position the ants. In areas where the detail was less specific, I would sprinkle the ants on.

What was the most challenging aspect of this piece of work? The work was challenging from start to finish, finding and acquiring the ants, figuring out what medium to use, getting the right image, working in the details. I also had a hard time carrying through with the project. Some people don't believe me that it was hard to kill them, but I think at that quantity you become hyper-aware of what you are doing.

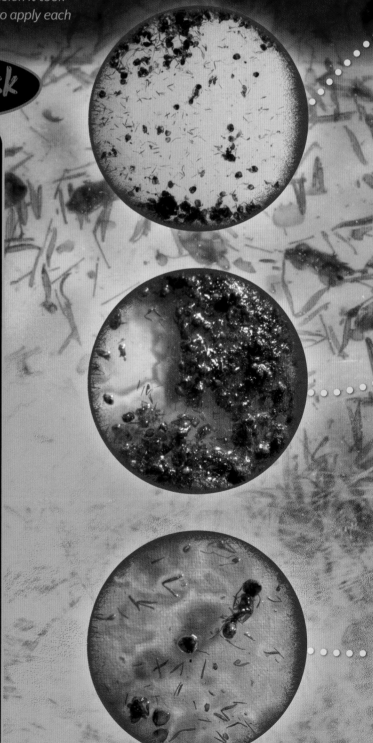

Red harvester ants are native to the southwestern U.S.A. and are relatively large, measuring ½ in (1.3 cm) long. They are venomous and will give a painful bite!

ESCAPE BID

A Tokyo Zoo worker dressed as an orangutan pretends to make a bid for freedom from his enclosure as part of the zoo's animal escape drill. Staff practice confronting the escapee, as well as surrounding him with nets, before pretending to shoot him with a tranquilizer dart.

monkey smuggler When customs officials at Mexico City International Airport noticed a passenger with a mysterious bulge in his clothing, they discovered that he had 16 live monkeys hidden inside his sweater.

ace ape Following a stint as a painter, where her works fetched up to $3,000, Nonja, an orangutan at Schoenbrunn Zoo, Vienna, Austria, turned her hand to photography. Keepers gave her a digital camera, which issued a fruit treat whenever a picture was taken, and set up a Facebook page for her on which thousands of fans viewed images of her food, her companion and climbing her rope.

eight lives left Sandy LaPierre's pet cat Smoka was found alive—after being buried deep in rubble for 26 days. Sandy had assumed that the cat had perished in the fire that destroyed her apartment in Franklin, Ohio, but almost a month later when demolition crews moved in to tear down what remained of the building, they found Smoka's head sticking out from under 16 ft (5 m) of debris.

parachuting pooches As part of their training, U.S. Army police dogs make parachute jumps, plummeting 12,500 ft (3,800 m) from a military helicopter at speeds of 120 mph (193 km/h).

shrinking sheep A breed of Scottish sheep has shrunk in body size by five percent over the last 24 years—because of climate change. The legs of the Soay sheep have got steadily shorter and their body weight has decreased as milder winters help smaller sheep to survive.

jumping cow Arriving home to find a damaged roof and smashed tiles, a woman in Somerset, England, phoned police to report a burglar—only to discover that the culprit was a cow that had somehow managed to jump 6 ft (1.8 m) up onto the roof.

extra leg Sydney May and Jamison Conley of Big Rapids, Michigan found a five-legged rat while working at a pet store.

bear-faced cheek A 125-lb (57-kg) black bear walked through the automatic doors of a Hayward, Wisconsin, grocery store in October 2009. He climbed 12 ft (3.6 m) onto a shelf in the beer cooler, and sat there happily for an hour before being tranquilized by wildlife authorities.

Lucky Lamb

A lamb in Shangdong Province, China, gets around well and is steady on his feet despite being born with only two legs. Sheep farmer Cui Jinxin would normally have killed the lamb at birth, but she was so moved by his determination to survive that she spared him and kept him as a pet.

spider fossil Scientists discovered a well-preserved, 165-million-year-old spider fossil in Inner Mongolia, China. It closely resembles a family of modern arachnids.

artistic dog Paintings by Sam, a pet dog owned by Mary Stadelbacher of Eastern Shore, Maryland, sell for up to $1,700. Sam has created more than 20 different works of art, each made by holding a tailor-made paintbrush in his mouth.

chimp chefs Chimpanzees in the mountain forests of Guinea, Africa, have been observed fashioning their own cutlery to eat food more comfortably. They have been seen using pieces of stone and wood to chop up their food into bite-size portions—this is the first time such behavior has been witnessed in a nonhuman species.

ticket seller A Chinese zoo recruited a baboon to work as a ticket seller. Tianjin Zoo in Tianjin, northeast China, said the baboon, named Chun Chun, accepted money from visitors, handed them their tickets and gave them their change—but still had to work with a human supervisor because he would only accept 100-yuan banknotes as they are red, his favorite color.

pig voter Pauline Grant took her pig Blossom to her local polling station in East Sussex, England, after the animal was sent a letter by the council asking it to vote at the 2010 general election. Owing to an administrative error, the pig receives several junk letters a month, plus repeated demands for overdue bills.

joyriding bear A bear climbed into an empty car outside a house near Denver, Colorado, honked the horn and knocked the gear shift on the automatic transmission into neutral, sending the vehicle rolling backward 125 ft (38 m) down the driveway into a thicket. The bear was still inside the car when deputies arrived on the scene. They suggested the bear had been attracted by a peanut butter sandwich left on the back seat.

guardian angel Eleven-year-old Austin Forman of Boston Bar, British Columbia, Canada, was saved from a cougar attack by his 18-month-old Golden Retriever, Angel, who leaped in front of the cougar and blocked its path, giving Austin time to escape. Angel survived, too, despite receiving puncture wounds around her head and neck.

DETERMINED DINER

Believe it or not, this incredible photograph shows a python attempting to haul a wallaroo out of a watering hole in Kimberly, Western Australia, in order to eat it. The wallaroo is a marsupial related to the kangaroo and can reach a length of 6½ ft (2 m), while the predator is an olive python, examples of which can stretch over 13 ft (4 m)—making it one of the biggest snakes in Australia.

Snake Stories

● IN 2009, A FAMILY IN KATHERINE, AUSTRALIA, DISCOVERED THAT AN 8-FT (2.5-M) OLIVE PYTHON HAD NOT ONLY EATEN THEIR PET RABBIT OSCAR BUT ALSO TAKEN UP RESIDENCE IN HIS RABBIT HUTCH.

● AN OLIVE PYTHON, MEASURING 6½ FT (2 M) LONG, WAS DISCOVERED TRAPPED INSIDE A WASHING MACHINE IN MIRANDA SEIB'S HOUSE IN BATCHELOR, AUSTRALIA, IN 2008. THE SNAKE HAD SLITHERED UP THROUGH THE PLUMBING.

● THREE MALAYSIAN FISHERMEN GOT MORE THAN THEY BARGAINED FOR WHEN THEY HAULED IN A NET AND DISCOVERED THEY HAD CAUGHT A 22-FT (6.6-M) PYTHON, COMPLETE WITH A 6½-FT-LONG (2-M) MONITOR LIZARD INSIDE ITS STOMACH.

Ripley's Believe It or Not!
animals

hero hugo A cat saved a neighbor's life by rescuing him from his burning home. Andrew Williams was asleep when the fire broke out in his bungalow in Berkshire, England, and he would almost certainly have died but for his neighbor's cat Hugo coming in through a catflap and waking him by clawing at his face. Hugo and his brother Harvey are regular visitors to the home of cat-lover Mr. Williams.

jack's journey A Whippet-Terrier cross called Jack was reunited with his owners in Sheffield, England, after a marathon 31-hour trek that took him across the M1—one of Britain's busiest expressways—four major roads and miles of treacherous moorland. The dog, who got separated from his owners on a walk, was especially brave considering he suffers from a fear of traffic, and walks with a limp after being knocked down by a truck in 2005.

wasp stings A 53-year-old woman from Attleboro, Massachusetts, survived being stung more than 500 times after falling onto a wasp nest outside her home. Firefighters used a carbon dioxide chemical fire extinguisher to blast the aggressive insects off the woman's body.

plunging parrots A mystery illness caused hundreds of lorikeets to fall out of the sky over Darwin, Northern Territory, Australia, in 2010. The birds appeared groggy and listless, as if they were suffering from a bad hangover, but recovered over a period of a few weeks.

POTTY PLANT
The mountain treeshrew of Malaysia has a handy place to go to the bathroom. There is a particular type of pitcher plant shaped conveniently like a treeshrew-sized toilet bowl that attracts the small creatures with its sweet nectar. And while the shrew feeds on the pitcher's nectar, the plant has been found to extract food of its own from the shrew droppings.

living larders Some members of honeypot ant colonies eat until they are unable to walk. They then become living food storage containers, regurgitating food for their nest mates as needed.

painful ritual To prove they are real men, teenage members of the Setere-Mawe people of Brazil subject themselves to being stung repeatedly by bullet ants, the sting of which is so painful it has been compared to a gunshot wound. For the initiation, boys wear a pair of gloves each laced with hundreds of live bullet ants, stingers pointing inward, for ten minutes—and they must go through this agonizing ritual 20 times.

faithful fowl Of the thousands of pairs of mating swans studied over 40 years at the Wildfowl and Wetlands Trust in Slimbridge, England, only two have ever "divorced" and found new partners.

air miles Arctic terns migrate about 43,000 mi (70,000 km) each year, which, during their lifetime of 30-plus years, works out at a distance equal to three round trips from the Earth to the Moon.

adaptable lungs Elephant seals collapse their lungs before they dive for food and can stay underwater for up to two hours.

population boom Under ideal conditions, a population of five pregnant female German cockroaches could grow to 45 million—in just a year.

Antarctic Escape
In 2005, a lucky gentoo penguin narrowly escaped a pod of hungry killer whales off the coast of Antarctica when it jumped from the water into an inflatable boat full of tourists that happened to be floating nearby. The penguin then swam away,

death dance Male Australian redback spiders, which weigh only one percent as much as females, must dance for well over an hour when approaching a female, otherwise they will be eaten before they can finish mating.

fisherman's luck? While fishing 80 ft (25 m) above the water from a cargo ship off the coast of Queensland, Australia, Filipino engineer Algerico Salise was stung by a tentacle from a thimble-sized irukandji jellyfish. The potentially fatal sting happened when the engineer's face was splashed with seawater that contained the jellyfish as he reeled in a fish. Urgent hospital treatment saved his life.

bird deodorant Scientists in New Zealand are seeking a deodorant for some of the country's smelly birds in a bid to make them less attractive to predators. Unlike their overseas counterparts, birds native to New Zealand did not evolve alongside traditional land mammals, and they emit a strong smell when preening themselves to produce the wax needed to protect their feathers. The kiwi emits a mushroom-like scent, while the kakapo parrot smells like a musty violin case—and these odors attract newly introduced foreign predators.

WHALE WHISPERER

Andrew Armour from the Caribbean island of Dominica is able to pet Scar, a vast sperm whale that he has befriended. The "whale whisperer," as Andrew is known, first encountered Scar as an injured calf ten years ago, and soon struck up a relationship when Scar, now 32 ft (10 m) long, began recognizing his boat. Andrew's unique relationship with Scar and the other whales in his pod gives a rare insight into the behavior of these mysterious animals, which can grow up to 65 ft (20 m) long, weigh more than five school buses and live for 70 years.

lost gator In 2010, a 5-ft-long (1.5-m) freshwater alligator was found swimming with whales 20 mi (32 km) out to sea in the North Atlantic off the coast of Georgia. It is thought the reptile had been washed out to sea from the mouth of the Altamaha River during heavy rains.

thieving spiders Rather than build their own webs, dewdrop spiders steal food or eat the leftovers from the webs of larger spiders.

bifocal bugs The principal eyes of the larvae of the sunburst diving beetle have bifocal lenses. The bifocals have been found in four of the larvae's 12 eyes and allow it to switch its vision from up-close to distance—all the better for seeing and catching its favorite prey, mosquito larvae.

KAMIKAZE CARPENTERS

A species of carpenter ant found in Borneo has a gruesome way to defend its colony. Designated soldier ants wait until a predator is close by and then sacrifice themselves by exploding glands that run along their bodies. These glands contain a sticky poisonous glue that ensnares the would-be invader, but also kills the carpenter ant in the process.

shark rider Attacked by a 14-ft-long (4.3-m) tiger shark off the coast of Hawaii, 68-year-old surfer Jim Rawlinson grabbed its fin, pulled himself on to its back so that he was straddling the shark and then rode it for about 10 seconds. Sliding off the beast's back and watching it swim off, Jim returned to what remained of his board (after the shark had bitten a chunk out of it) and surfed for another 45 minutes before returning to the beach uninjured.

false legs Meadow, a calf born in New Mexico who lost her two back hooves to frostbite, was able to walk again after being fitted with a pair of prosthetic legs by veterinarians at Colorado State University.

boating otter Wolfgang Gettmann of Dusseldorf, Germany, has a pet otter that accompanies him on kayaking trips.

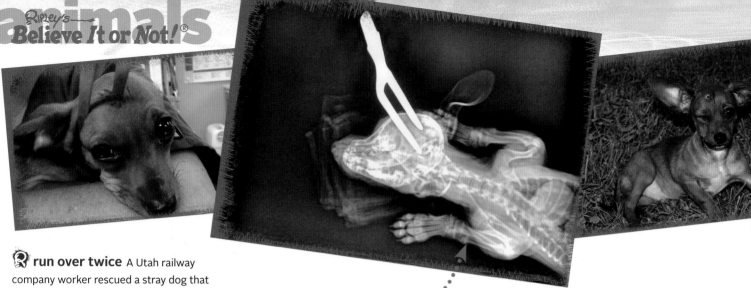

run over twice A Utah railway company worker rescued a stray dog that had been run over by a freight train twice on the same day—April 4, 2010. Although hit by the train's snowplow, the small dog survived and was nursed back to health by Fred Krause and his family.

car wash To raise funds, three African elephants at the Wildlife Safari Park in Winston, Oregon, were taught to wash visitors' cars. For $20 a time, the elephants scrubbed the cars with sponges and rinsed the water off with their trunks.

PAWS FOR THOUGHT

Hope, a cat owned by Nicole Kane from County Carlow, Ireland, has 24 digits—six on each paw.

UNLUCKY PUPPY

Smokey, a 12-week-old Chihuahua puppy from London, Kentucky, survived a freak accident at a garden party that left him with a barbecue fork stuck in his head. Despite having the 3-in-long (8-cm) fork prongs lodged in his brain for three days, veterinarians were eventually able to operate and save Smokey's life, and he was soon back at home with his owners.

vegetarian spider Unlike other spiders, *Bagheera kiplingi*, discovered recently in acacia trees in the forests of Central America, is vegetarian. It is almost exclusively herbivorous, only nibbling on ant larvae for an occasional change of diet. The males are also the only spiders that are known to help the females look after their eggs and young.

hunter hit In January 2010, a 53-year-old hunter in Los Banos, California, was shot and injured by his own dog when it stepped on the trigger of his loaded gun.

sex change A cockerel in Tuscany, Italy, changed sex after a fox raid on his enclosure killed all his hens. Within days of the 2010 raid, the bird that was previously a rooster suddenly started laying eggs and trying to hatch them.

irwin legacy A new, rare species of Australian tree snail has been named *Crikey steveirwini* in honor of the country's famous wildlife advocate, Steve Irwin, who was tragically killed by a stingray barb in 2006.

sixth sense A lost cat found her way to an animal rescue center in Fife, Scotland, despite having a can of cat food stuck on her head! The cat was thought to have been scavenging for food when she came across the discarded can. Unable to see where she was going, she somehow managed to avoid being hit by a car and wandered into the Scottish SPCA unit in Dunfermline where the tin headgear was removed.

Swallowed Diamond When a gem dealer dropped a $20,000 diamond in a Washington, D.C., jewelry shop, it was immediately gobbled up by a dog! The dealer got his diamond back three days later after nature took its course.

frozen journey In January 2010, a dog was rescued by the crew of a Polish ship after being found huddled on an ice floe 15 mi (24 km) out in the Baltic Sea. The shivering dog had floated at least 75 mi (120 km) down the Vistula River and out into the sea as temperatures dipped to below −4°F (−20°C).

domesticated deer Since being abandoned by her mother five years ago, Dillie the deer has shared the Canal Fulton, Ohio, home of the Butera family, where she has learned to turn lights on and off and fetch one of her favorite meals, ice cream, from the refrigerator.

diving dachshund Sergei Gorbunov, a professional diver from Vladivostok, Russia, has taught his pet Dachshund Boniface to scuba dive in a specially built wetsuit, complete with helmet.

high-rise heifer A cow was rescued from the 13th floor of an apartment block in Chelyabinsk, Russia, in 2009. No one knows how it got there, but when fire crews arrived they found it trying to get into an elevator. They decided bring it down the stairs instead.

Alien Monster?

Tomas Rak uses macro photography to make tiny, harmless British jumping spiders look like alien monsters from a horror movie. He scours the country in search of the spiders, which measure just ¼ in (6 mm) long, but can jump six times their own height. Tomas sometimes waits for up to three weeks to get the right shot.

bird slippers A baby African Crowned Crane was able to walk properly after keepers at a wildlife park in Cornwall, England, fitted its feet with a pair of tiny bright green slippers. The hand-reared chick had been born with a slight defect that left it with curled toes, but the slippers helped to straighten them out.

happy reunion Twelve-year-old Brierley Howard was reunited with her pet Labrador dog Iggy in 2010—nearly five years after he vanished. Amazingly, Iggy turned up 130 mi (209 km) away from the family home in Lancashire, England.

bewildered bear An inquisitive black bear in Vermont had a milk can stuck on its head for more than six hours in 2010. After the bear had been seen running around aimlessly, bumping into trees and boulders, rescuers successfully cut the can from the animal's head.

wine buffs Baboons invaded the vineyards in South Africa's Franschhoek Valley in early 2010 and ate thousands of bottles' worth of grapes right from the vines.

fox's revenge A wounded fox turned the tables on a hunter in the Grodno region of Belarus by accidentally putting its paw on the trigger of the hunter's rifle and shooting him. The hunter, who had been trying to finish the animal off with the butt of his rifle, was taken to hospital with a leg wound while the fox made its escape.

slow progress Lottie the tortoise disappeared from her home in Essex, England, in 2008— and was found safe and well nearly two years later, having traveled just 1½ mi (2.4 km).

FEARSOME FURRY FAMILY

In the wild, predators Shere Khan, Baloo and Leo would be mortal enemies, but at the Noah's Ark animal center in Georgia, the 350-lb (159-kg) Bengal tiger, 1,000-lb (454-kg) American black bear and 350-lb (159-kg) African lion live, eat and sleep together in the same custom-built cabin. The three gentle giants, all male, were rescued as a group of cubs in 2001 and their amazing relationship has developed as they've grown up together.

high hound Giant George, a blue Great Dane owned by David Nasser of Tucson, Arizona, stands 43 in (1.1 m) tall from paw to shoulder and weighs 245 lb (111 kg). He eats around 110 lb (50 kg) of food each month and is so tall that some children mistake him for a horse!

bad habits In 2010, Zhora, a chimpanzee at a zoo in Rostov, Russia, was sent to rehab to cure the smoking and beer-drinking habits he had picked up. He used to pester visitors at the zoo for cigarettes and alcohol.

beefy beetles Some male bull-headed dung beetles fight off love rivals by developing the strength to haul loads 1,000 times their own body weight—the equivalent of a human pulling six fully laden double-decker buses.

Lizard Boy

Navratan Harsh is the lizard boy of India, spending most of his time with the creatures, particularly his favorite geckos. In his local village in Rajasthan, he is known as the Gecko King owing to his love for the wild reptiles that he seeks out and trains. Navratan even enjoys the lizards biting his skin, crawling over his face and climbing inside his mouth.

extra teeth Martin Esquivel of Chaparral, New Mexico, owns a Chihuahua dog with two rows of front teeth.

speed queen In 2009, Sarah, a cheetah at the Cincinnati Zoo, Ohio, ran 100 m (109 yards) in 6.13 seconds—three seconds faster than Usain Bolt's best time. Sarah's time was all-the-more impressive because, at eight years old, she is middle-aged in big cat terms.

wasps' nest A giant wasps' nest measuring 6 x 5 ft (1.8 x 1.5 m)—almost as big as a king-size bed—was discovered in the loft of a pub in Southampton, England, in 2010.

rare reptile A two-headed, albino hognose snake was unveiled at a Venice Beach, California, sideshow in June 2010. Todd Ray paid $20,000 for the bizarre serpent—called Lenny and Squiggy—which he saw on an online reptile message board. Each of the snake's heads is fed twice a week.

bravery medal In 2010, a nine-year-old black Labrador dog named Treo was given Britain's Dickin medal—the highest military honor an animal can receive—for his work sniffing out explosives in Afghanistan. The medal has been awarded to more than 60 animals since its inception in 1943, including 32 carrier pigeons, three horses and a cat.

tongue tied Some chameleons have tongues that measure an incredible 4 in (10 cm) longer than their bodies. When at rest, the tongue sits rolled up at the bottom of the chameleon's throat, behind its head.

Artistic Ape For at least 30 minutes a day, Jimmy, a chimpanzee at Niteroi Zoo, Rio de Janeiro, Brazil, dips a brush into plastic paint containers and uses bold, broad strokes to create works of art. His keeper had tried everything to keep him entertained but Jimmy showed little interest in the usual chimp toys until the paints were introduced.

clever crocs Two dwarf crocodiles at an aquarium in Merseyside, England, have been taught to recognize their names. The Cuvier's caiman—named Paleo and Suchus—have also learned to open their mouths when requesting their food.

bat speak Just like people, bats have regional accents. A study of about 30 bat species living in the forests along the coast of New South Wales, Australia, found that their calls varied depending on their location.

MUSCLE HOUND

No, this is not trick photography, and this dog has not been pumping iron. Her oversized muscles are perfectly natural, albeit very unusual. Wendy, from Canada, is a "Bully" whippet, a mutation of the breed that causes muscles to grow to double their normal size, meaning Wendy is twice as heavy as a regular whippet.

Ripley's
Believe It or Not!®

Creepy Cr

They might look like strange extraterrestrial beings, but these creatures, photographed in Germany, are called harvestmen.

Although they look like spiders, harvestmen are actually another type of arachnid, only recently discovered in Europe. Different types of harvestmen often mass together in groups of tens of thousands, moving as one to resemble a single large organism. This seething carpet of tangled legs, which can each span 6 in (15 cm), is thought to deter predators—it also multiplies the effect of the unpleasant odor that harvestmen secrete when under threat.

Ripley's Believe It or Not! animals

CLOSE-UPS

Dr. Richard Kirby of the University of Plymouth, England, has taken high-magnification photographs of sea angels (*Clione limacina*), microscopic plankton that live in the ocean around the U.K. Despite their size, they anchor the entire marine food chain by providing fish with food and the world with oxygen, and they also play a key role in the global carbon cycle.

stunt baboon Moco, a baboon at China's Changzhou Yancheng Wild Animal Park, is such a talented gymnast and daredevil that he has joined a circus. He specializes in the flying rings but can also perform stunts involving the horizontal bars, parallel bars, balance beam, fire hoops and even bike riding!

SPOT THE CATERPILLAR

Believe it or not, there's a hungry caterpillar standing on this leaf! The Baron caterpillar—*Euthalia aconthea gurda*—of Southeast Asia is almost invisible against the background of this mango tree leaf in Kuala Lumpur, Malaysia.

doggy stroller Jenny, a pug owned by Ellen Zessin of Portland, Oregon, loves to stand on her hind legs and push her soft toy pugs around the garden in a baby stroller.

underground fish *Stygichthys typhlops*, an extremely rare blind fish that lives underground in Brazil, was recently rediscovered almost 50 years after the only known specimen was collected. Biologists believe that the fish may be a living relict that has survived deep below ground while its relatives above ground became extinct.

draining experience Three weeks after disappearing from Susan Garr's home in Salt Lake City, Utah, Millie, a four-year-old Australian Shepherd mix, was found stuck in a storm drain. Rescue crews freed the dog, whose weight had dropped from 35 lb (16 kg) to 22 lb (10 kg) during her ordeal.

hen-pecked A cockerel and his three hens gained revenge for a series of attacks by killing a young fox that broke into their pen in Essex, England. A table in the corner of the coop had been kicked over, knocking the fox out, allowing Dude the cockerel and hens Izzy, Pongo and Pecky to peck the intruder to death.

giant squid In July 2009, a 19.5-ft-long (6-m) giant squid was caught in the Gulf of Mexico—the first live giant gulf squid captured for more than 50 years.

helpful marking In case anyone has any doubt as to what sort of animal she is, Polly, a tabby kitten owned by Garry and Joan Marsh of Staffordshire, England, has the word "cat" clearly spelled out in her fur on her left side.

long lives Splish and Splash, two goldfish won at a funfair in Gloucestershire, England, by Hayley and Matthew Wright in 1977, were still alive 33 years later.

turtle surprise A monster grouper fish that died after being washed up on a beach in Townsville, Queensland, Australia, was found to have a whole sea turtle inside its stomach. The green turtle had a shell measuring 16 in (40 cm), while the fish, estimated to be 25 years old, weighed a mighty 330 lb (150 kg). Although the cause of the turtle's death was probably the grouper, veterinarians said it was unlikely that the turtle caused the grouper's death.

lucky by name... Lucky, a cat belonging to Keri Hostetler of New York City, survived a 26-story fall from the ledge of her apartment building.

NATURAL HAIRCUT

A manatee living off the coast of Florida receives a natural haircut from dozens of tiny blue gill fish, which crowd around the gentle sea mammal and eat algae, parasites and dead skin off its body.

Herd for Heights

These Alpine ibexes think nothing of climbing the near-vertical face of the Cingino Dam in the Italian Alps to lick minerals from the stones. Alpine ibex have incredible agility and balance, which enable them to cling to the rough rock of the 160-ft-high (49-m) dam with their hooves.

one big eye Although sea urchins don't have actual eyes, they see by using the entire surface of their body as one big eye. They have light-sensitive molecules, mainly in their tube feet and around their spines, and use these to avoid predators or find dark corners to hide in. Therefore, the sea urchins with the most densely packed spines are the ones with the best vision.

greyhound wedding Inseparable greyhounds Pete and Zoe were married in a canine ceremony at an animal shelter in Cambridgeshire, England. The bride wore a specially made dress and afterward she and her spouse devoured a three-tier liver cake. Staff thought a wedding would be a good way to seal the dogs' love for each other and to ensure they would be adopted together.

master of disguise The blue-striped fangblenny, a reef fish found off the coasts of Australia and Indonesia, can change its color at will to mimic other fish so it can get close enough to take a bite.

swallowed soccer ball Bracken, a two-year-old Labrador Retriever owned by John Grant of East Dunbartonshire, Scotland, needed emergency surgery after swallowing a whole toy soccer ball. The deflated ball—measuring 5 in (12 cm) long—had become lodged next to his heart, causing him to cough incessantly.

Scary Ride A tiny kitten that was just a few weeks old survived a 20-mi (32-km) journey in the engine of a car in Perthshire, Scotland. The cat had crawled under the hood of John Kellas' car. When the unsuspecting car-owner heard miaowing the following day, he drove the vehicle to a garage where mechanics found the terrified kitten stuck in a wheel arch. The kitten was given the name Farmer, after the garage that saved it.

ram raid A ram smashed through the glass patio door of a house in Lancashire, England, and ran amok, butting the stove door, knocking over a TV, smashing up furniture and wrecking carpets. It is believed the animal, which had fled from a nearby field and was agitated because of the breeding season, charged at the patio door after seeing his own reflection in the glass.

four wings A guin—a rare hybrid between a chicken and a guinea fowl—was born in Worcestershire, England, in 2010 with four wings. Although the strange chick had two extra wings at the front, it was unable to fly. Lyn Newman had introduced two guinea fowl into her coop to act as lookouts, unaware that they could breed with her hens.

lucky turtle In 1922, a giant turtle amazingly survived being swallowed by a shark. Suffering from nothing worse than cuts and shock, the turtle was rescued and taken to the New York Aquarium where he was named Jonah.

terrible tusks Babirusas, the "deer pigs" of the Indonesian archipelago, have a set of tusks that push straight through their nose and can grow long enough to curve back around and poke a hole in their forehead.

bee careful Ellie, a Labrador Retriever owned by Robert and Sandra Coe of Santee, California, survived after eating a beehive containing pesticides and thousands of dead bees. The inquisitive dog has also eaten wooden toy train tracks and laptop computer keys.

parrot alarm Burglars who broke into a house in London's Docklands in July 2010 were scared off when owner Gennadi Kurkul's green Lory parrot, Kuzya, let out a screech that could be heard several streets away.

bat cave Bracken Cave, near San Antonio, Texas, is home to 20 million bats that feed on more than 100 tons of insects every night.

panda puzzle Giant pandas possess the genes needed to digest meat, but none of the genes required to digest their only significant food source—bamboo.

BEE-STUNG LIPS

The 2010 Clovermead bee beard competition was abuzz with excitement as competitors were loaded with some of the millions of bees kept on the Clovermead farm in Ontario, Canada. A queen bee was attached to each competitor's neck, her smell attracting entire bee colonies. The champion beard belonged to Tibor Szabo, who wore a bee mask that covered his face. He was congratulated by a particularly courageous spectator.

OPEN WIDE

This fearsome deep-sea creature sports what appear to be humanlike teeth at the center of its tentacles. An unusual species of squid, the *Promachoteuthis sulcus* was discovered at a depth of 6,560 ft (2,000 m) in the South Atlantic Ocean. In reality it is far less terrifying than it appears—what look like teeth are fleshy lips around its beak, and this specimen is actually only 1 inch (2.5 cm) long.

ACTUAL SIZE ACTUAL SIZE ACTUAL SIZE ACTUAL SIZE

camel freed Fire crews shoveled mud for several hours to free a 1,500-lb (680-kg) camel that had fallen into an 8-ft-deep (2.4-m) sinkhole in Oregon City, Oregon.

allergic alsatian Joey, a sensitive Alsatian-Collie cross who lives in Hamilton, Scotland, gets a nasty rash if he chases a cat. He is also allergic to running through grass, jumping into water—and all types of food except potatoes and porridge.

beaver attack A large beaver weighing around 42 lb (19 kg) hospitalized fisherman Russ McTindal in 2010 after launching an unprovoked attack on him. The animal swam across Georgia's Chattahoochee River and launched at him, gnawing at his arm while he tried fending it off by hitting it with his fishing rod.

pinocchio frog On a 2008 expedition to West Papua, Indonesia, Australian scientist Paul Oliver found a tree frog with a long nose that points upward while the frog sounds a call.

IDENTITY THEFT

Pet dogs at the Dahe Pet Civilization Park in Zhengzhou, China, went undercover disguised as wild animals in 2010. With the help of some expertly applied paint, a Golden Retriever and a pack of Chow Chows were surprisingly convincing as the endangered tigers and pandas of China.

BEFORE

AFTER

Ripley's Believe It or Not!®

full house A 60-year-old woman shared her home in a suburb of Stockholm, Sweden, with her mother, her sister, her son—and 191 cats.

four ears A four-eared kitten was found living at a gas station in Vladivostok, Russia, in 2010. Luntik's second, smaller pair of ears do not have any canals, however, so his hearing is no better than that of the average cat.

fish hospital Patit Paban Halder runs a hospital for pet fish at his home in Chandannagore, West Bengal, India. The fish doctor does his rounds of the 32 aquariums, takes blood samples, checks the patients for fungus and bacteria and even gives them tiny injections.

heat alert A chocolate Labrador trapped in a car in Macungie, Pennsylvania, on a 90°F (32°C) day in July 2010 honked the horn until he was rescued. Max's owner had gone shopping and forgot that the dog was still in the car, but when she heard the sound of the horn she went outside and saw Max sitting in the driver's seat, honking the horn.

ice dive The dagger-shaped bill of the common kingfisher is so sharp that the bird can dive straight through a thin layer of ice to catch fish.

smoking viper Po the viper enjoys two cigarettes a day after picking up on his owner's 20-a-day habit. When Sho Lau of Taipei, Taiwan, casually threw a cigarette butt away, the snake went for it and seemed to enjoy having it in his mouth, subsequently becoming hooked on nicotine.

ankle biters A police officer who was escorting a teenager home following a traffic violation was hospitalized after being attacked by a gang of angry Chihuahuas. The five dogs ran from the boy's home in Fremont, California, and rushed the officer, leaving him with a number of injuries, including bites to his ankle.

ONE EAR

Rabbit breeder Franz-Xaver Noemmer from Egglham, Germany, holds his pet white rabbit born in February 2010 with only one ear.

BAT LINE

More than 130 orphaned bats were wrapped in dusters and hung on clothes lines while they recovered after being rescued from the devastating floods that hit Queensland, Australia, in January 2011. Vulnerable after coming to the ground to feed, the baby bats were picked up by the Australian Bat Clinic and then bottle-fed and housed in the cloths to keep warm.

gallant granny A 60-year-old grandmother fought off an attack from a 5-ft-long (1.5-m) shark by repeatedly punching and kicking it after it had ripped off chunks of her flesh. Paddy Trumbull suffered deep bite wounds and lost a huge amount of blood in the incident, which occurred while she was snorkeling off the coast of Queensland, Australia.

breast-fed calf After a calf's mother died when it was just three days old, Chouthi Bai of Kilchu, Rajasthan, India, saved the young animal's life by breast-feeding it three or four times a day. As well as giving the calf her own milk, Bai supplemented its diet with chapatis and water. Many people in India consider the cow to be a sacred animal.

rooster arrested A rooster was taken into police custody in Benton, Illinois, after it confronted a woman and her child in an aggressive manner. It was the latest in a series of incidents involving the bird, which had been bothering local residents and preventing them from going about their business.

zucchini attack When a 200-lb (91-kg) bear tried to force its way into a house near Frenchtown, Montana, in September 2010, a woman sent the animal fleeing by pelting it with a large zucchini. As the bear stuck its head through the doorway, the woman grabbed a 14-inch-long (35-cm) zucchini from the kitchen counter and hurled the vegetable at the bear, hitting it on the top of its head and causing it to run off.

swallowed glass A German Pointer dog had to undergo emergency surgery after downing a shot of Jägermeister liqueur—and the glass—at a party in Australia. Billy made a full recovery following a three-hour operation to remove the glass from his stomach.

burpless sheep Australian scientists are working on a program to breed sheep that don't burp in a bid to reduce greenhouse gas emissions. The agriculture sector in Australia produces about 16 percent of the country's total emissions, and two-thirds of that figure comes from livestock, chiefly the result of methane being released from the guts of grazing sheep and cattle.

crab crawl The 100 million red crabs living on Christmas Island in the Pacific Ocean walk from the inland forest to the island's shoreline and back in an annual breeding migration. Roads are closed and special tunnels dug as the entire island is turned into a creeping crimson carpet.

food sharing Bonobos—a sister species of chimpanzees—share things just like humans. A scientific study of bonobos in the Democratic Republic of the Congo showed that they voluntarily shared their food with other members of their group, making them the only species known to do this apart from humans.

cat nap A house fire in Port Townsend, Washington State, was started by a cat that managed to depress a toaster lever while sleeping on top of the toaster oven. The cat, which slept there to avoid the family's dog, escaped unharmed.

permanently pregnant European brown hares are capable of being pregnant twice at the same time—and can therefore potentially be permanently pregnant. Researchers in Berlin, Germany, fertilized female hares in late pregnancy and found they became pregnant again about four days before delivery, a phenomenon known as superconception. Simultaneous pregnancies mean the hares can give birth to up to a third more offspring each reproductive season.

clean kitten A kitten had an incredible escape after climbing into a washing machine and going through a full wash cycle. Liz Fear's seven-month-old Burmese cat Suki was soaked, rinsed and then spun dry after climbing in with a load full of dirty clothes at the family home in Melbourne, Australia. Despite her ordeal, Suki was later given a clean bill of health.

Pretty Boy

Despite his bug eyes, crooked mouth and distinctive teeth, Ug, a partially blind two-year-old Pointer cross, proved a big hit with the ladies. April Parker from Doncaster, England, paid £200 ($320) for him— and renamed him Doug—after her two teenage daughters fell in love with him on an animal sanctuary's website.

Ripley's—
Believe It or Not!®

PRETTY IN PINK
This rare, bright pink grasshopper was found in the garden of a house in Havant, England, in July 2010. Grasshoppers are normally green and this one's colorful pigmentation is bad news, as it makes the insect more vulnerable to attack from predators.

® RIPLEY RESEARCH
A grasshopper can either be born pink as the result of a genetic mutation or turn pink as an adult because of infection. During the summer, a parasitic worm may enter the insect's body through its food, and this can alter the grasshopper's physiological status and cause it to change color.

® **dog on wheels** Tillman, a five-year-old bulldog owned by Ron Davis of Oxnard, California, can skateboard 325 ft (100 m) in under 20 seconds. The 60-lb (27-kg) dog began skateboarding at the age of nine months and has now mastered it so well that he can do turns and tricks. Tillman has also been trained to surf and snowboard. "He's an adrenaline junkie," says Davis.

® **yoga bear** Santra, a female brown bear at Ahtari Zoo, Finland, performs a 15-minute yoga routine every morning. Visitors watch in amazement as she calmly stretches both legs before balancing on her bottom and pulling them up around her ears.

® **pigs can fly** Scarlet, a Hungarian mangalitza pig, loves to bounce around on a trampoline at her home in Shropshire, England. Gwen Howell discovered her pet's hidden talent after leaving her on the family's trampoline in the garden, and soon the pig was spending 45 minutes a day on it.

® **swooping hawk** Canada Post temporarily suspended mail service to 150 homes in a suburb of Calgary, Alberta, in September 2010 because a hawk repeatedly swooped down from the sky and attacked the postman. The bird was so aggressive it even broke a bike helmet the mail carrier was wearing for protection.

® **too small** An owl chick had an incredible escape at Paignton Zoo, Devon, England, after it fell from its nest and landed right next to an adult lioness. The tawny owls nest in a tree in the lion enclosure, but this one got lucky because the lioness, Indu, decided it was too small to eat.

® **watch bird** Lorenzo the parrot was arrested in Colombia in 2010 for trying to tip off a local drug cartel while police officers carried out an undercover raid. Police suspicions were confirmed when Lorenzo spent the whole of his first morning in custody squawking: "Run, run, you are going to get caught."

Ripley's Help Ripley
When the My Heart's Desire animal rescue group in Louisiana found this abandoned poodle in a ditch, he was in such an unbelievable condition that they named him Ripley, after *Ripley's Believe It or Not!* According to shelter co-director Tracy Lapeyrouse, "You would have never believed there was a dog under there. He didn't even look like a dog. He looked like the elephant man. All you could see was his snout." Ripley's fur was so overgrown and twisted that he couldn't see or even get up and walk.

When *Ripley's Believe It or Not!* heard about Ripley's predicament, they stepped in to help, making a donation to the animal rescue center and pledging to help his new owners cover Ripley's food and grooming expenses. At the shelter, Ripley was shorn of 2 lb 8 oz (1.2 kg) of thick matted hair, given a wash and a feed, and was soon looking like a dog again, ready for adoption.

bionic cat A cat that lost both of his back paws in an accident can run and jump again after being fitted with two bionic legs. The mechanical implants were drilled into Oscar's ankles by British veterinarian Noel Fitzpatrick, and then treated with a substance that allows bone and skin to grow around them. To give Oscar full movement, fake paws were then fitted on "see-saw" joints at the ends of the prosthetics.

mini horse Einstein, a horse born in April 2010 in Barnstead, New Hampshire, weighed just 6 lb (2.7 kg) and stood only 14 in (35 cm) tall at birth.

chewed toe Kiko the Jack Russell terrier saved his owner's life by eating his big toe. After Jerry Douthett of Rockford, Michigan, passed out one day, Kiko sensed an infection festering in his master's right big toe and chewed most of it off. Douthett woke up to find lots of blood and rushed to a nearby hospital where doctors diagnosed him with diabetes with a dangerously high blood-sugar level. A bone infection meant the toe needed to be amputated.

tiny frog A new species of frog found in Borneo measures a tiny 0.4 in (10.2 mm) long as an adult—that's about the size of a fingertip. The micro species *Microhyla nepenthicola*, which was named after a plant that is also found on the island, had been documented before, but scientists had wrongly assumed it was a juvenile of another species of frog instead of an adult in its own right.

SEAGULL SNIPER

A seagull was seen flying around the seaside town of Scarborough, England, for more than a month with a crossbow bolt through its head. Local animal rescue officers tried to catch and treat the bird, but to no avail. The victim of a mystery sniper, the seagull was able to survive because the bolt miraculously missed its brain.

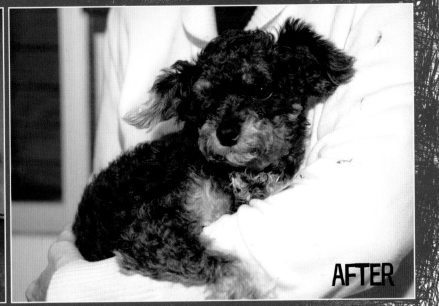

world tour Together with his South African owner Joanne Lefson, Oscar the dog visited five continents and 29 countries in 2009. During their nine-month world tour, Oscar walked on the Great Wall of China, posed beneath the Statue of Liberty and took in such sights as the Eiffel Tower and the Taj Mahal.

swollen tongue Penny, an 18-year-old dog from Paisley, Scotland, nearly suffocated after a freak accident caused her tongue to swell to four times its normal size. She was eating her favorite treat of pig's heart when membrane from the pig's aorta wound itself around the base of her tongue, cutting off the blood supply and causing it to swell up. As she tried to paw her tongue free, blood began gushing from her mouth. Luckily, veterinarian Dermot Mullen managed to separate the aorta from her tongue.

quicker by pigeon A carrier pigeon proved faster than a rural broadband connection in an English race to determine which was more efficient at sending a video from East Yorkshire to Lincolnshire. Rory the pigeon made the journey carrying the five-minute video loaded onto a computer memory card in 80 minutes, reaching his destination while the computer was still uploading the video.

colorful cat Natasha Gregory from Swindon, Wiltshire, England, dyed the white fur of her cat pink with food coloring so that it matched her own pink hair.

BEFORE

AFTER

Toadally Cool

You've heard of leather made from cows, and even alligators and kangaroos, but what about toads? Marino Leather Exports, from Cairns, Australia, has been making bags, purses and hats from giant Cane Toads since 1994. There are now more than 60 items in the range, some using the entire toad, which can grow to a length of 15 in (38 cm)—and that's not counting the legs.

---

spat out A new species of chameleon was discovered in 2009—inside the mouth of a snake. The tiny lizard, *Kinyongia magomberae*, small enough to sit in the palm of a human hand, was spat out dead by a twig snake that had been disturbed by a scientist in Tanzania's Magombera forest.

croc house Shaun Foggett from Oxford, England, shares his semi-detached house with his fiancée, their three young children and 24 crocodiles and alligators. He spends $12,000 a year feeding the reptiles.

ALIEN FROG

This may look like a weird alien creature, but it is really a close-up of an eye of a sleeping red-eyed tree frog photographed by Igor Siwanowicz at his studio in Munich, Germany. Igor has spent over seven years studying insects and amphibians and has captured such strange natural phenomena as a praying mantis posing like a kung-fu fighter and two stag beetles wrestling.

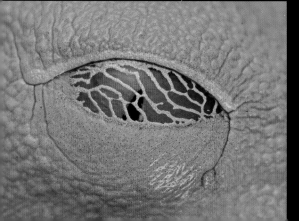

clever collie Whereas most dogs can recognize about 15 commands, Betsy, a seven-year-old Border Collie in Austria, can recognize more than 340 words. She can also fetch an object after seeing a picture of it.

no hurry At its average speed of 0.03 mph (0.05 km/h), a garden snail would take 34,519 days to slide around the world—that's nearly 95 years.

giant amphibians The giant salamanders of China and Japan can grow to more than 5 ft (1.5 m) in length and live for as long as 50 years.

insect velcro A species of South American ant—*Azteca andreae*—has its own Velcro-like device that enables it to hold on to about 6,000 times its body weight—the equivalent of a domestic cat holding on to a humpback whale. The ant's claws are shaped like hooks and fit neatly into fibrous loops on the undersides of the leaves where it lives, enabling it to trap much bigger insects as prey.

yap nav Taxi driver Andrzej Szymcakowi from Lodz, Poland, decided to switch off his GPS after realizing that Bobo, his Yorkshire Terrier, is better at giving him directions. Bobo, who has traveled in the cab since he was a puppy, knows all the routes. He yaps and raises his right paw to indicate a right turn, lifts his left paw for a left turn, and barks and wags his tail for straight on.

ant invasion Millions of crazy Rasberry ants—a newly recognized species named after Tom Rasberry, an exterminator from Pearland, Texas—have been swarming over the state. They are attracted to electrical equipment and have ruined pumps at sewage pumping stations, fouled computers and gas meters, and caused fire alarms to malfunction. Rasberry had to clear the ants from the Johnson Space Center, one of NASA's major facilities, for fear that they would destroy the computer systems.

gambling rabbit Daisy the pet white rabbit has become a regular at the Prince of Wales pub in Malvern, England, where he enjoys a drink of cider while playing the fruit slot machine. His owner says the rabbit loves the flashing lights.

slippery surface A highway in northern Greece was closed for two hours in May 2010 after millions of frogs emerging from a nearby lake caused three drivers to skid off the road.

goat land-scraping City officials in Chattanooga, Tennessee, use herds of goats to control invasive kudzu vines, one of their favorite foods.

toxic rub Lemurs of Madagascar rub millipedes over their bodies, covering themselves in toxic chemicals, before eating the bugs.

big stink An infestation of stinkbugs hit Brooklyn, New York City, in January 2010. The small, brown flying beetles, which are native to the Far East, emit a smell like rotting cheese when they are squashed or even vacuumed.

golf balls When Chris Morrison from Dunfermline, Scotland, noticed a strange rattling sound coming from the stomach of his black Labrador, Oscar, he took the five-year-old dog to a veterinarian—who removed 3 golf balls from the animal's stomach. One of the balls had been in Oscar's stomach so long that it had turned black and was decomposing.

long journey A cat traveled an amazing 2,000 mi (3,200 km) over a period of two years to track down his owners after they had moved house without him. Ravila Hairova thought her gray cat, Karim, would find the move from Gulistan, Uzbekistan, too traumatic, so she asked neighbors to take him in, but in 2010 she found her bedraggled pet waiting on her doorstep at her new home in Liska, Russia.

in the doghouse A dog named Bruno was found safe and well 20 mi (32 km) away from his home in Gesztered, Hungary, after he and the kennel he was in were sucked into the sky by the wind during a violent storm. Agnes Tamas had chained her pet, whom she has renamed Lucky, to the kennel and could only watch helplessly as the doghouse was lifted up into the air with the animal cowering inside.

PSYCHIC OCTOPUS

Paul the Psychic Octopus became a worldwide celebrity after correctly predicting all of the German national soccer team's results at the 2010 World Cup. Before each match, two plastic boxes, one with a German flag and one with the flag of their opponents, were lowered into his tank at the Oberhausen Sea Life Center in Germany. Each box contained a tasty mussel, and the box that Paul opened first was judged to be the predicted winner. After correctly forecasting five German victories, he upset the nation by choosing Spain to win their semifinal clash. Spain duly defeated Germany, and Paul maintained his 100 percent record by predicting that Spain would beat the Netherlands in the final.

mutant frogs Ribeiroia trematodes, a parasitic flatworm, infects tadpoles, causing them to grow several additional legs as they develop into adult frogs.

defence mechanism In addition to their venomous fangs, many species of tarantula defend themselves with a patch of barbed, inflammatory hairs on their abdomen, which they kick off into the air.

shark fight Fishermen were reeling in a 10-ft-long (3-m) great white shark off the coast of Australia in October 2009 when a second great white—estimated to be 20 ft long (6.1 m)—bit it nearly in half.

sacred whale In February 2010, nearly 10,000 people gathered in a small Vietnam village to pay homage to a 15-ton whale that had died offshore.

croc jailed A cranky crocodile was thrown in jail for three days in 2009 for loitering around the town of Arrkuluk Camp in Australia's Northern Territory. Rangers seized the 6-ft-6-in (2-m) saltwater croc and placed it in a police cell after it had been spotted acting suspiciously near a residential area.

six-legged calf An otherwise healthy calf, born in Leizhou, Guangdong Province, China, in March 2010 had two extra legs—complete with hooves—and a second tail growing out of its back.

water catastrophe An octopus flooded California's Santa Monica Pier Aquarium by swimming to the top of its tank and disassembling the water recycling system's valve—causing around 200 gal (757 l) of seawater to gush on to the floor.

nut house Veined octopuses, found off the coast of Indonesia, occasionally carry empty coconut shells as portable homes.

curious eater Polly, an Australian cattle dog, underwent surgery to remove 1,000 magnets from her stomach. The dog, who took the magnets from the office of her owner, Cathy James of Mickleham, Victoria, had previously swallowed a computer mouse, gardening gloves and several rolls of fax paper.

MATCH	PAUL'S PICK	RESULT	
Germany vs. Australia	Germany	Germany 4	Australia 0
Germany vs. Serbia	Serbia	Serbia 1	Germany 0
Germany vs. Ghana	Germany	Germany 1	Ghana 0
Germany vs. England	Germany	Germany 4	England 1
Germany vs. Argentina	Germany	Germany 4	Argentina 0
Germany vs. Spain	Spain	Spain 1	Germany 0
Germany vs. Uruguay	Germany	Germany 3	Uruguay 2
Netherlands vs. Spain	Spain	Spain 1	Netherlands 0

Ⓡ **shell slice** When veterinarians at Brazil's Anhembi Morumbi University discovered that a pregnant tortoise was unable to deliver her eggs naturally, they cut away a small square section of her shell with an electric circular saw and safely retrieved the eggs. They then replaced the piece of shell and left the tortoise to recover.

Ⓡ **cliff plunge** Oscar, a five-year-old Cocker Spaniel owned by Rupert and Emma Brown, survived despite running over the edge of a 120-ft-high (37-m) cliff in Dorset, England. He emerged from his death-defying leap with nothing worse than a slight limp after being rescued from the rocks below by a canoeist who had witnessed the accident.

Ⓡ **eggs-hausted** A chicken belonging to Chris Schauerman of Honeoye Falls, New York State, laid a 5-oz (140-g) egg (two-and-a-half times normal size), along with five normal eggs—but the stress was so great that the bird died.

Ⓡ **splash of color** A beluga whale at the Qingdao Polar Ocean World in China paints pictures that sell for hundreds of dollars. Xiao Qiang paints with the brush in his mouth while his keeper holds the paper. Belugas are able to manipulate a brush because they have more soft tissue around their mouth than other whales and the turning of the head to paint is a natural movement that they perform in the wild when cleaning sand from their food.

Ⓡ **purr-fect day** In an unofficial ceremony, postman Uwe Mitzscherlich, from Possendorf, Germany, "married" his cat Cecilia in May 2010 after being told that the animal did not have long to live. As marrying an animal is illegal in Germany, Uwe paid an actress $395 to officiate at the ceremony.

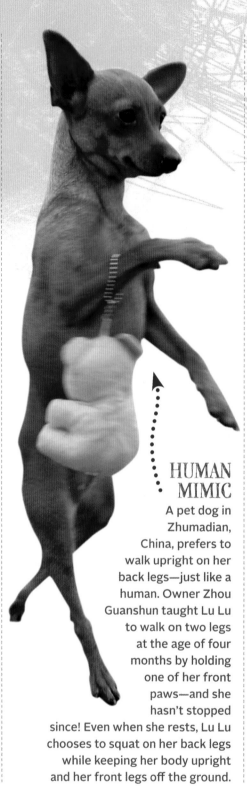

HUMAN MIMIC

A pet dog in Zhumadian, China, prefers to walk upright on her back legs—just like a human. Owner Zhou Guanshun taught Lu Lu to walk on two legs at the age of four months by holding one of her front paws—and she hasn't stopped since! Even when she rests, Lu Lu chooses to squat on her back legs while keeping her body upright and her front legs off the ground.

Ⓡ **royal lineage** Queen Elizabeth II has owned more than 30 Corgis, nearly all descended from her first dog, Susan, who died in 1959, and was a gift from her parents on her 18th birthday.

Ⓡ **rabbit whisperer** Cliff Penrose, of St. Austell, Cornwall, England, has treated hundreds of rabbits with behavioral problems by hypnotizing them. By massaging certain parts of a rabbit's body, particularly the belly, he is able to relax the animal in a matter of seconds. He then "bows" to the rabbit by lowering its head so that it does not feel threatened before shutting its eyelids, leaving it in a trance. He says the rabbit emerges from the trance a happier, more relaxed pet.

Ⓡ **mosquito killer** In a contest organized by an insect trap company Huang Yuyen, a pig farmer from Taiwan, killed and caught more than four million mosquitoes in a month. Her haul weighed in at just over 3 lb 5 oz (1.5 kg).

Ⓡ **sewer snake** In 2005, a 10-ft-long (3-m) python lived for three months in a neighborhood sewer system in Manchester, England, moving from toilet to toilet before it was eventually caught.

Ⓡ **selective breeding** Researchers at Yale University are working to bring back to life a species of giant Galapagos tortoise that became extinct hundreds of years ago. The selective breeding program, based on the D.N.A. of the tortoises' great-great-great-grandchildren, will take over a century to complete owing to the reptiles' long lifespan and the fact that they don't reproduce until they are 20 to 30 years old.

Ⓡ **turtle eggs** In 2006, scientists in Utah discovered a 75-million-year-old fossil of a pregnant turtle, with a clutch of eggs inside.

CRASH LANDING

A couple on a whale-watching trip off Cape Town, South Africa, got a closer view than they expected when a 40-ton, 33-ft-long (10-m), southern right whale suddenly jumped on to their yacht. After snapping the mast on impact, it thrashed around before sliding back into the water. A species with notoriously bad eyesight, the whale navigates by sound, and as the boat had its engine off, the whale probably hadn't realized it was there.

LIGHTNING STRIKE!

A cow miraculously survived after being struck by lightning near the town of Gladstone in Queensland, Australia. The animal was left with blistering burns and ankle wounds after the bolt apparently entered via its front legs and exited out the back legs. Cows are particularly susceptible to lightning strikes because they graze with all four legs on the ground and eat grass from the ground, where electricity is conducted from the strike.

swooping swan A motorcyclist in Worcestershire, England, suffered a broken collarbone after being knocked off his bike by a low-flying swan.

wire walk At a zoo in Fuzhou, Fujian Province, China, visitors flock in their hundreds to see a goat walking a tightrope while being ridden by a small monkey!

regurgitates fish A performer with the Great Moscow Circus swallows and regurgitates a live fish. Local authorities banned her act when the circus visited Australia in 2010 for being cruel to the fish.

good disguise A zebra's black-and-white stripes are effective camouflage because lions, who hunt them, are colorblind.

uninvited passenger In February 2010, a turkey vulture crashed through the windshield of a helicopter being flown by Paul Appleton over Miami, Florida, and landed on his lap. It sat there until the chopper landed, then flew away. Appleton sustained a scratch to his forehead and the bird partially knocked off his headset and glasses, but luckily it didn't knock his hand from the controls.

▲The lion approaches the white Toyota and tries the door handle with its teeth.

▲Curiosity gets the better of the cat as it starts to open the unlocked door.

▲The lion pulls the door open, leaving the occupants momentarily frozen in fear before they drive off.

ANY CHANCE OF A RIDE?

A couple visiting Lion Safari Park, Johannesburg, South Africa, had the fright of their lives when a 300-lb (136-kg) lion opened the rear door of their car with its teeth. As they drove off, the lion chased the car to the park gates, where a game warden managed to shoo it back into the enclosure.

pet wash Animal owners in Japan can wash their cats and dogs in specially designed washing machines at pet supermarkets. The machines, which are claimed to be entirely safe, give the animals a shampoo, a rinse and a dry in a half-hour cycle for around $10.

bison family The last wild European bison was killed in 1927 and the 3,000 animals alive today are all descendants of 12 captive bison.

secret growl Scientists at San Diego Zoo, California, have discovered that, in addition to the familiar trumpeting call, elephants communicate in a secret language that is largely inaudible to humans. They say two-thirds of the elephants' growling sound is at a frequency too low to be picked up by human ears.

bringing up baby A Chinese woman rocked an abandoned bear cub to sleep each night and put him in diapers so that he didn't soak the wooden box she had made for his bed. Huang Lijie adopted the cub, which she called Hu Niu, at her home in Dandong, Liaoning Province, and fed him milk and baby food four times a day until he was big enough to be released back into the wild.

pink hippo British wildlife photographers Will and Matt Burrard-Lucas were picnicking on the banks of the Mara River in Kenya's Masai Mara game reserve in 2010 when they spotted a pink hippo emerge from the water onto the opposite bank! The animal's rare coloring is a result of leucism, a condition in which pigmentation cells fail to develop properly, causing pale skin color.

missing in action Sabi, a bomb-sniffing dog for the Australian Special Forces in Afghanistan, was lost during a battle in September 2008 and wandered the countryside until an American soldier found her 14 months later.

tortoise masks Following a fire at Poestlingberg Zoo in Linz, Austria, fire crews saved the lives of six giant tortoises by strapping oxygen masks onto their heads. Although the masks were designed for humans, they fitted the 140-lb (63.5-kg) tortoises and prevented them dying from smoke inhalation.

pigeon spy A white pigeon that landed in the Indian state of Punjab, close to the border with Pakistan, was taken to a police station where it was held under armed guard and accused of spying. It had a ring around its foot and a Pakistani phone number and address stamped on its body in red ink, but the message it was suspected of carrying was never found.

TUG-OF-WAR

A thirsty baby elephant that ventured to the edge of a waterhole in South Africa's Kruger National Park got the fright of its life when a lurking crocodile suddenly grabbed it by the trunk. As the croc tried to drag its prey into the water, the baby's distress calls alerted the rest of the herd and they managed to scare off the reptile by trumpeting loudly and stamping their feet.

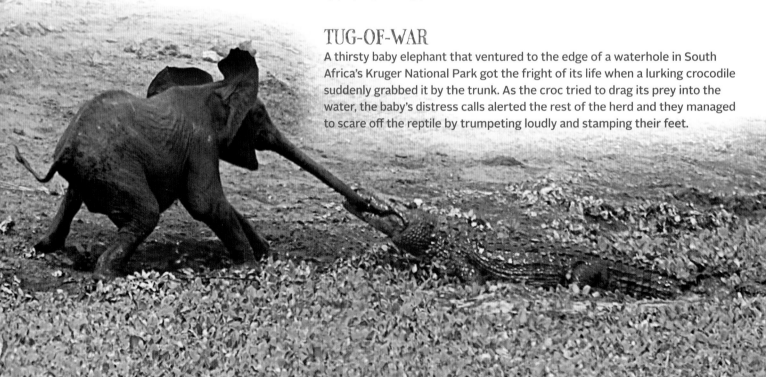

bear steals teddy A black bear broke into a house in Laconia, New Hampshire, in 2010 and stole a teddy bear! The burglar bear ate a selection of fruit, and drank from the Parkinson family fishbowl, before making off with the stuffed toy after being scared by the sound of the garage door being raised.

lone wolverine Buddy, California's last wolverine, was discovered roaming the Tahoe National Forest in 2008—almost 90 years after the species was declared extinct in the state. He was seen marking his territory to attract a mate—even though the nearest other wolverines are thought to be more than 800 miles (1,290 km) and two states away.

romantic stork A stork named Rodan flies 8,080 mi (13,000 km) each year from South Africa to Brodski Varos, Croatia, to visit his handicapped mate, Malena, who is unable to fly. They have chicks each year and Rodan teaches them to fly. He then takes them with him to South Africa for the winter and returns with them to Malena in the spring.

ink intact Even though it died around 155 million years ago, scientists were still able to extract ink from the fossilized remains of a squid-like creature discovered in a rock in Wiltshire, England. The odds of finding a squid's delicate ink sac intact after so many centuries are put at a billion to one.

rubber crocs Pansteatitis, a disease normally associated with cats, caused the body fat of more than 200 crocodiles in South Africa's Kruger National Park to turn to the consistency of shoe rubber in 2008, eventually killing them. The disease, which results from eating too much rancid fat, led the reptiles' body fat to solidify, leaving them heavy, lethargic and unable to hunt. When their bodies were opened up, the crocodiles' insides were found to be orange, hard and rubbery.

vet trapped A female veterinarian had to be rescued by fire crews in Devon, England, after becoming trapped under a sedated horse. She was called to a farm to treat a horse that was stuck in a fence, but when she sedated it, the animal fell asleep on top of her.

Monster Bug

Giant isopods are a cousin of the humble wood louse and often measure up to 15 in (38 cm) long. They live 1,000–7,000 ft (300–2,100 m) deep in the ocean and can weigh almost 4 lb (1.8 kg). In April 2010, oil workers in the Gulf of Mexico discovered a giant isopod double this size, measuring 2½ ft (76 cm) long!

ACTUAL SIZE!

RIPLEY RESEARCH
The giant isopod is an example of deep-sea gigantism, where creatures living at great depths are often much larger than their shallow-water counterparts. This is thought to be because deep-sea animals need a sturdy body to withstand the colder temperatures and intense pressure in the watery depths, plus the slow pace of life, which delays sexual maturity and results in greater size.

Balancing Act

A pig in Xincai County, Henan Province, China, can walk despite being born with only its two front legs. Owner Wang Xihai started training the two-legged piglet to walk when it was just a few days old by lifting it up by its tail, and after a month it was able to walk upside down without help. Named by villagers Zhu Jianqiang ("strong-willed pig"), it can balance and move well on its front trotters even though it weighs over 110 lb (50 kg).

fishing dog A dog in China's Hubei Province has become a local celebrity after taking up fishing. Mr Lin's dog, Ding Ding, had always loved swimming in Donghu Lake, but in 2009 he suddenly started catching live fish. His owner says the dog locates the fish by watching bubbles coming from the water.

busy beavers A beaver dam in Wood Buffalo National Park, Northern Alberta, Canada, is more than 2,800 ft (850 m) long. The construction, which has been worked on by several generations of beavers since the 1970s, is so big that it can be seen on NASA satellite photographs taken from outer space.

clever horse Lukas, a 17-year-old thoroughbred horse owned by Karen Murdock of Chino Hills, California, has mastered 35 feats of intelligence—including counting, spelling and shape sorting. He can spell his own name, Karen's name, and that of Karen's husband Doug. Lukas has also learned to nod his head for "yes" and shake it for "no," curtsy, and pretend to be lame.

rodent infestation Police who raided an apartment in Aachen, Germany, discovered that it was overrun by 300 guinea pigs—and in some rooms the pile of droppings was 4 in (10 cm) high.

hero buddy Buddy the German Shepherd saved his owner's home by guiding emergency service personnel to the blazing building. The dog was in the Caswell Lakes, Alaska, workshop of his owner, Ben Heinrichs, when a stray spark started a fire. Buddy then ran out, found an Alaskan Trooper at a crossroads and, by running in front of the patrol car, steered him through a series of back roads to the scene of the fire.

bee line A swarm of 20,000 bees attached themselves to colorful socks and underpants that were hanging on a woman's clothes line in Victoria, Australia.

replica romance Timmy, a 60-year-old tortoise who lives in a sanctuary in Cornwall, England, has fallen in love with a plastic toy tortoise. He never hit it off with other tortoises, but since Tanya the replica was introduced into his enclosure, he has started nuzzling and kissing her and fetching food for her.

thieving octopus Victor Huang was diving off the coast of Wellington, New Zealand, in April 2010 when an octopus suddenly lunged forward and grabbed his bright blue digital camera. The octopus quickly swam off with its booty but, after a five-minute chase, Huang used his speargun to extract the camera from its grasp.

musical fish Diane Rains from Hudson, Wisconsin, owns a goldfish that can play musical instruments, including the glockenspiel and handbells, in perfect time to music playing outside its tank. Jor Jor has been trained to play single notes, chords and four-part harmonies, using its mouth to tug on a string attached to each instrument.

old hen A hen in China is 22 years old—the equivalent of around 400 years in human age. Hens normally live for only seven years, but the bird owned by Yang Shaofu of Yunnan Province has reached three times that age, during which time she has laid over 5,000 eggs.

climbing fish The climbing perch of Africa and Southeast Asia is a fish that can breathe air and use its spiky gill covers and pectoral fins to "walk" on dry land from one body of water to another. It can live out of water for several days and will actually drown if it is held underwater.

drink tears Three species of worker bee drink human tears. Either singly or in groups of up to seven, the bees were observed in Thailand landing on people's lower eyelashes and sipping lachrymation. It is thought the insects have adapted to drink tears as a means of gaining extra protein.

FROGS IN THEIR THROATS

Humans might be divided on eating frog's legs, but they remain very popular in the natural world.

1 Tad and Karen Bacon from Maryland discovered this giant bullfrog snacking on another frog after taking a dip in their swimming pool. Bullfrogs can grow to over 12 in (30 cm) long.

2 Luis Fernando Espin from Ecuador came upon an Amazonian whipsnake slowly devouring a large tree frog. The frog has toxic chemicals in its skin but that didn't prevent the snake from eventually swallowing it whole.

3 A burrowing owl in Florida makes short work of a large frog—legs included.

beyond belief

believe it!

world

animals

sports

body

transport

feats

mysteries

food

arts

science

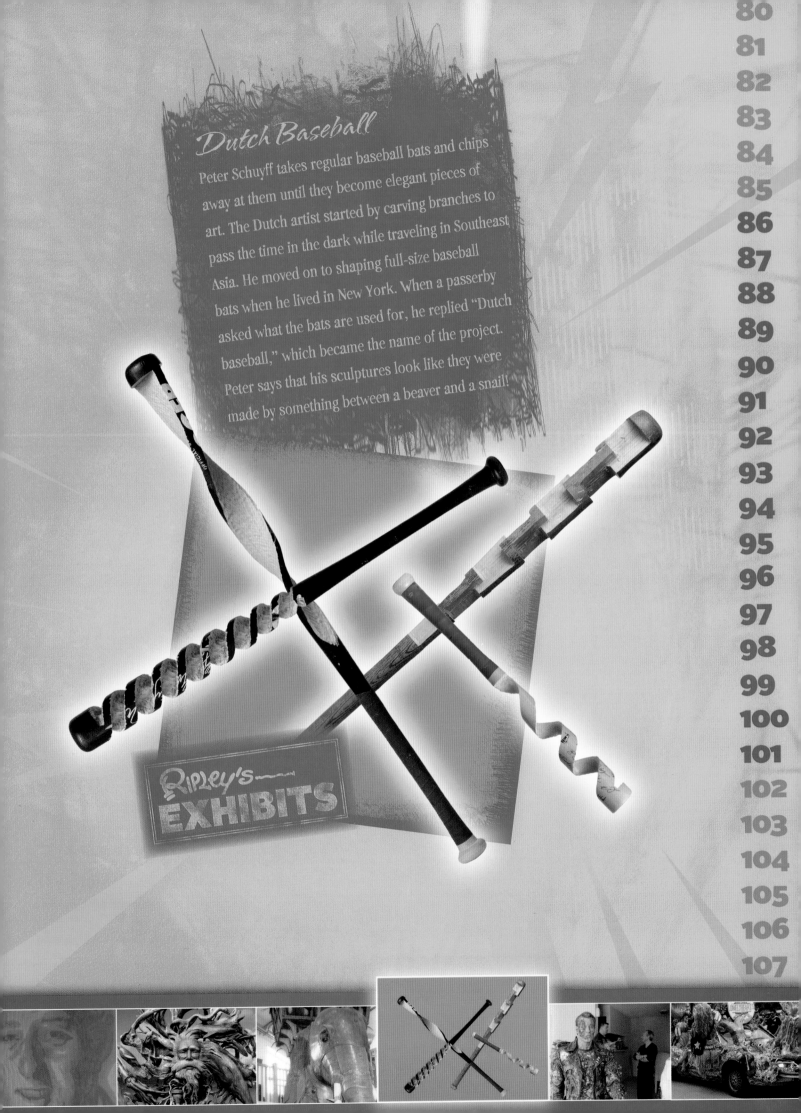

80
81
82
83
84
85
86
87
88
89
90
91
92
93
94
95
96
97
98
99
100
101
102
103
104
105
106
107

Dutch Baseball

Peter Schuyff takes regular baseball bats and chips away at them until they become elegant pieces of art. The Dutch artist started by carving branches to pass the time in the dark while traveling in Southeast Asia. He moved on to shaping full-size baseball bats when he lived in New York. When a passerby asked what the bats are used for, he replied "Dutch baseball," which became the name of the project. Peter says that his sculptures look like they were made by something between a beaver and a snail!

Ripley's
EXHIBITS

The modern Olympic Games were established by a Frenchman—Baron de Coubertin—who was inspired by the ancient Greek competition of the same name.

They are hosted by different countries and, with the exception of three cancellations due to world wars (in 1916, 1940 and 1944), have been staged every four years since 1896. Both Summer and Winter Games are held, and today more than 13,000 athletes compete in 400 events representing 35 sports. While every Olympics delivers great tales of sporting prowess, it is perhaps some of the lesser-known tales that are the most remarkable...

THE ANCIENT OLYMPICS

Contested between representatives of several city states and kingdoms, the Ancient Olympics were staged every four years from 776BC until AD393, when Roman Emperor Theodosius banned them on the grounds that they were a pagan ritual. Believe it or not...

• The Emperor Nero of Rome competed in the AD66 Olympics, accompanied by 5,000 bodyguards, and won every event in which he took part.

• All the competitors at the Ancient Olympics were men, and they competed naked.

• Among the more unusual events was a contest for trumpeters.

• Three-time Olympic champions had statues erected in their honor and were offered exemption from taxation.

• Centurions demonstrated their speed and strength in races run in full suits of armor.

• The Pankration, or all-in wrestling, allowed any moves, including strangling your opponent.

• The 2004 Olympic marathon in Athens was raced over the same historic course first run by the messenger Pheidippides in 490BC when he announced the Greek victory over Persia in the Battle of Marathon.

THE EARLY DAYS

big chill The swimming races at the 1896 Athens Olympics were held in the Mediterranean Sea, which was so cold that many competitors, numb from the chill, gave up and had to be rescued by boat.

mystery cox To reduce the weight in their boat, Dutch pair Francois Antoine Brandt and Roelof Klein recruited a young French boy—believed to be about seven years old—to act as their coxswain in the rowing final at the 1900 Paris Olympics. The mystery boy helped them to win the Olympic title but then vanished into thin air and his name was

the pits! The track and field events at the 1900 Paris Olympics were staged on rough ground in the Bois de Boulogne—a large park on the edge of the city—where facilities were so basic that the jumpers had to dig their own pits and the obstacles for the men's 400 meters hurdles were 30-ft-long (9-m) telephone poles.

short distance Women were not allowed to compete in track and field events at the Olympics until 1928. However, some collapsed at the end of the 800 meters in that year so they were subsequently banned from running

how far? During the first several modern Olympics, the marathon was an approximate distance. In 1908, the British royal family requested that the marathon start at Windsor Castle so that the royal children could see its start. The distance from Windsor Castle to the Olympic Stadium was 26 miles and 385 yd. In 1924, this distance became the standard length of a marathon.

art prizes No medals were awarded at the 1900 Paris Olympics—winners were given pieces of art instead. At this, the second of the modern Olympics, more athletes than

OLYMPIC ODDITIES

not allowed Harvard University refused to give student James B. Connolly eight weeks' leave of absence in order to compete in the 1896 Olympics in Greece. So he resigned from the university, paid for the voyage himself—and went on to win the triple jump.

wrong anthem At the medal ceremony for the 1964 Tokyo Olympics marathon, won by Abebe Bikila of Ethiopia, the stadium band did not know the Ethiopian national anthem, so they played the Japanese one instead.

first gold India has 17 percent of the world's population, but the country did not win its first individual Olympic title until 2008 when Abhinav Bindra won the 10-meter air rifle shooting event.

bully-off As a reward for winning gold in the women's field hockey tournament at the 1980 Moscow Olympics, every member of the Zimbabwe team was presented with a live ox on their return home.

walk, don't run The three leading competitors in the women's 20-km walk at the 2000 Sydney Olympics were all disqualified for running in the final kilometer, leaving China's Wang Liping to claim an unlikely gold medal.

dirty laundry Competitors at the modern Olympics produce over 2,000,000 lb (907,000 kg) of dirty laundry. A family of four would take an estimated 264 years to get through that much laundry.

nine-hour bout The light-heavyweight Greco-Roman wrestling final at the 1912 Stockholm Olympics between Anders Ahlgren of Sweden and Ivar Böhling of Finland went on for nine hours without a decision being reached. So the judges called it a draw and awarded both men silver medals as neither had defeated his opponent to earn gold.

no gold Long-jumper Robert LeGendre, a 26-year-old graduate from Georgetown University, Washington, D.C., jumped further than anyone else and set a new world record of 25 ft 5½ in (7.76 m) at the 1924 Olympics—but he didn't win a gold medal because he was competing in the pentathlon, where he could finish only third overall.

OLYMPIC HEROES

dislocated arm Konrad von Wangenheim helped Germany's equestrian team to win gold at the 1936 Olympics despite riding with a broken collarbone and his left arm in a sling.

incredible double At the 1924 Paris Olympics, Finland's Paavo Nurmi won the men's 1,500 meters final and then just over an hour later he won the 5,000 meters final, setting Olympic records in both events.

veteran rider At the 2008 Olympics in Beijing, equestrian rider Hiroshi Hoketsu represented Japan at the age of 67. He had also taken part in the Tokyo Olympics—44 years earlier.

heroic horsewoman Despite being paralyzed below the knees after contracting polio, Denmark's Lis Hartel, who had to be helped on and off her horse, won silver medals in the individual dressage event at both the 1952 and 1956 Olympics.

wooden leg American gymnast George Eyser won six medals in one day at the 1904 Olympics in St. Louis, Missouri—three of them gold—despite having a wooden leg. His left leg had been amputated after he was run over by a train. He even won gold in the long horse vault, which he jumped without the help of a springboard.

duck escort Partway through his quarter-final race against Victor Saurin of France at the 1928 Olympics, Australian rower Henry Pearce stopped rowing to allow a family of ducks to pass in single file in front of his boat. He recovered to win the race and later the gold medal, too.

changing hands Hungarian pistol shooter Károly Takács lost his right hand in 1938 when a grenade that he was holding exploded. So he taught himself to shoot left-handed and won a gold medal at the 1948 London Olympics, successfully defending his title four years later in Helsinki.

Ripley's
sports
Believe It or Not!®

OLYMPIC HOWLERS

calendar chaos After spending over 16 days at sea, the U.S. team arrived in Athens for the first modern Olympic Games in 1896 believing that they still had 12 days to prepare for the competition. In fact, the Games started the very next day—the Americans had forgotten that Greece still used the Julian calendar and was therefore 12 days in advance.

joined picnic Exhausted by the heat of the 1912 Olympic marathon in Stockholm, Sweden, Japan's Shizo Kanaguri stumbled into the garden of a family who were enjoying a picnic and stayed with them rather than rejoining the race.

lost medal After winning a rowing gold medal at the 1956 Olympics, 18-year-old Russian Vyacheslav Ivanov quickly lost it. He threw the medal into the air in celebration, but it landed in the lake. He dived in but was unable to find it.

hot stuff To prepare himself for the heat of Rome, where he won the 50-km walk at the 1960 Olympics, Britain's Don Thompson kept the heat on at all times in his bathroom for 18 months—and ran up a gas bill of over £9,000. He returned home from his triumph to find that the gas had been cut off.

lost in translation American athlete Loren Murchison was left at the start of the 1920 Olympic men's 100 meters final in Antwerp, Belgium, because he didn't understand French. When the starter said "prêt" ("get set"), Murchison thought that the crouching runners had been told to stand up and was doing so when the starting gun went off.

missing gloves Moments before he was due to fight at the 1992 Barcelona Olympics, Iranian boxer Ali Kazemi was disqualified because he had forgotten his gloves.

feeling crushed Having arrived in Canada in preparation for the 1976 Montreal Olympics, the Czech cycling team lost all of their wheels and spare tires after garbage collectors mistakenly took them away to be crushed.

shot in foot U.S. Lieutenant Sidney Hinds won gold in the free rifle team event at the 1924 Olympics in Paris, shooting a perfect 50—despite having been accidentally shot in the foot partway through the competition when the Belgian rifleman positioned next to him threw his loaded weapon to the ground during an argument with an official.

pot luck Sweden's Svante Rasmuson was set to win the modern pentathlon at the 1984 Olympics until, a few yards from the finish of the cross country, he stumbled over a potted plant, placed there by the Los Angeles organizers to brighten up the course. Italy's Daniele Masala passed him to snatch gold.

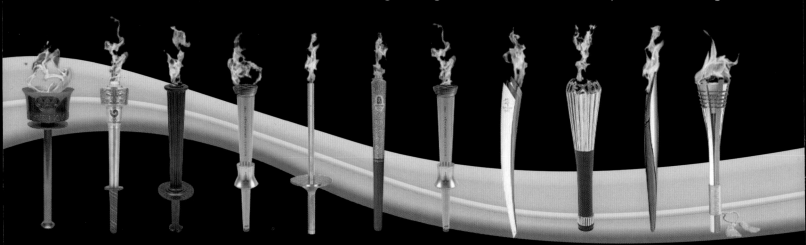

UNUSUAL OLYMPIC EVENTS

**Vertical rope climb
(1896, 1904, 1906, 1924, 1932)**
So hard was this event that in 1896 only two of the climbers made it to the top, prompting officials to send the rope back for alterations.

Men's Sailor's 100 meter freestyle (1896)
This event was only open to sailors in the Greek Royal Navy. Only three competitors took place in the event. And the winner was from... Greece!

Long jump for horses (1900)
A horse named *Extra Dry* won at the Paris Olympics with a jump of 20 ft ¼ in (6.1 m)— that's shorter than the men's record in 1901.

Underwater swimming race (1900)
Not the most thrilling visual spectacle, this race was held over 60 meters with competitors being awarded points for each meter swum and time spent underwater.

Pigeon shooting (1900)
Paris 1900 featured the only Olympic event in history at which animals were deliberately harmed—300 live pigeons. Belgium's Leon de Lunden won gold, bagging himself 21 birds.

200m obstacle swimming race (1900)
Held in Paris' River Seine, competitors had to climb over a pole, clamber over a row of boats and then swim under another row of boats.

Pistol dueling (1906)
Participants shot over 20 and 30 meters at mannequins that wore fancy frock coats with bull's-eyes embroidered on the chest.

Tug of war (1900, 1904, 1908, 1912, 1920)
The Ancient Greeks staged the first tug in 500BC, but in modern Olympic rules, a team of eight had to pull the opposition 6 ft (1.8 m) to win. London 1908 saw the sport at its most intense, when America was beaten in just a few short seconds by Great Britain. The unhappy losers accused the British team—all policemen—of wearing illegal spiked boots, so they were offered a rematch, with the British in their socks. They still lost.

FAMOUS OLYMPIANS

- Lieutenant George S. Patton, one of the leading generals during World War II, finished fifth in the modern pentathlon at the 1912 Olympics.

- Johnny Weissmuller of the United States won three gold medals in freestyle swimming at the 1924 Olympics plus a bronze in the men's water polo, and two more swimming golds in 1928—feats that helped him earn a lucrative Hollywood career playing Tarzan.

- Buster Crabbe of the U.S.A. won a swimming gold medal at the 1932 Olympics and also went on to play Tarzan in the movies.

- Britain's Philip Noel-Baker won silver in the 1,500 meters at the 1920 Olympics—and in 1959 was awarded the Nobel Peace Prize.

- Crown Prince (later King) Constantine of Greece won a sailing gold medal at the 1960 Olympics.

- Hollywood actress Geena Davis took part in the trials for the U.S. archery team for the 2000 Olympics.

- Baby care expert Dr. Benjamin Spock was a member of the Yale University eight that won rowing gold for the U.S.A. at the 1924 Olympics.

- Harold Sakata won a weightlifting silver for the U.S. in 1948 before going on to play the evil Oddjob in the James Bond movie *Goldfinger*.

- Princess Anne, daughter of Queen Elizabeth II, was a member of the British equestrian team at the 1976 Montreal Olympics.

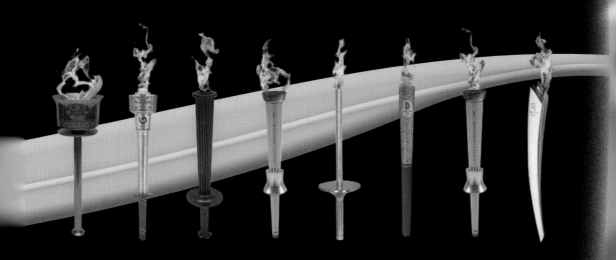

REMARKABLE TORCH RELAYS

Tokyo 1964 This torch relay featured the most torchbearers ever used—101,866—comprising a carrier, two reserve runners and up to 20 accompanying people for every kilometer of its land journey.

Grenoble 1968 In the later stages of the relay, a diver swam across the French port of Marseilles holding the torch's flame out of the water.

Mexico City 1968 The relay retraced the steps of Christopher Columbus to the New World and featured one of his direct descendants, Cristóbal Colón de Carbajal, as the last runner on Spanish soil before the torch made its way across the Atlantic.

Montreal 1976 The Canadians organized the transmission of the flame by satellite between Athens and Ottawa by transforming it into a radio signal that was sent by satellite to Canada, where it triggered a laser beam to relight the flame on Canadian soil.

Lillehammer 1994 The flame was transferred between two parachute jumpers—in midair—and then made an impressive entry at the opening ceremony of the Games when it was carried by a ski jumper during his actual jump!

Atlanta 1996 and Sydney 2000
The Olympic torch (but not the flame) was carried into space by astronauts.

SHINE A LIGHT

One of the enduring symbols of the Games is the Olympic flame, which burns for the duration of the competition. A few months before each Games, at the Temple of Hera at Olympia, Greece—the site of the ancient games—a woman in ceremonial robes lights the torch, using just a mirror and the sun. The flame is then carried by relay to the host city, where it ignites the Olympic cauldron in the stadium and burns until the closing ceremony. During its journey, it must never go out. The route to each stadium is often long and tortuous.

In 2004, to celebrate the Games held in Athens, Greece, the torch went on a global tour, covering 48,470 mi (78,000 km) in the hands of some 11,300 torchbearers.

Over the years, it's been carried by dogsled, horseback, camel and canoe, as well as by an army of runners.

When the flame has to travel in an airplane, special security lanterns are used, and every night of its journey the flame is kept burning in custom-made cauldrons, attended by three guards, one of whom must be awake at all times.

Eighteen authentic Olympic torches are displayed in the Ripley's Believe It or Not! Museum in London, England, among them the torch from the Sydney 2000 Olympiad that was carried, lit, underwater by divers near the Great Barrier Reef.

Mighty Mouth

A man in Lagos, Nigeria, lifts a bar carrying 110 lb (50 kg) of iron weights with his mouth!

solo sailor At age 16, Jessica Watson of Queensland, Australia, finished a 210-day, 23,000-nautical-mile (42,600-km), solo, nonstop and unassisted voyage around the world. In her 34-ft-long (10-m) yacht *Ella's Pink Lady*, she battled 39-ft (12-m) swells and a ripped sail and ate 576 chocolate bars.

jail jaunt In June 2009, 194 French inmates made a 1,430-mi (2,300-km) bicycle trip through the country in a prisoners' Tour de France.

head-to-head Croatian tennis player Goran Ivanisevic needed stitches when he tried to head the ball over the net at the 1998 Canadian Open, only to bang heads with his doubles partner Mark Philippoussis, who had tried to do the same thing. Philippoussis got away with only a bruised forehead.

dodgeball tournament In October 2009, more than 235 teams in three divisions competed in a dodgeball tournament in Richmond, Virginia, involving more than 4,000 players.

novice at 90 Ninety-year-old Mary Tattersall from West Yorkshire, England, hit a hole-in-one at a golf course near Bradford in 2010. She had been playing golf for only two years.

world cup miss Spain's international goalkeeper Santiago Cañizares missed the 2002 soccer World Cup after dropping a bottle of aftershave onto his right foot, severing one of his tendons.

board marathon A team of ten wakeboarders (a cross between waterskiing and surfing) completed 1,448 laps of a Cincinnati, Ohio, cable wakeboard park in 24 hours in June 2010. They traveled just over 506 mi (814 km)—roughly the distance from Cincinnati to Atlanta, Georgia.

delayed game Twenty-one years after a 1989 New Jersey high-school hockey championship game between Delbarton and St. Joseph's was canceled because of a measles outbreak, the players—now in their late thirties—finally took to the ice to play the deciding game for charity.

surf club The Palestinian territory's Gaza Strip has its own surf club, which was founded after a Jewish surfer donated a dozen surfboards to the community.

fast match In October 2009, Jo-Wilfried Tsonga of France and Spain's Fernando Verdasco played a tennis match on board a train traveling at 268 mph (431 km/h). The mini-tennis court was laid out in one of Shanghai's high-speed Maglev trains, where the players were traveling faster than their serves.

round-the-world In 2010, 34-year-old Vin Cox from Cornwall, England, cycled 18,225 mi (29,330 km) around the world in just 163 days. Starting and finishing his journey in London, he took 12 plane and boat transfers, crossed six continents—Europe, (northern) Africa, Asia, Australia, South America and North America—and cycled through 17 countries.

big haul In August 2010, Jeff Kolodzinski caught 2,160 fish—mostly small bluegills and perch—from Lake Minnetonka, Minnesota, in a 24-hour period.

one-legged wrestler Michigan-based Zach "Tenacious Z" Gowen, who lost his leg at age eight, made his debut at 19 as a one-legged professional wrestler.

thrown away Jesus Leonardo of Wanaque, New Jersey, earns about $45,000 a year examining discarded horse-racing tickets for winning stubs accidentally thrown away.

insect aside Spotting that an insect had landed on his ball at the 1950 U.S. Open Golf Championship, Lloyd Mangrum of the U.S.A. instinctively picked up the ball and flicked the insect away. However, he was penalized two strokes for his misdemeanor, which ultimately cost him the title.

blind catch Sheila Penfold, a legally blind grandmother from London, England, caught a catfish that weighed in at a whopping 214 lb (97 kg) and measured 8 ft 2 in (2.5 m) long on Spain's Ebro River in January 2010. It took Mrs. Penfold, who stands just 5 ft 3 in (1.6 m) tall, 30 minutes to reel in the monster.

master jockey Since 1974, Canadian jockey Russell Baze has won more than 11,000 horse races. In the space of just two days—October 17 and 18, 2007—he won no fewer than 11 races.

seven out In 2009, in his first game as a pitcher for the St. Louis Cardinals, John Smoltz struck out seven hitters in a row—something he had never managed to do in 708 trips to the mound with his previous team, the Atlanta Braves.

first female In 2010, Kelly Kulick of the U.S.A. became the first woman to qualify for the Professional Bowlers' Association's Tournament of Champions—and she went on to beat an all-male field of 62 to claim the title.

extra load In 2009, former British soldier Kez Dunkley ran the 26.2-mi (42-km) Leicester Marathon in 5 hours 53 minutes with an 84-lb (38-kg) tumble-drier strapped to his back. The previous year he had run the race with a bag of cement on his back.

BIKE CLIMB

In November 2010, Colombian cyclist Javier Zapata rode up the 649 steps of the Piedra del Peñol monolithic formation in Guatapé, Colombia, in just 43 minutes. Zapata is no stranger to epic climbs. In 2003, he rode his bike up the 1,318 stairs of Mexico City's Torre Mayor, the tallest building in Latin America.

Bill emerges from the seawater following his surfing extravaganza with bloodshot eyes and dusted in salt.

SURF'S UP!

Surfer extraordinaire Bill Laity of San Clemente, California, surfed for 26 hours straight at the state's Huntington Beach in November 2010, during which time he caught 147 waves.

Bill paddled his board into the water at 7.24 a.m. on a Saturday morning—he didn't stop surfing until 9.26 a.m. on Sunday!

The super-surfer's fingers appear severely wrinkled as a result of being submerged in the water for 26 hours straight.

AIRBED RACE

At the annual Glen Nevis River Race in Scotland, competitors on inflatable airbeds don helmets and lifejackets to navigate a treacherous 1½-mi (2.4-km) course along the Glen Nevis River, tackling white-water torrents, rapids and even a 30-ft (9-m) waterfall.

bowling star Retired high-school principal Allen Meyer of Toronto, Canada, was still bowling twice a week in a league that he ran at the age of 106.

foul ball After years of attending Philadelphia Phillies baseball games, Steve Monforto made a great grab to catch his first foul ball. He high-fived his three-year-old daughter Emily and handed her the prize ball... which she then threw back over the railing! The family still went home with a ball after Phillies officials saw what happened and took a ball up to him. What's more, spectators threw back every foul ball caught for the remainder of the game so that Emily didn't feel bad for losing her dad the special ball.

extreme hole The "Extreme 19th" hole at the Legend Golf and Safari Resort in Limpopo, South Africa, has a tee-off on a mountain that is accessible only by helicopter—and sits 1,300 ft (400 m) above a green designed in the shape of the continent of Africa. In 2008, Ireland's Padraig Harrington became the first golfer to make a par-3 at this hole.

welly wanging Under the British rules of "welly wanging" (or gum-boot throwing), competitors take a maximum run-up of 42 paces before hurling a size 9, non-steel toecap gum-boot through the air as far as possible. Finland's Jouni Viljanen has hurled a gum boot more than 208 ft (64 m).

anvil blast In the U.S. sport of competitive anvil shooting, participants use black gunpowder to launch 100-lb (45-kg) anvils up to 200 ft (60 m) into the air. One anvil is placed upside down on the ground, the brick-shaped cavity in its underside is filled with gunpowder, and then a second anvil is placed on top of it. A fuse is lit—and the anvil-shooter runs as fast as he can out of the blast radius.

rabbit jumping As well as pioneering show jumping, where horses clear obstacles, Sweden established the sport of rabbit jumping, in which domestic rabbits are trained to jump miniature fences without touching them.

double faults In her first-round ladies' singles match at Wimbledon in 1957, Brazilian tennis player Miss M. de Amorim began by serving 17 consecutive double faults.

flying kayak Miles Daisher of Twin Falls, Idaho, paddles a kayak... across the sky at an altitude of 13,000 ft (4,000 m). The daredevil has invented a new sport, skyaking, a combination of skydiving and kayaking. Sitting in his kayak he jumps from a plane, pulls the chute at about 5,000 ft (1,525 m) and descends at nearly 100 mph (160 km/h), reducing to half that speed as he finally swoops to land spectacularly on water.

solo row In her 19-ft-long (5.8-m) rowboat *Liv*, Katie Spotz, 22, from Mentor, Ohio, rowed solo 2,817 mi (4,533 km) across the Atlantic Ocean from Dakar, Senegal, to Georgetown, Guyana, in just over 70 days in 2010. Previously she has swam the entire 325-mi (520-km) length of the Allegheny River, run 150 mi (240 km) across the Mojave and Colorado deserts and cycled 3,300 mi (5,310 km) across the U.S.A. from Seattle, Washington, to Washington, D.C.

FIERY BULL

In a festival dating back to the 16th century, a Bull of Fire runs through the streets of Medinaceli, Spain. The bull's body is covered in mud to protect it from burns and it wears an iron frame on its horns that bears two torches. The bull is chased through the streets until the torches go out.

Cold Climb

In February 2010, Andreas Spak from Norway, Christian Pondella from California and Canadian Will Gadd became the first adventurers to scale the Vøringfossen waterfall in Norway, one of the highest in Europe. In warmer weather, the water surges at 40 ft (12 m) per second, but winter temperatures of 5°F (−15°C) transformed the torrent into a 650-ft (198-m) ice skyscraper.

sports
Believe It or Not!®

tennis marathon At the 2010 Wimbledon Tennis Championships, John Isner of the U.S.A. beat France's Nicolas Mahut in a match that lasted more than 11 hours over three days. The match began at 6.18 p.m. on Tuesday, June 22 and finished at 4.49 p.m. on Thursday, June 24, Isner eventually winning 6-4, 3-6, 6-7, 7-6, 70-68 in a final set that lasted 8 hours 11 minutes.

mirror image U.S. golfer Phil Mickelson is right-handed in everything but golf. He plays left-handed after mirroring his father's right-handed swing as a child.

every ground In February 2010, Scott Poleykett from Kent, England, completed a 50,000-mi (80,000-km) journey to visit every soccer ground—professional and amateur—in England and Wales. In the course of his ten-year mission, he took photographs of 2,547 soccer fields.

commentator's nightmare The finish of an August 2010 race at Monmouth Park, New Jersey, was fought out between horses named *Mywifeknowseverything* and *Thewifedoesn'tknow*. The two horses were unconnected, with separate trainers and owners.

TATTOO TRIBUTE

Colombian soccer fan Felipe Alvarez has had his upper body tattooed to resemble a jersey of his favorite team, Atletico Nacional. The tattoo is in honor of Andrés Escobar, the Colombian player who was shot dead as a result of scoring an own goal, which lost his side the match, while playing against the U.S.A. at the 1994 World Cup. Seen here with Atletico player Victor Aristizábal, Alvarez now has Escobar's number 2 permanently marked on his back.

one hand At 6 ft 10 in (2.1 m) tall, Kevin Laue of Pleasanton, California, received a scholarship to play basketball for Manhattan College despite having only one hand.

flying shot In 2010, Tyler Toney, a student from Texas A&M University, made a basketball shot he threw from a low-flying airplane!

atlantic crossing A four-man crew led by Scotsman Leven Brown overcame 40-ft (12-m) waves, two capsizes and an outbreak of food poisoning to row 3,500 mi (5,600 km) across the Atlantic from New York to the Scilly Isles, which lie off the southwest coast of England, in 43 days in 2010. They were following the route of a Norwegian crew who had made the same crossing in 55 days back in 1896.

veteran coach Soccer coach Ivor Powell finally hung up his boots in 2010—at age 93. A former Welsh international forward, he went on to train more than 9,000 players during his 53-year coaching career.

wrestling champs In 2010, Blair Academy of Blairstown, New Jersey, won its 30th consecutive National Prep School Wrestling Championship.

monkey guards Organizers at the 2010 Commonwealth Games in New Delhi, India, hired monkeys to work as guards at the athletes' village. They hoped that the team of 40 gray langur monkeys would chase off the packs of smaller rhesus monkeys that had been breaking into buildings and stealing from the competitors' quarters.

switch hitters It took 134 years for the Arizona Diamondbacks' Felipe Lopez to become the first baseball player in history to switch-hit homers from both sides of the plate on Opening Day. It took just one inning, in the same 2009 game, for Tony Clark to become the second.

SAND SKIS

Germany's Henrik May prefers to ski on sand rather than snow—and in the Namibian Desert he reached a speed of 57.24 mph (92.12 km/h) while skiing down a 246-ft-high (75-m) dune. He has developed a special type of wax that enables the skis he uses to slide over sand.

flying fish One of the favorites to win the 2010 Missouri River 340—a grueling 340-mi (550-km) canoe and kayak race—Brad Pennington from Houston, Texas, was forced to quit just hours into the event after a 30-lb (13.6-kg) Asian silver carp leaped out of the water and hit him in the head. He described the blow as like being hit with a brick, and it left him with a pounding headache.

tug-of-war Fishing on the Victoria Nile River in Uganda, Tim Smith from Enniskillen, Northern Ireland, landed a 249-lb (113-kg) Nile perch, which at 6 ft (1.8 m) long, was taller than him. He battled for 45 minutes to reel in the monster—and then had to pry his catch from the jaws of a crocodile that launched itself at his tiny boat in a desperate bid to snatch the fish.

soccer saints An executive box at the Hamburg stadium of German soccer club St. Pauli is decorated like a Gothic chapel, complete with stained glass windows, candles, an altar to football and depictions of the team's players as saints.

frozen toe The U.S.A.'s Rulon Gardner, the 2000 Olympic Greco-Roman wrestling gold medallist, lost a toe to frostbite in 2002 and kept it in a jar in his refrigerator for years, apparently to remind him of his mortality.

free throws Perry Dissmore, a pastor from Hartford, Illinois, made 1,968 successful basketball free throws in an hour in September 2010—an average of one throw every 1.8 seconds.

matador fled Matador Christian Hernandez quit his job mid-bullfight in Mexico City in 2010—by running away from the charging bull, jumping over a wall and fleeing the stadium to a chorus of boos.

loyal fan Nesan Sinnadurai, a U.S.-based fan of English soccer club Arsenal, has flown more than 6,000,000 mi (9,600,000 km) supporting the club since 1967. Every other weekend during the soccer season, the Sri Lankan I.T. consultant makes the 9,000-mi (14,500-km) round trip from Columbus, Georgia, to London to watch his favorite team.

blind abseiler Blind extreme sports enthusiast Dean Dunbar abseiled down the 658-ft-high (200-m) Eas a' Chual Aluinn waterfall in Scotland. He has also competed in power boating, mountain biking, sea kayaking and hill running events, bungee jumped from a helicopter and been hurled through the air as a human catapult.

super sprinter Irish sprinter Jason Smyth can run the 100 meters in 10.32 seconds—even though he is legally blind. He suffers from Stargardt's disease, a disorder that has reduced his vision to about ten percent of that of a fully sighted person, but can run so fast that he competed against able-bodied athletes at the 2010 European Championships.

too much yelling Manchester United goalkeeper Alex Stepney dislocated his jaw while shouting at his defenders during a 1975 soccer match against Birmingham City.

Sky Walker

Californian Dean Potter walked across a highline 100 ft (30 m) long and over 1,000 ft (305 m) above the ground in Yosemite National Park in 2009. He walked barefoot, and unattached. Dean has many years of experience on the highline—if he does slip off, he grabs the line with his arms or legs.

HOCKEY HORROR

Buffalo Sabres' goaltender Clint Malarchuk narrowly escaped death after a collision caused a player's skate to cut the cartoid artery in his neck during a 1989 hockey match against the St. Louis Blues. If the skate had hit Malarchuk $1/8$ in (3 mm) higher, he would have been dead within 2 minutes. The injury was so horrific that 11 fans fainted and two had heart attacks, while three players vomited on the ice. Malarchuk needed 300 stitches to fix the wound, but was back playing in goal ten days later.

These heroic athletes and fans have the scars to show how sport can be dangerous. Incredibly, all have survived and, believe it or not, returned to the arena for more.

When baseball player Kelly Shoppach of the Cleveland Indians let the bat slip at a game against the Texas Rangers in Arlington, Texas, in 2006, this unfortunate fan failed to notice Shoppach's bat flying straight toward his face. In 2009, Shoppach claimed another victim when he struck a female fan in the face with a foul ball during a game against the Kansas City Royals.

FACEBALL BAT

10 MOST DANGEROUS SPORTS IN THE U.S.A.

(Injuries per year)

1. Basketball 512,213
2. Cycling 485,669
3. Football 418,260
4. Soccer 174,686
5. Baseball 155,898
6. Skateboarding 112,544
7. Trampoline 108,029
8. Softball 106,884
9. Swimming/diving 82,354
10. Horseback riding 73,576

DANGEROUS RING

Celebrating a goal for Swiss team Servette in 2004, recently married Portuguese soccer player Paulo Diogo jumped on the stadium fence and caught his wedding ring on the top. When he jumped off, he left the ring and half his finger behind. To add insult to injury, the referee showed him a yellow card for time wasting as the doctors searched for the missing finger! Although doctors were unable to reattach the digit, Diogo quickly resumed his career.

UNLUCKY BREAK

Brazilian-born Croatian soccer player Eduardo suffered a horrific broken leg when playing for his club team, Arsenal, in England's Premier League in 2008. A tackle by Birmingham City's Martin Taylor left Eduardo's anklebone sticking through his sock and kept him out of the game for almost a year.

BRUTE FORCE

Spanish matador Julio Aparicio was gored through the neck with such force by a bull in Madrid in 2010 that the end of the animal's horn can be seen coming out of the bullfighter's mouth. The horn went through Aparicio's tongue and penetrated the roof of his mouth. His life was saved after two operations and, incredibly, he returned to the ring two months later.

DIVING BELLE

Seventeen-year-old Columbus, Ohio, diver Chelsea Davis smashed the bridge of her nose on the diving board while competing at the 2005 World Swimming Championships in Montréal, Canada. She was lifted on to a stretcher, her face covered in blood, but she never lost consciousness and was soon back competing.

believe it!

world

animals

sports

body

transport

feats

mysteries

food

arts

science

beyond belief

The Terminator

In 2011, Ripley's acquired a life-sized statue of Arnold Schwarzenegger as the Terminator, created by Mexican artist Enrique Ramos. Made from an assortment of materials, including a dead bat, the sculpture is a tribute to Hollywood films and icons, and features images of Spiderman, Homer Simpson, E.T., Jaws and Frankenstein among many others.

Ripley's
EXHIBITS

102
103
104
105
106
107
108
109
110
111
112
113
114
115
116
117
118
119
120
121
122
123
124
125
126
127
128
129

HEADS OF STATE

Chinese micro-artist Jin Y. Hua has painted the face of every President of the U.S.A. from George Washington to George W. Bush—that's 42 portraits—on a single human hair less than ½ in (1.3 cm) long and just 0.0035 in (0.09 mm) thick. Jin uses a brush made from a single rabbit hair to apply the paint.

Thomas Jefferson 1801–1809

ACTUAL SIZE!

Lyndon B. Johnson 1963–1969

Ronald Reagan 1981–1989

George Washington 1789–1797

John Adams 1797–1801

Thomas Jefferson 1801–1809

James Madison 1809–1817

James Monroe 1817–1825

John Quincy Adams 1825–1829

Andrew Jackson 1829–1837

Martin Van Buren 1837–1841

William Henry Harrison 1841

John Tyler 1841–1845

James K. Polk 1845–1849

Zachary Taylor 1849–1850

Millard Fillmore 1850–1853

Franklin Pierce 1853–1857

James Buchanan 1857–1861

Abraham Lincoln 1861–1865

Andrew Johnson 1865–1869

Ulysses S. Grant 1869–1877

Rutherford B. Hayes 1877–1881

James A. Garfield 1881

Chester A. Arthur 1881–1885

Grover Cleveland 1885–1889 & 1893–1897

Benjamin Harrison 1889–1893

William McKinley 1897–1901

Theodore Roosevelt 1901–1909

William Howard Taft 1909–1913

Woodrow Wilson 1913–1921

Warren G. Harding 1921–1923

Calvin Coolidge 1923–1929

Herbert Hoover 1929–1933

Franklin D. Roosevelt 1933–1945

Harry S. Truman 1945–1953

Dwight D. Eisenhower 1953–1961

John F. Kennedy 1961–1963

Lyndon B. Johnson 1963–1969

Richard Nixon 1969–1974

Gerald Ford 1974–1977

Jimmy Carter 1977–1981

Ronald Reagan 1981–1989

George H. W. Bush 1989–1993

Bill Clinton 1993–2001

George W. Bush 2001–2009

John F. Kennedy 1961–1963

Richard Nixon 1969–1974

snake twins In June 2009, in Xiaogan, eastern China, Hui Chung gave birth to conjoined twins, who were known as the "snake babies" because they were attached at the waist. The siblings shared one long body with a head at each end, and as they did not have external sexual organs, it was impossible to say what sex they were.

long hair When 79-year-old Tran Van Hay died in Kien Giang, Vietnam, in February 2010, his hair was more than 22 ft (6.7 m) long and weighed 23 lb (10.5 kg). He began to let his hair grow more than 50 years ago, because he often became sick after a haircut. As his hair grew, he balanced it on his head like a basket.

LICK OFF
Actor Nick Afanasiev from California has an incredible role all to himself—as the owner of America's longest tongue! Stretching to an unbelievable 3.5 in (9 cm), it means that Nick can lick his own nose and even his elbow, a bizarre feat that most people find impossible.

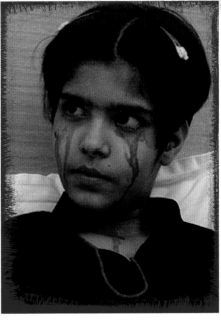

BLOOD, SWEAT AND TEARS
Twinkle Dwivedi from Lucknow, India, is one of the strangest and rarest medical cases in the world. From the age of 12, Twinkle began to bleed at random through the skin on any part of her body—without any visible wounds or pain—from the soles of her feet to her eyes. Although the cause of her spontaneous bleeding remains a mystery, experts believe that she may suffer from a blood disorder, or hematohidrosis, an extremely rare but recognized condition where the patient sweats blood through the skin.

miracle escape A Japanese toddler who wandered onto rail tracks in Suzaka City escaped with only scratches after a train came to a halt on top of her. After spotting the girl, the driver applied the emergency brakes and the train stopped with the girl beneath. She survived because she was trapped in the 20-in (50-cm) gap between the train and the tracks.

scorched footprints For two weeks in 2009, Sikeli Nadiri left a trail of scorched footprints on grassland around his home village in Fiji. There was no explanation as to why the grass had burned away beneath his feet, as he had not stepped on any chemicals or anything else that would cause scorching.

dangerous operation In March 2010, U.S. Army medical staff at Bagram airfield in Afghanistan donned armor in the operating room while removing a live high-explosive round from the scalp of a soldier from the Afghan Army.

A Bicycle Made for Two

Although Charles B. Tripp had no arms and Eli Bowen had no legs, they were able to ride a bicycle—together. Known to circus audiences as "The Armless Wonder" and "The Legless Wonder," they simply combined their physical attributes on a tandem bicycle—Tripp pedaling with his legs and Bowen steering with his arms.

Charles B. Tripp was born without arms in 1855 in Woodstock, Ontario, Canada, but soon learned to dress himself and write using his feet. Remarkably, he made his living as a skilled carpenter until joining Barnum's Circus, which was the start of a 50-year career as a performer. He specialized in penmanship, portrait painting and paper cutting—holding the implements between his toes. Around the turn of the century, he developed an interest in photography and became known as "The Armless Photographer." He died in 1939 in Salisbury, North Carolina, at the grand age of 84.

Eli Bowen was born in Ohio in 1844. He was one of ten children, all of whom were able-bodied except for Eli who had seal limbs, or phocomelia, a condition that left him with no legs and with two feet of different sizes growing from his hips. As a child he walked on his arms, perfecting a technique whereby he held wooden blocks in his hands that enabled him to swing his hips between his arms. The strength he gained from this helped him become a talented acrobat and, at the age of 13, he joined his first circus troupe.

Despite his condition, Eli was considered by many to be the most handsome man in showbusiness and, age 26, he married Mattie Haight who was ten years his junior. The couple had four healthy sons. He continued performing into his eighties, and his death, from pleurisy in 1924, was just days before he was due to appear at The Dreamland Circus at Coney Island, New York.

Eli Bowen with his wife and son

Charles Tripp having a cup of tea

swallowed cutlery When 52-year-old Margaret Daalmans went to a hospital in Rotterdam, Holland, complaining of stomach pains, surgeons removed 78 different items of cutlery—including spoons and forks—that she had swallowed.

seven-foot worm Sailing on board the ship *Elizabeth* from Cork, Ireland, to Quebec, Canada, in June 1825, 12-year-old Ellen McCarthy fell ill and coughed up three intestinal worms, the longest of which measured 7 ft 3 in (2.2 m).

Ice Man Wearing just trunks, goggles and a swimming cap, Lewis Pugh of Devon, England, swam 0.62 mi (1 km) across the glacial Pumori Lake, which lies 17,400 ft (5,300 m) up Mount Everest and has a water temperature of just 2°C (36°C). The man, dubbed the "human polar bear," took 22 minutes 51 seconds to breaststroke across the lake. He had to find a delicate balance between going too fast and going too slowly—too quickly he could have lost energy and drowned, but too slowly and he would have suffered hypothermia.

lightning strike Dog-walker Brad Gifford of Kettering, England, had a miraculous escape after he was knocked unconscious, burst both eardrums and exploded into flames when a 300,000-volt bolt of lightning struck him on the ear. The lightning was traveling at 14,000 mph (22,500 km/h) and had heated the air around it to 54,032°F (30,000°C)—five times hotter than the surface of the Sun.

big baby At ten months old, Lei Lei, a baby from Hunan Province, China, weighed 44 lb (20 kg)—equivalent to the weight of an average six-year-old.

parachute plunge When her parachute became entangled seconds after she exited an airplane above South Africa, skydiver Lareece Butler plunged 3,000 ft (915 m) before hitting the ground—she survived with a broken leg, broken pelvis, bruises and concussion.

ate finger In a protest over unpaid wages, a Serbian union official chopped off his finger and ate it. Zoran Bulatovic, a union leader at a textile factory in Novi Pazar, was so angry because some of his fellow workers had not been paid for several years that he used a hacksaw to chop off most of the little finger on his left hand and then ate it to underline the fact that the workers could no longer afford to eat conventional food.

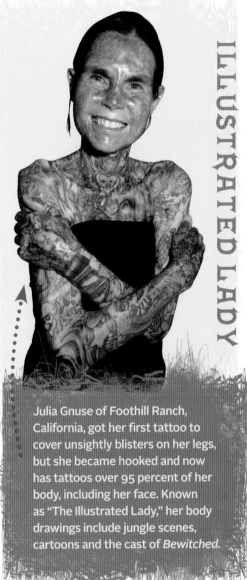

ILLUSTRATED LADY

Julia Gnuse of Foothill Ranch, California, got her first tattoo to cover unsightly blisters on her legs, but she became hooked and now has tattoos over 95 percent of her body, including her face. Known as "The Illustrated Lady," her body drawings include jungle scenes, cartoons and the cast of *Bewitched*.

MAGNETIC FINGERS

By having tiny magnetic implants inserted in their fingers, people are able to pick up metal items, such as paper clips or bottle tops, seemingly by magic. Some people have even had magnets inserted in the backs of their hands or on their ears!

RIPLEY RESEARCH

A small incision is made either at the front or to the side of the fingertip, a tiny dermal elevator is used to separate the layers of the skin, and then the magnet covered in silicone is inserted slightly to the side of the finger pad. The incision is then closed with a stitch. With a finger magnet, people can detect live electrical cables but they can't erase computer hard drives or credit cards or get stuck to refrigerators. The magnets are effective at lifting small items, but this shouldn't be done for longer than 20 minutes at a time in case the skin over the magnet becomes damaged.

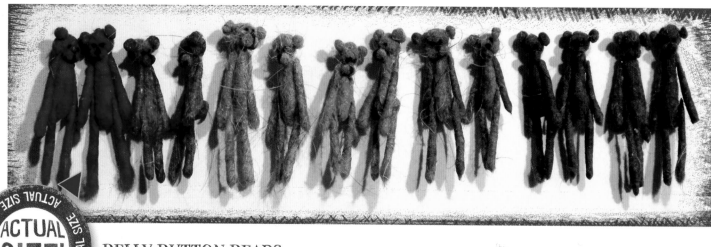

ACTUAL SIZE! ACTUAL SIZE ACTUAL SIZE

BELLY BUTTON BEARS

Artist Rachel Betty Case from Bethlehem, Pennsylvania, turns belly button fluff into tiny bears. She collects the lint from the belly buttons of male friends and sells her cute fluffy creations in small glass jars.

bullet surprise A 35-year-old Polish man who went to a hospital in Bochum, Germany, worried about a small lump on the back of his head, was unaware that he had been shot five years earlier. It was only when doctors removed a .22 caliber bullet that he remembered receiving a blow to the head around midnight at a New Year's Party.

metal muncher Doctors in Cajamarca, Peru, removed 2 lb 3 oz (1 kg) of metal from a man's stomach, including nails, coins, copper wire and scrap metal. Requelme Abanto Alvarado said he had been eating metal for months and had once swallowed 17 5-in (13-cm) nails in one day.

talented toes Since having both arms amputated at age ten after an accident, Liu Wei of Beijing, China, has learned to do everything with his feet. He uses his toes to eat, dress himself, brush his teeth and surf the Internet. He even plays the piano with his toes and earned a standing ovation when he performed on the TV show *China's Got Talent*, which he then went on to win.

not twins In 2010, Angie Cromar from Murray, Utah, found herself pregnant with two babies at the same time—but they weren't twins. She was born with a rare condition called didelphys, meaning two uteruses, and she conceived in both, at odds of one in five million.

long lobes Jian Tianjin, a farmer from Taiwan, has stretchy earlobes that make his ears 6½ in (16 cm) in length. His lobes are so long and flexible that they reach his shoulders and can be wound around his chin.

eight limbs Before having an operation to remove them when he was seven years old, Deepak Paswaan of Bihar, India, had four extra limbs—the result of being born with the arms, legs and buttocks of a parasitic twin protruding from his chest. Although the parasitic twin's arms were small and withered, its legs grew at the same rate as Deepak, meaning the youngster had to carry a heavy weight around.

single handed Despite being born with just one hand, Kevin Shields from Fort William, Scotland, is an accomplished rock climber and has even mastered treacherous ice climbs.

GALL STONES

Doctors in Shenyang, Liaoning Province, China, removed more than 880 stones from the gall bladder of a 67-year-old woman. Mrs. Miao's gall bladder was so full of stones it had swollen to the size of a fist, forcing doctors to remove the whole bladder. They estimated that the stones had been forming inside her for about 20 years.

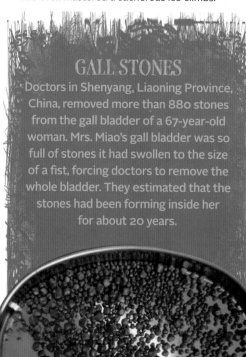

new language A 13-year-old Croatian girl woke from a 24-hour coma speaking fluent German. The girl was no longer able to speak Croatian but was able to communicate perfectly in German, a language that she had only just started studying at school.

sum girl! A 15-year-old schoolgirl with a love of math was awakened from a coma when her father began asking her simple sums. Vicki Alex of Northamptonshire, England, had been unconscious for three days and had failed to respond to other attempts to stimulate her brain, but after her father's intervention she soon regained full consciousness.

hairy hands Since becoming the first American to undergo a double hand transplant, Jeff Kepner from Augusta, Georgia, has noticed that his new hands are considerably hairier than the rest of his body because the donor had more hair than him.

self-amputation Ramlan, an 18-year-old construction worker who was trapped by a fallen concrete girder in the rubble of a building that collapsed during a 2009 earthquake in Padang, Indonesia, survived by sawing off his own leg.

toddler plunge Two-year-old Zhu Xinping had a miraculous escape after falling from the 21st floor of an apartment block in Jianyang City, Sichuan Province, China. She escaped with nothing worse than a broken leg after landing on a freshly dug pile of soil that cushioned her fall.

large family After giving birth to two sets of quadruplets (in 2004 and 2005), Dale Chalk of Sydney, New South Wales, Australia, had twins in 2009, giving her a total of 11 children under the age of seven.

self-service After badly cutting his leg in an accident at home, a 32-year-old man became so frustrated at having to wait an hour at Sundsvall Hospital in northern Sweden that he picked up a needle and thread and sewed up the cut himself.

tugged off In June 2009, a man from Shenzhen, China, was competing in a game of tug-of-war when he had his hand pulled off.

born twice Doctors in Texas performed prenatal surgery at 25 weeks to remove a grapefruit-sized tumor from Macie McCartney, while she was still inside her mother's womb. The procedure involved pulling out the uterus of mother Keri and then half of Macie. Once free from the tumor, Macie was returned to the womb, where she recovered and grew for another ten weeks before being "born" again.

baby's tail Surgeons in China performed an operation to remove a 5-in-long (13-cm) tail from the body of a four-month-old baby girl. Hong Hong, from China's Anhui Province, was born with the tail, but it quickly doubled in size. X-rays had shown that it was connected to a fatty tumor within her spinal column.

reverse walker Rotating his feet nearly 180 degrees, Bittu Gandhi of Rajkot, Gujarat, India, can walk backward while facing forward!

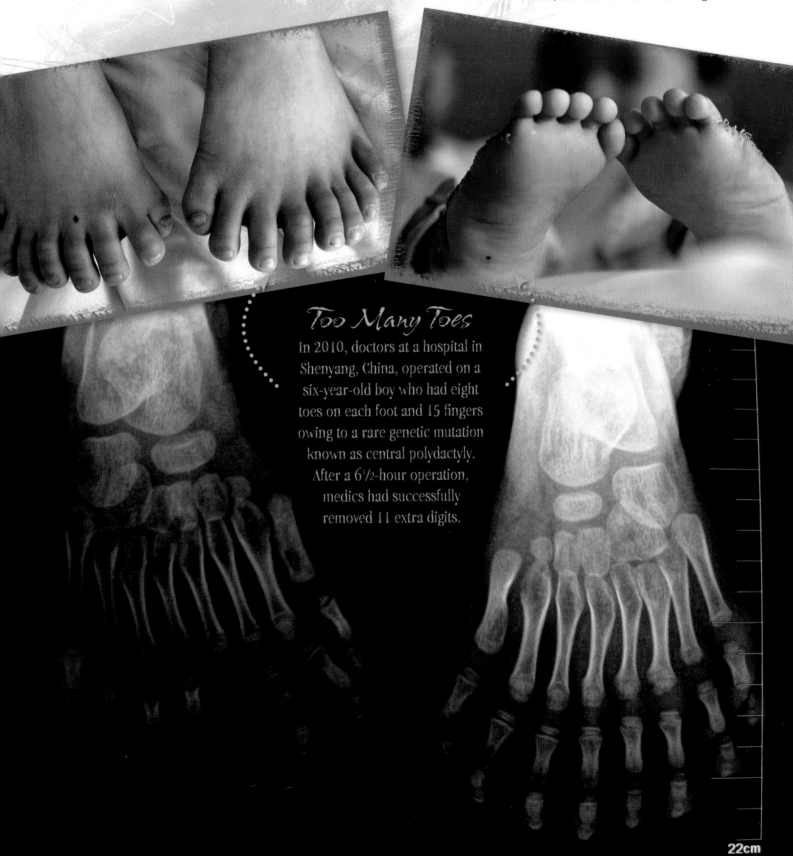

Too Many Toes

In 2010, doctors at a hospital in Shenyang, China, operated on a six-year-old boy who had eight toes on each foot and 15 fingers owing to a rare genetic mutation known as central polydactyly. After a 6½-hour operation, medics had successfully removed 11 extra digits.

22cm

determined dan Dan Netherland of Gatlinburg, Tennessee, can keep his fingers gripped together while ten people try to pull his arms apart.

tongue typist Legally blind and unable to use his hands, Josh LaRue of New Concord, Ohio, wrote a book by tapping out the words in Morse Code using his tongue.

lucky break When Raymond Curry overturned his car near his home in Northumberland, England, he was rushed to hospital with a fence post speared through his chest. There, doctors were relieved to see that the post had amazingly missed all of his vital organs—and they found a four-leafed clover stuck to his back.

saving lives Ben Kopp, a U.S. Army Ranger Corporal, was killed while saving six soldiers in a firefight and then helped save the lives of 75 others by donating his organs and tissues.

sprouting pea Doctors in Cape Cod, Massachusetts, investigating the cause of a patient's sickness, were stunned to find that he had a pea plant growing in his lung. They believe Ron Sveden, from nearby Brewster, had eaten a pea at some time in the previous couple of months but it had gone down the wrong way, and the seed had split inside him and started to sprout about ½ in (1 cm).

beatle tattoo Beatles fan Rose Ann Belluso of Downington, Pennsylvania, took a sign to Paul McCartney's Philadelphia show in August 2010 asking him to sign her back with a marker pen that she had brought along. After the singer called her up on stage and obliged, she decided to make the inscription permanent the next day by getting a tattoo artist to ink over the signature.

puff, puff... boom! Unlucky Andi Susanto of Indonesia lost six of his teeth when a cigarette he was smoking mysteriously exploded in February 2010.

route 66 Ron Jones of Bartlesville, Oklahoma, gets his kicks out of having Route 66 tattoos all over his body. He has more than 80 tattoos dedicated to destinations along the 2,448-mi (3,940-km) highway, including the Ariston Café in Litchfield, Illinois, and the arch on the Santa Monica Pier in California,

bee therapy Bed-ridden multiple sclerosis sufferer Sami Chugg from Bristol, England, was able to get back on her feet after being stung 1,500 times by bees. The Bee Venom Therapy, carried out over a period of 18 months, involved holding a bee in a pair of tweezers and deliberately stinging an area of skin around her spine.

little miss dynamite Dr. Thienna Ho, 5 ft (1.5 m) tall and weighing barely 95 lb (43 kg), deadlifted 104,846 lb (47,557 kg) in one hour in San Francisco. The barbell she lifted weighed 46 lb (21 kg)—nearly half her body weight. She has previously completed more than 5,000 sumo squats in an hour.

chinese accent After suffering a severe migraine headache in March 2010, Sarah Colwill of Plymouth, Devon, England, suddenly started speaking with a Chinese accent—despite never having been to that country. Doctors say she has Foreign Accent Syndrome, a rare condition that damages the part of the brain that controls speech and word formation.

deep sleep A Polish man woke up from a 19-year coma to find the Communist Party no longer in power and food no longer rationed. After being hit by a train in 1988, railway worker Jan Grzebski also slept through the weddings of four of his children and the births of 11 grandchildren.

head returned Lewis Powell, a conspirator in the assassination of U.S. President Abraham Lincoln, was hanged in 1865 and was buried headless. His skull had been missing for 127 years when it was found in storage in the Smithsonian Museum and returned to the body.

migraine cure In order to relieve crippling migraine headache pains, teenager Melissa Peacock from Bradford, England, has to "drink" her brain fluid every day. At the age of nine she was diagnosed with intracranial hypertension, a condition that causes her body to produce too much spinal fluid. This collects in her skull and pushes on her brain, leaving her with such bad migraines and blurred vision that sometimes she could not walk in a straight line. On nine separate occasions, doctors punctured her skull to drain the fluid, but when it kept returning they decided to fit a tube that siphons fluid from her brain straight into

odd reaction Desiree Jennings from Ashburn, Virginia, claimed she couldn't walk forward after suffering a freak reaction to a seasonal flu shot. Her forward motion suddenly became awkward with a twisted gait and she also had difficulty speaking, reading and remembering things—yet the symptoms disappeared when she ran or walked backward.

frozen fingertip After losing her right pinky fingertip in an accident at her home in Davis, California, Deepa Kulkarni took it to doctors—and when they said they were unable to reattach it, she decided to investigate a new procedure called tissue regeneration. Eventually, she persuaded a local doctor to carry out tissue regeneration on her fingertip and after seven weeks of treatment it grew back. However, she still keeps the original fingertip in her freezer.

armless pitcher Tom Willis of San Diego, California, can throw a baseball the entire 60½ ft (18.5 m) distance from the mound to home plate without the ball bouncing—with his feet. Born with no arms, he has used his feet to throw the first pitch of a game at more than ten Major League Baseball stadiums in the U.S.A.

hidden bullet Eighty-three-year-old World-War-II veteran Fred Gough from the West Midlands, England, thought that he was suffering from painful arthritis—until doctors told him in 2010 that a German bullet had been lodged in his hip for the past 66 years.

light lunch U.S. sideshow performer Todd Robbins has chewed and swallowed more than 4,000 lightbulbs.

bunny girl Rabbit-loving grandmother Annette Edwards of Worcester, England, has spent $16,000 on cosmetic surgery to make herself look like Jessica Rabbit, the sultry heroine of the 1988 movie *Who Framed Roger Rabbit?* As well as the surgery, she went on a rabbit-style diet for three months, eating just salads and cereals.

tattoo marathon In December 2009, Nick Thunberg was tattooed for 52 straight hours by body artist Jeremy Brown in

Self-styled

Etienne Dumont, a journalist from Geneva, Switzerland, has some of the most stunning body modifications in the world. He is tattooed from head to toe with vibrant images including skulls, flowers and animals, but most striking are the designs covering his face and a hole stretched in his chin, held open by a transparent disk through which you can see his teeth. He also has a synthetic horn implant protruding from his scalp and has also used progressively larger disks to stretch his earlobes.

body

Ripley's Believe It or Not!®

Iron Man

In 1848, a man working on the Vermont railway survived having an iron rod blasted right through his face and out of the top of his skull. Phineas Gage had been using explosives to clear space for the tracks by packing gunpowder into holes in rock with a heavy iron rod when a spark ignited the powder and the rod shot through his head.

Unbelievably, Gage survived this horrific accident and remained physically able for the rest of his life, although damage to his brain significantly altered his character. His injury became famous in medical circles, and contributed to an understanding of how the brain works. Gage returned to work as a coach driver and died in 1860, 12 years after his accident.

Identified as Gage in 2009, this photo shows him with the same 13-lb (6-kg) tamping iron that pierced his brain, which he kept as a gruesome souvenir. He lost the sight in his left eye when the rod passed behind it.

R hair insured American football player Troy Polamalu, a defender with the Pittsburgh Steelers, has had his hair insured for $1 million by Lloyd's of London. His 3-ft-long (90-cm) black curls are so famous that he has not cut them since 2000. Although he wears a helmet while playing, his hair is still at risk—in 2006 he was tackled by his ponytail by Larry Johnson of the Kansas City Chiefs after intercepting a pass.

R magnetic disruption Placing a magnet on your head can temporarily turn a right-handed person into a left-hander. By positioning a powerful magnet on the left posterior parietal cortex—a region of the brain that deals with planning and working out the relationship between three-dimensional objects—researchers at the University of California, Berkeley, found that normally right-handed volunteers started to use their left hand more frequently for tasks such as picking up a pencil. This is because the magnet disrupted and confused the volunteers' brains.

R epic climb Three U.S. war veterans climbed 19,341-ft (5,895-m) Mount Kilimanjaro in Tanzania in 2010—despite having only one good leg between them. Amputees Dan Nevins, 37, of Jacksonville, Florida, who lost his legs in Iraq; Neil Duncan, 26, of Denver, Colorado, who lost both legs in a roadside bomb attack in Afghanistan; and Kirk Bauer, 62, of Ellicott City, Maryland, who lost a leg in Vietnam in 1969, made the climb on their prosthetic legs in just six days.

FACE BOOKED

In 2010, Chang Du from Lishuguo, China, went public with an offer to sell advertising space on his oversized chin. After a small pimple in his mouth swelled massively over a period of five years, Chang made the bizarre proposal in order to raise funds to reduce his chin back to normal size. He confirmed that an $8,000 offer would be enough to secure the space on his face.

R fridge raider Anna Ryan of Blue Springs, Missouri, put on 126 lb (57 kg) over several years—by eating food from her refrigerator while sleepwalking. She was puzzled why her weight ballooned to 266 lb (121 kg) despite adhering to a strict low-fat diet. However, when she awoke one morning to find cookies in her bed it emerged that, unbeknown to her, she had been getting up regularly in the night to eat cheese, chocolate and even meat.

R human heads When airport workers in Little Rock, Arkansas, noticed a package that was not labeled properly, they checked the contents and found a shipment of 60 human heads. Further investigation revealed the heads were on their way to a company in Fort Worth, Texas, to be used by neurosurgeons for the study of ear, nose and throat procedures.

R heroic landing In early 2010, Lt. Ian Fortune of Britain's Royal Air Force was shot between the eyes while piloting a helicopter in Afghanistan. He survived the incident and continued flying for another eight minutes before making a successful landing, saving all 20 people on board.

R full bladder After a 14-year-old boy in India was admitted to hospital complaining of pain and urinary problems, doctors were shocked to find a ¾-in-long (2-cm) fish in his bladder.

sucked hair After her car swerved off the road in Colorado, Cynthia Hoover survived for five days in the freezing wilderness of the Rocky Mountains by sucking water from her wet hair into her mouth. She was eventually found because she managed to crawl 450 yd (410 m)—despite having 11 broken ribs, a punctured lung and several broken vertebrae—to where she heard voices coming from a disused mine.

snowshoe beard David Traver of Anchorage, Alaska, was the winner of the 2009 World Beard and Moustache Championships with his 20½-in-long (52-cm) beard woven to resemble a snowshoe.

What is the best thing about having such long hair?
My long locks are my pride and joy and my baby. They can be bundled and used as an extra pillow. I also bundle them behind my lower back when driving long distance, because they work better than a pillow for back support. They work as a great scarf in the winter when I visit cold states.

How do you keep your hair under control on a day-to-day basis?
For chores and running errands, I tie my locks in a wrap on my lower back, just like African women carry their babies. It secures my locks and allows me total freedom of movement, which is brilliant as I am very over-protective of my locks.

How often do you wash it, and how long does that take? For 20 years I washed my locks three times a week. Now I wash them only once a week, as per advice from a locks stylist. It takes about 30 minutes to wash them, about 40 minutes wrapped in a huge bath towel to absorb the water, and between 15 and 24 hours to totally dry.

Would you ever get your hair cut? Never is a strong word, but I will NEVER cut my locks. My locks are my baby... my crown... they hold 22 years of my sorrows and my joys, they're like another person... yet it's me... no, I will never cut my locks.

celebrity tattoos Steve Porter from Nottingham, England, has 12 autographed pictures of celebrities—including Alice Cooper, Anastacia and Ozzy Osbourne—inked onto his skin as tattoos. In total, he has more than 20 tattoos of actors and rock stars covering his body.

body bacteria There are as many as ten times the number of living bacteria and bugs in and on our bodies as there are human cells. Of the estimated 100 trillion microbes, the most densely populated areas of flesh are the belly button, the bottoms of the feet and between the fingers.

still singing After suffering a stroke, singer Ann Arscott of Birmingham, England, was left unable to speak—but she could still sing. She has aphasia, a condition caused by damage to the areas of the brain responsible for language. It impairs speech, but some people with it can still sing, as music activates a different part of the brain.

cat boy A boy in Dahua, China, has bright blue eyes that glow in the dark and enable him to see in the pitch black. Nong Youhui can read perfectly in complete darkness and also has good vision during the day. Medical experts think he was born with a rare condition called leukodermia, which has left his eyes with less protective pigment and made them more sensitive to light.

sneezed nail Prax Sanchez, 72, of Colorado Springs, Colorado, had an MRI scan for an ear problem, which dislodged a nail in his head that he then coughed up after the procedure. He had no idea the nail was there and it could have been decades old.

LONG LOCKS
Asha Mandela from Clermont, Florida, has hair that measures an incredible 19 ft 6 in (6 m), longer than a pickup truck. Asha has not cut her hair for an astonishing 22 years.

what knife? Julia Popova of Moscow, Russia, was attacked by a mugger in February 2010 but walked home not aware that she had been stabbed and that the knife was still impaled in her neck.

miss plastic A 2009 beauty contest in Budapest, Hungary, was open only to women who had undergone cosmetic surgery. "Miss Plastic" featured contestants who had enhanced their bodies with everything from new breasts and liposuction to hair transplants.

nasty shock In 2003, librarian Susanne Caro of Sante Fe, New Mexico, opened a 115-year-old medical book and found an envelope containing scabs from smallpox patients.

skeleton growth A person's skeleton continues to grow until around age 25, when the collarbone finally finishes developing.

strong boy Kyle Kane, a 12-year-old schoolboy from the West Midlands, England, lifted a 308-lb (140-kg) weight—more than twice his own body weight—at a junior bodybuilding event in 2010.

HUMAN SKELETON

Billed as the "Skeleton Dude" at Coney Island's Dreamland Circus in 1917, Eddie Masher of Brooklyn, New York, stood 5 ft 7 in (1.7 m) tall, but he declared he weighed just 38 lb (17 kg). Other records have put him at 48 lb (22 kg) or as much as 67 lb (30 kg), but even those weights were astonishingly light for an adult man. He was so skinny that tailors struggled to make a suit that would fit him. He died in 1962 at 70 years old—a good age for a skeleton!

secret bullet Vasily Simonov of Togliatti, Russia, has lived with a bullet in his lung for 70 years. As a child in 1941, he was playing with a rifle cartridge when he decided to take out the bullet and shove it up his nose. After trying in vain to remove it, he then breathed it in. He forgot all about it and the lodged bullet never caused him any problems, only coming to light during an MRI scan in 2009. Even then, doctors decided it was best to leave the bullet where it was.

body sale In 2010, anatomist Gunther von Hagens launched a mail-order service for his Plastinarium museum in the German town of Guben, selling human and animal body parts that had been preserved with a special plastic solution. Items for sale included a smoker's lung ($4,440), a chunk of human head ($2,000), a slice of a human hand ($228) and a cross-section of giraffe neck (price unspecified).

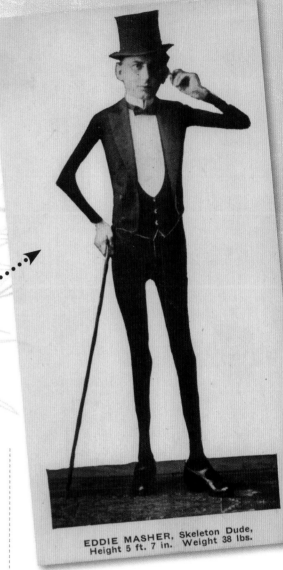

EDDIE MASHER, Skeleton Dude, Height 5 ft. 7 in. Weight 38 lbs.

kept "dying" Motorcyclist Steven Nixon from Derbyshire, England, suffered a massive heart attack after being in collision with a car—but he pulled through even though he had technically "died" 28 times over the next few hours when his heart repeatedly stopped beating.

tall guy Sultan Kosen of Turkey stands 8 ft 1 in (2.5 m) tall. His hands measure 10¾ in (27.5 cm) and his feet 14¹/₃ in (36.5 cm). He lives with his parents, three brothers and a sister, all of whom are of normal height and normal size.

bionic bottom After suffering massive internal injuries in a motorcycle crash, a man from South Yorkshire, England, now presses a remote control to open his bowels and go to the toilet. Surgeons rebuilt his bottom by taking a muscle from above his knee, wrapping it around his sphincter, and then attaching electrodes to the nerves. The electrodes are operated by a handset that he carries in his pocket and switches to on or off to control his bowel movements.

BIG BABY

At age two, Fan Sijia of Yuncheng City, Shanxi Province, China, was 3 ft 7 in (1.1 m) tall and weighed 100 lb (45 kg)—about four times the average weight for a girl her age.

constantly seasick Jane Houghton from Cheshire, England, went on a week-long Mediterranean cruise—and still feels permanently seasick more than nine years later. She suffers from the rare Mal de Debarquement Syndrome, which causes people to feel as though they are constantly bobbing about on a rough sea. She feels so nauseous and wobbly that she has even had to stop buying clothes with stripes or busy patterns because she is unable to focus to iron them.

chute terror Skydiver Paul Lewis survived after falling 3,000 ft (900 m) onto the roof of a hangar at Tilstock Airfield, Shropshire, England, in August 2009. His main parachute failed to open at 3,000 ft (900 m) and although his reserve chute opened at 2,000 ft (600 m), a problem caused him to spiral out of control from 1,000 ft (300 m) with the canopy only partially opened. Luckily, the parachute became snagged on the hangar roof, preventing him from plunging to the ground and almost certain death.

busy brain The number of neurons in your brain—100 billion—is about the same as the number of stars in the Galaxy.

matching horns A Chinese grandmother who grew a 2.4-in (6-cm) horn on the left side of her forehead in 2009 began to develop a similar growth on the right side of her forehead a year later. Zhang Ruifang from Linlou has cutaneous horns—growths made of keratin, the same substance that makes up fingernails. Most cutaneous horns are just a few millimeters long, but occasionally they can extend a number of inches from the skin.

weight loss In January 2010, former postman Paul Mason of Suffolk, England, weighed 980 lb (444.5 kg)—but then he instantly lost 294 lb (133.5 kg) after undergoing gastric bypass surgery. The operation involved having part of his stomach stapled off so that all the food he eats goes into a small pouch, vastly restricting the amount he can consume. At his heaviest he ate 20,000 calories a day—eight times the amount needed by an average man.

coal-powered bike Sylvester H. Roper of Roxbury, Massachusetts, built a steam-powered velocipede in the 1860s that drove like a motorcycle but was instead fueled by coal.

teenage toddler Although she is old enough to drive a car, Brooke Greenberg of Reisterstown, Maryland, weighs just 16 lb (7.2 kg), is 30 in (75 cm) tall and rides around in a stroller pushed by her mother. The teenager has the body and behavior of a tiny toddler, thought to be the result of a mutation in the genes that control her aging and development, and which has apparently left her frozen in time.

tooth test Scientists can determine the ages of people born after 1943 to within 18 months by examining the amount of radioactive carbon in their teeth, caused by above-ground nuclear weapons testing in the 1950s and 1960s.

Twisted Tiger

Double contortionists Hassani Mohammed (right) and Lazarus Mwangi of Cirque Mother Africa bend over backward to entertain the audience at a show in Hamilton, New Zealand.

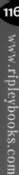

Ripley's Believe It or Not!®

Major Mite

▼ At only 28 in (71 cm) tall when fully grown, Major Mite was no bigger than the average toddler.

▲ Major Mite would travel with his normal-sized parents Frank and Helen Howerton. Frank entered Major Mite in local sideshows before he was snapped up by the Ringling Brothers for their traveling circus. Each of his four brothers grew to be 6 ft (1.8 m) tall.

Clarence C. "Major Mite" Howerton *was born in February 1913, and was billed by the press in the 1930s as the smallest man in the world. He stood only 28 in (71 cm) tall and weighed just 20 lb (9 kg).* He was so small that he once traveled from New York to Chicago to find a tailor who would make a tuxedo for his diminutive size. He wore custom-made shoes just 2.5 in (6 cm) long.

The Ringling Brothers and Barnum & Bailey Circus signed up Major Mite in 1923, when he was ten years old, and he starred in its sideshow for more than 25 years. As well as being a big draw on the sideshow circuit, Major Mite featured in several Our Gang comedy shorts and played a trumpet-playing munchkin in the 1939 film The Wizard of Oz.

After a life in showbusiness, he died in Oregon at the age of 62.

▲ The Ringling Brothers Circus was the biggest of its kind, featuring 800 performers and more than a thousand animals.

MAJOR MITE
AGE 20 YEARS
WEIGHT 20 POUNDS
HEIGHT 26 INCHES

▼ Major Mite plays cards with 7-ft-8-in-tall (2.3-m) Jack Earle during downtime while performing for the Ringling Brothers Circus in the early 1930s.

▲ Tiny Major Mite being held aloft by his friend, giant Jack Earle.

• Clarence C. Howerton was not the only "Major Mite," although he was by far the most famous. A 33-in (84-cm) comedian who died in New York in 1900 also shared the name, as did other little people on the circus sideshow circuit.

• Major Mite became a mascot for the U.S. Marine Corps recruitment before retiring from the entertainment industry in 1948.

▲ Major Mite performed with many extreme individuals, such as 700-lb (318-kg) Ruth Pontico.

◄ Reports suggest that Major Mite had a rebellious streak, sometimes dressing in children's clothes and then shocking the public by smoking, shouting—or posing on a motorbike.

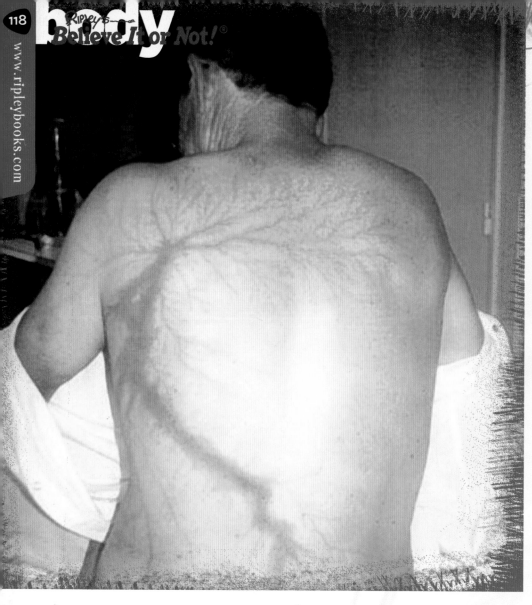

HEAVENLY STRIKE

This beautiful and unusual treelike pattern is the result of a lightning strike. The patient survived with no permanent injuries, and the red markings disappeared within two days. Known as a Lichtenberg Figure, or "lightning flower," the pattern on the skin is rarely seen and not fully understood. Experts believe that it may be caused by damage to small blood vessels along the path of the electric current, or bruising from shock waves in the air above the skin.

parasitic twin Eighteen-month-old Kang Mengru of Henan Province, China, had her dead twin removed from her stomach. Her parents were puzzled by her increasingly swollen stomach, which made her look pregnant, until medical scans revealed that she was carrying the parasitic fetus of her unborn twin in her belly. In such rare cases—affecting one in 500,000 births—one twin in the womb grows larger than the other and envelops its smaller sibling. The second fetus never fully develops, but continues to grow within the first baby, feeding off it like a parasite.

baby frozen Sixteen-week-old Finley Burton of County Durham, England, was put in a hospital "deep freeze" for four days to keep him alive when complications arose after heart surgery. His heart had started to beat alarmingly quickly, so his body was placed in a "cool bag," through which cold air was pumped to keep his temperature down. This slowed his metabolism, which in turn slowed his heart rate.

rare quads In December 2009, Lisa Kelly of Middlesbrough, England, gave birth to a set of quadruplets made up of two sets of identical twins—a ten-million-to-one chance!

vulture tonic In southern Africa, vultures' brains have become so popular as a traditional medicine that it has contributed to seven of the region's nine vulture species becoming endangered.

kangaroo care Having been told by doctors at a hospital in Sydney, Australia, that her premature baby Jamie had not survived the birth, Kate Ogg cuddled her lifeless son—born at 27 weeks and weighing just 2 lb (900 g)—next to her body and said her tearful goodbyes to him. Incredibly, after two hours of being hugged, touched and spoken to by his mother, baby Jamie began showing signs of life and was soon breathing normally and opening his eyes. The doctors called it a miracle but Kate put it down to "kangaroo care," a technique named after the way kangaroos hold their young in a pouch next to their bodies, allowing the mother to act as a human incubator and keep the baby warm.

knife horror Xiao Wei, a 16-year-old from Jilin, China, had a knife stabbed through his head that went in one side and out the other—but he survived after a two-hour operation to remove the blade.

big baby Muhammad Akbar Risuddin was born on September 21, 2009, in North Sumatra, Indonesia, at a weight of 19 lb 3 oz (8.7 kg)—more than twice the weight of an average baby.

DENTAL DIRT

This is what your used dental floss looks like when magnified more than 500 times. Dental plaque, formed from bacteria and saliva, is clearly visible on the tiny floss fibers. Photographer Steve Gschmeissner from Bedford, England, used an electron microscope capable of magnifying objects more than 500,000 times to show everyday household items in a completely new light.

canadian citizen On December 31, 2008, a Ugandan woman gave birth on an airplane flying over Nova Scotia, Canada. Her newborn daughter was granted Canadian citizenship.

scaly growths Muhammad Yunusov from Kyrgyzstan was born with the rare skin condition *Granulomatous candidiasis*, which left his face and head covered in scaly barnacle-like growths. Cruelly dubbed "dragon boy," he never went out without wearing a mask to cover his face. After six years of torment, he was finally cured when a dermatologist got rid of the unsightly growths in just 17 days with a mixture of creams and medication.

star wars tattoos *Star Wars* fan Luke Kaye from Wiltshire, England, has undergone more than 100 hours of pain to cover his back, arms and legs with tattoos of over a dozen characters from all six *Star Wars* movies, including Luke Skywalker, C3PO and Darth Vader.

churchill's chompers A pair of gold-plated false teeth owned by former British Prime Minister Winston Churchill sold at auction for £15,000 in 2010. Without his dentures, Churchill would never have been able to make his rousing wartime speeches—in fact, they were so valuable to him that he carried a spare set at all times.

tiny tot A premature baby boy born at the University of Goettingen Hospital, Germany, in 2009 survived despite weighing less than 10 oz (283 g) at birth. The tiny tot weighed just 9.7 oz (275 g)—which is 75 grams below the weight doctors consider the minimum birth weight for a baby to survive.

human magnet Metal items such as coins, keys, safety pins and spanners can stick to the body of 50-year-old Brenda Allison from London, England, for up to 45 minutes without falling off. All through her life, her mysterious magnetic powers have set off car alarms, interrupted TV signals and blown out lightbulbs.

Beautiful Bite

To enhance their beauty, women in the Mentawai Islands of Indonesia have their teeth filed into sharp points. The unusual rite of passage, in which the teeth are chiseled into shape with no anesthetic, conforms to local opinions of beauty rather than any practical purpose. Observers have commented that Mentawai women seem to feel no pain during the process, and that they willingly undergo the ritual.

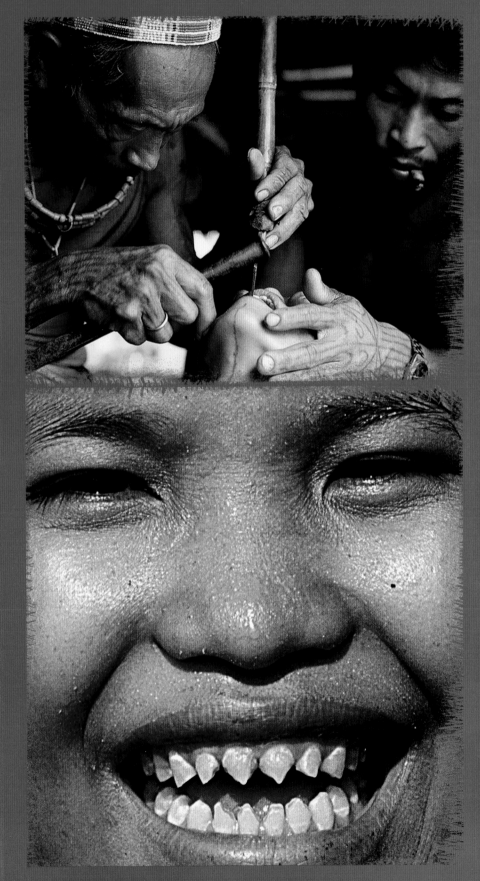

RUSTY NAIL

A man had a rusty 4.7-in-long (12-cm) nail removed from his left kidney in Zhengzhou, Henan Province, China. The nail had been in Mr. Gao's body for 20 years following an accident at home. Although it had cut into his stomach and entered his body, he had sterilized the wound and it healed. In time, a membrane formed around the nail, preventing it penetrating deeper into his body.

glass eater Wang Xianjun of Sichuan Province, China, has eaten more than 1,500 lightbulbs. He started snacking on broken glass when he was 12 because it was "crispy and delicious," and now regularly eats a bulb for breakfast. He smashes the bulb and swallows it piece by piece while sipping from a glass of water. Although his bizarre diet has apparently not affected his health, it did cost him his marriage. He had kept his glass munching a secret from his wife, but when she caught him, she thought it was too weird and they separated.

blood camp The Indian political party Shiv Sena collected 24,200 bottles of blood in a single day at a blood donation camp in Goregaon.

impaled by tree A 13-in-long (33-cm) tree limb crashed through the windshield as Michelle Childers of Kamiah, Idaho, and her husband were driving down the road, impaling her through the neck. Amazingly, she survived.

titanic tumor Doctors in Buenos Aires, Argentina, removed an enormous tumor weighing 50 lb 11 oz (23 kg) from the womb of a 54-year-old woman in 2010. It had been growing inside her body for 18 months. She entered a hospital for the operation weighing 308 lb (140 kg), but after the removal of the tumor she was discharged weighing just 231 lb (105 kg).

saved by implants When a gunman opened fire with a semiautomatic assault rifle in a dentist's office in Beverly Hills, California, Lydia Carranza's life was saved by her size-D breast implants, which took the force of the blow and stopped bullet fragments from reaching her vital organs.

sticky situation Irmgard Holm, 70, of Phoenix, Arizona, sealed her eye shut after mistakenly using quick-drying glue instead of eye drops. She had confused the two products' similar-looking bottles. Doctors cut off the glue covering her eye and washed out the remainder to prevent serious damage.

MONSTER STONE

A kidney stone the size of a coconut was removed by surgeons in Hungary from the stomach of Sandor Sarkadi. Whereas even the largest kidney stones are seldom bigger than a golf ball, this one measured a whopping 6¾ in (17 cm) in diameter and weighed 2½ lb (1.1 kg).

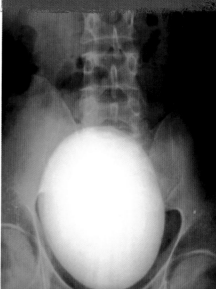

Kidney Hoard

In an operation that took four hours, doctors in Dhule, India, removed a staggering 172,155 kidney stones from the left kidney of 45-year-old Dhranraj Wadile in December 2009.

guardian angel Angel Alvarez survived despite being shot 23 times by New York City police officers during a disturbance in August 2010. Although he was shot in the arms, legs, abdomen and jaw, all the bullets somehow missed his vital organs.

self-amputation Jonathan Metz of West Hartford, Connecticut, saved his own life by partially sawing off his left arm after it had become trapped in his furnace boiler and started to turn gangrenous. Taking a blade from his toolbox, he began sawing through the arm to prevent the infection spreading to the rest of his body. To stem the flow of blood, he used first his shirt and then a telephone cord as a tourniquet. After more than two days —during which his only drink was rust-colored boiler water scooped into his mouth with a flip-flop he had been wearing— he was rescued and taken to hospital where doctors completed the amputation.

reading mystery On July 31, 2001, Canadian mystery writer Howard Engel awoke from a stroke and discovered he could no longer read—but could still write. He was diagnosed as having *alexia sine agraphia*, which meant that newspapers and even his own books appeared to be written in indecipherable oriental script.

supersized son At age three, Xiao Hao of Guangzhou, China, weighs a massive 140 lb (63.5 kg)—as much as an adult man. He dwarfs his mom and has been banned by some nurseries as a hazard to other children.

lucky bounce An 18-month-old boy escaped without a scratch after falling 80 ft (24.4m) from his seventh-floor apartment in Paris, France, bouncing off a café awning and into the arms of a passing doctor. The café was closed for the day and the awning was out only because a mechanism had jammed.

deadly device U.S. Army Private Channing Moss survived a direct body hit from an anti-vehicular rocket in Afghanistan. Luckily, the explosive head failed to detonate, but he was impaled by the rocket shaft.

on the run Former British Army soldier Mike Buss from Swindon, England, completed 517¼ mi (832.4 km) on a treadmill over seven grueling days. He ran the equivalent of nearly three marathons a day, sleeping for just two hours a day, and lost two toenails in the process.

Foreign Bodies

- SURGEONS IN CHINA FOUND A PIECE OF GRASS, 1 ⁵⁄₁₆ IN (3 CM) LONG, GROWING IN THE LUNG OF A TEN-MONTH-OLD BABY GIRL.

- AFTER SWALLOWING A BONE AT DINNER, A CALIFORNIAN BOY HAD IT STUCK IN HIS LUNG FOR THE NEXT 11 YEARS.

- A FRAGMENT OF A PLASTIC EATING UTENSIL WAS FOUND IN THE LEFT LUNG OF JOHN MANLEY FROM WILMINGTON, NORTH CAROLINA. HE HAD INHALED IT TWO YEARS EARLIER WHILE EATING AT A FAST-FOOD RESTAURANT.

- QIN YUAN FROM CHONGQING, CHINA, ACCIDENTALLY SWALLOWED HIS FALSE TEETH, WHICH WERE LATER FOUND LODGED IN ONE OF HIS LUNGS.

- SURGEONS IN INDIA REMOVED A TOOTHBRUSH FROM THE STOMACH OF ANIL KUMAR, WHO HAD ACCIDENTALLY SWALLOWED IT WHILE BRUSHING HIS TEETH IN FRONT OF THE TV.

- DEREK KIRCHEN FROM NORFOLK, ENGLAND, HAD A CASHEW NUT STUCK IN HIS LUNG FOR 18 MONTHS.

- A SMALL BRANCH OF WHITE CEDAR WAS FOUND IN THE LUNG OF A 61-YEAR-OLD JAPANESE WOMAN.

- CHRIS BROWN OF GLOUCESTERSHIRE, ENGLAND, COUGHED UP A 1-IN-LONG (2.5-CM) TWIG THAT HAD BEEN WEDGED IN HIS LUNG FOR 20 YEARS.

- A 62-YEAR-OLD FRENCHMAN SWALLOWED 350 COINS, AN ASSORTMENT OF NECKLACES AND SEVERAL NEEDLES. THE INGESTED MASS WEIGHED 12 LB 2 OZ (5.5 KG)—THE EQUIVALENT OF A BOWLING BALL—AND WAS SO HEAVY THAT IT HAD PUSHED THE MAN'S STOMACH BETWEEN HIS HIPS.

WEIRD INHALATION

After Artyom Sidorkin started coughing blood and complaining of chest pains, surgeons in Russia found a 2-in-long (5-cm) spruce tree inside his lung. He must have inhaled the piece of tree, which then got lodged in his lung, causing it to become seriously inflamed.

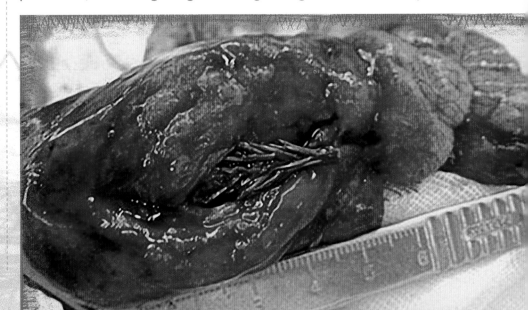

Accidental Discovery

X-rays were first observed in 1895 by German physicist Wilhelm Roentgen, who found them accidentally while experimenting with vacuum tubes. A form of electromagnetic radiation, they have gone on to become one of the most useful tools in medical history, employed for identifying everything from broken bones to accidentally swallowed toothbrushes.

chopstick removal A Chinese man had a chopstick removed from his stomach 28 years after swallowing it. Mr. Zhang had swallowed the chopstick in 1982, but thought it had been digested until he started suffering stomach pains. X-rays revealed that the remains of the chopstick were still inside him. Surgeons in Shanghai extricated it by making a small incision in his stomach.

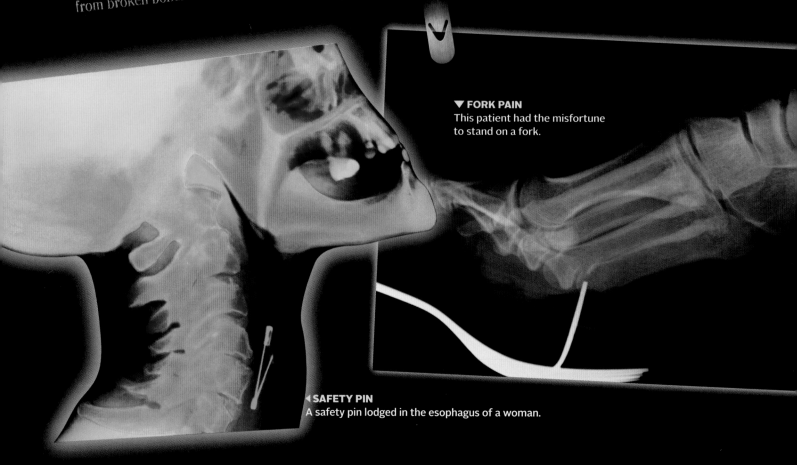

▼ FORK PAIN
This patient had the misfortune to stand on a fork.

◄ SAFETY PIN
A safety pin lodged in the esophagus of a woman.

einstein scan An X-ray of Albert Einstein's skull fetched more than $35,000 at a 2010 auction in Beverly Hills, California. The genius scientist had the scan in 1945, ten years before his death at age 76.

botox cure A stroke victim who had been paralyzed for more than 20 years was able to walk again after being injected with Botox, a substance usually associated with smoothing wrinkles. Having been told by doctors that he would never regain his mobility, Russell McPhee of Victoria, Australia, was able to stand up and walk a few yards just a month after his first Botox injection.

chance discovery An X-ray of a 35-year-old woman from Para, Brazil, who complained of earache revealed that she had over 20 steel needles in her body. She had inserted the needles into herself as a child.

fatal pick In September 2008, a man from Manchester, England, died from a nosebleed caused by his aggressive nose picking.

horned man Jesse Thornhill of Tulsa, Oklahoma, has two devil horns on his head, created by surgically implanting Teflon lumps under the skin to stretch the scalp. The heavy-metal fan also boasts tattooed eyebrows, lengthened earlobes and implant earrings on his head.

echo location A blind English boy has learned to "see" again after adopting a technique used by dolphins and bats to detect where objects are. Jamie Aspland from Ashford, Kent, navigates his way around obstacles by means of echolocation, whereby he utters high-pitch clicks and then interprets the sound that rebounds off the surfaces.

tortoise woman For nearly 30 years, Sun Fengqin from Inner Mongolia carried a 55-lb (25-kg) tumor on her back, which resulted in her being nicknamed "Tortoise Woman." The tumor started as a yellow birthmark but grew so large that in the end she struggled to walk upright.

rubber man Vijay Sharma of Rajasthan, India, is so flexible that he can pass his body through a tennis racket, wind his arms around his back so that his hands grip each other at the front of his waist, wrap his legs over his head, and drink from bottles that he has gripped between his toes.

souvenir finger After losing part of his small finger, Matthew Tipler of Bend, Oregon, took the tip, encased it in clear plastic and made a keychain out of it.

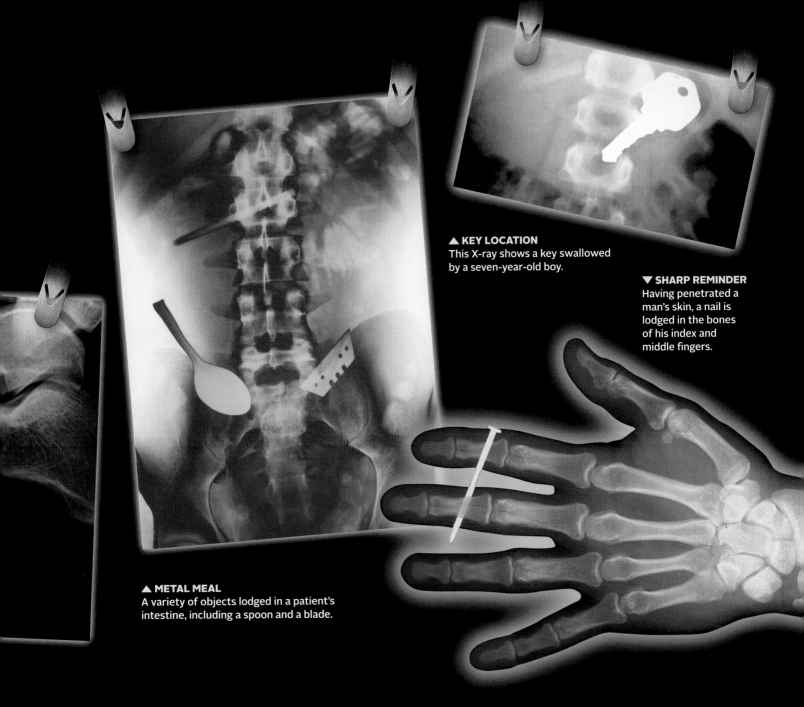

▲ KEY LOCATION
This X-ray shows a key swallowed by a seven-year-old boy.

▼ SHARP REMINDER
Having penetrated a man's skin, a nail is lodged in the bones of his index and middle fingers.

▲ METAL MEAL
A variety of objects lodged in a patient's intestine, including a spoon and a blade.

bumpy landing In June 2009, window cleaner Alex Clay from Eau Claire, Wisconsin, fell six floors, bounced off a concrete first-floor roof and landed on the ground—surviving with nothing worse than a broken foot bone and a cut on his leg.

amnesia victim In 2009, a man later identified as Edward Lighthart walked out of a park in Seattle, Washington, with $600 in his sock but with no idea of who he was and how he got there—the victim of a rare form of dissociative amnesia.

too tall In 2010, at age 14, Elisany Silva from Belem, Brazil, already stood 6 ft 9½ in (2.07 m) tall—and was unable to go to school because she could not fit on the bus. She is believed to be suffering from gigantism, a condition in which the body produces excessive amounts of growth hormones.

facial transplant Thirty Spanish doctors at the Vall D'Hebron Hospital in Barcelona worked for 22 hours in March 2010 to perform a full facial transplant on a patient, which included skin, nerves, muscles, nose, lips, cheekbones, teeth and a jawbone. The recipient, a 31-year-old man, is eventually expected to regain up to 90 percent of his facial functions.

foot skills Born without arms, Ren Jiemei from Shandong Province, China, has learned to use her feet to eat, wash, comb her hair, draw pictures and cut paper. She is so skilled with her feet that when she uses them to thread a needle she is always successful on the first attempt—in fact, she is said to be the best embroiderer in her village. In her school days, she often topped the class despite having to write with her feet and use her mouth to turn book pages.

arm wrestler Joby Mathew from Kerala, India, may be only 3 ft 5 in (1.05 m) tall but he is a champion arm wrestler. Despite having severely underdeveloped legs, he is able to defeat able-bodied opponents who are twice his height. He can also jump up steps using only his hands and perform push-ups on just one hand.

first-aid app During the 65 hours that U.S. filmmaker Dan Woolley was trapped following the Haitian earthquake in January 2010, he used an iPhone first-aid application to treat his fractured leg and head wound.

skydiving champ Despite losing both his legs in a bomb explosion in Northern Ireland in 1992, former paratrooper Alistair Hodgson of Cumbria, England, is a freestyle skydiving champion and has made more than 5,000 jumps.

MINI MAN

At age 22, Wu Kang from Wuhan, China, wears the clothes of a nine-month-old toddler and stands just under 2 ft 3 in (68 cm) tall. Wu suffers from panhypopituitarism, which decreases the secretion of hormones, including growth hormones, produced by the pituitary gland in the brain.

body-building granny At age 73, grandmother Ernestine Shepherd of Baltimore, Maryland, gets up at 3 a.m. and spends her days running, lifting weights and working out. She runs 80 mi (130 km) a week—the equivalent of three marathons—bench-presses 150 lb (68 kg) and lifts 20-lb (9-kg) dumbbells.

heart stopped Joseph Tiralosi of Brooklyn, New York City, miraculously survived after his heart stopped beating for 45 minutes. The 56-year-old father had gone into sudden cardiac arrest inside the emergency room at New York-Presbyterian/Weill Cornell Medical Center, and it was nearly an hour before doctors succeeded in getting his heart going again. Usually if a person cannot be revived within six minutes, they die. Equally incredible, he came through the whole episode without suffering any form of brain damage.

poke-a-nut During a 2009 martial-arts demonstration in Malacca, Malaysia, Ho Eng Hui pierced four coconuts with his index finger in 31.8 seconds.

mass extraction Between the ages of seven and 12, Chelsea Keysaw of Kinnear, Wyoming, underwent three oral surgeries to remove a total of 13 extra permanent teeth and 15 baby teeth.

turtle boy Maimaiti Hali from Heping, China, was born with a hard, mutated growth covering most of his back, its shell-like appearance leading bullies to call him "Turtle Boy." The growth was removed from the eight-year-old's back in a two-hour operation in 2010 and replaced with skin grafts from his scalp and legs.

second face A baby born in China's Hunan Province has two faces. Kangkang was born in 2009 with a transverse facial cleft that extends nearly all the way up to his ears, making it look as if he is wearing a mask.

free flights Thirty-one-year-old Liew Siaw Hsia gave birth on an AirAsia flight over Malaysia in October 2009, and as a result the company granted her and her child free flights for life.

sandwich bag To keep the body temperature of a tiny premature baby warm, medics at Worcestershire Royal Hospital in England used the smallest insulating jacket they could find—a 6-in (15-cm) plastic sandwich bag from the hospital kitchens. The improvised insulator did the trick and saved the life of little Lexi Lacey who had been born 14 weeks early weighing just 14 oz (396 g) and had been given only a ten percent chance of survival.

making antivenom Snake antivenom is commonly produced by injecting horses with snake venom, then collecting the appropriate antibodies from their blood.

rope bed Gao Yang of Liaoning Province, China, can sleep on a single length of rope tied between two trees for up to seven hours at a time. He was taught special balancing skills at age 12 but it took him nearly a quarter of a century to master this feat by practicing on a 10-ft-high (3-m) rope in his local park every morning.

gold tattoo A business in Dubai offers temporary body tattoos made of real gold. The 24-carat gold-leaf tattoos are in demand for glitzy parties and weddings and can be bought for as little as $50. The company is also offering the tattoos in platinum.

BREATHE IN!

Steve McFarlane of South Jordan, Utah, can displace some of his internal organs to suck his stomach in with spectacular effect.

BEFORE

AFTER

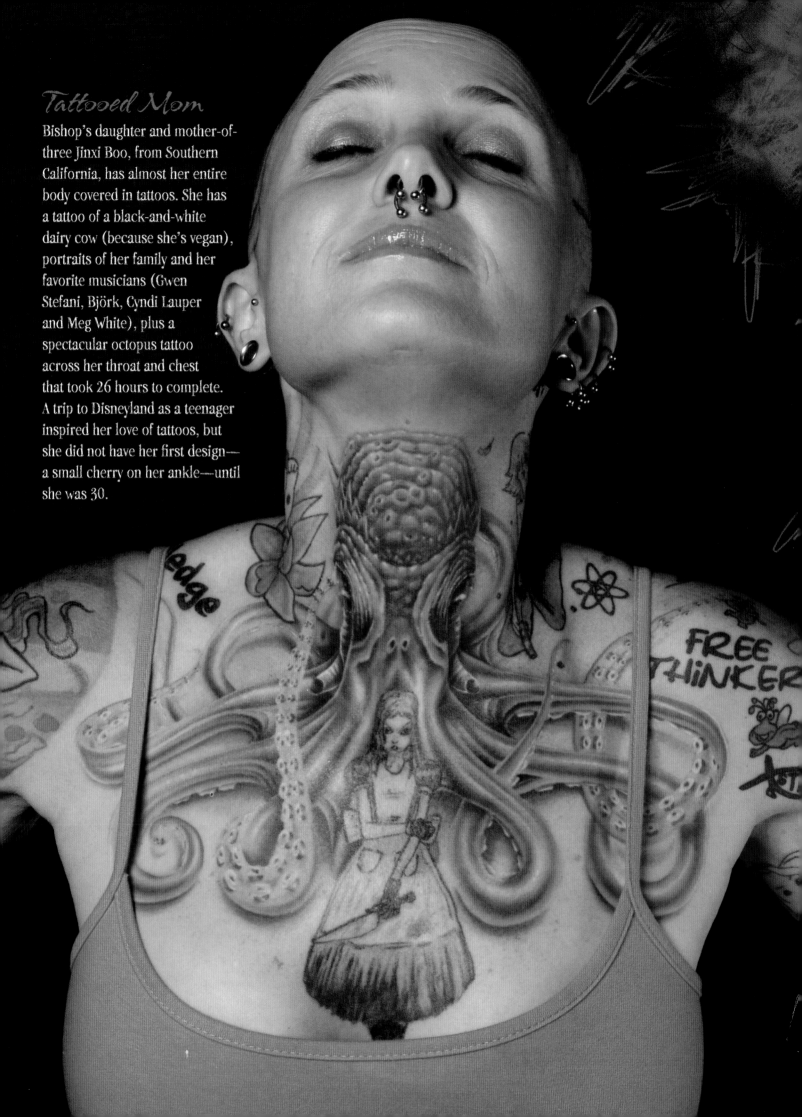

Tattooed Mom

Bishop's daughter and mother-of-three Jinxi Boo, from Southern California, has almost her entire body covered in tattoos. She has a tattoo of a black-and-white dairy cow (because she's vegan), portraits of her family and her favorite musicians (Gwen Stefani, Björk, Cyndi Lauper and Meg White), plus a spectacular octopus tattoo across her throat and chest that took 26 hours to complete. A trip to Disneyland as a teenager inspired her love of tattoos, but she did not have her first design—a small cherry on her ankle—until she was 30.

Ripley's Believe It or Not!®

nickel allergy Kim Taylor from Northamptonshire, England, is unable to touch hundreds of everyday items like keys, coins, zippers, scissors, door handles and saucepans because she is severely allergic to nickel. She takes her own wooden-handled cutlery to restaurants and has to cover everything nickel—even her eyeglasses, bra clasp and buttons—in nail varnish so that her skin doesn't come into contact with the metal.

extra bones Dan Aziere of Danbury, Connecticut, suffers from multiple hereditary exostoses, a rare genetic disorder that causes extra bones to keep growing in his body. He estimates that he has about 50 excess bones—some as large as 4 in (10 cm) long— and since the age of five he has had more than a dozen operations to remove them.

name jinx The parents of a boy who has failed to grow since being born on Dwarf Street claim the name has jinxed their child. Four-year-old Liu Chengrui from Wuhan, China, still weighs just 11 lb (5 kg) and stands only 2 ft (60 cm) tall.

eye twitch Barbara Watkins of Halifax, England, suffers from a rare and bizarre condition that causes her to wink thousands of times a day. She has blepharospasm, an incurable condition that causes frequent muscle contractions around the eyes and affects just a handful of people in every million.

BEARDED LADY

When she suddenly started to grow facial hair in the 1920s, Mrs. Baker B. Twyman of Peoria, Illinois, supported her family by joining the circus as a bearded lady. She later had the surplus hair surgically removed.

miracle boy Seventeen-month-old Jessiah Jackson of Leland, North Carolina, fell from a chair in July 2010 and a metal hook pierced his skull. It penetrated 2 in (5 cm) into his brain, but he survived.

high life Husband and wife Wayne and Laurie Hallquist of Stockton, California, measure a combined height of 13 ft 4 in (4.07 m). He stands 6 ft 10 in (2.1 m) and she is 6 ft 6 in (1.97 m).

hidden needle Doctors in China's Henan Province removed a needle from a man's brain that may have been there for 50 years. Following a seizure, Lin Yaohui, 51, was rushed to hospital where X-rays revealed the 2-in-long (5-cm) metal needle embedded in his skull. As an adult's skull is hard, surgeons believe the needle must have penetrated his head before he was 18 months old.

sneezed bullet A man who was shot in the head during New Year's Eve celebrations in Naples, Italy, survived after sneezing the bullet out of his nose. The .22 calibre bullet went through the right side of Darco Sangermano's head, behind his eye socket, and lodged in his nasal passage. Bleeding heavily, he was rushed to a hospital but while waiting to be seen by doctors, he sneezed and the bullet flew out of his right nostril.

tiny tot At 21 years old, Hatice Kocaman from Kadirli, Turkey, has the body mass of an eight-month-old baby. She suffers from a rare bone disease and stands just 28 in (70 cm) tall and weighs only 15 lb (6.8 kg).

TALL TEEN

At age 14, Brazilian teenager Elisany Silva towers over her sisters because she is already 6 ft 9 in (2.06 m) tall. She is so tall that she had to stop going to school because she could not fit on the bus. Medical experts believe she could be suffering from gigantism, a condition in which the body produces excessive amounts of growth hormones. If left untreated she could continue to grow up to 6 in (15 cm) more a year.

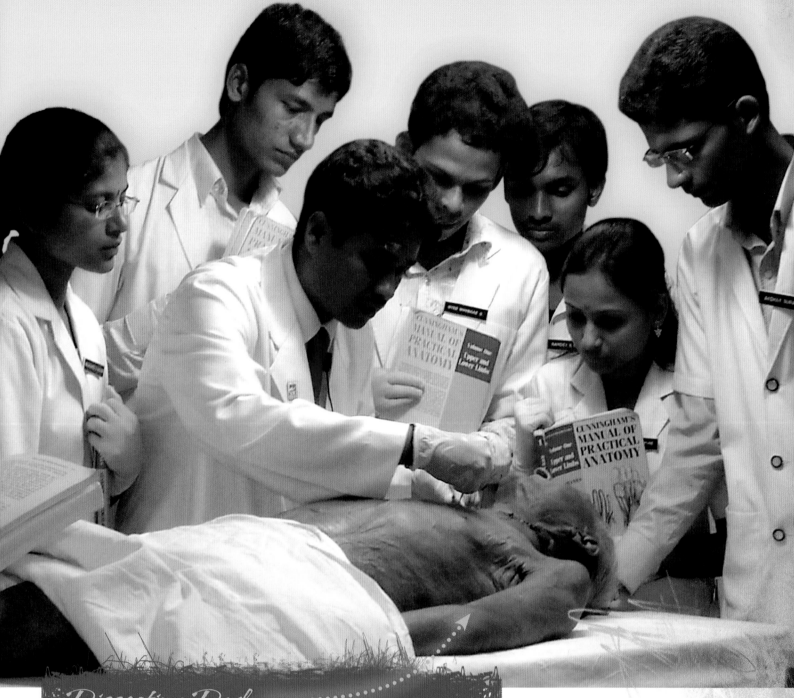

Dissecting Dad

To help teach anatomy to his students, Dr. Mahantesh Ramannavar dissected the body of his father, Dr. Basavanneppa Ramannavar, which had been embalmed for exactly two years. His father had specified in his will that his body should be donated to the university in Belgaum, India, where his son worked and that his son should perform the dissection, which was shown live on Indian TV.

serial sleeper Claire Allen from Cambridge, England, falls asleep 100 times a day. Her condition—an extreme form of narcolepsy—causes her to fall into a trancelike state where she is unable to see or move. Each episode lasts between 30 seconds and five minutes and is triggered by emotions such as surprise and anger, and especially sufaces when she laughs.

turning the screw After an operation to remove a tumor left a gaping hole in his leg, 14-year-old Simeon Fairburn from Brisbane, Australia, saved the limb by turning surgical screws on a leg brace four times every day for over two years to stretch the bone by 1 ft (30 cm). He initially faced amputation, but after wearing the brace and undergoing 20 operations, he can once again dream of becoming a basketball player.

skewered neck Twelve-year-old Garret Mullikin from Houston, Texas, survived after a 9-in-long (23-cm) stick skewered his neck. Falling off a dirt bike, he hit the ground and the piece of tree branch, as thick as a broom handle, plunged into his neck and down into his chest, through his lung, past vital arteries and his heart. Doctors said that if the stick had been pulled out before he was rushed to hospital, he could have bled to death.

worm's-eye view After John Matthews of Bellevue, Iowa, noticed two spots obscuring the vision in his left eye, doctors diagnosed the cause—a worm had got into his eye. The worm—thought to be either a hookworm or a raccoon roundworm—was then killed by medics who shot a laser into his left eyeball. "I could see it from behind," he said, "moving, trying to dodge the laser."

Ripley's Believe It or Not!®

JOIN THE DOTS

Inspired by the idea of getting her birthmarks numbered, Colleen A.F. Venable from New York City has a connect-the-dots tattoo that creates the shape of a giraffe on her left leg.

nose leech *Tyrannobdella rex*, a new species of leech with savage, sawlike teeth, was first discovered in the nose of a nine-year-old Peruvian girl. Named after the most ferocious dinosaur in history, the 2-in (5-cm) bloodsucker came to light after the girl, who regularly swam in tropical rivers and lakes, complained of feeling a sliding sensation in one of her nostrils.

latin tattoos As a subject, Latin is ten times more popular in British schools than it was a decade ago. One theory for the ancient language's surge in popularity is that it is because celebrities such as Angelina Jolie, David Beckham and Colin Farrell have body tattoos with Latin inscriptions.

body piercing In April 2010, Ed Bruns of Gillette, Wyoming, had more than 1,500 16-gauge needles inserted into his arms, back and legs by a body-piercing artist in less than 4½ hours.

tattoo proposal When San Diego, California, tattoo artist Joe Wittenberg decided to propose to his girlfriend, he inked the words "Rachel, will you marry me?" on his own leg.

organs awry Bethany Jordan from the West Midlands, England, was born with her internal organs in unexpected places in her body. Her heart is behind her lungs, her liver and stomach are on the opposite side of her body from normal and she has five tiny spleens instead of just one.

free leg Needing a $60,000 bionic leg so that he could walk again, David Huckvale of Leicestershire, England, happened to go to his local pub on the same day as surgeon Alistair Gibson, who specializes in fitting the computer-controlled limbs. When the two got talking, Mr. Gibson mentioned he had a spare leg and could fit it for free!

hiccup cure After hiccupping an estimated 20 million times over a period of three years, Chris Sands of Lincolnshire, England, finally stopped in 2009 following brain surgery. It is thought that a tumor on his brain stem had been pushing on nerves, causing him to hiccup every two seconds, 24 hours a day.

diamond tattoo South African jeweler Yair Shimansky designed a temporary tattoo made of 612 diamonds and carrying a price tag of $924,000. It took more than eight hours to encrust the ornate floral design on the skin of a model using a special water-based adhesive.

rare phenomenon A woman who had been pronounced dead hours earlier at a hospital in Cali, Colombia, following a series of unsuccessful resuscitation attempts suddenly started breathing again in a funeral home as workers began to apply formaldehyde to her body. Doctors later diagnosed her condition as a case of Lazarus Syndrome, an extremely rare phenomenon in which the body's circulation spontaneously restarts after failed resuscitations.

changing beard Sameer Mehta, a businessman from Gujarat, India, makes weekly trips to the barber and has had more than 60 styles of short beard in the last four years. These have included a heart-shaped beard and another trimmed in the design of his country's flag.

rod removed While playing on a construction site, 12-year-old Kalim Ali from Malegaon, India, was skewered by a rod 3 ft 4 in (1 m) long that pierced ten internal organs, including his rectum, small intestine, lungs and liver. Incredibly, the 0.6-in-thick (1.5-cm) pole didn't damage any major blood vessels, and surgeons successfully removed it after a three-hour operation.

26 digits Heramb Ashok Kumthekar from Goa, India, has six fingers on each hand and seven toes on each foot, giving him a total of 26 digits. He is proud of his condition, called polydactylism, even though he has insufficient nerve endings to feel all his fingers and toes.

tall teen At just 16 years old, schoolgirl Marvadene Anderson stood 6 ft 11 in (2.1 m) tall, making the New Jersey school basketball star 5 in (12.5 cm) taller than her idol, Michael Jordan. Height must run in the family because the Jamaican-born teenager's older sister, Kimberly, is 6 ft 4 in (1.9 m) tall.

bullet in head After being shot at point-blank range by a German soldier in 1944, Ivan Nikulin of Chita, Russia, lived happily with a bullet lodged in his head for nearly 70 years.

Furry Features

Supatra Sasuphan from Bangkok, Thailand, was born with Ambras Syndrome—or congenital hypertrichosis—a rare genetic disease that causes excessive hair growth on the face and other parts of the body. It affects one person in a billion, and there are fewer than 40 known cases in the world. There is no permanent cure for the condition, but nine-year-old Supatra doesn't let it affect her life and enjoys the same activities as her schoolfriends. She hopes eventually to become a teacher.

world

animals

sports

body

transport

feats

mysteries

food

arts

science

beyond belief

believe it!

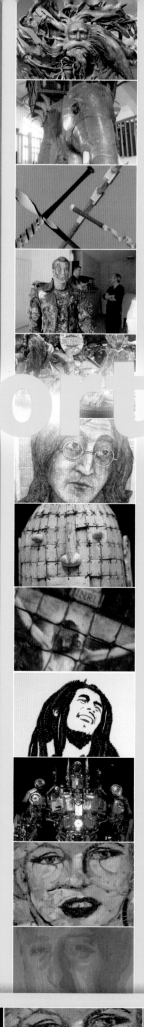

Beatlemania

Art teacher Rebecca Bass and her students in Houston, Texas, won "Best of Show" at the 2010 Houston Art Car Festival with this dazzling vehicular tribute to the music of The Beatles. Each extravagant decoration is inspired by lyrics from Beatles songs. Ripley's soon snapped up the car, named *Lucy in the Sky with Diamonds*.

124
125
126
127
128
129
130
131
132
133
134
135
136
137
138
139
140
141
142
143
144
145
146
147
148
149
150
151

RIPLEY's
EXHIBITS

THE LOST

Glacier Girl flying above Nevada in 2006. More than 80 percent of the new aircraft was built from original parts retrieved from deep beneath Greenland's ice and snow. In October 2002, before a crowd of 20,000 spectators, Glacier Girl took to the skies once again—60 years after her fateful crash in the Arctic. Now the plane can be seen at air shows across the U.S.A.

SQUADRON

A World-War-II fighter plane was rescued and restored to flying condition after spending 50 years buried beneath 268 ft (82 m) of solid snow and ice in Greenland.

The Lockheed P-38F Lightning, since nicknamed "Glacier Girl," was part of an eight-strong squadron making its way across the Atlantic to fight in Europe in June 1942. Bad weather forced the squadron to crash-land on a remote ice cap in Greenland. The crews were rescued after ten days on the ice, but the planes had to be sacrificed.

Later attempts to recover the aircraft proved unsuccessful because decades of snowstorms and shifting ice had carried them 2 mi (3.2 km) from their original location, and buried them so deep no one could find them. Then, in 1988, Glacier Girl was tracked down by a combination of magnetometers (to detect underground magnetic fields) and radar. A daring rescue and restoration project then swung into action.

To access the plane, hot water was passed down through long copper pipes to melt a 4-ft-wide (1.2-m) hole. Technicians rappelled down the hole for 20 minutes to reach the plane and used hot-water hoses to create a 50-ft-wide (15-m) chamber around it. Although the ice had crushed the canopy, the rest of the plane was intact. It took four months in 1992 to disassemble the plane and bring the parts to the surface, one piece at a time. The team, funded by businessman Roy Shoffner, had to sink five shafts to excavate a hole big enough for the last piece, the 17-ft-long (5.2-m), three-ton center section. The parts were taken to Middlesboro, Kentucky, for painstaking reconstruction.

transport
Ripley's Believe It or Not!®

all at sea American sailor Reid Stowe returned to shore in June 2010 after spending more than three years at sea without touching dry land. He set off from New Jersey in his 70-ft (21-m) schooner *Anne* in April 2007 and docked in Manhattan at the end of a 1,152-day voyage, to be greeted by his girlfriend, who had joined him on part of the voyage, and their 23-month-old son, whom he had never seen before.

high security The $400-million, 557-ft-long (170-m) yacht owned by Russian billionaire Roman Abramovich is equipped with a swimming pool, two helipads, a mini-submarine and a missile defense system.

highway party Some 20,000 tables were set up along a 37-mile (60-km) section of a German autobahn between Dortmund and Duisberg for a street party with a difference. The high-speed road was closed to motorists and turned over to cyclists, skaters and picnickers in an event attended by more than three million people.

toilet car Dave Hersch of Lakewood, Colorado, spent four years designing a twin-bowl motorized toilet capable of reaching speeds of 30 mph (48 km/h). His "toilet car" has a 6.5 horsepower motor, can seat two people and features six toilet rolls and a magazine rack.

yellow lines Sally Baker left her Peugeot 206 on a street in Manchester, England, because the road had unrestricted parking—but when she returned she found the vehicle was facing the other way, had double yellow lines painted underneath and had a parking ticket on the windshield. In her absence, council workmen had hoisted her car into the air so that they could paint double yellow "no parking" lines beneath it.

homemade lamborghini Truck driver Chen Jinmiao of Hunan Province, China, built a replica Lamborghini supercar—complete with the famous wing doors—for just $3,000. He downloaded the drawings from the Internet and bought materials from markets and bargain stores to construct a working car with a top speed of 50 mph (80 km/h)—compared to a real Lamborghini's 200 mph (320 km/h).

GatorBike

Jim Jablon from Florida has made a wild custom motorbike from a real-life alligator. Each year a number of wild alligators in the state are culled to control the population, and Jim decided to put one to good use. The reptilian chopper, named the GatorBike, took over a year to build, and features the full skull and skin of an alligator. Worth $80,000, the bike was created to raise funds for Jablon's wildlife rehabilitation park, which has its own rescued alligators alongside other animals, such as Arctic, the large albino Burmese python pictured above on the chopper.

Amphibious Bike In 2010, Lei Zhiqian of Hubei Province, China, rode an amphibious bicycle on a return trip across the 3,250-ft-wide (990-m) Hanjiang River in under 30 minutes. The bike, which is of normal design but has eight barrels for buoyancy and a propeller to push it forward in water, is the invention of Li Weiguo. Out of water the buoyancy barrels fold away so that it can be ridden like an ordinary bike.

bottle track Li Guiwen, a military driver from Beijing, China, gently steered a car along a track made up of two rows of upright bottles for more than 195 ft (60 m). His journey along the 1,798 bottles of beer took 8 minutes 28 seconds.

ship found In 2010, archeologists excavating the World Trade Center site in New York City discovered the remains of a wooden ship believed to have been buried there more than 200 years ago.

lucky leap During a traffic accident in August 2009, Carl Brewer of Canton, Ohio, saved himself by leaping from his motorcycle on to the back of a moving pickup truck.

persistent offender A Saudi-Arabian student racked up $97,000 in driving fines—the result of 400 traffic violations in Dubai over a period of less than two years.

HANG TIME
An Oklahoma driver escaped disaster after reversing his Mercedes sedan through the exterior wall of a parking garage—seven floors up! The driver's foot had become stuck on the gas pedal, but luckily the vehicle lodged itself halfway through the exterior wall. Falling debris damaged several cars, but no one was injured and the driver exited his vehicle safely.

BULLION BUGATTI
Made from solid 24-carat gold and platinum and featuring a large, flawless diamond on the front grille, the Bugatti Veyron Diamond must be the most expensive toy car ever made. It may be only toy-size, weighing 15 lb (7 kg) and measuring 10 in (25 cm) in length, but it costs a cool $2 million to buy—that's almost twice as expensive as a real, regular-size Bugatti Veyron! Jewelry designer Stuart Hughes from Liverpool, England, and Swiss model expert Robert Gulpen spent two months creating this intricate replica, which also features functional steering and a detailed engine.

SPARKLING BLADES

War correspondent Michael Yon captured an unusual phenomenon while working in Afghanistan. When U.S. Air Force helicopters come into land, the dust in the air reacts with the spinning blades to create static electricity that throws out bright sparks around the chopper. Michael named this the Kopp-Etchells effect, after U.S. soldier Benjamin Kopp and British soldier Joseph Etchells, both of whom Yon knew and who died in the conflict.

emergency landing Pilot Matt Conway was forced to make an emergency landing on a busy Atlanta, Georgia, highway after his plane experienced engine problems. He touched down on Interstate 85, a few miles from Peachtree DeKalb Airport, and skidded to a halt without hitting any cars. However, the plane did block four lanes, causing a long traffic jam until it was hauled away a few hours later.

flame thrower Fed up with car drivers cutting him off on the road, James Bond fan Colin Furze from Lincolnshire, England, designed the ultimate revenge—a gadget that fires 15-ft-long (4.5-m) flames out the back of his moped.

ejector scare A civilian passenger in a South African air force display plane accidentally activated the ejector seat while reaching for something to steady himself during a spectacular midair maneuver. The startled passenger instantly shot through the jet's Perspex canopy and was blasted 300 ft (90 m) into the sky by the rocket-powered emergency chair. He subsequently floated down to the ground on a parachute that opened automatically.

coal-powered bike Sylvester H. Roper of Roxbury, Massachusetts, built a steam-powered velocipede in the 1860s that drove like a motorcycle but was fueled by coal.

flying car A company from Massachusetts has devised a road car that can convert into an airplane in just 30 seconds. The Terrafugia Transition, which has four wheels, two folding wings, and a propeller at the rear, can reach speeds of 80 mph (130 km/h) on the ground and 115 mph (185 km/h) in the air. It can be stored in a conventional garage yet has a flight range of more than 490 mi (790 km).

personal potholes In an attempt to finance the repair of its crumbling roads, the village of Niederzimmern, Germany, put its many potholes up for sale in 2010. For $68, people could buy a hole in the road, and in return the authorities repaired it and put a personal message on top. TV channels and newspapers soon bought some of the potholes for advertising.

busy airport London's Heathrow Airport is six times the size of the country of Monaco and has three chaplains—Anglican, Catholic, Free Church—and representatives for the Jewish, Muslim, Hindu, Buddhist and Sikh faiths. Nearly 70 million passengers pass through each year, and 10 percent of Britain's perfume sales take place at the airport.

homemade sub In October 2009, Tao Xiangli, a farmer from Beijing, China, made a successful maiden voyage in his homemade submarine. Without any expert advice, he spent 18 months building the 4-ft-10-in-high (1.5-m), 21-ft-long (6.5-m), one-man, battery-powered sub from used scrap. The body is made out of five oil drums, the sonar is improvised from a stethoscope, and the periscope is an old camera. He tested the vessel by taking it down to the bottom of a local river and staying there for nearly five minutes.

JET BUS

It wouldn't take long to get to school in Paul Stender's jet-powered school bus. *School Time* is equipped with a massive Phantom jet-fighter engine with the power of more than 250 family automobiles, propelling the 35-ft (10.5-m) bus to speeds more than 350 mph (560 km/h). Turbine-crazy Paul has also built a 10,000-horsepower Dodge pickup that can reach 400 mph (645 km/h), and a jet-powered outhouse featured in *Ripley's Believe It or Not! Seeing is Believing.*

hypersonic flight Flying off the coast of southern California in May 2010, an unmanned X-51A Waverider aircraft flew for more than three minutes at Mach 5—that's five times the speed of sound and more than 3,800 mph (6,115 km/h).

police tractor To combat crime in rural areas of Lincolnshire, England, a farm tractor has been converted into a police vehicle, complete with a flashing blue light.

back to life A 1929 Austin 12/4 car that had been languishing idly in a garage in Lincolnshire, England, instantly roared into life in 2010 when its starter handle was turned for the first time in nearly 50 years. The car had been owned by Roger Bulled's late father, Leslie, who had last driven it in 1961.

helicopter rescue A Swiss van driver and his vehicle had to be rescued by helicopter after his GPS sent him up a remote mountain footpath near Bergun. Robert Ziegler found himself stranded on the narrow track, unable to go forward or turn around.

wrong nuts In May 2009, a car traveling down a Swiss highway lost all four of its wheels at the same time. The owner had used the wrong nuts to secure them.

lost torpedo The Taiwanese navy offered a reward of nearly $1,000 in 2010 after sailors aboard the submarine *Sea Dragon* lost a torpedo during a routine training exercise.

much traveled German police who stopped a double-decker Latvian tour bus in Berlin in 2010 found that it had 1.1 million mi (1.8 million km) on the clock—enough to go to the Moon and back twice.

barbie ban Forty-year-old Paul Hutton of Essex, England, was banned from the road after being caught drunk driving in a toy Barbie car that had a top speed of 4 mph (6 km/h). The electric car was designed for three-to-five-year-olds.

melon-coly motorists A busy motorway near Basel, Switzerland, was closed for two hours after a Spanish truck carrying melons lost its load and splattered fruit all over the road. Drivers in the 3-mi-long (5-km) traffic jam eased the pain of their delay by getting out of their cars and helping themselves to the melons.

Off the Rails

One of the most bizarre rail accidents in history occurred in 1895, when a steam locomotive thundered into the Montparnasse station in Paris, France, at full speed. The engine plowed through the platform and then the station wall, crashing into the street 30 ft (9 m) below and killing a pedestrian. The train had been 2 mi (3.2 km) from the station and traveling at 55 mph (90 km/h) when the driver realized that the brakes had failed. Despite the driver's best efforts, the locomotive hit the station at 35 mph (55 km/h). All those aboard escaped serious injury.

GREAT BALL OF FIRE

Pilot Captain Brian Bews parachuted to safety seconds before his $30-million CF-18 fighter jet crashed and exploded in a devastating ball of fire at Lethbridge County Airport, Alberta, Canada. Having completed his practice routine for the 2010 Alberta International Air Show, he was returning to land at the airport when the plane suddenly nose-dived on approach. Just 100 ft (30 m) from the ground, he managed to escape using the plane's rocket-powered ejector seat. Moments later, the plane smashed into the ground and was engulfed in smoke and flames, but Captain Bews survived with only minor injuries.

CHEATED DEATH

Stunt pilot Dino Moline cheated death by a split second by deploying his built-in parachute after a wing of his plane fell off at an air show in Santa Fe, Argentina. After performing a series of daring, acrobatic maneuvers, Moline was flying upside down when he felt an explosion and saw the shadow of the detached wing pass the cockpit. As the plane spiraled out of control, he instantly activated its parachute, which slowed the aircraft's descent and allowed it to float gently to the ground where it caught fire. Moline escaped with only one small injury—a burned foot.

GLIDER CRASH

Former racing-car driver Mike Newman escaped unharmed except for three broken vertebrae after the glider he was piloting crashed at high speed into the runway in front of 15,000 spectators at an air show in West Sussex, England. After performing his routine, he prepared to land but a malfunction caused the glider to plunge almost vertically to the ground, striking its wing first. The nose section crumpled around him and the cockpit burst open, leaving him dangerously exposed. He lay stunned amid the wreckage for a minute before managing to stumble out onto the runway.

PLANE SAILING

Is it a boat? Is it a plane? Actually, it's a bit of both—a plane–boat. Visitors to Fort Lauderdale, Florida, can charter Dave Drimmer's *Cosmic Muffin*, a boat recycled from movie-producer Howard Hughes' old Boeing B-307 airplane. The historic Stratoliner plane was rescued from landfill in 1969 by pilot Ken London, who bought it for $69 and spent four years removing the wings and converting it into a luxury boat. The cockpit of the original plane still houses the controls that pilot the boat.

When is a Stratoliner airplane not an airplane?

school flight When a ferry service was stopped in late 2009, the school children of Papa Westray in Scotland's Orkney Islands were forced to take a 96-second air flight to school each day.

horse-drawn hummer Jeremy Dean of New York City spent $15,000 on his Hummer H2 sport utility vehicle, and then turned it into a horse-drawn carriage.

warthog alert In November 2009, an Air Zimbabwe plane made an emergency stop after hitting a warthog on the runway in Harare, Zimbabwe.

mini motorbike Santosh Kumar of Mysore, India, built an electric motorcycle less than 18 in (45 cm) long and less than 1 ft (30 cm) tall, but capable of carrying a person.

cone fall Shortly after takeoff, a 20-lb (9-kg) engine tailcone, measuring 4 ft (1.2 m) long and 3 ft (90 cm) in diameter, plummeted thousands of feet from a Delta Air Lines jet and landed on the lawn of a home in Roosevelt, New York. None of the crew noticed that the part had fallen off, and the plane—a Boeing 777—was able to complete its journey from Kennedy Airport to Tokyo, Japan.

Monster Limo

The Midnight Rider, a giant tractor-trailer limo, is 70 ft (21 m) long, 13 ft 8 in (4.2 m) high, has 22 wheels, weighs about 50,560 lb (22,930 kg) and has room for 40 passengers. Owned by Pamela Bartholomew Machado from California, the monster vehicle, which costs $1,000 an hour to hire, boasts three lounges, a bar and a bathroom. To refuel it with a full tank of gas costs about $700 and a full oil change costs around $1,000.

Five decades later, when it's a boat...

... with steering controls in the cockpit.

sole owner Ninety-two-year-old Rachel Veitch of Orlando, Florida, bought her Mercury Comet Caliente new in 1964 and has since driven it nearly 600,000 mi (965,500 km).

wooden bicycles Max Samuelson of Cape May, New Jersey, builds functional bicycles out of wood, using as many as 120 pieces of wood in a single bike.

motorized unicycle In 2009, Japanese manufacturer Honda unveiled a motorized unicycle designed mainly for the country's aging population. It has a series of smaller, motor-controlled wheels inside the main wheel, so that to steer the 22-lb (10-kg) battery-powered device on a busy sidewalk all you have to do is perch on it and lean in the direction you want to go.

welcome tip Taxi driver Don Pratt from Cornwall, England, retired from work in 2010 after a grateful passenger left him a $375,000 tip in her will. Don had spent 20 years ferrying pensioner Mary Watson to and from her local shops.

electric bullet In August 2010, the Buckeye Bullet 2.5, an electric car designed by a team of students from Ohio State University, clocked an average speed of 307.7 mph (495.2 km/h) on Utah's Bonneville Salt Flats. The Bullet is powered by nearly 1,600 compact lithium-ion batteries, the kind that power laptops.

parking space An uncovered, outdoor parking space in Boston, Massachusetts, was sold for $300,000 in June 2009.

out to launch Having spent nearly 30 years building a boat in his mother's back garden in Hampshire, England, Owen Warboys finally launched the 40-ft-long (12-m) sloop in 2010. He got the 20-ton vessel out of the garden by hiring a crane that lifted it 40 ft (12 m) into the air over the house and onto a truck.

viking land boat Matt Norris of Austin, Texas, spent two years building a 45-ft-long (14-m) human-powered road vehicle in the style of a Viking longboat. Made of steel and corrugated plastic, it glides on trailer tires, has the axle of a golf cart and is propelled by its crew of 13 people who "row" a system of pulleys and cables.

close encounter A motorist in London, England, tried to avoid a fine for driving in a bus lane by claiming aliens had forced him into it.

extended journey Given permission to drive the family pickup truck to the end of the driveway to unload trash at their home in Damascus, Oregon, a 12-year-old boy kept going for nearly 100 mi (160 km) until he was stopped by police.

modern sailing To cut fuel costs by 20 percent and reduce greenhouse emissions, the 10,000-ton German cargo ship MV *Beluga Skysails* is partially powered by a huge kite. In a throwback to old sailing ships, the 433-ft-long (132-m) vessel is pulled by a computer-guided 1,720-sq-ft (160-sq-m) kite, which is tethered to a 49-ft-high (15-m) mast.

WHEELIE WIZARD

Tyler Shepard, the "Wheelie Wizard" of Middletown, Ohio, rides near-vertical wheelies on a Honda XR 50 motorbike without a front wheel. His wheelie shows include such incredible feats as riding his one-wheeled bike in a wheelie while blindfolded, and maintaining a wheelie for 1 hour 30 minutes nonstop during a parade.

FAKE PORSCHE

Austrian artist Hannes Langeder spent six months building a life-size Porsche sports car from plastic pipes, tape and cardboard. The aluminum-foil-covered Ferdinand GT3-RS has no engine, but is powered by a hidden bicycle, which is why it has handlebars instead of a steering wheel.

floating palace At 1,187 ft (362 m) long, the Finnish-built liner *Oasis of the Seas* is four times the length of a football field and, at 236 ft (72 m) high, it is taller than Nelson's Column in London. Over 3,300 mi (5,310 km) of electrical cabling and 150 mi (240 km) of pipework run through the ship, which took 8,000 man years to build (three years in actual time). Around 160,000 gal (600,000 l) of paint were used to decorate the luxury vessel, which boasts every conceivable facility, including basketball courts, ice rinks, a hospital, a landscaped park and a wedding chapel. Some 55 tons of ice are produced onboard every day to supply the ship's 37 bars and 20 cafés and restaurants, and no fewer than 50,000 pieces of cutlery are housed in the main dining room.

last orders Matthias Krankl of Maulburg, Germany, was banned from driving by police after converting a beer crate into a motorized mini quad bike.

bottle boat Four months after leaving San Francisco, California, the *Plastiki*, a 60-ft (18-m) catamaran built from 12,500 recycled plastic bottles, reached Sydney, Australia, in July 2010 at the end of an 9,550-mi (15,370-km) voyage across the Pacific Ocean. The boat's bottles were lashed to pontoons and held together with glue made from cashew nut husks and sugar cane. Even the sails were made from recycled plastic.

versatile vehicle Dave March of the Californian company WaterCar has created the Python, a $220,000 amphibious supercar that can reach speeds of 125 mph (200 km/h) on land and 60 mph (96 km/h)—faster than many speedboats—on water. All the driver has to do before entering the water is put the gears into neutral, engage the jet drive, then push a button to raise the wheels.

lucky escape A driving lesson on Good Luck Road, Lanham, Maryland, ended with a large family car crashing through the wall of a ground-floor apartment and finishing up on a bed where the homeowner had been lying just minutes earlier.

backward driver Indian taxi driver Harpreet Dev drives everywhere in reverse. His backward driving skills have become so famous in his hometown of Bhatinda that he has even been given a special government license allowing him to drive in reverse anywhere in the state of Punjab. His enthusiasm for driving backward at speeds of up to 50 mph (80 km/h) began one night in 2003 as he was returning home from a party. He discovered that, owing to a mechanical fault, only the reverse gear of his Fiat Padmini worked. He has since redesigned the car's gearbox so that it has four reverse gears and just one forward one.

super model Tony Nijhuis of East Sussex, England, has built a balsa wood and plywood model airplane that weighs more than 100 lb (45 kg) and, with a 20-ft (6-m) wingspan, is as wide as a house. The model is so large it is classed as a light aircraft and has to be licensed by the Civil Aviation Authority. He spent two years and £8,000 constructing the 1:7 scale version of a 1950s U.S. Air Force Boeing B-50 Superfortress bomber, which has four electric motors, 96 batteries and can reach a speed of 40 mph (64 km/h).

long leak The World-War-II ruin of the battleship U.S.S. *Arizona* is still leaking oil into the ocean nearly 70 years after it was sunk in Pearl Harbor, Hawaii.

ZIPPER BOAT

Japanese artist Yasuhiro Suzuki has designed a boat that looks like a zipper—and the wake it leaves behind it in the water makes it look like it's unzipping the ocean as it goes along.

built to last School caretaker Owen Hook of Cambridgeshire, England, has ridden the same bicycle for nearly 60 years. He bought the top-of-the-line three-speed Raleigh cycle in 1953 and still rides it half-a-mile to and from work every day.

maiden flight After six years of design and construction, a Chinese cobbler, who left school with only a basic education, completed a maiden flight in his homemade airplane. Huang Jianjun of Hunan Province spent more than $15,000 on the project—and in June 2010 his plane soared to a height of over 1,640 ft (500 m) before landing successfully.

Inflatable Weapons

Russian balloon manufacturer Rusbal has created a range of full-size inflatable weapons—including fighter planes and tanks (see above)—that look realistic to the enemy from as near as 330 ft (100 m). The country's defense department commissioned the models as decoys in order to protect real combat units from strikes.

Such inflatables are not a new invention. During World War II, the British army used blow-up rubber tanks as decoys. Designed to look just like a U.S. Sherman tank—and easily carried by four men—they were deployed before the Normandy Landings in 1944 in an attempt to deceive the German Army.

animals

sports

body

transport

feats

mysteries

food

arts

science

beyond belief

believe it!

world

144
145
146
147
148
149
150
151
152
153
154
155
156
157
158
159
160
161
162
163
164
165
166
167
168
169
170
171

Dial - a - Portrait

Alex Queral's celebrity portraits, carved from whole phone books, jumped out of the pages of an earlier Ripley's Believe It or Not! book—*Enter If You Dare!* Ripley's now have several of his creations on display at a number of museums, including Marilyn Monroe, Jack Nicholson and, seen here, John Lennon.

Ripley's
EXHIBITS

GREAT ESCAPES

At 32 years old, Akash Awasthi is already one of the most daring escapologists in India, risking life and limb to escape from a burning haystack, a locked box deep underwater and a coffin placed in the path of a speeding truck.

He has also ridden a motorbike through the packed city streets of Trivandrum, Kerala, while blindfolded. He is following in the footsteps of his father, Anand Awasthi, one of the most famous magicians in the country.

1

THE GREAT FIRE ESCAPE

Akash's most dangerous feat is to escape from a giant burning haystack. First he is bound with 25 locks and a 25-ft-long (7.5-m) chain, and hoisted into the air on a 120-ft (37-m) crane.

Akash is hoisted into the air by a 120-ft (37-m) crane.

2

Akash fights his way out of the burning haystack, which becomes an inferno within seconds.

UNDERWATER ESCAPE

Akash has twice taken on the famous underwater box escape. It was first performed by the legendary Harry Houdini in 1912 in New York, and he took 57 seconds to free himself. Akash's father also performed the stunt in 1970, taking 40 seconds to emerge. This escape is one of the most dangerous performed by escapologists. In 1983, Dean Gunnarson failed to escape from a coffin submerged in a Canadian river and stopped breathing before being resuscitated. In his first attempt at the underwater record in Hyderabad, Akash took just 15 seconds to reach the surface. His second attempt was in the harbor at Trivandrum. Handcuffed and chained, he was locked inside a box and lowered into water 150 ft (46 m) deep. Akash surfaced after only a few seconds. When the box was retrieved from the water, it was intact, with the chains and handcuffs still inside.

The box containing Akash, who has been bound with chains, is lowered into the water.

The fearless escapologist emerges from the locked box.

Akash emerges from the flames, unchained, moments before the haystack is completely engulfed. He is tended to by volunteers.

FAMOUS ESCAPES

1. Matt the Knife (U.S.A.) took just 11 seconds to free himself from handcuffs while underwater.

2. Dorothy Dietrich (U.S.A.) escaped from a straitjacket while suspended from a burning rope hundreds of feet in the air.

3. Dean Gunnarson (Canada) escaped from a straitjacket while hanging upside down from a trapeze 726 ft (221 m) above the gorge of the Hoover Dam.

4. David Merlini (Hungary) escaped from a shark-filled pool while in a straitjacket, weights and restraints.

5. Zdenek Bradac (Czech Republic) escaped from a pair of real police handcuffs in 1.6 seconds.

6. David Straitjacket (U.K.) escaped from a straitjacket while on stilts in 1 minute 38 seconds.

7. David Blaine (U.S.A.) took 15 minutes to free himself from shackles and a gyroscope that had been spinning him around 50 ft (15 m) above Times Square, New York, for 52 hours.

Stilt Stunt

In 1891, Sylvain Dornon from Landes, France, walked from Paris to Moscow, Russia, on stilts! He completed the 1,830-mi (2,945-km) journey in 58 days, averaging more than 30 mi (50 km) each day. Earlier in the 19th century, stilts were a fairly common means of getting around marshy terrain in certain parts of France, especially among shepherds, but, by 1891, Dornon was considered very strange indeed.

UNDERWATER JUGGLER

With a single breath, Merlin Cadogan from Devon, England, was able to juggle three objects underwater for 1 minute 20 seconds.

spinning yo-yos At the 2010 London Toy Fair, Ben McPhee from Australia kept 16 yo-yos spinning simultaneously. He had yo-yos hanging off hooks, his fingers, and even his ears and teeth.

young climber At just five years old, Sail Chapman of East Yorkshire, England, achieved his ambition of scaling all 214 peaks listed in Alfred Wainwright's famous Lake District guidebooks. He began walking the Cumbrian hills with his family at the age of two and completed the Wainwright peaks when he reached the top of his namesake fell, Sale, which stands at 2,536 ft (773 m).

tough granny Pint-sized Sakinat Khanapiyeva, a 76-year-old grandmother from Dagestan, Russia, can tear through phone books, lift a 52-lb (23.5-kg) dumbbell while standing on a bed of nails, and break iron horseshoes. She first realized how strong she was at the age of ten when she moved a 660-lb (300-kg) box of grain—equal to the weight of four grown men.

NOSE-TO-NOSE

In March 2010, Robert Officer and John Milhiser from the Serious Lunch comedy group touched noses together for 10 hours 34 minutes, with no breaks or interruptions. Robert and John's record-breaking task included a trip on the New York subway and bathroom breaks together before appearing live on the Jimmy Fallon show.

Into the Skies

wheelchair wheelie Nineteen-year-old Michael Miller of Ellington, Wisconsin, performed a 10-mi (16-km) wheelie in a wheelchair. Michael, who was born with spina bifida, completed 40 laps of a high-school track on two wheels in just under 4 hours. He performed his first wheelchair wheelie when he was just four years old.

text exchange Nick Andes and Doug Klinger, two friends from central Pennsylvania, exchanged a thumb-numbing 217,033 texts during March 2009. At the end of the month, Andes received an unexpected itemized bill for $26,000—for the 142,000 texts he had sent and the 75,000 he had received from Klinger.

happy hugger In Las Vegas, Nevada, on Valentine's weekend 2010, 51-year-old Jeff Ondash (a.k.a. Teddy McHuggin) of Canfield, Ohio, gave out 7,777 hugs in just 24 hours—the equivalent of more than five hugs a minute.

senior student Hazel Soares of San Leandro, California, received her college diploma in May 2010—at age 94! "It's taken me quite a long time because I've had a busy life," said the mother-of-six, who has more than 40 grandchildren and great-grandchildren.

tea potty Over a period of 25 years, Sue Blazye from Kent, England, has built up a collection of more than 6,000 teapots—and they take up so much room that she has converted her home (called Teapot Island) into a museum. Her favorite teapot is in the shape of Princess Diana's head, and was made when she got engaged to Prince Charles.

mayor moore Hilmar Moore has served as the mayor of Richmond, Texas, for more than 60 years. He was first appointed in 1949 and has been re-elected every two years since, although the last time he had an opponent was 1996.

bat breaker At the Riverwalk Stadium, Montgomery, Alabama—home of the Montgomery Biscuits Minor League baseball team—Steve Carrier broke 30 baseball bats over his leg in less than a minute. The 6-ft-4-in (1.9-m), 290-lb (131-kg) Carrier, from Dallas, Texas, also bends steel with his teeth.

Aerial adventurer and qualified pilot Jonathan R. Trappe from North Carolina made history in May 2010 by traveling 76 mi (122 km) across the English Channel attached to a bunch of 55 helium balloons. Drifting from Ashford, England, toward France, Jonathan reached speeds of 35 mph (56 km/h) and heights of 7,000 ft (2,135 m). Three hours 22 minutes after taking off, and after a flight adjustment to avoid Belgium, he landed safely in a cabbage field near Dunkirk, France.

Ripley's Ask

Why did you first start balloon flying? I first became interested in balloon flight as a child—I wondered at a balloon, and how it floated upon the air. Then I thought "If I just get enough of these, couldn't I go into the sky?" As an adult, I left behind the idea that such a thing isn't possible and awakened a dream that had grown quiet.

What inspired you to cross the channel? The English Channel is a challenge that has called to aviators for generations. There is romance in flying over the famous White Cliffs of Dover and the Lighthouse at Dunkirk.

What was it like when you were in the sky? A quiet dream. I was 1,000 feet above the water and I could hear only the waves. When you're in the air, you move perfectly with the wind, not knowing where you'll land.

Was it a bumpy landing? The landing was smooth, but after the landing, as I worked to release the helium and take my balloons down, the winds kicked up!

What are your balloon ambitions? I would like to launch out of California, within sight of the ocean, and then fly inland, above the Sierra Nevada mountains, into the heart of America.

Ripley's Believe It or Not!®

WALL OF DEATH

The crowd peers over the Wall of Death as the powerful motorbikes roll into the ring. The sound inside the track grows deafening as the motorbikes accelerate, tires rumbling. As they pick up speed, the bikes climb the steep, wooden walls until the riders flash inches past the faces in the audience.

Tubular tracks with steep walls, Walls of Death, or Motordromes, evolved in the early 20th century. Riders would start at the bottom of the circular track, increasing their speed and the angle, until they were racing at just over 55 mph (88 km/h) at right angles to the wooden wall. One slip could spell disaster—early Wall of Death riders had little or no safety equipment, often neglecting to wear helmets because the force of gravity would make it hard to keep their heads straight. Soon riders started to increase the risk, racing two or three abreast, crossing each other and even introducing motorcars. Optimum speed was essential. If the bikes went slower than 55 mph (88 km/h), they would drop off the wall; too much faster and the riders were in danger of blacking out as the centrifugal force could drain blood from the brain. Motordromes are now rare—few exist in North America and Europe, but they continue to draw big crowds in Asia.

Cookie Crum, still riding motorbikes and now living in Oregon, was one of the few female Motordrome riders. She first started to ride the Wall of Death in 1949, when only 17 years old, and toured the U.S.A. for eight years. Cookie also rode in what became known as "liondromes." To thrill the crowd even further, fully grown lions were let loose on the boards, the idea being that they would chase the rider around the ring. Incredibly, they were also trained to sit in vehicles as they tore round the Motordrome (see bottom right). ▼

Ripley's Ask

Cookie, how did you start out riding on the wall of death? I can't remember when I didn't have a love for motorcycles. My mother used to say, "By the time you're 16 you won't even notice one going by." Well, here I am 79 years old and still riding—on the street—not the Wall of Death."

How hard was it to learn? I lived in Sarasota, Florida, where a boy named Kenny Kennedy taught me to ride. A few years later I saw an advertisement in the Sarasota newspaper for a female exhibition rider in a Motordrome. So I went for the interview and got the job! Learning to ride is different to how you would imagine. The instructor pushes you around the floor until you get over trying to "straighten up." Then you get one cylinder (the other one they have pulled the spark plug out of) until you can ride around the floor without putting your feet down. Then you get two cylinders and keep working up in stages till that wonderful day (six or eight weeks down the line) when you finally make it up to the straight wall!

Did you ever crash? Because my instructor was very slow and easy, I learned without an accident. Which is not to say I didn't "slide" off the wall a few times!

Were you ever frightened by the liondrome? I don't think I was ever "frightened" by the lion that was on the one show I played on. I do remember one thing about him, though. His cage was next to my stool out in front and almost every time the boys put him in it, he would stroll over to my side, lift his leg, and... you guessed it. Maybe he didn't like me?

What did it feel like to ride on the wall of death? I loved performing for the crowds, especially the children. I could walk inside, start my Indian motorcycle and take off up the wall like most people would open the door and go into a restaurant for a cup of coffee—that relaxed! Yet when I would go upstairs to watch one of the guys ride, I was as amazed as some of the crowd. I thought I couldn't possibly do that! To this day, all these years later, I still get the same feeling whenever I see a Motordrome. Which, by the way, there aren't too many of, so if you get the chance to see one—DO!"

▶ Stuntmen perform death-defying feats on motorbikes and in cars whizzing around the walls of "Wells of Death" at fairs across India. A modern twist on the original Walls of Death, these dromes attract large crowds wherever they spring up.

Ripley's feats
Believe It or Not!®

everest landing British skydivers Leo Dickinson and Ralph Mitchell and Indian Air Force officer Ramesh Tripathi successfully landed their parachutes at an altitude of 16,800 ft (5,120 m) on Mount Everest in September 2009. After jumping out of a helicopter at 20,500 ft (6,250 m), they had just five seconds of free fall in which to open their chutes. The trio had to home in on Gorak Shep—a narrow, sand-covered lakebed and the only safe landing spot for miles around. "It was pretty hairy," said 62-year-old Dickinson. "If you missed that or overshot it, you were either going to die or end up with something important broken."

chopper leap Defying potentially dangerous turbulence, U.S. daredevil motorcyclist Travis Pastrana successfully backflipped a dirt bike over a helicopter that was hovering off the ground in front of Australia's Sydney Harbour Bridge, clearing the revolving chopper blades by about 13 ft (4 m).

paper round Ted Ingram has been delivering newspapers in Dorset, England, for nearly 70 years. He started his job in 1942 and estimates that he has since delivered more than half a million papers.

mass waltz More than 1,500 couples—from children to pensioners—danced a waltz in the main square of Tuzla, Bosnia, in 2010. Organizers estimated that as many as 25,000 people danced in the surrounding streets, but the square had to be sealed off so that the couples had enough room to move.

free haircuts Working round the clock, a team of ten stylists from Pump Salon completed 618 free haircuts in 24 hours in Cincinnati, Ohio, in September 2010.

old scout Reg Hayes, 95, of Oxford, England, retired in 2010 after 87 years as a Boy Scout. He joined the 2nd Oxford Wolf Cub pack in 1923 and moved up to the SS Mary and John 2nd Oxford Scouts in 1930, where he stayed for the next 80 years.

human wheelbarrow In Helsinki, Finland, Adrian Rodrigues Buenrostro from Mexico and Sergiy Vetrogonov from Ukraine completed a 131-ft (40-m) human wheelbarrow race in just 17 seconds.

car wash Students from Bloomington High School South, Indiana, cleaned 1,207 cars in ten hours in a marathon car-wash.

STILL LIFE
S.C. Naganandaswamy of Karnataka, India, can float in 20 ft (6 m) of water for 22 hours continuously without moving any limbs.

bulky wear Croatia's Kruno Budiselic managed to wear 245 T-shirts—ranging in size from medium to extra large—at the same time. The extra clothing added around 150 lb (68 kg) to his overall weight.

king gnome Andy and Connie Kautza of Wausau, Wisconsin, built a concrete garden gnome that stands 15 ft (4.5 m) tall and weighs more than 3,500 lb (1,590 kg).

HUMAN SPARKLER
Dr. Peter Terren of Bunbury, Western Australia, shot more than 200,000 volts of electricity down his body to create a spectacular version of Rodin's *The Thinker*. He turned himself into a human sparkler for 15 seconds by using a homemade Tesla coil, which transforms a feed of domestic electricity into a supercharged bolt of power. He was saved from electrocution by wrapping his torso, arms and legs in builders' insulating foil—the electricity traveled through the foil and out to the earth from his foot. He also wore a tin-foil cap and a wire-mesh mask and taped steel wool to the bottom of his left shoe to create the shower of sparks from his foot.

backward running Germany's Achim Aretz ran 10,000 m backward in a time of 41 minutes 26 seconds at the third Retrorunning World Championships in Kapfenberg, Austria, on August 8, 2010.

beach towel A beach towel covering a whopping 24,110 sq ft (2,240 sq m) of beach was unveiled near Las Palmas on the Canary Islands. A team of 25 people spent 15 days making the towel, and more than 50 people were needed to roll it out on the beach.

heavy suit U.S. Air Force Staff Sergeant Owen Duff ran a mile (1.6 km) in 9 minutes 22 seconds at Kirkuk Regional Air Base, Iraq, in 2010 while wearing an 80-lb (36-kg) bomb suit.

wheelchair crossing Setting off from his home in Lynn, Massachusetts, in June 2010, Matt Eddy crossed the U.S.A. by wheelchair in just over four months. Matt has been confined to a wheelchair since the age of ten and suffers from Duchenne Muscular Dystrophy, as a result of which he is strong enough only to move two fingers and requires a ventilator to breathe. Traveling on the quieter back roads to reach his destination of Long Beach, California, he averaged at least 25 mi (40 km) a day.

Milk Man

New Yorker Ashrita Furman once walked more than 80 mi (130 km) around a track in Queens, New York, with a full milk bottle on his head.

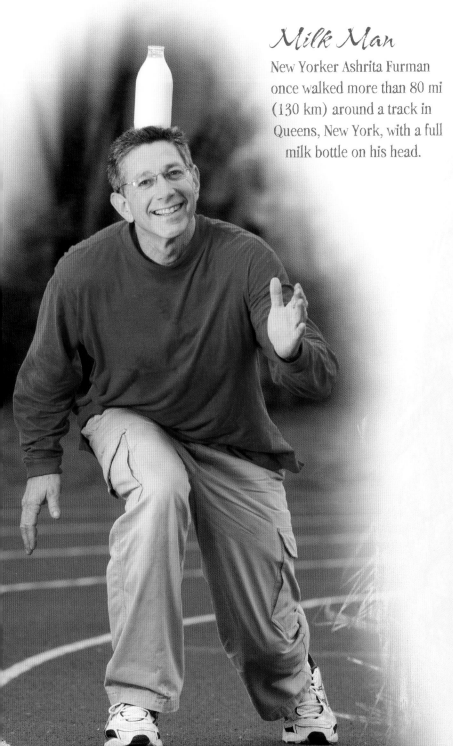

Anthony Martin has been an escape artist for more than 30 years, during which time he has performed a number of truly death-defying stunts.

ANTHONY'S GREAT ESCAPES

- In 1984, Anthony escaped after being bound in 20 lb (9 kg) of chains secured with six padlocks and nailed inside a coffin. The coffin was tied twice at both ends with heavy rope, weighted with rocks and submerged in more than 6 ft (1.8 m) of water.

- After being chained hand and foot, tied with six sets of handcuffs and locked behind six prison doors, he escaped from the Waushara County Jail in Wautoma, Wisconsin, in only 4 minutes 45 seconds.

- Wearing two sets of handcuffs and chained to the inside of a locked freight box, he was pushed out of an airplane at 13,500 ft (4,115 m) in 1988. He escaped at 6,500 ft (1,980 m) and parachuted safely to the ground.

- In 1990, he freed himself from a padlocked chain while locked in a metal cage submerged in icy water in 1 minute 45 seconds.

- Bound with handcuffs, he leaped from an airplane at 11,000 ft (3,350 m) above Idaho's deadly Snake River Canyon and, with just 30 seconds to pick the lock and open the parachute, he successfully escaped in free fall and landed on the north rim.

- Handcuffed in a chain of 12 handcuffs that included a 20-lb (9-kg) ball and chain, Anthony was locked in a cell at the Porter County Jail, Indiana, in 2009. He overcame the handcuffs and three locked jail doors to walk free in 8 minutes 13 seconds.

But if you think these are amazing...

TURN THE PAGE...

LEAP OF FAITH

Escape artist and evangelist Anthony Martin performed a daring skydive from an airplane flying at 13,500 ft (4,115 m) over Illinois—wearing handcuffs that were locked to a chain around his neck and linked to leather cuffs fastened above each elbow.

To add to the stunt's death-defying nature, the safety device attached to his parachute that automatically deploys the chute at 700 ft (215 m) was turned off. Without this backup, he had just 45 seconds, while spinning to Earth at 180 mph (290 km/h), to free himself from the handcuffs and chains and to reach back to pull the release handle and activate the canopy.

Falling in a sitting-back position, Anthony seemed to struggle with the lock for about 25 seconds before working himself free and safely deploying the chute.

The 45-year-old from Sheboygan, Wisconsin, has been picking locks since he was a child and made his first authenticated escape at age 12, when he managed to work his way out of a regulation police straitjacket. He jokes that he comes from the "School of Hard Locks."

Since then he has broken out of a locked box thrown from an airplane, escaped from being buried alive beneath 2,000 lb (907 kg) of sand and freed himself from a heavily secured coffin submerged underwater. He has even requested permission to break out of Fort Knox—where most of the U.S. gold bullion reserves are stored—but the U.S. Government refused to allow the escape bid.

How did you first get into escapology?
I became interested in escapes as a result of becoming disappointed in magicians' tricks. Although I can appreciate the talent required to do tricks, I didn't want to fool people—I wanted to do something real. With the proper tools and training, locks can be legitimately compromised. My goal is to thrill, not deceive.

What was your first escape? It was around the age of six, with the help of my ten-year-old cousin. He used to padlock a chain around my wrists from which I would try to escape.

Which has been your most dangerous escape? Aerial escapes, whether in a box or not, are always the most dangerous. Once you leave the airplane there is no going back.

Have you ever thought during an escape that you weren't going to come out alive? There have been times in my career when I did not have 100 percent certainty that I was going to make it unscathed. However, I never thought I would fail and pay the ultimate price. If I believed that, I simply wouldn't do it.

What went through your mind when you jumped from the airplane? When I am "in the zone" and in the middle of an escape, I am thinking of nothing but the required tasks that must take place to succeed. Everything else is blocked out of my mind, yet I always seem to have an internal clock that knows how much time I have.

How difficult was it trying to focus on your hands while you were spinning in midair? The difficulty of a skydiving spin is that centrifugal force wants to take my eyes off the work I need to do. Sometimes in these situations I can alter the position of my legs and stop the spin, but that requires me to divide my attention (something I don't like to do).

How do you prepare for your escapes? When preparing for an escape, I practice with the specific type or model of restraint I expect to be facing. This process can take several weeks to several months depending on the complexity of the stunt.

How satisfying is it to break free from a seemingly impossible situation? The Great Escape strikes a cathartic cord in all of us. How many of us haven't been in a sticky situation we wish we could get out of?

Ripley's Believe It or Not!®

WITH RINGLING BROS.

Millie Betra, WORLD'S GREATEST SHOWS.

J. V. Brown,

THE SERPENT QUEEN.

PHOTOGRAPHER.

Milwaukee

SERPENT QUEEN

While working for Ringling Bros. Circus in the 1880s, petite American Millie Betra, billed as the "Serpent Queen," regularly handled dozens of huge pythons that were almost twice her size, even wrapping many of the snakes around her body simultaneously.

maggot transfer In May 2009, Charlie Bell of London, England, moved 37½ lb (17 kg) of live maggots from one container to another—in his mouth. He practiced at home with rice for months before finally replacing the grains with the "revolting" maggots.

bike jump At Reno, Nevada, in 2009, U.S. motorcyclist Ryan Capes soared an astonishing 316 ft (96.3 m) through the air from one ramp to another.

yoga queen At the age of 83, Bette Calman of Williamstown, Victoria, Australia, still teaches up to 11 yoga classes per week. She can perform headstands, "bridges" and, from lying on her front, raise her whole body off the ground, using only her arms.

mighty pen Three men in Hyderabad, India, have created a pen that is not only mightier than a sword but is the size of a giraffe! The brass pen, which cost more than $5,000 to make, stands 16 ft (4.9 m) tall, 1 ft (30 cm) wide, weighs 88 lb (40 kg) and is embossed with Indian cultural illustrations.

free-fall solution After jumping from an airplane at an altitude of 14,000 ft (4,300 m), Ludwig Fichte of Dresden, Germany, flew through the air while sitting in a rubber dinghy while solving a Rubik's Cube puzzle. It took him 31.5 seconds during a free-fall descent of 5,900 ft (1,800 m) to solve the cube, at which point he deployed his parachute.

KING BOARD

Californians Joe Ciaglia and Rob Dyrdek built a giant skateboard that measures 36 ft 7 in (11.15 m) long, 8 ft 8 in (2.6 m) wide, 3 ft 7 in (1.09 m) tall and weighs more than 3,600 lb (1,634 kg). It is 12 times larger than a standard board and is so big it is fitted with car tires and has to be transported on a flatbed truck.

Completely Hooked

Massachusetts stuntman Ses Carny, "the American Madman," entertains audiences by inserting two stainless-steel fishing hooks into his eyes. With the sharp hooks resting on the orbital bones at the base of the eyes, he then pulls down on the hooks to reveal what it looks like under his eyeballs!

top of the world Jordan Romero of Big Bear Lake, California, reached the summit of Mount Everest in May 2010—at the age of just 13. He climbed with his father and three Sherpa guides, and on getting to the peak of the world's highest mountain he telephoned his mother and said: "Mom, I'm calling you from the top of the world." Jordan has conquered many of the world's highest mountains, and climbed Africa's Mount Kilimanjaro when he was only ten.

limbo queen Shemika Charles from Buffalo, New York State, weighs 140 lb (63.5 kg) and stands 5 ft 9 in (1.75 m) tall, but can limbo under a bar just 8½ in (22 cm) off the ground—while carrying a tray with three fuel canisters in each hand.

happy meals Kelvin Baines of Devon, England, began his collection of McDonald's Happy Meal toys in the 1980s and he now has more than 7,500.

rubber bands Allison Coach, 11, from Chesterfield Township, Michigan, has created a rubber band chain that measures more than 1.3 mi (2.1 km) long. She keeps the chain, which consists of more than 22,000 rubber bands, wrapped around a wooden stand made by her grandfather.

clog dance More than 2,500 people in Pella, Iowa, took part in a mass clog dance in May 2010. To ease the discomfort of the wooden shoes they were wearing, many of the dancers put on extra-thick socks or stuffed their clogs with sponges.

blind speedster Turkish pop singer Metin Senturk drove a car at 182 mph (292.9 km/h)—even though he is blind. He drove a Ferrari F430 unaccompanied along the runway at Urfa airport, with a co-driver giving him instructions through an earpiece in his helmet from a car following behind.

giant clock The family clock-making firm Smith of Derby, England, built a huge mechanical clock 42 ft 8 in (13 m) in diameter with a minute hand 25 ft 7 in (7.8 m) long. The 11-ton clock took a year to design and build and was delivered to its final home—in Ganzhou, China—in 2010 for installation in the 371-ft-high (113-m) Harmony Tower.

cucumber man Frank Dimmock, 87, from Oxfordshire, England, grew a cucumber 41¼ in (104.8 cm) long in 2010. Known as the "Cucumber Man," he has been growing vegetables since before World War II when he became an apprentice to a gardener.

tower leap In May 2010, Algerian-born rollerblader Taig Khris leaped from the 131-ft-high (40-m) first floor of Paris's Eiffel Tower and landed safely onto a 98-ft-high (30-m) ramp.

▼ HEAD IN THE SAND

Some Hindu sadhus—such as this gentleman photographed in the 1970s—will bury their heads in the ground for extended periods of time. In 1837, the English newspaper The Daily Telegraph reported that a famous Indian sadhu, Haridas, had survived being buried alive for an unbelievable 40 days without food or water. Witnesses claimed that when the casket in which he lay was opened, Haridas was revived within half an hour.

▲ FEET OF ENDURANCE

Robert Ripley photographed this Hindu sadhu in Calcutta, India, in 1923. As part of his religious devotion, the sadhu had contorted his body into this position for so long that his leg was permanently twisted behind his back, leaving his foot forever resting on his shoulder.

◄ HAND HELD HIGH

Many Hindu sadhus make a pilgrimage every four years to the Kumbh Mela festival at the Ganges River, India. In 2010, this man claimed to have held his right arm aloft, and not cut his nails, for more than 20 years.

NO SITTING ▲

This Hindu holy man from India remains standing for 24 hours a day. When he needs to sleep, he does it upright resting in a sling.

Extreme Devotion

These religious devotees are masters of mind over matter, performing totally unbelievable feats that require intense physical and mental discipline and endurance.

Sadhus, sometimes known as fakirs by people in the West, are largely Hindu mystics from India. Following an ancient practice of spiritual devotion, sadhus remove themselves from normal life and dedicate themselves to extreme physical feats, often for their entire lifetime. They often claim to be able to control pain using the power of thought, and some have demonstrated this by walking on razor-sharp blades, or piercing their flesh with metal pins. Some go for years without sitting down—or standing up.

◄ ON ALL FOURS

In 1936, Robert Ripley encountered a bizarre religious ascetic at the holy site of Bodh Gaya, India. He had assumed the shape of a monkey and taken to walking on all fours at all times.

◄ NAP ON NAILS

In 1907, English photographer Herbert Ponting took this picture of a sadhu in Varanasi, India He appears to be resting quite comfortably on a bed of nails.

® **shark incentive** Spain's David Calvo solved two Rubik's Cube puzzles one-handed simultaneously in just 76 seconds while inside a tank with six sharks at the Terra Natura Park in Benidorm, Spain.

® **tightrope walk** Chinese tightrope walker Adili Wuxor spent more than five hours a day for 60 days gingerly walking across a 1.3-in-thick (3.3-cm) steel wire strung across Beijing's Bird's Nest stadium at a height of more than 200 ft (60 m) above the ground. He walked about 12 mi (19 km) a day, so that he covered around 700 mi (1,130 km) in total.

® **gorilla run** More than 1,000 people dressed in gorilla suits to take part in the 2009 Denver Gorilla Run, a 3½-mile (5.6-km) charity run/walk through the streets of the city to help mountain gorilla conservation.

® **poker session** Professional poker player Phil Laak of Los Angeles, California, played poker for more than 115 hours from June 2 to June 7, 2010, at the Bellagio Hotel in Las Vegas, Nevada. He finished $6,766 up.

® **hang tough** Strapped into special gravity boots and hanging upside down from a frame, Zdenek Bradac from the Czech Republic juggled three balls for 2 minutes 13 seconds, during which time he made 438 consecutive catches.

® **california wingwalk** Traveling at speeds of 100 mph (160 km/h), often in the face of strong winds, Ashley Battles of Tulsa, Oklahoma, stood on the wing of a biplane for more than four hours in June 2010. Her wingwalk took place over San Francisco, California, giving her fabulous views of the Golden Gate Bridge and Alcatraz.

® **speedy mower** Don Wales drove a lawn mower at a speed of more than 87 mph (140 km/h) at Pendine Sands in Wales, in May 2010. His grandfather, Sir Malcolm Campbell, broke the world land speed record, in a car, at the same venue in 1924.

® **stiletto sprinters** Running along a 263-ft (80-m) course at Circular Quay in Sydney, New South Wales, Australia, a relay team comprising four women from Canberra—Brittney McGlone, Laura Juliff, Casey Hodges and Jessica Penny—completed the four legs in 1 minute 4 seconds—while wearing 3-in-high (7.5-cm) stiletto heels.

® **bathtub voyage** Rob Dowling of Dublin, Ireland, sailed 500 mi (800 km) down the Amazon River in a motorized bathtub in 2006. The 5-ft-7-in (1.72-m) fiberglass tub was supported by six 36-gal (136-l) steel drums and propelled by a 15-horsepower motor. He had intended to sail from Iquitos in Peru to the Atlantic—2,465 mi (3,967 km)—but his journey ended after just over 500 mi (800 km) when Brazilian authorities told him he didn't have a licence for the bathtub!

Ice Bath

Wearing only swimming trunks, Jin Songhao and Chen Kecai immersed themselves in ice up to their necks for 120 minutes and 118 minutes, respectively, high up on Tianmen Mountain in China's Hunan Province in January 2011. Jin was even able to write Chinese calligraphy during his ordeal.

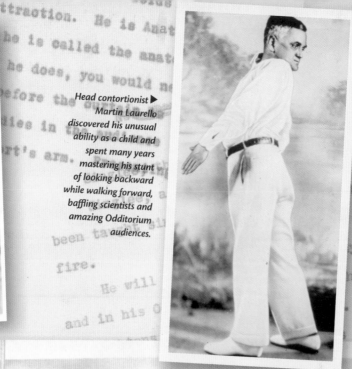

Head contortionist ▶ Martin Laurello discovered his unusual ability as a child and spent many years mastering his stunt of looking backward while walking forward, baffling scientists and amazing Odditorium audiences.

Grace McDaniels ▶ complained about her early billing as "the ugliest woman in the world," but nevertheless was a popular sideshow draw for many years, later becoming known by her preferred moniker, "The Mule-Faced Woman." After fielding several marriage proposals, she settled down and had a son, Elmer (pictured here), who later became her manager.

▲ Freda Pushnik from Pennsylvania was born with no arms or legs, but she was determined to master everyday tasks. Aged just ten years old, she wowed audiences at the 1933 World's Fair with her cheerful repartee and demonstrations of writing and sewing. Freda performed in Ripley's Odditoriums for six years, and went on to have a successful sideshow career before retiring from the stage in the 1950s.

Ripley's C

Habu Koller ▶ from Germany could lift over 100 lb (45 kg) using a hole in his tongue. According to his Ripley backstory, Habu reportedly received a split tongue as punishment in Asia after refusing to bear arms in World War I.

Professor A. L. Morrell, the "Jack-Knife King" was billed as the world's greatest whittler. Assisted by his wife, he wowed audiences with his astonishing exhibit of carved objects displayed in a variety of small-necked bottles. ▼

RUBBER SKIN GIRL

SKIN STRETCHES 14 INCHES. CAN BE PIERCED IN ANY PLACE WITHOUT PAIN — OR DRAWING BLOOD

AGNES SCHMIDT HAMBURG GERMANY

▲ Agnes Schmidt from Hamburg, Germany, was known as the "Rubber Skin Girl." Her skin stretched for 14 in (35 cm) and could be pierced in any place without pain or drawing blood.

▲ Arthur Loos was known as the "Rubber-Skinned Man," because the skin of his neck would hang 18 in (45 cm) down onto his chest.

▲ Captain Ringman Mack—seen here holding two ge[n] shrunken heads—was a European strongman who cou[ld] pull cars and suspend heavy weights with hooks throu[gh] his nipples without any sign of pain. He had performe[d] sideshows since the early 20th century.

CHICAGO'S SKY LINE · FIELDS MUSEUM · SEARS-ROEBUCK BLDG · SHEDD AQUARIUM · 12TH ST BRIDGE · 18TH ST BRIDGE · SOLDIER'S FIELD · LAMA TEMPLE · AVENUE OF FLAGS · HALL OF SCIENCE · GENE[RAL]

◀ With his unique ability to make his eyes pop out of his head, Leonard "Popeye" Perry from Richmond, Georgia, was an Odditorium sensation. He went on to work in other Ripley's Odditoriums for many years after the Chicago Fair.

▲ Singlee, the "Fireproof Man," belonged to an Indian fire-worshipping sect. He said that fire was part of his religion and as long as he was faithful to his fire god, fire could not harm him.

▲ Known as the "Anatomical [Wonder,]" displace his entire abdomen, r[evealing his] chest. Ladies in the audience w[ould take a] firm grip on [their] escort's ar[m]

Chicago World's Fair

Between 1933 and 1934, about 48 million people visited the Chicago World's Fair—a showcase of thousands of exhibits including the latest scientific, architectural and transport innovations.

The Century of Progress Exposition, as the Fair was known, was held to commemorate Chicago's 100th anniversary and to illustrate the amazing technological developments that had taken place worldwide in that time. It was staged on an area of 427 acres (173 ha) along the shoreline of Lake Michigan, and opened on May 27, 1933. It closed on November 12, but had proved so popular that it was re-opened the following May, and ran until the end of October 1934.

Also appearing at the Fair was the first-ever Ripley's Odditorium, which was one of the most popular crowd-pullers, attracting over two million visitors. Show-business agent Clint Finney had been assigned by Robert Ripley to find the best performers to appear at this Odditorium, and Finney managed the show in 1933 and 1934 with C.C. Pyle. With their help, Ripley scoured the world for unusual performers, his "human rarities and oddities." Ripley's many international contacts also sent him photographs and telegrams suggesting possible people to include.

A CENTURY OF PROGRESS — CHICAGO 1933 — INTERNATIONAL EXPOSITION

SERIAL No. 11303 1933
IDENTIFICATION CARD
(NOT A PASS)
S. B. Ricketts 2
EMPLOYEE OF CONCESSIONAIRE
International Oddities, Inc.
AT A CENTURY OF PROGRESS
PAY ROLL No.
S. B. Ricketts
EMPLOYEE'S SIGNATURE
ACCEPTED SUBJECT TO CONDITIONS ON PASS
ISSUED BY
A CENTURY OF PROGRESS
Lenox R. Lohr
General Manager
FORM S. C. 44

NOTICE TO KULI ALI BEI, FAKIR CEKANAVICIUS AND OTHERS

People with peculiar characteristics or peculiar physical built (freaks), are wanted for worlds fair in Chicago, from June 1 to November 1, 1934. A certain firm will pay a round trip passage fare and living expenses such as meals, board etc. to all such exponents that will be demonstrated at the fair. The firm will cover all expenses and pay wages to guides who will accompany non English speaking exponents. It will also furnish all documentary ... ities for the entrance into the United ...

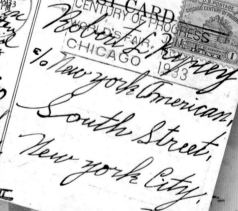

Official Post Card of
RIPLEY'S
"BELIEVE-IT-OR-NOT"
ODDITORIUM
A CENTURY OF PROGRESS

The name & address on this card was written upside down and backwards and at ease. Now see if you can read this just fill in the closed spaces, not the open ones
WHATS ½ of 12, vrs
I.D. MORENO & CO., PRINTERS, CHICAGO, U.S.A.

POST CARD

CENTURY OF PROGRESS
CHICAGO 1933

Robert L. Ripley,
c/o New York American,
South Street,
New York City,
N.Y.

Postal Telegraph
THE INTERNATIONAL SYSTEM
Commercial Cables — All America Cables
Mackay Radio

New York Aug. 21, 1933

Goio
Imperial Hotel
Dubrovnik Jugu Slavia

to bring small man and father to America at once all expenses and reasonable salaries Send their ... mediately

Ripley

Postal Telegraph
THE INTERNATIONAL SYSTEM
Commercial Cables — All America Cables
Mackay Radio

This is a full rate Telegram, Cablegram or Radiogram unless otherwise indicated by signal in the check or in the address.
DL — DAY LETTER
NL — NIGHT LETTER
NM — NIGHT MESSAGE
LCO — DEFERRED CABLE
NLT — NIGHT CABLE LETTER
WLT — WEEK END CABLE LETTER
RADIOGRAM

54 WIRELESS COLLECT VIA MACKAYRADIO=N MANILA 1048A MAR 7 1934

RIPLEY KINGSYN=
NEWYORKNY (RIPLEY KINGS FEATURES SYNDICATE 235 EAST 45 ST)=

...NABLE TWELVE MALE FEMALE PRIEST MAGNUNUS FIRE WALKERS
...AST DAGGER CEREMONY PRECEDING WALK STOP OBTAINABLE UP
...PONTOC IGOROT HEADHUNTERS ARMS WAR
...CORRECTLY EXECUTED

INTERNATIONAL G...
666 LAKE SHORE DRIVE
CHICAGO, ILLINOIS

May 8, 1934.

...VE-IT-OR-NOT" EXHIBITION
...URY OF PROGRESS
... TO OCTOBER 31, 1934

Memo for Mr. Simpson:

In regard to the Chinese man t...
you believe could be dressed in Korean religious co...
and be a good attraction, beg to advise that there ...
many giant... are fr... 8½ feet tall wh...
tower ov... re this ...
any goo... le to ...
...sul...

Billy Cunningham
817 So. 4th St
Louisville Ky.

W. A. Cunningham
817-So-4th St
Louisville Ky

S WORL...
Too Coney
...STAIN "PINK MAN" FRO...
THIS IS GOOD, DO...
STORY ABOUT PILL.

CAN'T GET BORNEO BELLES
"   " CARVED FACE MEN
BUT TRY ALEKO E. LILIUS
P.O. Box 3220 Manila. Cable address
AEOLUS

OBTAIN WILLIAM D'ANDREA
88 - SOUTH ELM St
...

At Chicago Exhibit of Believe-It-Or-Nots

Thousands of Americans who have followed the famous Believe-It-Or-Not Cartoons of Robert Ripley are seeing the actual Believe-It-Or-Nots housed in the palatial Ripley "Odditorium" at the Chicago Century of Progress. Included among the exhibits are (left) Singhlee, a Hindu who can grasp a red-hot metal bar and put it to his mouth; (below left) Albert Nelson and his one-man mechanical band of thirty instruments; and (below right) Blystone, the rice writer.

E L BLYSTONE
of ARDARA, PA
WROTE 2871 LEGIBLE LETTERS
ON A SINGLE GRAIN OF RICE

Our next presenta...
off Hin...
r who be...
fire.
...pley Odd...
...s back...
...f his...
...to prov...
...is a...
...he sa...
...re car...
...rehip...

▲ Kanichka, or "The Man with the Ostrich Stomach," swallowed billiard balls, goldfish, silver dollars, watches and doorknobs—and would then regurgitate them. As a finale, he would swallow electric lights, visible within his stomach when switched on. He was described as having an ostrich stomach because they swallow stones.

▲ Lydia McPherson of Los Angeles was billed as having the longest red hair in the world, which stretched 7 ft 5 in (2.3 m) in length.

to the Ripley's
fire-eaters, eye-poppers
...tion proved so popular
...ent on to open many
...tates.

CHRYSLER MOTORS BLDG.

GOODYEAR FLYING FIELD

TRAVEL & TRANSPORT

GENERAL MOTORS BLDG.
CAMP WHISTLER

GETTYSBURG

THE MIDWAY

PANTHEON

ORIENTAL VILLAGE

VILLAGE

PANORAMA
OF
A CENTURY OF PROGESS EXPOSITION
CHICAGO · 1933

A seasoned ▶ performer known variously as the "Human Pincushion" or the "Painless Wonder," Leo Kongee would drive pins and nails into his face, and even had a button sewn onto his tongue, and seemingly felt no pain.

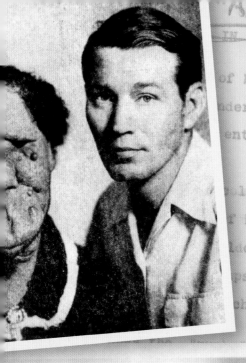

Charles Romano, ▶ the "Rubber Arm Man," could twist and turn and throw his arms around in such a way that audiences were amazed that he could return his body to its normal shape and position.

J.T. Saylors from ▶ Georgia had never demonstrated his talent for jaw-dislocation and pulling funny faces professionally, despite offers from show people and motion picture companies, until he appeared at the Odditorium in Chicago.

dditorium

More than two million visitors flocked
Odditorium to see sword-swallowers,
and many other curiosities. The attrac
that Ripley's founder, Robert Ripley, w
other Odditoriums across the United S

Egyptian Hadji Ali could ▶ drink up to 50 glasses of water in quick succession and then return it all to a receptacle in a steady stream, turning himself into a "human fountain." He also swallowed a range of other items before regurgitating them in any order requested.

Sword-swallower ▶ Joseph Grendol had worked a season for the Ringling Circus before joining Ripley's Odditorium. He would swallow a 20-in (50-cm) bayonet attached to the butt of a rifle and then fire the gun while the bayonet was in his stomach!

• FAIR FACTS •

- The electric lighting for the 1934 Fair came from 250,000 incandescent bulbs and totaled 30,000,000,000 candlepower—enough electricity to supply the needs of a town of 10,000 people.

- More than six million people rode in the Sky Ride elevators in the first 5½ months of the Fair.

- If all the steel cable in the Sky Ride had been stretched out in a single cable, it would have been more than 100 mi (160 km) long.

- The fountain at the 1934 Fair shot water 45 ft (14 m) into the air, pouring out 68,000 gal (260,000 l) a minute.

- A restaurant seating 3,500 people was a replica of the Old Heidelberg Inn, Germany.

- On October 26, 1933, the 776-ft-long (238-m) German airship *Graf Zeppelin* visited the Fair.

- The 1933 Fair employed 350 painters to create a "carnival of color" by using 25 different exterior colors and 36 interior colors of more than 25,000 gal (113,500 l) of paint to cover 10,500,000 sq ft (975,500 sq m) of surface area.

All the fun of the Fair

The Fair featured a multitude of dazzling exhibitions and displays that wowed audiences both by presenting cutting-edge technologies and by celebrating the diverse nature of the world in which they lived. Alongside exhibits demonstrating homes and cars of the future were re-creations of villages from over a dozen different countries—including England, France, Italy, Morocco, Belgium and Mexico—and newborn babies in incubators, which were a great scientific novelty at the time. Also on show was the ship belonging to Antarctic explorer Richard Byrd, and "Midget City," which was full of miniature houses inhabited by 60 "Lilliputians"—small people who included 18-year-old, 18.75-in-tall (46.8-cm) Margaret Ann Robinson, who weighed only 19 lb (8.6 kg).

star light The Fair was opened in spectacular style—when its lights were switched on with energy gathered from the rays of a distant star, Arcturus. With the aid of powerful telescopes, Arcturus' rays were focused on light-absorbent photoelectric cells in a number of astronomical observatories and then transformed into electrical energy, which was transmitted to Chicago. Arcturus was chosen because it was thought to be 40 light years away from Earth, and Chicago's previous World Fair had been 40 years earlier in 1893.

assembly line The central feature of the Fair's General Motors building was a complete automobile assembly plant, where 1,000 people at a time could watch cars being made from start to finish.

rainbow lights At night, the city and Lake Michigan were illuminated by an ever-changing rainbow provided by a color scintillator composed of 3-ft-wide (1-m) arc searchlights arranged in two banks of 12. The scintillator operators changed the color filters and the positions of the searchlight beams according to a prearranged schedule.

steel house Among the innovative exhibits at the Homes of Tomorrow Exposition was a fireproof house built from steel and baked iron enamel. After the Fair it was moved to Palos Heights, Illinois, where it remained until being demolished in 1992.

36A29   SKY RIDE, CHICAGO WORLD'S FAIR

3A-H8

HAVOLINE THERMOMETER   *Century of Progress International Exposition* CHICAGO 1933

ROCKET TRAVEL
The most recognizable symbol of the Fair was the Sky Ride, an aerial tramway that visitors used to travel from one side of the Fair to the other. It had a span of 1,850 ft (564 m) and two towers 628 ft (191 m) tall. Visitors could travel to the top of the towers using high-speed elevators that ascended at a rate of 700 ft (213 m) per minute, and from the top, four different states were visible on a clear day. Suspended from the tramway 220 ft (67 m) above ground were rocket-shaped cars, each carrying 36 passengers across the Fair.

HIGH-RISE TEMPERATURE
Another principal landmark of the Fair was the 218-ft-high (67-m), 21-story thermometer that was sponsored by the motor oil manufacturer Havoline. The air temperature was shown by means of neon light tubes on the outside of the building.

lunge runner Jamasen Rodriguez of Modesto, California, is an expert in lunge running, where instead of running, the athlete lunges to his knees, alternating left and right with each step. In August 2010, he completed a lunge mile in just more than 25 minutes, taking 1,370 lunges.

human dominos Thousands of people in Ordos, Inner Mongolia, China, formed a human domino chain. Arranged in lines, the 10,267 participants slowly fell backward onto each other in sequence from a sitting position like a line of toppling dominos.

back handsprings At Valmeyer, Illinois, 13-year-old Chelsey Kipping did 32 consecutive back handsprings. She has been doing gymnastics since age four and practices for at least nine hours a week.

harley jump California stunt rider Seth Enslow jumped 183 ft 8 in (56 m) on a Harley-Davidson motorcycle near Australia's Sydney Harbour in March 2010. Three years earlier, the bike ace had performed a 200-ft (60-m) jump over a Convair 880 passenger jet airplane.

cat statues Winnie Ferring has a collection of more than 1,000 cat statues arranged on every available space inside and outside her home in Lansing, Iowa. She has been collecting them for more than 50 years, and each piece is numbered and documented.

africa trek French adventurers Alexandre and Sonia Poussin spent three years walking 8,700 mi (14,000 km) from Cape of Good Hope, South Africa, to Israel, living solely on the hospitality of people they met along the way.

trapeze veteran In his early seventies, Tony Steele still performed as a trapeze artist with the Gamma Phi Circus of Illinois State University, the oldest collegiate circus in the U.S.A.

karate kid Varsha Vinod from Alappuzha, India, became a karate black belt in May 2009—the highest grade in the martial art—at the age of just five. She has been training since she was two and already has more than 15 katas, or karate disciplines, to her name.

manhole museum Stefano Bottoni has collected manhole covers from across the world—including from Holland, Finland, Cuba, the Czech Republic, Austria and Romania—for exhibition at his International Manhole Museum in Farrara, Italy.

liberty walk French high-wire walker Didier Pasquette crossed a 150-ft-long (46-m) wire tied between two replicas of the Statue of Liberty on top of the 23-story Liberty Building in Buffalo, New York State, in September 2010. The feat took him about three minutes, and he stopped twice during his walk to wave to the crowds on the ground some 230 ft (70 m) below.

ball control Twenty-five-year-old schoolteacher Rohit Timilsina of Kathmandu, Nepal, managed to hold 21 standard tennis balls on the palm of his hand for more than 14 seconds in 2008. It took him three years of practice to achieve the feat.

Balancing Act

One man rode a bicycle 165 ft (50 m) along a tightrope suspended 26 ft (8 m) above a tiger enclosure while another hung below him on a ladder at China's Changzhou Yancheng Zoo in March 2010. The pair, who were part of a stunt that involved a three-year-old girl walking the rope behind them, narrowly avoided tragedy when one of the zoo's Siberian tigers leaped high off the ground and grabbed at the ladder, nearly causing the men to fall into the enclosure.

UNDERPANTS MAN

Gary Craig from Newcastle, England, also known as the Geordie Pantsman, took 25 minutes to clamber into an incredible 211 pairs of underpants in an unusual charity challenge in April 2010. Gary initially planned to wear 200 underpants, but an Australian rival had achieved this landmark only a few days before, so Gary was forced to set his sights higher and find bigger pairs of pants. This caused problems, as the smaller the underpants the greater the pressure, making it a painful physical challenge.

stamp collector Postman Alan Roy from Dorset, England, spent 70 years painstakingly peeling off two million stamps from envelopes. He soaked each envelope in water and then carefully removed the stamp with tweezers. His collection is so big it fills up 40 packing crates that stack as high as a house.

emerald hunter Jamie Hill of North Carolina has dug up nearly 18,000 carats of emeralds in his home state since 1998.

pi chart Using only a single standard desktop computer costing less than $3,000, French software engineer Fabrice Bellard calculated pi to nearly 2.7 trillion decimal places. The complex calculation took him 131 days.

beer house In Schleiden, Germany, Sven Goebel spent three months building a five-room apartment made entirely from 300,000 beer mats. It featured a table, chairs and a fireplace—all made of beer mats. After spending up to eight hours a day, seven days a week, on construction, he then had to knock down the finished building to prove that it had been held together only with static, not adhesive.

plane pull In Jilin, China, in 2010, martial-arts expert Dong Changsheng took less than a minute to pull a half-ton airplane for 16 ft (5 m)—by a rope hooked to his eyelids! He had previously pulled a car with his eyelids but this was his first attempt with a plane.

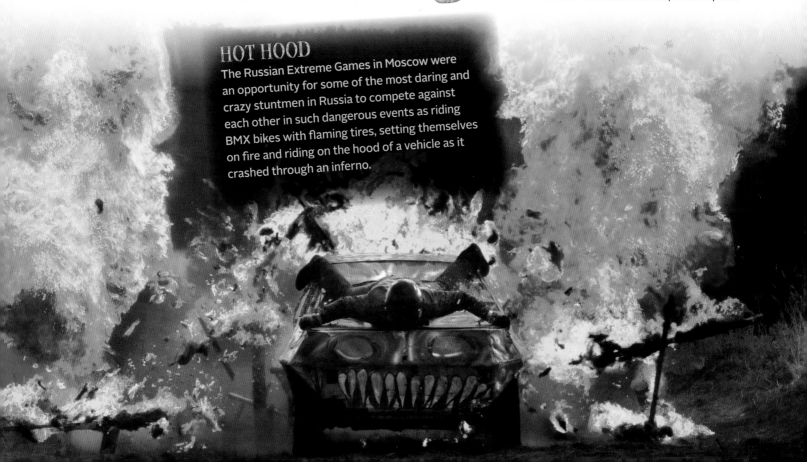

HOT HOOD

The Russian Extreme Games in Moscow were an opportunity for some of the most daring and crazy stuntmen in Russia to compete against each other in such dangerous events as riding BMX bikes with flaming tires, setting themselves on fire and riding on the hood of a vehicle as it crashed through an inferno.

Poker Face

Bai Deng from Shandong, China, can hurl a regular playing card so hard and with such accuracy that he can slice a cucumber in two. It's not as impossible as it might seem, given that in 2002 U.S. magician Rick Smith Jr. threw a playing card a distance of 216 ft 4 in (66 m) at over 90 mph (145 km/h).

human fly Jem Stansfield climbed the side of a 30-ft (9-m) wall of a school in Brighton, England, in 2010 using nothing more than suction from two vacuum cleaners. The 168-lb (76-kg) aeronautics graduate adapted the household appliances' motors into giant suckerpads, which were strong enough to support him and enabled him to cling to the wall.

flying lanterns More than 10,000 twinkling white paper lanterns were released simultaneously into the night sky from a beach in Jakarta, Indonesia, in December 2009. The flying lantern is a Chinese tradition. It is basically a paper bag containing a block of paraffin with a wick suspended by wire across the opening. When the wick is lit, the air inside is warmed like a hot-air balloon and the lantern lifts off into the sky.

rubber bands Eleven-year-old Allison Coach of Chesterfield Township, Michigan, created a chain of 22,140 rubber bands that stretched nearly 7,000 ft (2,130 m)—or 1.3 mi (2 km)—long.

champion plowgirl Thirteen-year-old schoolgirl Elly Deacon beat experienced farmers for first place in a plowing competition in Hertfordshire, England. Elly, who had driven a tractor for the first time only four days before the event, impressed judges with her straight and smooth plow marks on a 53,000-sq-ft (4,900-sq-m) patch of land, while at the wheel of the six-ton tractor.

turbo terry Terry Burrows from Essex, England, cleaned three windows, each measuring 45 sq in (290 sq cm), and wiped the sills in just 9.14 seconds during a 2009 window-cleaning competition in Blackpool, Lancashire. "Turbo Terry" actually finished the task in 8.14 seconds, but was handed a one-second time penalty for leaving two water marks on the glass.

rain dance More than 230 dancers took to the wet streets of Bath in Somerset, England, with umbrellas in May 2010 to perform a five-minute version of Gene Kelly's classic "Singin' in the Rain."

sand burial As part of the 2010 Clogherhead Prawn Festival in County Louth, Ireland, 524 people simultaneously buried themselves up to their necks on a sandy beach.

sports

body

transport

feats

mysteries

food

arts

science

beyond belief

believe it!

world

animals

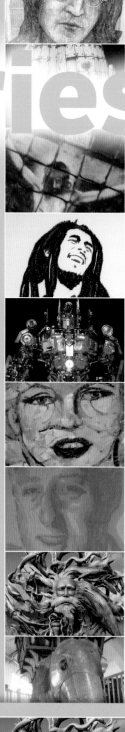

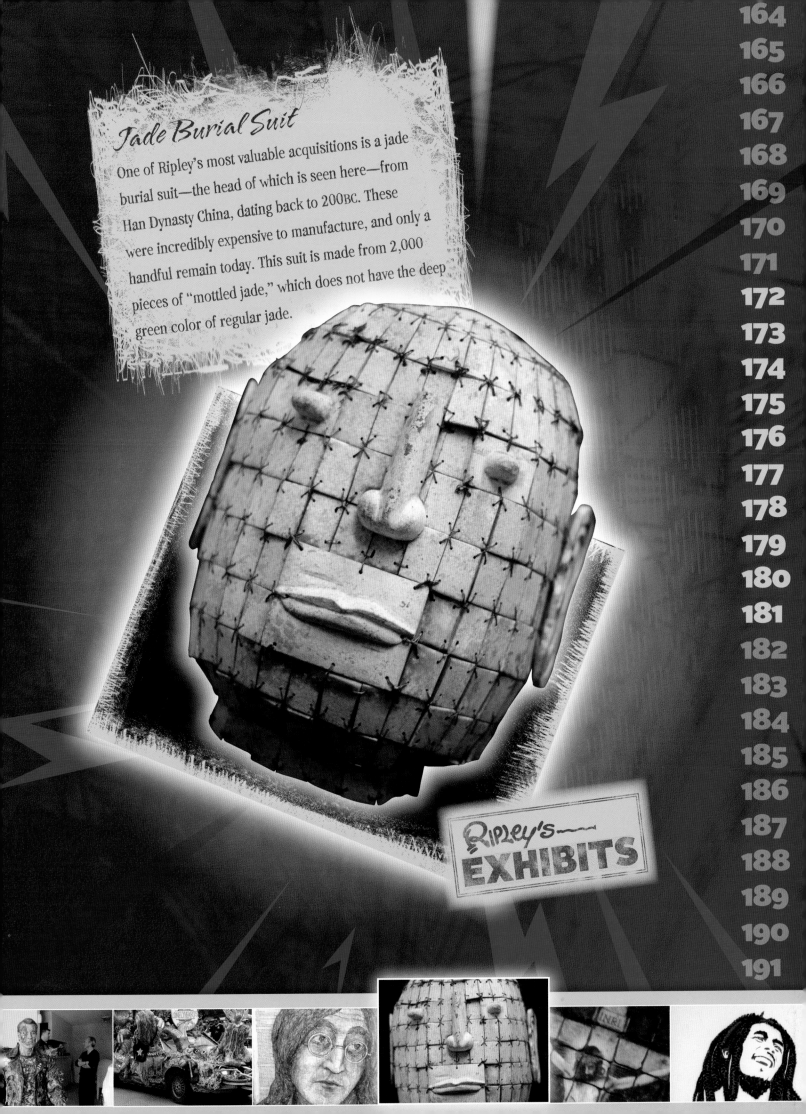

Jade Burial Suit

One of Ripley's most valuable acquisitions is a jade burial suit—the head of which is seen here—from Han Dynasty China, dating back to 200BC. These were incredibly expensive to manufacture, and only a handful remain today. This suit is made from 2,000 pieces of "mottled jade," which does not have the deep green color of regular jade.

Ripley's
EXHIBITS

164
165
166
167
168
169
170
171
172
173
174
175
176
177
178
179
180
181
182
183
184
185
186
187
188
189
190
191

Ripley's Believe It or Not!®
mysteries

raining birds More than 5,000 dead red-winged blackbirds rained from the sky over Beebe, Arkansas, on January 1, 2011, littering the streets with corpses. Three days later, another 500birds—dead or dying—fell into the Louisiana Highway in Pointe Coupee Parish. Scientists say the birds, disturbed by New Year's Eve fireworks or a passing train, may have died after flying at night and crashing into trees, houses and power lines.

marfa lights For over a century, witnesses have been spooked by the Marfa Lights, a strange light phenomenon occurring around the Mitchell Flats, outside Marfa, Texas. Descriptions range from small dancing lights in the sky to a single, stationary bright light that changes color. In a failed attempt to solve the mystery, a former World-War-II pilot even chased the lights in an airplane.

tunguska explosion At 7.14 a.m. on June 30, 1908, a mysterious explosion took place in central Siberia that was 1,000 times more powerful than the atomic bombs dropped on Japanese cities of Hiroshima and Nagasaki in 1945. The Tunguska Explosion leveled a staggering 80 million trees over an area of 830 sq mi (2,150 sq m) and generated a huge shock wave that knocked people to the ground 37 mi (60 km) from the epicenter. Experts believe it could have been caused by a meteorite crashing into the Earth.

SOMETHING IN THE GARDEN

Phyllis Bacon believes a fairy fluttered into her life and out again one evening in her garden in London, England. She wasn't even looking through the camera when she held it at arm's length and clicked the button to take a picture of her backyard. She spent months scouring the Internet for butterflies, beetles and moths that might match the image, but came up with nothing.

FLOATING HEADS

This may look like the disembodied head of Alfred Hitchcock floating in a field, but it is actually the eerie work of Spanish artist Ibon Mainar. Ibon uses ingenious projector techniques to beam images of famous people or objects, such as chandeliers and spooky cats' eyes, onto natural settings around his home in San Sebastián, Spain. He employs a car-mounted unit to project the images onto water, trees and mountainsides, and when viewed in real life the pictures have a strangely lifelike 3-D effect.

tunnel network Ten large holes and a network of tunnels—some big enough for a person to stand up in—suddenly appeared in the ground in the Krasnoyarsk region of Siberia in 2006. It is thought they were either the work of unknown animals or were somehow related to an earthquake that had hit the area in 2003.

ghost yacht A 40-ft-long (12-m) yacht, the *Kaz II*, was found drifting off the coast of Queensland, Australia, in 2007, with its engine running and a table laid for dinner but no sign of its three-man crew. The radio was working, the computers were running and the lifejackets were still on board, but there was no evidence of foul play and no bodies were ever found.

yellow deposit An unexplained greenish-yellow goo fell from the skies and splattered houses and streets in Snyder, New York State, on January 18, 2011. As temperatures dropped, homes were coated in yellow or green icicles.

taos hum For years, people in and around the town of Taos, New Mexico, have been able to hear a curious low-frequency noise known as the Taos Hum. Not audible to everyone, it has been described as sounding like a distant diesel engine, but its source has never been traced.

desert mummies Excavations at a 4,000-year-old graveyard in China's remote Taklimakan Desert uncovered around 200 mummies—but their D.N.A. showed they had partly European ancestry. The mummies also had European features, such as long noses, high cheekbones and reddish-blond hair.

Real Fairies?

As reported in *Ripley's Believe It or Not! Enter If You Dare*, two cousins, Frances Griffiths and Elsie Wright, rocked the world in 1917 when they said they had photographed fairies in a leafy glen near Elsie's home in Cottingley, England. The five photographs were highly convincing and were published by Arthur Conan Doyle, author of the Sherlock Holmes novels, with an accompanying article. Many experts in photography and psychic research, who examined the pictures and questioned the girls, came to the conclusion that the images were genuine. It was only in the 1980s the girls admitted to faking the pictures with cardboard cutouts and hatpins. However, when Frances Griffiths' daughter appeared on the BBC TV show *The Antiques Roadshow* on January 4, 2009, with a camera given to her by Conan Doyle, she revealed that her mother claimed right up to her death that the fifth and final photograph, taken on a separate occasion and shown here, was genuine.

mysteries

Ripley's Believe It or Not!®

Ectoplasm

Communicating with the dead was a popular pursuit in the early 20th century, and mediums who went into a trancelike state were often seen to produce a peculiar white substance called ectoplasm from their mouth, ears, nose or navel. Participants at seances would then watch in amazement as the ectoplasm was apparently transformed into spiritual faces, fully functional arms and even entire bodies. It also appeared to give mediums the power to perform astonishing feats of telekinesis, such as raising tables and chairs without any physical contact. But was it all genuine or just an elaborate hoax?

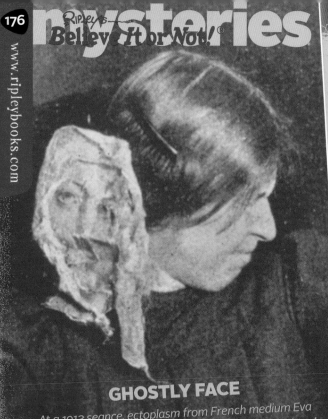

GHOSTLY FACE

At a 1912 seance, ectoplasm from French medium Eva C. (Eva Carrière) formed into the shape of a man's head, which, according to an observer, then made bowing movements. Eva C. was renowned for being able to produce ectoplasm, but skeptics said it was nothing more than chewed paper or fabric that had been regurgitated. Once, after the flow of ectoplasm had been reabsorbed into her mouth, she was given a powerful emetic and when she failed to vomit, the doubters were satisfied that she had not swallowed anything to fake the ectoplasm.

ⓇRIPLEY RESEARCH

Ectoplasm is the supposed residue left by ghostly spirits. The term was first used in 1894 by French scientist Charles Richet to explain a third arm that seemed to grow from Italian medium Eusapia Palladino. Ectoplasm was described as having a rubbery texture with a smell of ozone. Touching it or exposing it to light was said to cause injury to mediums, which was why they insisted on conducting seances in the dark. Skeptics said this was simply to hide their deception and indeed many mediums were caught creating their own fake ectoplasm by using thin strips of muslin, egg white, soap or paper. However, other respected witnesses maintained that ectoplasm moved as if it were genuinely alive and could change its shape at will.

Ⓡ **mockbeggar coffins** In the early 20th century, a number of wooden coffins—containing the remains of men, women and children—were discovered buried in mud at Mockbeggar, Newfoundland, Canada. The wood was not local, leading to speculation that the deceased could have been French fishermen, but the French did not usually take their families when they went fishing in the area. To this day, their identities remain a mystery.

Ⓡ **body glow** In 1934, Anna Monaro, an asthma patient at a hospital in Pirano, Italy, produced a flickering glow of blue light from her chest for up to 10 seconds at a time while she was asleep. Observed by doctors, scientists and government officials, the phenomenon occurred a number of times each night until it suddenly stopped several weeks later. Physicians suggested the glow might have been caused by certain compounds in the woman's skin.

Ⓡ **ringing rocks** Ringing Rocks Park in Upper Black Eddy, Pennsylvania, is home to a field of boulders, which, when hit with a solid object such as a hammer, produce melodious bell-like tones.

Ⓡ **fish deaths** In December 2010, more than 80,000 drum fish were found dead along a 20-mile (32-km) stretch of the Arkansas River and 10,000 red drum fish were mysteriously washed up dead in Chesapeake Bay, Maryland.

MYSTIC CAT

Oscar the cat has correctly predicted the deaths of over 50 patients at the Steere House Nursing and Rehabilitation Center in Providence, Rhode Island, by curling up next to them some two hours before they die. For more than two years, he was present at every death in the home—except one when relatives asked him to leave the room. Nurses once placed Oscar on the bed of a patient they thought was close to death, but he immediately went to sit beside someone in another room. The cat's judgment proved better than that of the medics, because while the second patient died that evening, the first lived for two more days.

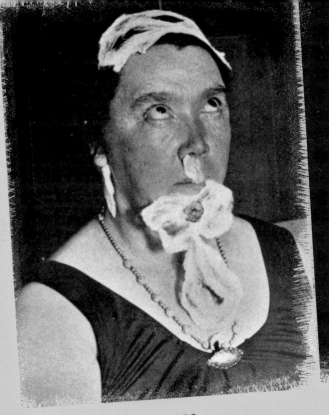

HOLMES MYSTERY

While in a trance in Winnipeg, Canada, in 1929, Scottish medium Mary Marshall produced nasal ectoplasm at the center of which was a face that her spirit guide—Walter—claimed was that of Sherlock Holmes creator Sir Arthur Conan Doyle, himself a confirmed believer in spiritualism. The necklace worn by Mary in the photograph is an "apport"—an object that materialized during the seance, but was not there before or after the event.

plain of jars Hundreds of ancient stone jars, some weighing up to 6 tons, can be found scattered across several square miles in northern Laos. Their purpose remains a mystery, but they may have been used to house the bodies of dead people until decomposition, after which the remains would have been removed for burial or cremation.

crystal tears Between March and November 1996, a 12-year-old Lebanese girl, Hasnah Mohamed Meselmani, produced glass crystal tears from her eyes. She wept tiny crystals at an average rate of seven a day, and although they were razor-sharp, she felt no pain. Physicians were mystified by her condition, which stopped as suddenly as it had started.

bacterial rain Over a three-week period in August 1994, gelatinous blobs rained down over Oakville, Washington State, leaving animals dead and people with flu-like symptoms. The blobs contained human white blood cells and two types of bacteria, one of which is found in our digestive system, but no one knows where the blobs came from.

GRAVE VISITS

When ten-year-old Florence Irene Ford was buried after dying of yellow fever in 1871, her distraught mother Ellen had steps built down to the head of the casket and a glass window installed so that she could comfort her child during the thunderstorms that had always terrified her during her short life. On many nights, Ellen would ride up to the cemetery in Natchez, Mississippi, and go underground to sit with her dead daughter and read or sing to her.

In the early 1990s, a woman took her 13-year-old daughter to visit the Ford grave at night. After descending the steps, the woman suddenly emerged screaming with a strange green glow all over her. As she rolled on the grass the glow diminished until a cemetery worker was able to scoop it into his hands. He later said it felt like compressed air or a tennis ball. He then released it into the air where it went up, sparkled and disappeared.

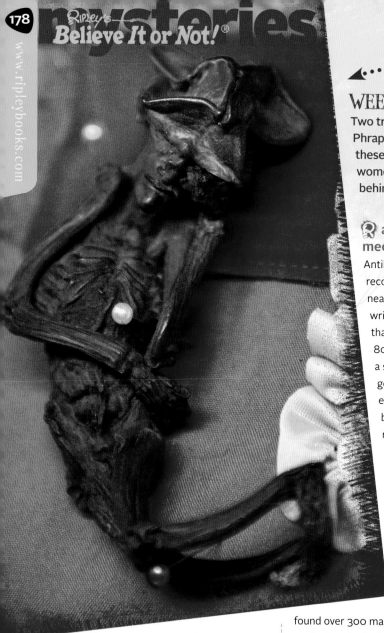

WEE FOLK

Two tree pods shaped like fairies are kept in a glass box at the Wat Phrapangmuni Temple near Sing Buri, Thailand. According to popular belief, these *Naree Pons* (or pod people) appeared to the Buddha as beautiful women while he meditated in a secluded area. They then vanished and left behind a miniature humanoid pod form on a nearby tree.

advanced mechanism When the Antikythera Mechanism was recovered from a shipwreck near Crete in 1900, the writing on its case indicated that it was made around 80 BC—but an X-ray revealed a system of differential gears not known to have existed until 1575 AD. It is believed to be an ancient mechanical computer designed to calculate astronomical positions, but its sophistication is in fact comparable to a 19th-century Swiss clock.

stone balls In the Costa Rican jungle in the 1930s, workmen found over 300 man-made stone balls, many perfectly spherical and varying in size from as small as a tennis ball to huge boulders 8 ft (2.4 m) in diameter and weighing 15 tons. The stones date back at least 500 years, but nobody knows who made them and how such spherical precision was achieved.

flaming fireball A massive fireball lit up the sky over five U.S. states—Missouri, Iowa, Wisconsin, Illinois and Indiana—on the night of April 14, 2010. Puzzled scientists say it could have been a meteor, a chunk from an asteroid, or rocket debris.

milk miracle For several hours on September 21, 1995, Hindu religious statues all over the world drank milk. When a worshiper at a temple in New Delhi, India, offered a spoonful of milk to the trunk of a statue of the elephant-headed deity Ganesha, the liquid was seen to disappear. Soon Hindu temples in the U.K., Canada, Dubai and Nepal were reporting similar occurrences. Scientists were baffled by the phenomenon, which stopped before the end of the day when statues suddenly refused to accept milk.

unfinished city Having spent years constructing 30-ft-high (9-m) walls from perfectly hewn basalt, the inhabitants of the ancient city of Nan Madol, in the Micronesia region of the Pacific, mysteriously abandoned it, leaving some of the walls unfinished.

who goes hare! In 1971, a rabbit was shot by Jasper Barrett near his home in Jefferson, South Carolina. On being prepared for the pot by his wife and a friend, the outline in black of a woman's face was found on the skinned flesh of one foreleg. It was about an inch across and had a rosebud mouth, curly hair and long lashes. Within a week of the news breaking, 4,000 people had trekked to see the face and extra police were called in to control the crowds.

GHOSTLY VISION

When Kevin Horkin downloaded this photo and saw a pale young woman peering from a window on the first floor of Gwrych Castle in Abergele, he knew something spooky was afoot. The huge Welsh castle has been derelict since 1985 and the floor crumbled away years ago, so no one could possibly have been standing there. Countless sightings, orbs, cold spots and cases of objects moving have been recorded at Gwrych, said to be the most haunted building in Wales.

ghostly pleas Sightings of the ghosts of tormented slaves from the 1830s have been reported at Lalaurie House, New Orleans. Servants who begged the assistance of outsiders when the house was burning are seen running back inside, slamming doors, shouting repeatedly. Several people have seen ghostly faces of the dead peering from upper windows.

eerie face The image of a child's face dating back over 100 years was found burnt onto an old oven door at a restaurant in Saint John, New Brunswick, Canada, in the 1980s. A lady visitor to the property at 31 Leinster Street had gone into the cellar to inspect the original brick oven, but when the dirt was cleaned away the smiling face of a young girl became visible in the iron door. It is believed the family living there in the late 19th century had used the oven as a crematorium to dispose of their dead daughter. The image on the door was caused by carbons given off by the body during burning, the bright light of the fire having acted as a lens.

Burning Mystery

When 92-year-old Dr. John Irving Bentley was found in the bathroom of his home in Coudersport, Pennsylvania, in December 1966, all that remained of him was a pile of ashes and the lower half of his right leg. He is thought to have been a victim of spontaneous human combustion, a phenomenon where people suddenly burst into flames for no apparent reason. Although almost his entire body had been consumed by an intense heat, the fire was confined to a small area and, apart from a hole in the floor where he had been standing, the rest of the room was largely undamaged. The rubber tips on his walking frame were still intact and a nearby bathtub was hardly scorched.

auto inferno Jeanna Winchester was riding in a car with a friend in Jacksonville, Florida, in 1980 when she was mysteriously engulfed in bright yellow flames. There was no spilled gas, she had not been smoking and the car window was up. Jeanna survived, although she suffered severe burns. The car interior, however, was virtually undamaged, with just a slight browning on Jeanna's white leather seat.

charred remains In March 1997, the charred remains of 76-year-old John O'Connor were found in a chair some distance from the hearth of his living room in County Kerry, Ireland. Only his head, upper torso and feet remained unburned, yet there was little smoke damage to the room or the furniture.

burning dress A dress being worn by Mrs. Charles Williamson of Bladenboro, North Carolina, unaccountably burst into flames in 1932. Her husband and daughter ripped off the blazing dress with their bare hands yet none of the three suffered any burns. Over the next four days, various items in the house suddenly caught fire, but each time the flames, which had neither smoke nor smell, simply vanished after the article had burned itself out.

fatal fire Mrs. Olga Worth Stephens, 75, of Dallas, Texas, suddenly burst into flames while waiting in her parked car in 1964 and died before anyone could rescue her. The car was undamaged and firemen concluded that nothing in the vehicle could have started the fatal blaze.

paper puzzle Anna Martin of West Philadelphia, Pennsylvania, was found incinerated at home in 1957, her body totally consumed by fire except for a piece of her torso and her shoes. The medical examiner estimated that temperatures must have reached at least 1,700°F (925°C)—far too hot for anything in the room to remain uncharred, yet newspapers lying just 2 ft (60 cm) away were found intact.

vaporized flesh At Blackwood, Wales, in 1980, a man's body was found burned beyond recognition in his living room. The armchair that he was sitting in was hardly damaged—neither were some plastic objects nearby—but the fire was so intense that it left a coating of vaporized flesh on the ceiling.

180 mysteries
Ripley's Believe It or Not!®
www.ripleybooks.com

FLORIDA MONSTER

Two boys playing on the beach near St. Augustine, Florida, in 1896 spotted the carcass of a huge creature half buried in the sand. It seemed to have a number of tentacles, some up to 30 ft (9 m) long, prompting the belief that it was some kind of giant octopus. However, a similar blob washed up in Chile in 2003 turned out to be a decomposing sperm whale. When some marine creatures decay, their form changes so much that they can look like unidentified sea monsters.

lake monster While fishing 900 ft (275 m) from shore on Russia's 770-sq-mi (1,990-sq-km) Lake Chany in 2010, a man saw his 59-year-old companion hook an unknown creature so powerful that it overturned his boat and dragged him beneath the surface to his death. At least 19 people have vanished on the lake since 2007. Most of the bodies have never been found, but some human corpses have been washed ashore with large bite marks on their bodies. Witnesses have described a snakelike beast with a long neck, a large fin and a huge tail.

baghdad battery An ancient clay vessel was an early example of a battery—even though batteries were not rediscovered for another 1,800 years. The 2,000-year-old Baghdad Battery contained a copper cylinder and an oxidized iron rod, both held in place by asphalt. When filled with an acid or alkaline liquid, it was capable of producing an electric charge.

metal spheres Over recent decades, miners in Klerksdorp, South Africa, have dug up hundreds of ancient metal spheres that look entirely man-made. However, they were found in Precambrian rock dating back 2.8 billion years—that's over 2.79 billion years before Neanderthal man! The mysterious spheres measure about 1 in (2.5 cm) in diameter and some are etched with three parallel grooves running around the middle.

unique stone The Mystery Stone of Lake Winnipesaukee, New Hampshire, has distinctive markings that make it unique. The egg-shaped stone—found encased in a lump of clay in 1872—has intricate man-made carvings and a hole bored through both ends, but its origins and purpose remain unknown and no matching stones have ever been discovered.

missing belt For reasons unknown, Jupiter loses or regains one of its two belts every ten to 15 years. The planet usually has two dark bands in its atmosphere—one in its northern hemisphere and one in its southern hemisphere—but pictures taken by astronomers in April 2010 showed that the Southern Equatorial Belt had disappeared. The dark belts are clouds created from chemicals such as sulfur and phosphorus, which are blown into bands by 350-mph (560-km/h) winds.

scary site The Borley Rectory in England has been the site of a vast number of mysterious phenomena reported by resident reverends and their families since 1863. The appearance of a ghostly nun, wall writings, stone throwing, windows shattering, bells ringing, unexplained footsteps, a woman becoming locked in a room with no key, and spirit messages tapped out from the frame of a mirror are just some of the incidences said to have occurred. Mediums contacted two spirits there: a French nun murdered on the site and a man who said he would burn down the house. Burn it did—in 1939.

APE MAN

On an expedition to Venezuela in 1920, Swiss geologist François de Loys claimed to have stumbled across a 5-ft-tall (1.5-m), red-haired, tailless ape that walked upright like a human. He shot the animal and photographed it, using a long stick to prop up its head, but the corpse went missing before it could be examined. If genuine, it would have been the first ape ever discovered in the Americas, thereby rewriting the theory of primate evolution, but scientists decided that the photo was merely a common spider monkey whose tail was conveniently hidden or chopped off.

ⓇRIPLEY RESEARCH

In early July 1947, an object described as a "flying disk" crashed near Roswell, New Mexico. The Roswell Army Air Force (RAAF) insisted the craft was a weather balloon, but speculation mounted that it was a U.F.O. A local rancher saw a shallow trench, several hundred feet long, gouged into the land and recovered metallic debris that turned liquid when dropped. Nurses said they saw small humanoid bodies being examined in a cordoned-off corner of the local hospital. A mortician at a Roswell funeral home revealed he had been asked to provide child-sized, hermetically sealed coffins. To this day no one knows whether the Roswell Incident was a cover-up or a flight of fancy.

Alien Autopsy

A display at the U.F.O. Museum at Roswell, New Mexico, re-creates the alleged autopsy of a dead alien killed when his spacecraft crashed in the area in 1947. The dummy extraterrestrial was originally made for the 1994 movie *Roswell*.

Ⓡ fearsome forest Aokigahara Forest, Japan, at the foot of Mount Fuji, is reportedly haunted by strange beasts, monsters, ghosts and goblins. One popular myth states that the magnetic iron deposits underground cause compasses to malfunction and travelers to get lost in the forest. It is the world's third most popular suicide location.

Ⓡ straight line Four ancient historical sites—Easter Island in the Pacific Ocean, the Nazca lines in southern Peru, the Inca city of Ollantaytambo, also in southern Peru, and the Great Pyramid of Giza, Egypt—are all exactly aligned along a straight line. Other world wonders that are within just one-tenth of a degree of this alignment include Persepolis, the capital of ancient Persia; Mohenjo Daro, the ancient capital of the Indus Valley; and the lost city of Petra in modern-day Jordan.

Ⓡ ghost ship Carrying a shipment of coal, the *Carroll A. Deering* was found run aground off the coast of North Carolina on January 31, 1921—but its 11-man crew had vanished. There was no sign of the crew's belongings or the ship's navigating instruments, log or clock, yet evidence in the galley indicated that food was being prepared for the following day's meals.

Ⓡ near miss Pilot David Hastings from Norwich, U.K., revealed a close encounter with a U.F.O. when flying over the Mojave Desert in the U.S.A. in 1987. He described how a mysterious black shape came at his plane head-on, then flashed overhead. Seconds later the object was moving at high speed at the plane's side. Hastings took photos and showed them to U.S. Navy officers, but they refused to comment.

Ⓡ band of holes Nearly 7,000 man-made holes are located on a plain near Peru's Pisco Valley—but their origins and purpose remain unknown. The Band of Holes stretches for 1 mi (1.6 km) and some of the holes are up to 7 ft (2.1 m) deep.

Ⓡ they're here! A 2010 April Fool's report in a Jordanian newspaper wreaked havoc in one town. Its front-page article described a U.F.O. landing near Jafr, 185 mi (300 km) from Amman. Residents panicked, keeping their children home from school; and Jafr's mayor even sent security forces in search of the aliens. He was at the point of emptying the town of its 13,000 residents when newspaper journalists came clean.

Ⓡ aliens welcome Bob Tohak has believed in U.F.O.s since he was a kid. He is so eager to make contact with aliens that he has put a 42-ft-high (13-m) U.F.O. landing port on his property in Poland, Wisconsin. "I'm just hoping that something will show up," he says.

FIRE STARTER

A ghostly young girl was pictured in a building on fire in the town of Wem, England, in 1995. Many were convinced that the photograph captured the ghost of a girl that died after accidentally setting the same building alight in the 17th century. In 2010, after the photographer had died, it was suggested that the 1995 photograph was a fake. The ghostly girl in the fire had been copied from a 1922 Wem postcard, which was spotted in the local newspaper by an eagle-eyed reader.

Ⓡ perfect fit The ancient site of Sacsayhuaman, Peru, features three huge stone walls built so expertly that it is impossible to insert a piece of paper between the different-shaped stones, some of which are 9 ft 10 in (3 m) high and weigh 200 tons.

body

transport

feats

mysteries

food

arts

science

beyond belief

believe it!

world

animals

sports

175
176
177
178
179
180
181
182
183
184
185
186
187
188
189
190
191
192
193
194
195
196
197
198
199
200
201
202

Toast Crucifixion

Ripley's have recently added their largest ever piece of toast art to their collection, depicting the Crucifixion. British artist Adam Sheldon first created the piece to hang in a church in Lincolnshire, England, but it is currently on display in the Ripley's museum in Branson, Missouri. The artwork was made using conventional toasters, blowtorches and scrapers, and 153 pieces of toast.

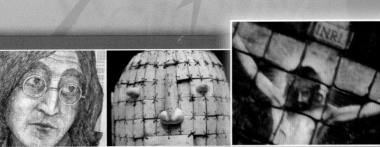

Ripley's
EXHIBITS

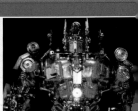

FAST FOOD

Patrick "Deep Dish" Bertoletti from Chicago is one of the world's most successful competitive eaters. In 2008, he became an official pizza-eating world champion, devouring 47 slices of 16-in (41-cm) deep dish in 10 minutes. Most people might not finish even half of one large pizza in that time.

Highlights of Patrick's career include finishing off more than 10 lb (4.5 kg) of Key Lime Pie in 8 minutes and 275 pickled peppers in 10 minutes. These and many more appetite-busting achievements mean that Patrick is ranked in the top five eaters in the world by the sport's Major League Eating organization. In 2010, in Black Hawk, Colorado, Patrick swallowed 3 lb 11¾ oz (1.7 kg) of deep-fried bull's testicles in 10 minutes.

You don't need to be extremely heavy to be an eating champion; in fact many are in good shape. Culinary-school graduate Patrick weighs in at 190 lb (86 kg), relatively lightweight given his 6-ft-2-in (1.88-m) frame and the vast amounts that he consumes at eating competitions—regularly gulping down more than 10,000 calories in just a few minutes. Fittingly, Patrick works as a chef and hopes to open his own restaurant— serving regular-sized portions.

Ripley's Ask

How did you start speed eating?
My first professional event involved me eating 5 lb (2.3 kg) of pizza in 15 minutes, but I have been doing it my entire life and I was genetically predisposed for speed eating.

What is your favorite speed-eating food? And do you have to like what you are speed eating to win? I love ice cream in contests, as I don't suffer any of the dreaded effects. If I am in eating shape and have a good day, I would eat shoe leather in a contest. I don't like oysters or pickled jalapenos, but I block that out and have records in both.

What is the worst thing to speed eat and why? Any type of sea oysters, raw, or rocky mountain oysters (bull testicles). The texture of both make speed eating quite difficult.

Do you do much training? And what is your diet like when you are not competing? I stay on a strict diet outside of contests because my appetite is truly insatiable. I have to keep my eating on lockdown because my appetite gets unleashed with a fury. I will eat a giant meal with a few gallons of water two days before as a final stretch, but my stomach has been trained so I don't need much extra training, perhaps a few practices for technique if I'm a little rusty.

Are there any downsides to speed eating? Heartburn and indigestion, but I keep the Pepto Bismol close. You have to be conscious of calories because it's very easy to gain weight if left unchecked when eating tens of thousands of calories.

Is it ever dangerous? All events have paramedics so there is little risk for healthy individuals at contests.

What are your tips for top speed eating? You can't train for speed eating; it's something you are born with.

What are your speed-eating ambitions? I would like to be the best eater in the world and to win the annual hot-dog contest, also to translate my eating fame into the opening of a gourmet diner in Chicago.

Patrick's Menu

Food	Amount	Time
Blueberry pie	9 lb (4 kg)	8 minutes
Slushie	22 fl oz (650 ml)	9 seconds
Hotdogs	55	10 minutes
Pizza (16 in/41 cm)	47 slices	10 minutes
Hamburgers	94	8 minutes
Chicken wings	227	30 minutes
Chili spaghetti	11.5 lb (5.2 kg)	10 minutes
Ribs	8.5 lb (3.85 kg)	12 minutes
Subs (8 in/20 cm)	14	10 minutes

food
Believe It or Not!®

Headless Chickens

In parts of Asia, no part of the chicken goes to waste. In Bangkok, the capital of Thailand, barbecued chicken head kebabs are available to buy as fast food. Once cooked, the brain and soft tissue can be eaten. Roasted, boiled and deep-fried chicken heads are also popular.

slice of luck A restaurant in Hankou, China, selected from 15 applicants for the post of chef by asking the candidates to slice a melon on a woman's stomach. The successful candidate, Hu Gua, chopped up his melon in less than a minute without hurting the woman who was protected from the blade by just a thin sheet of plastic.

lime pie During the Key West, Florida, 2010 Conch Republic independence celebration, locals used 1,080 Key limes to prepare a 450-lb (204-kg), 7-ft-wide (2.1-m) Key lime pie.

taste test As a designer and tester with Fox's Biscuits, Simon Pope of West Yorkshire, England, is paid to eat more than 7,000 cookies a year.

margarine marge Restaurant owner Simon Smith of Staffordshire, England, celebrated the 20th birthday of *The Simpsons* by making a 4-ft-high (1.2-m) bust of his favorite character, Marge, out of margarine. He used 26 lb (12 kg) of special heat-resistant puff pastry margarine on the sculpture and achieved the shape by wrapping it around chicken wire.

chicken feast At the 2010 Canoefest in Brookville, Indiana, 1,654 lb (750 kg) of fried chicken was served up in a donated canoe. Up to 200 volunteers had cooked the 2,700 lb (1,225 kg) of raw meat.

cake tower Chef Gilles Stassart and architect Jean Bocabeille designed a cake for display in Paris, France, in July 2010 that was nearly 26 ft (7.8 m) tall—that's as high as a two-story house. The "Tower without Hunger" was made from 1,385 lb (628 kg) of flour, 1,120 lb (508 kg) of sugar, 350 eggs and 40 lb (18 kg) of butter. The towering cake was meant to last four days outdoors but sweltering temperatures made it soft and unstable and it had to be taken down after just 24 hours.

haute dog New York City restaurant Serendipity 3 introduced a $69 hot dog in 2010. The Haute Dog comes with white truffle oil, a salted pretzel bed, truffle butter, duck foie gras, Dijon mustard, Vidalia onions and ketchup.

locust topping When a plague of millions of locusts hit the town of Mildura, Victoria, Australia, in April 2010, pizza café owner Joe Carrazza put dozens of the dead insects on his pizzas as a topping.

placenta drink A new drink from Japanese health food manufacturer Nihon Sofuken tastes of peaches but contains 0.3 oz (10,000 mg) of pigs' placenta, a substance said to be able to restore youthful looks and help with dieting.

long fry John Benbenek of Buffalo, New York, was eating lunch at Taffy's Hot Dog Stand in 2010 when he found a 34-in-long (85-cm) French fry in his meal.

fiery sauce Eight teenagers in Augsburg, Germany, were treated in a hospital after a test of courage in which they drank chili sauce that was more than 200 times hotter than Tabasco. The sauce clocked 535,000 on the Scoville scale, which measures the hotness of sauce, compared to 2,500 for normal Tabasco sauce.

bridge picnic More than 6,000 people sat down to breakfast on Sydney's famous Harbour Bridge in October 2009 after it was closed to traffic and carpeted with grass for a giant picnic.

double yolks Fiona Exon from Cumbria, England, beat odds of more than a trillion to one when she discovered that all six eggs she had bought in a single carton from her local supermarket had double yolks.

bacon envelopes U.S. company J & D's, whose motto is "Everything should taste like bacon," have created "Mmmvelopes," envelopes that have a bacon flavor when you lick them.

chocolate landmark A team of Chinese confectioners built a 33-ft-long (10-m) replica of the Great Wall of China entirely out of chocolate. The wall was made of dark chocolate bricks held together by layers of white chocolate. It was unveiled at the 2010 World Chocolate Wonderland exhibition, which also featured 560 chocolate replicas of China's famous 2,200-year-old Terracotta Army.

giant pumpkin Christy Harp of Jackson Township, Ohio, took first place at the 2009 Ohio Valley Giant Pumpkin Growers' annual weigh-off with a pumpkin that weighed 1,725 lb (783 kg)— nearly ten times the weight of an average man. At one point her prizewinning pumpkin grew at a rate of 33 lb (15 kg) per day.

earthy taste Thuli Malindzi, 22, of Cape Town, South Africa, is addicted to eating soil and consumes a chunk every day. She has been eating earth for more than ten years and although she has tried to give up, she cannot resist hard lumps of clay, which she says taste like fudge.

salsa bowl During the 2010 Jacksonville Tomato Fest in Texas, a team of 20 volunteers made a 2,672-lb (1,212-kg) bowl of salsa.

1821 bun A hot cross bun baked on Good Friday, 1821, has been kept in a Lincolnshire, England, family for 190 years— and still shows no sign of mold. The fruity bun, which has the date March 1821 on its base, was made by Nancy Titman's great-great-great-grandfather, William Skinner, who owned a bakery in London. It was not eaten at the time and has been preserved in a box ever since, passed down through generations of the family as an unusual heirloom. The bun is now rock hard and the currants have disintegrated, but the shape of the cross is still visible.

PARTY BUG
Bug-eating parties are all the rage in Tokyo, Japan, where guests tuck into dishes such as grilled cockroaches, fried grasshoppers, cricket pie and this red moth larvae soup.

chocolate wall To mark the 20th anniversary of the fall of the Berlin Wall, French chocolate-maker Patrick Roger constructed a 49-ft-long (15-m) replica of the landmark in chocolate. Over three weeks in 2009, he used 1,980 lb (900 kg) of chocolate to build the wall, and even added graffiti and artwork to the surface by spraying it with cocoa butter mixed with food coloring.

scorpion snack Li Liuqun of Hunan Province, China, is addicted to eating live scorpions and estimates he has eaten more than 10,000 over the last 30 years. Stung by a huge scorpion one day, he angrily bit off its head and enjoyed the taste so much that he now eats up to 30 in a single sitting. Luckily, he appears immune to the venom, which can paralyze and even kill people.

curry favor Feeding curry to sheep could help save the planet by lowering methane emissions. The spices used in curry kill the "bad" bacteria in a sheep's gut, reducing the amount of methane produced by up to 40 percent.

CREATIVE CAKES
Debbie Goard of Oakland, California, has created hundreds of incredibly lifelike custom-made cakes in the shape of animals, foodstuffs and everyday objects. Her cake designs include dogs, a scorpion, a warthog, a burger, popcorn, spaghetti, sneakers, a Blackberry, a camera and a baby giraffe that was nearly 2 ft (60 cm) tall. Her life-sized Chihuahua cake was so realistic that restaurant patrons were concerned there was a dog on the table!

expensive bottle In London, England, in 2009, jeweler Donald Edge unveiled a gold, pearl and diamond-encrusted bottle of Chambord raspberry liqueur that was valued at over $2 million. The bottle featured 1,100 individual diamonds.

banana bonanza Banana peels make up more than half of the trash collected on Scotland's Ben Nevis mountain. During a September 2009 survey, more than 1,000 discarded banana skins were found on the summit plateau.

chocolate coin Chocolatiers Gary Mitchell, Jess Nolasco and Rita Craig, from Purdy's Chocolates, Vancouver, Canada, spent more than eight hours creating a 25-lb (11.3-kg) chocolate coin, measuring 24 in (60 cm) wide and 1½ in (4 cm) thick, and valued at $625.

fast food "Humble" Bob Shoudt from Royersford, Pennsylvania, won first prize of $2,500 for eating 7 lb 14½ oz (3.58 kg) of French fries in ten minutes at the Curley's Fries Eating Championship at Morey's Piers, Wildwood, New Jersey, in May 2010.

vintage cognac A French entrepreneur bought a bottle of Cognac dating back to 1788—the year before the French Revolution—for nearly $37,000 at a Paris wine auction in December 2009.

sushi roll In November 2009, hundreds of students at the University of California, Berkeley, assembled a 330-ft-long (100-m) sushi roll. They used 200 lb (90 kg) of rice, 180 lb (82 kg) of fish, 80 lb (36 kg) of avocado and 80 lb (36 kg) of cucumber. To cater for vegetarians, the final 15 ft (4.5 m) contained tofu instead of seafood.

moon beer In its thirst to create even better beer, the family-owned Brewery Caulier in Péruwelz, Belgium, has begun producing beer made by the light of a full moon. The full moon speeds up the fermentation process, shortening it from seven days to five, which adds extra punch to the beer, giving it a stronger flavor.

triple yolker Bob Harrop from Devon, England, beat odds of 25 million to one when he found a triple-yolk egg while preparing his breakfast. The former hotelier has fried more than 155,000 eggs over the years and has seen hundreds of double yolkers, but this was the first time he had ever come across an egg with three yolks.

FAT DRAGON
Japanese-born pastry chef Naoko Sukegawa created a sculpture of a dragon made from margarine. The dragon, built over a steel and mesh frame, stood 29 in (74 cm) high, weighed 35 lb (16 kg) and took four months to make.

super spud Amateur gardener Peter Glazebrook of Northampton, England, grew a potato that weighed 8 lb 4 oz (3.74 kg)—the weight of a newborn baby and 25 times more than the weight of an average potato. The supersized spud would make 66 bags of potato chips, 33 portions of fries, 80 roast potatoes or 44 portions of mash.

pizza chain A chain of 2,200 pizzas stretching 1,630 ft (496 m) was laid out in 14 rows at Bucharest, Romania, in 2009. The pizza chain required 1,320 lb (600 kg) of flour, 880 lb (400 kg) of mozzarella, 440 lb (200 kg) of tomato sauce, 4 gal (15 l) of olive oil and 6 lb 10 oz (3 kg) of yeast.

sundae lunch A London ice-cream parlor offered a new twist on the traditional British Sunday roast, with each course being a frozen dessert. The "Sundae Lunch," designed by Italian mixologist Roberto Lobrano, comprised a starter of fresh pea sorbet with mint, followed by a main course of beef bouillon and horseradish sorbet topped with a Yorkshire Pudding wafer. The final course was an apple-and-blackberry-crumble gelato.

status symbols Pineapples were status symbols in 17th-century Britain, and wealthy people would rent them by the day to place on their dinner table and impress their friends.

big dipper Students from Miami-Dade, Florida, filled a 13-gal (49-l) bucket with homemade guacamole. The guacamole weighed 4,114 lb (1,866 kg) and was made from 3,500 lb (1,588 kg) of avocados, 500 lb (227 kg) of tomatoes, 100 lb (45 kg) of mayonnaise and 500 limes.

lot of dough Using a secret 1950s sourdough recipe involving Somerset flour, Cotswolds spring water and Cornish sea salt, baker Tom Herbert from Gloucestershire, England, creates loaves of bread that cost over $30 each. Each 4½-lb (2-kg) hand-crafted shepherd loaf takes him two days to make from start to finish.

MICE LUNCH

While making sandwiches for his family in 2010, a father from Oxfordshire, England, found an unwelcome ingredient in the bread he had bought from a local supermarket—a dead mouse baked into the half-eaten loaf. To make matters worse, the unfortunate rodent was missing its tail, leading Stephen Forse to wonder whether his family had already eaten it.

YUCKY FOOD FACTS

- For every 3½ oz (100 g) of product, the U.S. Food and Drug Administration allows a certain amount of alien material before taking action. This includes up to three rodent hairs and 60 insect fragments in chocolate, five fly eggs and one maggot in tomato juice, and one rodent hair and 30 insect parts in peanut butter.

- In 2010, an English chef opened a tin of baked beans and discovered a dead rat inside. Tests showed that it had not eaten any beans.

- A family from Kentucky drank from a container of milk for three days before they noticed that a mouse had died inside it.

- In 2009, a Florida man found an entire mouse inside his can of cola after complaining that it tasted strange.

chocolate fashion At the 15th Paris Salon du Chocolat in Shanghai, China, chefs and clothes designers from across the world combined their talents to create dresses, jackets, shoes and handbags all made from chocolate.

edible plates To save on washing up after school dinners, catering boss Tiziano Vicentini from Milan, Italy, has devised a range of edible plates made from a kind of dough that is tough enough to last a lunchtime, but tasty enough to eat afterward.

Frog's Heart

Customers in Japan who order Frog Sashimi eat the still-beating heart of a freshly killed American bullfrog. The rest of the frog is eaten as a raw dish, with any leftovers, including the feet, turned into soup.

barter system In 2010, a bar owner on Estonia's Hiiumaa Island in the Baltic Sea revived the age-old barter system to allow customers to pay for drinks with goods. Tarvo Nomm agreed to sell beer in return for bundles of firewood and catches of fish to help the locals beat economic hardship.

banana boxers Australian company AussieBum has unveiled a range of men's underwear made from bananas. The eco-friendly range incorporates 27 percent banana fiber, making the garments lightweight and absorbent without actually smelling of bananas.

half-mile pizza In August 2010, chefs in Krakow, Poland, used 3.5 tons of flour to make a pizza measuring 3,280 ft (1,000 m) in length—that's more than half-a-mile long!

chocolate shoes Confectioner Frances Cooley from Bristol, England, sells shoes and handbags made of chocolate. She has developed a line of individual, high-heeled shoes—including zebra-striped and polka-dot versions—which she makes by hand in her own kitchen. The largest shoe is 6¾ in (17 cm) long and made from two 3½-oz (100-g) bars of Belgian chocolate.

$1,000 burger Joe El-Ajouz's restaurant in Sydney, New South Wales, Australia, has a burger on the menu that costs $1,000. It weighs 210 lb (95 kg), requires 178 lb (81 kg) of mince, 120 eggs, 120 cheese slices, 16 tomatoes, 4½ lb (2 kg) of lettuce, 46 lb (21 kg) of bread and 1.1 lb (500 g) of barbecue sauce. It takes over 12 hours to cook and serves more than 100 people.

nacho tray At Northstar Church, Frisco, Texas, more than 300 volunteers built a 3,555-lb (1,613-kg), 48-ft-long (14.6-m) tray of nachos, loaded with 2,200 lb (998 kg) of yellow tortilla chips, 600 lb (272 kg) of nacho cheese, 250 lb (113 kg) of sour cream, 250 lb (113 kg) of jalapenos, 200 lb (90 kg) of shredded Cheddar cheese and 200 lb (90 kg) of sauce.

soluble gum Scientists at Bristol University, England, have devised a nonstick chewing gum. Rev7 has the same taste and texture as normal gum, but it disintegrates over time and can be removed from shoes, hair and other surfaces with just soap and water.

SWEET SKULLS
Marina Malvada, an artist from Montreal, Canada, uses genuine human skulls—borrowed from a tribal art collector who specializes in collecting cannibal skulls—to cast life-sized skulls in chocolate. Each head is solid chocolate, takes four days to complete and is entirely edible, although weighing 5½ lb (2.5 kg) each, one is more than a mouthful.

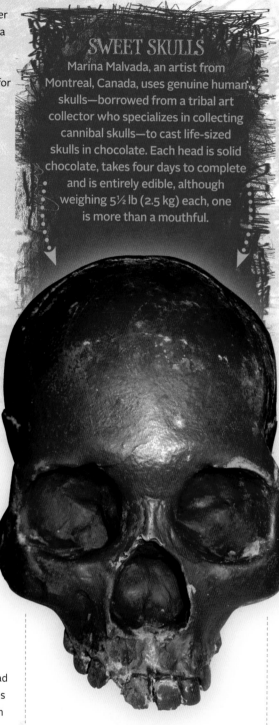

tea nation Britons drink 165 million cups of tea every day—around three cups a day for every adult and child. Although Great Britain accounts for less than 1 percent of the world's population, it is responsible for around 4 percent of its tea consumption.

dogs' dinner An ice-cream van exclusively for dogs attended a 2010 pet festival in London, England. Created by a team of scientists, the canine-friendly, K99 ice cream comes in two flavors—Dog Eat Hog World, a gammon and chicken sorbet topped with a biscuit bone and served in a cone, and Canine Cookie Crunch, dog biscuits and ice cream topped with a biscuit bone.

testicle cooking At the 2010 Testicle Cooking World Championship in Ozrem, Serbia, chefs produced dishes made from the testicles of animals including bulls, wild boar, horses, sharks, ostriches, kangaroos, donkeys, turkeys, goats, reindeer and elk.

scott's butter Two blocks of New Zealand butter nearly a century old were found intact in 2009 in an Antarctic hut used by British explorer Robert Falcon Scott on his doomed 1910–12 expedition.

humongous hummus Chefs in Beirut, Lebanon, prepared a massive plate of hummus weighing over two tons. They used 2,976 lb (1,350 kg) of mashed chickpeas, 106 gal (400 l) of lemon juice and 57 lb (26 kg) of salt to make the dish that weighed 4,532 lb (2,056 kg).

exotic tea Made from older leaves, Puer tea is renowned in China for its exotic taste and healing properties, and is so coveted that just one third of an ounce (10 g) of century-old tea can sell for $10,000.

double banana Having bought a bunch of bananas at a supermarket in Somerset, England, Cedric Hooper got home and found that one skin contained two bananas!

burger candle Columbus, Ohio-based fast-food chain White Castle offered customers a new way to sniff its produce by introducing candles that smell like its oniony Slider hamburgers.

mega meatball In 2009, Nonni's Italian Eatery in New Hampshire created a meatball that weighed a colossal 222 lb 8 oz (101 kg). The giant ball of mince took three days to cook.

hot chocolate In 2009, scientists at Warwick University, England, unveiled an environmentally friendly racing car, built partly from vegetables and powered by chocolate. The bodywork of the WorldFirst car is made from plastic bottles and scraps from airplanes, the seat from flax and soy, and the steering wheel from the waste of juiced carrots. The car, which can reach speeds of 135 mph (217 km/h), uses plant-oil based lubricants and can run on biodiesel made from chocolate factory waste and stale wine.

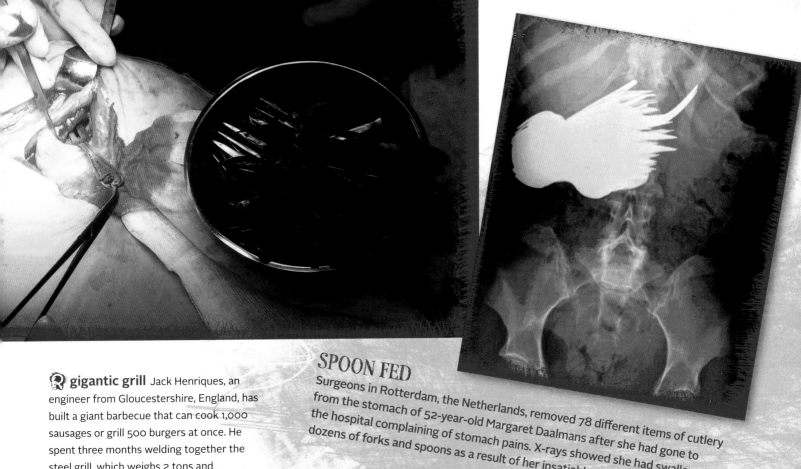

gigantic grill Jack Henriques, an engineer from Gloucestershire, England, has built a giant barbecue that can cook 1,000 sausages or grill 500 burgers at once. He spent three months welding together the steel grill, which weighs 2 tons and measures 16 ft (5 m) long, 6 ft 3 in (1.9 m) wide and 11½ ft (3.5 m) tall. The $15,000 barbecue, which requires 14 bags of coal to fill fully, is so big it can cook seven whole lambs, three whole pigs or two whole cows at the same time.

curry boom In 1950, there were only six Indian restaurants in the whole of Britain, but by 2004 their number had grown to around 9,000.

Bacon Kevin Bacon

J & D Foods in Seattle commissioned Pennsylvania artist Mike Lahue to create a sculpture of actor Kevin Bacon, from crispy bacon bits! The tasty Hollywood head took three months to complete, but unfortunately it is inedible owing to a protective lacquer coating. A bacon-obsessed food company from Seattle, J & D Foods produce bacon soda, "baconnaise" mayonnaise, bacon popcorn, envelopes that taste of bacon when you lick the seal and even bacon lip balm. Their company slogan is "Everything should taste like bacon."

SPOON FED

Surgeons in Rotterdam, the Netherlands, removed 78 different items of cutlery from the stomach of 52-year-old Margaret Daalmans after she had gone to the hospital complaining of stomach pains. X-rays showed she had swallowed dozens of forks and spoons as a result of her insatiable appetite for cutlery.

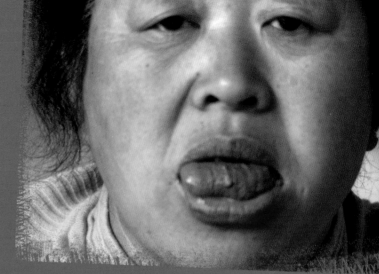

food

Ripley's Believe It or Not!®

SHE'S CRACKED IT

Zhou Yuqin from Chongqing, China, says she has cured all her ailments by eating up to 50 eggshells every day for 13 years. She has even persuaded her children to copy her. When eggshells aren't enough to satisfy her appetite for the unusual, she also nibbles on sand and cullet (broken glass).

DIRT DISH

Fan Qianrong from China's Hebei Province has stayed healthy by eating soil and mud for more than 40 years. Millions of people around the world consume soil, a practice known as geophagy. Eating soil can supply useful minerals and fight nausea, indigestion and diarrhea.

Dig In!

Some people eat the strangest things—wood, glass, metal, clothing, stones, hair and even excrement. The Glore Psychiatric Museum in St. Joseph, Missouri, has a display of 1,446 unusual items swallowed by a patient and removed from her intestines and stomach—including 453 nails, 42 screws and assorted safety pins, spoons and salt and pepper shaker tops. She died during surgery from bleeding caused by her weird diet.

Prickly Eaters

THE CONSUMPTION OF ODD OBJECTS IS CALLED PICA. HERE ARE SOME EATING HABITS TO KICK:

- HYALOPHAGIA IS THE EATING OF GLASS. FRENCH ENTERTAINER MICHEL LOTITO ("MONSIEUR MANGETOUT") ATE GLASS, METAL, RUBBER, BICYCLES, SHOPPING CARTS, TV SETS AND EVEN A LIGHT AIRPLANE, WHICH TOOK HIM TWO YEARS TO DEVOUR.

- TRICHOPHAGIA IS THE EATING OF HAIR. SURGEONS IN CHICAGO RECENTLY REMOVED A 10-LB (4.5-KG) HAIRBALL FROM THE STOMACH OF AN 18-YEAR-OLD WOMAN.

- XYLOPHAGIA IS THE EATING OF WOOD. PEOPLE WITH THIS CONDITION OFTEN EAT PAPER, PENCILS AND TREE BARK.

- COPROPHAGIA IS THE EATING OF FECES. CENTURIES AGO, DOCTORS USED TO TASTE THEIR PATIENTS' EXCREMENT TO DIAGNOSE THEIR STATE OF HEALTH.

- UROPHAGIA IS THE DRINKING OF URINE. MARTIAL-ARTS FIGHTER LYOTO MACHIDA FROM BRAZIL DRINKS HIS OWN URINE EVERY MORNING AS PART OF HIS TRAINING ROUTINE. HE SAYS IT'S A FAMILY TRADITION, PASSED DOWN TO HIM FROM HIS FATHER.

- AUTOSARCOPHAGY IS THE DISORDER OF SELF-CANNIBALISM. IN 2007, CHILEAN ARTIST MARCO EVARISTTI HOSTED A DINNER PARTY FOR FRIENDS WHERE THE MAIN COURSE WAS PASTA TOPPED BY A MEATBALL MADE WITH THE ARTIST'S OWN FAT, REMOVED EARLIER IN THE YEAR BY LIPOSUCTION.

DIET OF BUGS

Mr. Zhu from Sichuan Province, China, has eaten live centipedes since he was a child. In just one month, he and his friends consumed over 3,000 bugs and worms.

Squirrel Ale

In 2010, a Scottish brewery packaged bottles of its new beer, "The End of History," inside the bodies of dead animals. BrewDog sold bottles of its strong, limited-edition Belgian ale—made with juniper berries and containing a staggering 55 percent alcohol—for $1,000 if housed inside a dead squirrel and $750 for bottles encased in a dead stoat. The limited edition of 12 dead animal bottles was hand-crafted by a Yorkshire taxidermist using creatures that had died of natural causes.

long lunch In September 2010, chefs in Italy served lunch on a table that was over a mile long. The 5,775-ft-long (1,760-m) spread was laid out for 2,700 diners and stretched from Bosco to nearby Borzano. The organizers' biggest problem was that it required a tablecloth 5,905 ft (1,800 m) long.

molto macaroni Chef John Folse cooked 2,469 lb (1,120 kg) of macaroni and cheese—enough for 6,500 servings—in New Orleans, Louisiana, in September 2010.

wee dram London-based designer James Gilpin has created whisky made from the high-sugar urine of elderly diabetic patients, including his own grandmother. Gilpin, who is himself diabetic, filters the urine by the same processes used to purify water, and in doing so removes the sugars, which are then used in fermentation. The drink, named Gilpin Family Whisky, is not for sale.

safe breakfast Scientists in the U.K. have developed a breakfast that won't make you sick if you go on a roller coaster shortly afterward. It consists of yogurt mixed with blueberries, grilled bacon in a wholemeal bun with tomato, served with a drink of celery and carrot juice with ginger. Staffordshire theme park Alton Towers were so confident in the product that they offered to refund anyone who was sick on a ride after eating the breakfast.

pub crawl Since 1984, Stuart Ashby of West Sussex, England, has drunk more than 8,500 pints of beer in over 17,000 British pubs, from Cornwall to the Shetland Islands, in the process traveling some 25,000 mi (40,000 km).

beers and spirits For more than nine months in 2009, a ghost apparently kept topping up drinkers' glasses at the Apsley House pub in Southsea, Hampshire, England. Landlady Janice McCormack complained that the specter was costing her a fortune because it was giving away her beer.

vegetable phobia Vicki Larrieux of Portsmouth, England, suffers from lachanophobia, a fear of vegetables. The only vegetables she can bear to eat, touch or see are potatoes. The sight of a carrot or a pea, not just on her plate but even on supermarket shelves, leaves her sweating and stricken with panic attacks.

giant cupcake Chefs in Boca Raton, Florida, unveiled a 1,500-lb (680-kg) chocolate cupcake. It stood 4½ ft (1.4 m) high, 6 ft (1.8 m) wide, and was topped with pink icing, handmade 5-in (12.5-cm) sprinkles and a cherry with a circumference of 12 in (30 cm). It was baked in an oven measuring 10 x 10 ft (3 x 3 m).

golden curry Restaurateurs Padma Prasad and Bhagat Saxena of Hyderabad, India, added finely ground flakes of gold and silver to create a chicken curry that costs $300 a serving.

ALTERNATIVE DINING

• IN SEVERAL COUNTRIES, DINNER IN THE SKY OFFERS A DINING TABLE SUSPENDED IN MIDAIR BY A CRANE 164 FT (50 M) ABOVE GROUND. IT SEATS 22 DINERS AND HAS FIVE STANDING STAFF.

• AN UNDERWATER RESTAURANT IN THE MALDIVES SEATS 14 PEOPLE AND IS LOCATED 15 FT (4.5 M) BELOW THE SURFACE OF THE INDIAN OCEAN.

• IN 2005, ADVENTURER BEAR GRYLLS, BALLOONIST DAVID HEMPLEMAN-ADAMS AND SKYDIVER ALAN VEAL STAGED A DINNER PARTY UNDER A HOT-AIR BALLOON AT AN ALTITUDE OF 25,000 FT (7,620 M).

• THE RESTAURANT AT THE CHACALTAYA SKI RESORT, CORDILLERA, BOLIVIA, IS 17,519 FT (5,340 M) ABOVE SEA LEVEL.

• TWENTY-TWO FLOORS BENEATH THE STREETS OF MOSCOW, RUSSIA, SITS A RESTAURANT BUILT IN WHAT WAS ONCE SOVIET LEADER JOSEF STALIN'S UNDERGROUND BUNKER.

• A CAFÉ IN ISTANBUL, TURKEY, IS LOCATED INSIDE A 1,500-YEAR-OLD UNDERGROUND BYZANTINE WATER CISTERN.

• THE FORTEZZA MEDICEA RESTAURANT NEAR PISA, ITALY, IS SITUATED INSIDE A PRISON WHERE THE WAITERS ARE ALL INMATES.

• IN 2007, 500 PEOPLE WEARING SCUBA-DIVING GEAR DINED UNDERWATER AT THE BOTTOM OF A SWIMMING POOL IN LONDON, ENGLAND.

SUPER SALAMI

A monster salami measuring 7 ft 3 in (2.2 m) long and weighing 143 lb (65 kg) went on show at the Agricultural Trading Exhibition in Anhui, China, in February 2010.

® **sausage drama** A cleaner was taken to hospital in May 2010 after his head and shoulders were sucked into a sausage machine at a factory in Danvers, Massachusetts. The victim, who was not seriously hurt, was cleaning the inside of a cylinder that draws marinade into the meat, when the machine was accidentally switched on.

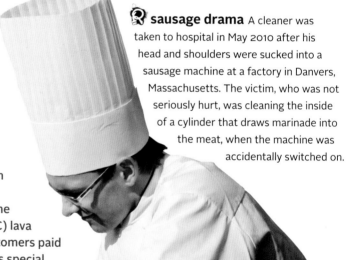

VOLCANO BARBECUE

When Iceland's Fimmvörðuháls volcano erupted in April 2010, Reykjavik chef Fridgeir Eiriksson cooked soup, flaming lobster, monkfish and shallots using the volcano's 390°F (200°C) lava as an oven. Two customers paid $1,000 to enjoy this special Champagne dinner on the bubbling volcano.

grass diet Fifty-year-old Li Sanju of Guangdong Province, China, has spent more than two years eating only leaves and grass. He says he enjoys his unusual diet but admits that he does smell strongly of grass.

full o bull The Cowtown Diner in Fort Worth, Texas, serves a chicken fried steak that weighs about 10 lb (4.5 kg) and packs 10,000 calories. The "Full O Bull," which comes complete with 6 lb (2.7 kg) of mashed potatoes and 10 slices of toast, normally costs $70—but if you can eat it solo, it's free!

jellyfish candy In response to an invasion of 6-ft-wide (1.8-m), 440-lb (200-kg) jellyfish, students at Obama Fisheries High School, Japan, harvested the creatures and turned them into caramel candies.

lion burger To mark the 2010 soccer World Cup in South Africa, a restaurant in Mesa, Arizona, added lion burgers to its menu. Cameron Selogie's Il Vinaio restaurant offered the burger (from farm-raised lion) at $21, served with spicy homemade chips and roast corn on the cob.

zebra pizza Alongside more familiar flavors, a pizza takeout store in Burnley, Lancashire, England, sells pizzas topped with the meat of zebras, crocodiles, kangaroos and buffalo. Owner Arash Fard sells around 20 of his exotic pizzas every week.

rich dish A 513-lb (233-kg) tuna sold for $177,000 at an auction in January 2010 in Tokyo's Tsukiji fish market. That works out to $345 a pound.

still bubbly In July 2010, divers exploring the wreck of a sailing vessel 180 ft (55 m) below the surface of the Baltic Sea off the coast of Finland discovered 30 bottles of champagne some 230 years old. As the bottles had been preserved in the ideal conditions of cold and darkness for so many years, experts said the champagne tasted remarkably good although it had lost some of its fizz.

long-life burger Wellness consultant Karen Hanrahan of Chicago, Illinois, has kept a burger for more than 14 years—without doing anything to preserve it—and it still looks as fresh as the day she bought it!

wrap artists In Lewisburg, Pennsylvania, cooks used 15 lb (6.8 kg) of bacon and 175 wraps held together with about 1,200 toothpicks to create a 102-ft-long (31-m) sandwich wrap.

tasty spider To raise funds for his school in Kent, England, headteacher Aydin Onac ate a baked Cambodian tarantula spider in front of a packed assembly. He said it tasted like burnt chicken.

deep-fried beer Texas chef Mark Zable has created a recipe for deep-fried beer. The beer is placed inside a pocket of salty, pretzel-like dough and dunked in oil at 375°F (190°C) for about 20 seconds. When customers take a bite, the hot beer mixes with the dough to give an alcoholic taste.

banana ketchup Made from mashed banana, sugar, vinegar and spices, banana ketchup is a popular Filipino condiment that is often colored red to resemble tomato ketchup. It was first produced during World War II when there was a shortage of tomato ketchup but an abundance of bananas.

Fast Grub

Eating insects is so popular in Thailand that the country even has its own insect fast food chain. Insects Inter has more than 30 outlets selling fried, crunchy grasshoppers, crickets, grubs and silkworms in $0.70 pots with ketchup or hot chili dips.

transport

feats

mysteries

food

arts

science

beyond belief

believe it!

world

animals

sports

body

196
197
198
199
200
201
202
203
204
205
206
207
208
209
210
211
212
213
214
215
216
217
218
219
220
221
222
223

Cassette Stars

Ripley's has bought a number of Erika Simmons' recycled cassette-tape portraits, depicting Bob Marley (seen here), Michael Jackson, Debbie Harry and Kurt Cobain, among others. The Atlanta artist, featured in *Ripley's Believe It or Not! Enter If You Dare!*, has since become an internet sensation after her tape art inspired the video for the Bruno Mars hit "Just the Way You Are."

Ripley's
EXHIBITS

Ripley's
Believe It or Not!®

Inflated Animals

Chinese artist Yang Maoyuan creates animal sculptures with a difference—he takes the skins of dead animals and inflates them to monstrous sizes, often dyeing them in lurid colors.

Beijing-based Yang travels to Hebei in northern China to buy horse, goat and sheep skins. He then stitches and processes the skins before blowing them up so that their bodies become bloated and round. He chooses animals from his Mongolian ancestry, making them larger than life to reflect his oldest dream symbols, and gives them a round shape that represents harmony in China. To make his sculptures even more grotesque, he gives some of the sheep two or three heads.

Yang's art has been a hit in galleries worldwide.

Yang's bright blue, three-headed, many-legged goat.

◀◀◀ **After**

Yang takes complete horse skins (right) and turns them into works of art that symbolize his philosophy and the nomadic traditions of his ancestors.

Before ▶▶▶

RIPLEY RESEARCH

Victor uses leaves from the maple-like Chinar tree, as they are particularly durable. The process takes around a month, involving as many as 60 individual steps. First he boils the leaf in water to soften it and remove any bacteria. Then he removes the layers of the leaf with a knife and needle, taking care to keep the delicate veins in place. Next he carefully cuts and sculpts the surface to create his chosen image. Then he brushes and shaves the leaf to make it appear transparent, coats it in an anti-aging treatment, dries it again, and finally waxes it before framing.

A NEW LEAF

Victor Liu collects dried old leaves from the streets around his home in Hebei Province, China, and very painstakingly carves into them beautiful images of subjects such as Barack Obama, Marilyn Monroe, the *Mona Lisa* and the Statue of Liberty.

new york bears Joshua Allen Harris placed inflatable polar bears made from discarded plastic bags above ventilation grates in the New York City subway so that the animals inflated and deflated with the passing of underground trains.

daily grind Instead of paint or ink, Bend, Oregon, artist Karen Eland creates replicas of famous artworks with coffee. Since her first espresso painting in 1998, she has completed more than 90 illustrations—many of which incorporate coffee drinking—including *Leonardo da Vinci's Mona Latte*, *Whistler's Mocha* and *Rodin's The Drinker*.

traveling bible A unique 1,500-page traveling Bible, written in 66 languages—one language for each book of the Old and New Testament—has toured more than 150 countries. The huge 15-lb (7-kg) book, which measures 18 x 12 in (45 x 30 cm), set off on its world tour from the Philippines in October 2008.

baseball mementos Mitch Poole, clubhouse manager with the Los Angeles Dodgers baseball team, turns milestones into mementos by painting significant game balls with details of the achievement. It is traditional for a clubhouse manager to retrieve the ball when an important hit, run, steal or win takes place, and for more than 20 years Mitch has decorated hundreds of balls. Using acrylic paint, he writes the player's name, opponent, accomplishment, date, box score and other information on the ball.

original nintendo In February 2010, a video-game collector paid $13,105 for an original Nintendo entertainment system and five game cartridges.

stage epic German producer Franz Abraham has created a stage version of the Roman epic *Ben-Hur* featuring 400 actors, 900 costumes, 50 scene designs, 46 horses, 120 doves, five chariots, two eagles and two vultures. The action takes place in a 26,000-sq-ft (2,415-sq-m) arena covered with 10 in (25 cm) of sand. The production uses 30 mi (48 km) of cable, 250 moving lights and 25 tons of sound equipment.

big business In Minneapolis, Minnesota, in 2009, entrepreneur Lief Larson presented a work contact with a giant business card that measured 60 x 34 in (150 x 85 cm).

CROCHET LIONS

English "crochetdermist" Shauna Richardson spent two years hand-crocheting three huge lions, each measuring 25 ft (7.5 m) long and 10 ft (3 m) high. She crocheted the skins in wool, accurately tracing the animals' muscular contours, over a polystyrene and steel framework. Shauna also crochets life-size pieces, which have included wild boars, bears and baboons.

tattooed pigs Belgian artist Wim Delvoye tattooed pigs with Louis Vuitton designer logos for an exhibit called *Art Farm*. He tattooed the LV logos on the animals when they were piglets and watched the designs increase in size as the pigs' bodies grew.

some yarn! Over the period of a week, Austin, Texas, artist Magda Sayeg covered a Mexico City bus from front to back with brightly colored knitted yarn. She has also knitted woolen coverings for trees, car antennas and signs in the U.S.A. as well as for the Louvre Museum in Paris.

typed portraits Keira Rathbone of Dorset, England, uses manual typewriters—some up to 70 years old—as her paintbrushes to create portraits of famous people, including Barack Obama, Marilyn Monroe and supermodel Kate Moss. After deciding which of her collection of 30 typewriters she wants to use, she turns the roller and selects different characters—numbers, letters and punctuation—to make the required shapes.

tan art James Titterton of London, England, endured a full body wax and eight sunbed sessions to have a fish, a cockerel and a ship's anchor bronzed onto his flesh. He masked off parts of his chest, arms and legs with vinyl stickers of the various images before having the outlines tanned on to his skin. Dressed in only underpants, he then exhibited his tanned artwork at a gallery in Sussex.

naked hug More than 5,000 people took off their clothes and embraced each other in the nude on the steps of Sydney Opera House, Australia, in March 2010 for a photo shoot by American artist Spencer Tunick.

$11 million book A copy of the book *Birds of America*, written and illustrated by Haitian-born John James Audubon in the early 19th century, was sold for more than $11 million in December 2010. Only 119 complete copies of the large-format book, which has foldout pages measuring 39½ x 29½ in (100 x 75 cm), are in existence, and all but 11 of those are in museums and libraries. To obtain such accurate likenesses of birds, Audubon stalked his subjects across the U.S.A. and shot them before hanging them from wires and painting them.

behind the smile Dr. Vito Franco of the University of Palermo, Sicily, Italy, believes the enigmatic smile on the face of Leonardo da Vinci's *Mona Lisa* was the result of very high levels of cholesterol. After studying the painting closely, the doctor says he can detect a build up of fatty acids around her left eye.

sound your horn! A giant, working vuvuzela horn 115 ft (35 m) long and 18 ft (5.5 m) in diameter was installed above a highway in Cape Town, South Africa, in 2010.

Living Dolls

When British artist Boo Ritson tells her subjects she wants to paint them, she means it literally. Boo covers her human volunteers in layers of water-based paint to create giant action figures, which she then photographs. She specializes in American symbols, which means that as well as painting subjects such as cheerleader and cowboy living dolls, she has also applied the technique to donuts.

arts

Ripley's Believe It or Not!®

Sticky Sculpture

When a popular adhesive tape company challenged people to come up with the best sculpture made entirely from sticky tape, they received some incredible entries. Artist Annie K. stuck together this giant jellyfish that appears to be floating in the air and ensnaring a bicycle in its tentacles. Some of the entries included an office desk made from 36 rolls of tape and a drum kit made from 48 rolls—that's over 7,770 ft (2,368 m), or enough tape to wrap round an aircraft carrier seven times.

ⓇⓇ cardboard scream Artist Mark Langan from Cleveland, Ohio, re-created Edvard Munch's haunting painting *The Scream* using discarded cardboard boxes. He spent 90 hours cutting up five old boxes with a craft knife and layering them to create a three-dimensional picture that measured 2.2 in (5.5 cm) deep. His cardboard creation sold for $2,500.

Ⓡ noncontact instrument The theremin is an electronic musical instrument that is played without any contact from the player! Named after Russian professor Léon Theremin, who invented it in 1919, it consists of two metal antennae that sense the position of the player's hands and send corresponding electric signals to a loudspeaker.

Ⓡ microbial art Dr. T. Ryan Gregory of the University of Guelph, Canada, is a pioneer of microbial art, where scientists design patterns by brushing fungi, deadly bacteria and dye around a petri dish. He creates images by using a small paintbrush and E. coli in liquid medium. These are then allowed to grow in a laboratory incubator, but the "living paint" soon dies, so the pictures are only temporary.

DEAD FLIES

Magnus Muhr collects dead flies from windows and lamps around his house in Sweden, places them on white paper, draws in legs and a crazy background, and then photographs them. The photos show the insects appearing to dance, sunbathe, dive, ride horses and perform acrobatic circus routines.

giant chair Furniture craftsman Radoslav Russev carved a wooden chair that was almost 15 ft (4.5 m) high and weighed more than 770 lb (350 kg). He made the oversized chair, which was placed in the main square of Razgrad, Bulgaria, from 70 cubic ft (2 cubic m) of pinewood.

leather portraits Welsh artist Mark Evans creates huge portraits of famous people—in leather. Using knives as his "brushes," he has scraped impressions of Muhammad Ali, Sir Winston Churchill and model Naomi Campbell into leather hides. He discovered his talent by accident after spilling blood on a new leather jacket. He tried to repair it with a palette knife but scratched too hard and ended up etching a portrait of Jimi Hendrix onto the back of the jacket.

cereal-ism With the help of 150 students, high-school teacher Doyle Geddes of Smithfield, Utah, used 2 tons of breakfast cereal to create a massive reproduction of Vincent van Gogh's painting *Starry Night* measuring 72 x 90 ft (22 x 27 m).

board game In 2009, board-game fanatic Luanga Nuwame created a 900-sq-ft (84-sq-m) wooden board game based on the city of Mississauga, Ontario, Canada... with real people as the pieces. He also built a huge dice with which to play it.

washington's fine New York Society Library says George Washington owes it $300,000 in library fines. Its ledgers show that the first U.S. President borrowed two books that were due to be returned on November 2, 1789, but are now more than 220 years overdue.

costly comic A copy of the 1938 edition of *Action Comics No. 1* sold in March 2010 for $1.5 million on an auction website. The issue, which features Superman's debut, originally sold for 10 cents.

french anthem Claude-Joseph Rouget de Lisle composed "The Marseillaise" in 1792 in return for a bottle of wine. The tune became the anthem of French Revolutionaries and was later adopted as the French national anthem. Ironically, Rouget de Lisle was a royalist who was thrown into prison during the Revolution and narrowly escaped being guillotined.

observation test To help improve their powers of deductive observation, a group of New York City police officers visited the Metropolitan Museum of Art to discuss with an expert what conclusions they could draw from the contents of pictures by the likes of Caravaggio and Guercino.

many parts Bollywood actress Priyanka Chopra played all 12 characters in the 2009 movie *What's Your Rashee?* Each character was one of the 12 zodiac signs.

serenading sharks Andy Brandy Casagrande IV, an American wildlife cinematographer, strummed a waterproof guitar and played a song underwater to sharks off the coast of Mexico—without a cage. He penned "The Great White Shark Song" to raise awareness of shark conservation and decided the best way to make his point was to don scuba gear and play his tune in shark-infested waters.

Kris Kuksi, a sculptor and painter from Kansas, creates macabre yet beautiful sculptures assembled from hundreds, sometimes thousands, of discarded toys, figurines and general trash. His work has been bought by celebrities and exhibited around the world.

Kris explains how Lies and Persuasion *came together:*

"My pieces are a collection of many different things. I started out by gathering miscellaneous figurines, small rocks, jewelry—anything I could incorporate. After I found some essential "supplies" that I felt were important for the individuality of the piece, I built a foundation, and everything after that is just assemblage. When it's all finished, the piece gets various coats of paint.

Lies and Persuasion *has so many little things in it and, interesting enough, the skull forms in the piece are actually the same skull split in half. I'll buy anything, anywhere, if I feel it's needed for a piece. I'd say that the whole assemblage, that is, the creation itself—withholding the mental preparation and shopping—lasted about a month."*

TURN THE PAGE...

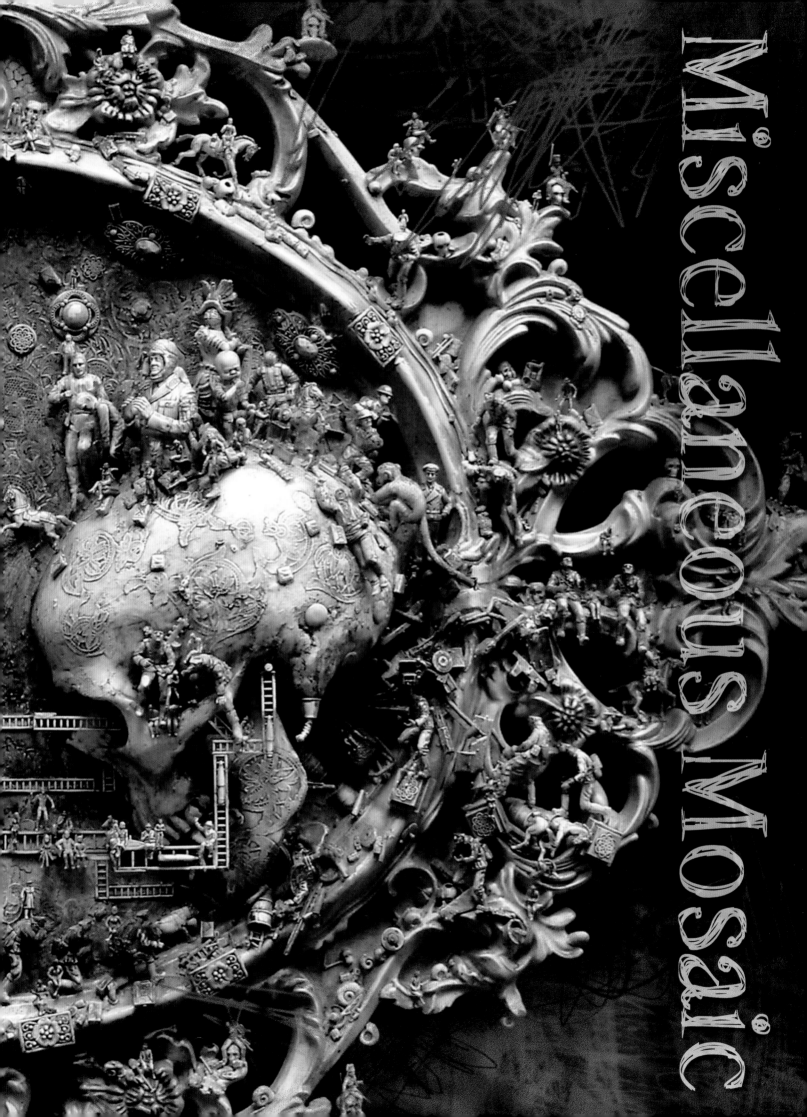

Miscellaneous Mosaic

arts
Ripley's
Believe It or Not!®

ILLUSION CONFUSION

There is a lot more to this portrait of legendary artist Salvador Dali than meets the eye. It is in fact a large three-dimensional illusion, consisting of a shark, a bull's head and a seal, among many other objects. These bizarre items appear to be randomly piled up but are actually meticulously placed to complete the image from just one perspective. Bernard Pras, the artist from Belgium, has been re-creating famous pictures out of junk for more than 30 years.

microscopic models Origami artist Mui-Ling Teh of Thornhill, Ontario, Canada, makes paper models so tiny—as small as 0.08 in (2 mm) long—that they look like a speck to the naked eye. She makes her microscopic models of objects such as birds, flowers and airplanes with scissors and tweezers. She first began to experiment with origami at age ten when she made small models out of candy wrappers.

auto robot A 33-ft-tall (10-m) version of Transformer Optimus Prime made from the bodies and tires of old cars and motorcycles was unveiled at Beijing's Green Dream Park in 2010. The Autobot sculpture weighed six tons and was assembled from five truckloads of recycled parts.

huge hammock Hansy Better Barraza, a professor at Rhode Island School of Design, created a 33-ft-long (10-m) hammock, covering an area of 264 sq ft (24.5 sq m) in Boston, Massachusetts, in 2010. The sculpture consisted of 4,278 ft (1,304 m)—that's nearly a mile—of "rope" made from recycled bottles woven over curved steel pipes.

avid reader Nonagenarian Louise Brown from Dumfries and Galloway, Scotland, has borrowed 25,000 library books in her lifetime. She has read up to a dozen books a week since 1946 without incurring a single fine for late returns.

smelly issue Issue No. 23 of the German magazine *mono.kultur* was infused with 12 smells suggested by Norwegian scientist, artist and odor expert Sissel Tolaas. Using a technique called microencapsulation, the smells were printed into the pages of the magazine, with the reader rubbing the paper to release them.

human ashes Dutch artist Wieki Somers makes 3-D printed sculptures of common household appliances—including bathroom scales, a vacuum cleaner and a toaster—out of human ashes.

gallery blunder Polish experimental artist Leon Tarasewicz sued a gallery for $30,000 after it ripped up one of his paintings and threw it in a trash can in the mistaken belief that it was a large bunch of scrap paper used for getting excess paint off brushes. The 25-ft-high (7.6-m) exhibit had been on display in the gallery in Katowice, but staff thought that it had been left behind by decorators.

beef bikini For the September 2010 cover shot of Japanese magazine *Vogue Hommes Japan*, U.S. singer Lady Gaga wore a bikini made of raw meat.

Tasty Shoes Israel's Kobi Levi has designed shoes in the shapes of bananas, cats, shopping baskets, dogs, rocking chairs—and one pair with a pink stiletto heel that makes it look as though the wearer has stepped in a piece of chewing gum.

GLASS HOLOGRAMS

Using special pencils, multiple layers of painted glass and between 14 and 30 glass panes, artist Xia Xiao Wan from Beijing, China, is able to transform ordinary 2-D glass into stunning 3-D holographic images.

fake porsche Austrian artist Hannes Langeder spent six months building a life-size Porsche sports car from plastic pipes and cardboard. The aluminum-foil covered Ferdinand GT3 RSX has no engine but is powered by a hidden bicycle, which is why it has handlebars instead of a steering wheel.

mosaic mural More than 130 artists and 500 children worked for three years to create a ceramic mosaic mural in Hanoi, Vietnam, that measures nearly 2½ mi (4 km) long. The brainchild of artist Nguyen Thu Thuy, the mosaic depicts images of Vietnam's history, life and culture.

whistle-stop tour German guitarist Vicente Patiz drove more than 600 mi (960 km) to give concerts in eight countries—Germany, Belgium, the Netherlands, France, Luxembourg, Switzerland, Lichtenstein and Austria—in just 24 hours.

bamboo dance More than 10,700 people assembled on March 12, 2010, to perform the Cheraw dance together in Aizawl, Mizoram, India. They spread out over an area of about 1¾ mi (3 km) to dance an eight-minute routine with bamboo sticks.

bargain buy A decade after buying 65 photographic plates at a garage sale in California for just $45, Rick Norsigian found that they could be the work of celebrated U.S. nature photographer Ansel Adams and therefore be worth around $200 million.

quick on the draw Singaporean artist Peter Zhou, aka Peter Draw, drew nearly 1,000 people nonstop, without food, for 24 hours.

Poo Shoes

British artist INSA created a pair of 10-in-high (25-cm) stiletto shoes with platforms made from elephant dung. He sourced the waste from the same family of elephants that provided the material for a famous series of elephant-dung collage paintings by Turner Prize-winning British artist Chris Ofili in the 1990s.

Roll the Dice Ari Krupnik, a software engineer from Silicon Valley, California, builds mosaics of famous people from hundreds of dice, achieving different shades of gray according to which face is up. He created a portrait of revolutionary leader Che Guevara from 400 dice and one of George Orwell, author of *Animal Farm*, from 1,925 dice. He has also made a 3-D image of actress Uma Thurman from hundreds of M&M's®.

pretty paddies Each year, the farmers of Inakadate Village, Aomori Prefecture, Japan, use different-colored varieties of rice to create works of art spanning entire rice paddies.

blind draft U.S. novelist Kent Haruf writes the first draft of each of his books blind! He takes off his glasses, pulls a stocking cap down over his eyes, and types his words in darkness.

rubik's replica Five artists in Toronto, Canada, spent two months making a replica of Leonardo da Vinci's *The Last Supper* measuring 8½ x 17 ft (2.6 x 5.2 m), using 4,050 Rubik's cubes.

poetry booth Starting in October 2009, an old-style telephone booth in Yellow Springs, Ohio, served as a stage for poetry readings, light shows and dance performances. People could walk into the booth, pick up the receiver and listen to a recorded reading of short poems or simply create their own experimental artworks.

vast violin In 2010, a dozen workers in Markneukirchen, Germany, created a playable violin that measured 13 ft 11 in (4.3 m) tall, 4½ ft (1.4 m) wide, and weighed more than 220 lb (100 kg).

gum-wrapper dress Elizabeth Rasmuson of Garner, Iowa, made her 2010 high-school prom dress out of hundreds of gum wrappers that she and her boyfriend, Jordan Weaver, had been collecting for six months. She also made him a matching vest out of blue-and-white gum wrappers.

in the dark London's Tate Modern gallery unveiled its latest giant installation in 2009—40 ft (12 m) of pitch darkness. It was created by Polish artist Miroslaw Balka who said that the darkness was a metaphor for life.

party poopers U.S. rock band Kings of Leon had to abandon a concert at the Verizon Amphitheater, St. Louis, Missouri, in July 2010 after they were bombarded with pigeon droppings. An infestation of birds in the rafters above the stage led to bassist Jared Followill being hit several times during the band's first two songs, including in the face.

lego plane LEGO™ enthusiast Ryan McNaught built a $5,500 replica of the world's biggest passenger plane—the Airbus A380— with more than 35,000 bricks. It took him more than eight months to build the model, which is 7 ft (2.1 m) long and 6 ft (1.8 m) wide, in the garage of his home in Melbourne, Victoria, Australia.

garbage pictures Richard Broom of Lincolnshire, England, spent hours photographing litter along Britain's roadsides and posting them on an Internet blog in an attempt to get the government to tidy up the country—but his photos, including discarded paper cups, old cans, a broken toilet and bottles of urine, proved so popular that they have turned into highly collectable art.

mini mansion Peter Riches of Hove, England, spent nearly 15 years creating an elaborately decorated doll house and sold it for $80,000—that's enough to buy a real home in some places. His miniature 23-room mansion boasted a music room with grand piano, a hand-crafted games room with snooker table, and a library with more than 1,000 individually bound books. He made the shell of the house from plaster and hand-etched 32,000 bricks on its walls. He cut the 5,000 roof tiles from cardboard. The finished house measured 4 ft (1.2 m) wide, 3 ft 3 in (1 m) high and 2 ft 7 in (80 cm) deep.

cloud graffiti U.S. pop artist Ron English created cloud graffiti in the skies above New York City in September 2009. He hired a skywriting plane and got it to spell the word "cloud" in puffy white dots several times over the city.

tiny tiger A Taiwanese artist has created a painted tiger sculpture that is smaller than a grain of rice. Chen Forng-shean spent three months carving the 0.04-in-high (1-mm) tiger from resin. He has also made delicate miniature sculptures from sand, dental floss, rice, ant heads and fly wings.

pinhead nativity In 2009, Italian craftsman Aldo Caliro sculpted a nativity scene—featuring hand-carved figures of the Virgin Mary, Joseph and an angel, plus a tiny baby Jesus in his crib—on the head of a pin! He painted the figures with a single paintbrush hair. He had previously carved nativity scenes on a lentil and a coffee bean.

chalk drawing *Head of a Muse*, a simple black chalk drawing on paper by Renaissance painter Raphael, sold at an auction in London, England, for $47.9 million in December 2009.

long story It will be nearly 1,000 years before the cover of the May 2009 issue of *Opium* magazine can be read in its entirety. It will take that long for the successive layers of ink to degrade—at the rate of one word per century—thereby revealing a nine-word tale created by U.S. conceptual artist Jonathan Keats.

precise worker U.S. bestselling horror writer Stephen King, originally from Portland, Maine, writes exactly ten pages (around 2,000 words) a day, whether he's in a creative mood or not.

coffee cups At the 2010 Rocks Aroma Festival in Sydney, Australia, a team of artists created a 21 x 18 ft (6.5 x 5.5 m) coffee mosaic of Marilyn Monroe. They formed the image by filling 5,200 cups of coffee with 180 gal (680 l) of milk and 205 gal (780 l) of coffee to varying levels.

enormous shirt A team of South-African tailors worked nonstop for three weeks to make a T-shirt bigger than the Statue of Liberty. About 6.5 million stitches held together the 208 x 140 ft (64 x 43 m) shirt, using over 22,965 ft (7,000 m) of fabric.

PENCIL TIPS

Dalton Ghetti of Bridgeport, Connecticut, has been creating miniature graphite masterpieces from the tips of pencils for more than 25 years, including a sculpture of Elvis wearing shades, carved from a single pencil tip. He uses three tools—a razor blade, a sewing needle and a sculpting knife—but no magnifying glass. He digs into the graphite with the needle, then scratches and creates lines, turning the pencil slowly in his hand. One piece—a pencil with interlinking chains—took him two-and-a-half years. He has made over 100 pencil-tip shapes in total, such as a saw, a screw, a key on a chain, a boot, a chair, a mini mailbox and all 26 letters of the alphabet.

Gum Dog

Gareth Williams of the U.K. created this sculpture of a dog, which was exhibited at London's Royal College of Art in 2009, with hair clippings from his own head stuck together with pieces of used chewing gum.

same glass For more than 35 years on an almost daily basis, Peter Dreher of Wittnau, Germany, has painted a portrait of the same drinking glass in the same position in his studio. He has so far completed more than 4,000 paintings of the glass.

lego repairs German artist Jan Vormann travels the world fixing crumbling walls and monuments with LEGO®. Among areas he has brightened up with the toy bricks are the old quarter of Tel Aviv in Israel and New York's Bryant Park.

midnight knitter Under the cover of darkness in early 2010, an unknown person dubbed the "Midnight Knitter" draped tree branches and lampposts in West Cape May, New Jersey, with small, brightly colored woolen sweaters.

cool music Norwegian composer Terje Isungset has recorded several albums with instruments made entirely of ice, including percussion, horns and trumpets.

movie veteran Aachi Manorama, a veteran of India's Tamil film industry, has appeared in more than 1,500 movies and 1,000 stage performances.

early watch In 2009, art experts discovered a 450-year-old painting that featured an image of a watch. The portrait, painted by Italian Renaissance artist Maso da San Friano around 1560, shows Cosimo I de' Medici, Duke of Florence, holding a golden timepiece. Watches first appeared shortly after 1500, making this one of the oldest paintings to depict a true watch.

tower cozy Robyn Love of New York City crocheted a yarn cozy for a wooden water tower on Broadway. Over a period of three weeks, she and six assistants used 60 balls of yellow and black yarn to transform the tower into a huge yellow pencil, complete with point.

sitting in silence Over a period of nearly three months in 2010, Serbian performance artist Marina Abramović spent 700 hours simply sitting and staring across a table at members of the public at New York's Museum of Modern Art. She sat on a chair for seven hours a day, six days a week, for her installation *The Artist Is Present*. Around 1,400 people—including singer Björk and model Isabella Rossellini—sat opposite her and returned her silent gaze. Some managed an entire day; others lasted just a few minutes.

expensive doll A French doll designed by Paris artist Albert Marque in 1915 was sold at auction in Atlanta, Georgia, for $263,000 in 2009. Only 100 examples of the doll were ever made and each was individually costumed, in styles ranging from 18th-century French court to traditional Russian folklore.

hay castle In January 2010, visitors flocked to Rob Marshall's sheep farm in West Victoria, Australia, to see a castle measuring 100 x 20 ft (30 x 6 m) that he had built out of hundreds of bales of hay. The castle remained in situ for six weeks until Rob dismantled it and used the bales to feed his sheep.

tree sculpture Inspired by a silver birch tree, Swedish furniture chain IKEA created a huge tree sculpture made from white kitchen appliances—including a washing machine, a dishwasher and a microwave oven—that was erected outside London's Barbican Centre in 2010.

holiday snaps A series of 19th-century watercolor paintings of European beauty spots by an unknown female British holidaymaker was sold in London for more than $5,000 in 2010. The paintings of such picturesque locations as Bavaria, the Swiss Alps and the Belgian city of Bruges were made in journals as holiday snaps by the woman following vacations she took with her husband in 1850 and 1853.

Ripley's Ask

Why did you start using your own blood for your paintings? I guess the easiest answer would be to prove to myself that I could. I have used every medium I could think of during the course of my artistic career, from oil paint, charcoal, graphite, automotive paints, inks, even coffee, so I think it was just to see if I could.

After my first one, I was so proud of my work and fascinated by the finish, even though my first one was somewhat clumsy in its execution, so I set off on my journey to perfect my blood work. And with each painting, I learned how to predict how it would handle on various surfaces, how it changes and how my blood itself varies depending on things like diet, hydration and so on.

How much blood do you use in a typical painting? This really depends on the image. As a guide, a 20 x 20 in (500 x 500 mm) painting will use between 1$\frac{1}{2}$ fl oz (40 ml) and 6$\frac{3}{4}$ fl oz (200 ml). It also depends on the tools I use—for example, airbrushed textures use a lot less than a paintbrush.

How much blood do you extract on a regular basis? Earlier on I was extracting up to twice per week. However, years of doing so has caused scar tissue in my vein walls so it is becoming increasingly painful to remove, so when we do, we take a lot, up to 1 pint (440 ml) at a time and then I store it in the refrigerator.

Is blood easy to use? How does it compare to regular ink? Not even close, it is by far the most difficult substance to use. It is not actually red—the cells within the plasma are—so essentially I'm painting with my body's tissue. These cells clog airbrushes, and don't give uniform coverage from a brush—once dry even the smallest amount of moisture will liquefy it again, so it's very easy to "burn" through what you have already painted. It has taken me a long time to master what I have, and I have almost completely given up all other mediums now because my blood painting has been deeply rewarding and proven very popular worldwide.

Blood Painter

Rev Mayers never runs out of the unique ink he uses for his paintings, because it's one hundred percent his own blood on the canvas. The extreme artist from Sydney, Australia, has the blood extracted from his arm using a syringe, just as a doctor would. He then applies the precious fluid with an airbrush or a standard paintbrush. More detail and depth becomes visible as the art ages. Rev estimates that he has so far used more than 12 pints of his own blood in his paintings, more than most adults have in their entire body.

BB-BALL GAGA

Sculptor and artist John O'Hearn of Gainesville, Florida, makes colorful mosaics from thousands of Airsoft BBs —the ¼-in (6-mm) plastic balls used in a BB gun. Among his designs are a portrait of Florida Gators quarterback Tim Tebow from 46,308 BBs, which measures 4 x 6 ft (1.2 x 1.8 m), and this larger-than-life mosaic of singer Lady Gaga that is 4 x 8 ft (1.2 x 2.4 m) and contains 61,509 BBs.

ℝ pothole scenes Urban artists Claudia Ficca and Davide Luciano from Montreal, Canada, travel North America transforming unsightly street potholes into works of art. They have been photographed in the guise of a woman washing her clothes in a pothole, a priest baptizing a baby in another, and a scuba diver taking a dip.

ℝ splendid sari A team of weavers in Chennai, India, spent 4,680 hours making a $100,000 sari, woven with precious metals and gems.

ℝ big monet At the 2010 Normandy Impressionist Festival, 1,250 fans of 19th-century French artist Claude Monet gathered in Rouen and held painted panels above their heads to create a giant, 6,460-sq-ft (600-sq-m) replica of his 1894 work *Rouen Cathedral at the End of the Day*. The result was captured by cameras perched 90 ft (27 m) above the city hall.

ℝ bone images Swiss-born artist and photographer Francois Robert, who is now based in the U.S.A., produces works of art from real human bones. He spent hours arranging bones into striking shapes for his photographic collection *Stop the Violence*, which featured bone images of a gun, a tank, a bomb, a grenade, a Kalashnikov rifle and a knife. He hit upon the idea after trading a wired-together human skeleton, found inside some school lockers he had bought, for a box of 206 human bones.

ℝ high horse Tony Dew from York, England, hand-carved a wooden rocking horse that stands 11 ft 10 in (3.6 m) high and 16 ft (4.9 m) long—more than twice the size of most real horses.

CART ART

Ptolemy Elrington trawls rivers and lakes near his studio in Brighton, England, for abandoned metal shopping carts and turns them into enchanting sculptures of animals, insects and birds. By breaking up the carts and welding them into the desired shapes, he has created such designs as a heron, a frog (with bulging eyes from the cart's wheels), a dragonfly with a 6-ft (1.8-m) wingspan, and this kingfisher eating a fish.

last suppers For his *Last Suppers* series, British artist James Reynolds re-created the final meals requested by American Death Row prisoners. He filled a succession of orange prison-issue trays with their genuine last meals, which included a single black olive; an onion, a packet of chewing gum and two bottles of coke; and six raw eggs.

dirt shirts Remembering how they always used to end up with manure on their clothes when they helped on the family farm as kids, Patti Froman Maine of Corry, Pennsylvania, and her brother Sonny Froman designed a range of T-shirts that are deliberately coated in the stuff. Their CowChipShirts don't smell and come in colors such as Udder Rose and Silage Brown.

gold painting Russian artist Elena Zolotaya created a 10-ft-wide (3-m) picture painted entirely with 14-carat gold.

DECORATIVE RECYCLING

Florida-based artists Alain Guerra and Neraldo de la Paz create stunning sculptures from discarded clothing. They drape old garments over a wire frame to form colorful designs including a rainbow, a snake, and a series of clothing trees that represent all four seasons of the year.

tall order For a wager, Norway's Ola Helland collected over one million giraffe pictures in 440 days. He was backpacking through South America when, as a keepsake to remember all the new friends he had met, he asked each to draw him a giraffe. When a friend bet him he couldn't collect a million, Ola set up a website and was soon deluged with giraffe pictures from 106 countries, including a giraffe made from a banana and another made out of bread.

new books Each year, in the U.S.A. alone, about 30 million trees are used to make paper to print new books.

turning heads After going bald in his twenties, Philip Levine of London, England, began using his scalp as a canvas for art. Every week, body painter Kat Sinclair transformed Philip's designs into a different piece of head art. He turned his head into a disco ball covered with 1,000 crystals, had it painted with flowers, cartoon characters and smiley faces, and even had acupuncture needles inserted into his scalp in the shape of a butterfly.

many hands At the 2010 Baltimore Book Festival in Maryland, 512 people contributed to a single piece of art. Local author K. Michael Crawford erected an easel with a blank canvas and invited passersby to add to the picture.

HELPING HAND

For his painting *The Hand With The Golden Ring*, Norwegian artist Morten Viskum said he used the hand of a human corpse as a paintbrush. He claims that he's been working with a severed hand as a brush for over a decade, and uses it to apply animal blood, acrylic paints and sometimes glitter to his canvases.

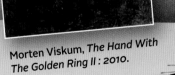

Morten Viskum, *The Hand With The Golden Ring II* : 2010.

comedy gig American comedian Bob Marley performed a 40-hour gig at the Comedy Connection in Portland, Maine, lasting 18 hours before having to repeat any jokes.

golden vuvuzela A Russian businessman bought an Austrian-made gold and diamond-encrusted vuvuzela horn for over $20,000. The plastic South African horns, sounded by soccer spectators at the 2010 World Cup, usually cost around $8 each.

embroidered map Textile artist Lucy Sparrow of Brighton, East Sussex, England, has embroidered a 97-sq-ft (9-sq-m) tapestry of the London Underground map. It took her 42 days to make the giant map, which is made up of 7,875 ft (2400 m) of thread and 142 buttons.

head banger Jim Bartek of Maple Heights, Ohio, listened to the album *Nostradamus* by heavy metal band Judas Priest once a day for 524 days in a row.

Paperback Titles On the bookshelves of his home in Wiltshire, England, Steve Hare has a collection of more than 15,000 Penguin paperbacks—including the first 2,000 titles published following their introduction in 1935. He has been collecting them for more than 45 years and has enough books to fill two trucks.

beach carving London, England, artist Everton Wright, aka Evewright, carved an outline of a 2,600-ft (800-m) artwork in the sand of a beach in Cumbria using a garden rototiller. A team of 20 horses and riders were then invited to walk along the outline to make the tracks deeper. The design took 18 months to plan, but lasted for only five hours until the tide came in and washed it all away.

long title When environmentalist Shripad Vaidya from Nagpur, India, released an anthology of eco-friendly poems in March 2010, the book's title consisted of no fewer than 355 words.

street strummers More than 850 ukulele players gathered in a London, England, street to play the Beach Boys' "Sloop John B" at the London Ukulele Festival in 2009.

cozy car Twenty grandmothers from Switzerland spent two months knitting nearly 70 lb (32 kg) of wool into a warm covering for a Smart car. The woolen car cover depicts a lace-up training shoe but exposes the car's wheels, giving it the appearance of a giant roller skate.

junk sculptures James Corbett of Ningi, Queensland, Australia, makes amazing sculptures out of old car parts that he picks up from junkyards. He's turned discarded spark plugs, exhaust pipes and radiators into such diverse artworks as a monkey, a yacht, a downhill skier, a kangaroo and, appropriately, a heavy metal guitarist.

RUBBER BEASTS

Artist Ji Yong-Ho from Seoul, South Korea, makes animal sculptures from old tires. Using the flexibility of the rubber to imitate skin and muscles, he has created powerful lions, dogs, rhinos and this 10-ft-long (3-m) shark, each work taking three months to make and selling for up to $75,000. To vary the skin texture, he uses different kinds of tread. For example, the neck and forehead of his rhinoceros are made from broad-treaded tractor tires layered beneath a rough outer skin of motorcycle tires.

Curioser Creation

Los Angeles art group LA Pop Art wrote out every word from the first 11 chapters of Lewis Carroll's novel, *Alice In Wonderland*, to create an illustration from the story. From a distance it appears to be solid color, but almost every inch of the artwork is formed from Lewis Carroll's own words, written clearly in felt-tip pens. The text was written upside down so that the artist didn't smudge the ink.

painting with wheels Ian Cook of Birmingham, England, created an artwork of a racing car 33 x 16½ ft (10 x 5 m)—painted with the wheels of remote-control cars, go-karts, a racing car, a sports car, a motorbike and a six-ton truck. He took a huge canvas, applied paint and then drove across it, creating the image with the different sizes and patterns of the tires. He said painting with the truck was particularly challenging because the back wheels were twice as wide as the front ones so it was difficult to see what he was doing.

guitar windmills Mimicking The Who guitarist Pete Townshend's windmill actions, Spencer Borbon of San Francisco whirled his arm around 79 times in 30 seconds at the 2009 San Francisco Treasure Island Music Festival.

tracker bob Bob "Tracker Bob" Hiemenz of Flora, Illinois, has a collection of more than 60,000 eight-track audio tapes. Since acquiring his first tapes in 1985, he has spent about $7,000 on his passion, which covers everyone from Abba to ZZ Top.

Sore Jaw Ken Parsons sang karaoke for more than two days straight at a church in Moose Jaw, Saskatchewan, Canada, in 2010. He finally put down the microphone after singing popular songs for an incredible 55 hours 11 minutes 30 seconds.

bard boost Performing William Shakespeare plays to cows can help boost milk production. After the Changeling Theatre Company entertained Friesian cows at a farm in Kent, England, with *The Merry Wives of Windsor*, milk yields increased by 4 percent.

finger portraits U.K.-based artist Kyle Lambert creates amazingly lifelike portraits of celebrities, including Jennifer Aniston and Beyoncé, using his fingers on an iPad.

sand sculpture A group of 30 artists took 75 days to create a 73-ft-tall (22-m) sand sculpture at the Zhoushan Sand Sculpture Festival in China. The sculpture depicted a Nigerian story of how a hummingbird managed to become king of all animals.

Tabletop Landscapes

New Jersey photographer and artist Matthew Albanese devises spectacular images of windswept tropical islands, tornadoes and volcanoes by building models from everyday items.

The azure sea in his tabletop D.I.Y. Paradise is actually melted sugar and tin foil, and the island is made from salt. He carefully arranged cotton wool over the scene to create clouds, and even the palm trees are not as they seem—the leaves are formed from feathers.

Matthew has also made convincing icebergs from sugar and waterfalls from salt, and re-created the surface of Mars with paprika, cinnamon, nutmeg and chili powder. His tornados are made from steel wool and he has created an impressive Aurora Borealis using a shower curtain, a corkboard and strobe lighting. His photographs of these homemade natural phenomena sell for over $900 each.

ticket tower British artist Robert Bradford created scale models of three U.K. landmarks—St. Paul's Cathedral, Edinburgh Castle and Blackpool Tower—from a total of 115,000 used train tickets.

moon scent Printers in Edinburgh, Scotland, have created a scratch 'n' sniff artwork that smells like the Moon. They developed it by talking to former NASA astronaut Charlie Duke, who was a member of the *Apollo 16* mission in 1972, and who described the Moon's surface as smelling like spent gunpowder.

victory at last Using an original wooden beam from the H.M.S. *Victory*, sculptor Ian Brennan from Hampshire, England, spent 17 years carving a 47-in-long (1.2-m) model of Admiral Horatio Nelson's 18th-century flagship. The model, accurate to the last detail, contains 200 ft (60 m) of rope, 104 miniature guns and 37 sails.

cow maze In a field near Berlin, Germany, workers cut corn and hemp into the shape of a giant cow. The maze depicted the bovine digestive system and was designed by the country's Federal Institute of Risk Assessment to promote healthy eating habits.

screw mosaic Saimir Strati spent two weeks creating a mosaic of a U.S. banknote 8 ft (2.4 m) high and 16 ft 1 in (4.9 m) long from 300,000 industrial screws. The giant bill features a portrait of the ancient Greek poet Homer in the center.

natural sculptures Peter Riedel, an artist and photographer from Toronto, Canada, spent five hours creating 42 temporary outdoor sculptures in the city's Humber River by balancing rocks and boulders on top of each other. He never uses glue in his works but arranges the rocks so that they don't fall.

still famous In the year following his death on June 25, 2009, Michael Jackson's estate earned one billion dollars.

same shot Except for the duration of World War II, Ria van Dijk had a photograph taken of herself at the same shooting gallery in Tilburg, the Netherlands, every year for 74 years. The first picture was taken in 1936 when she was 16.

poem boxing Japan hosts the National Poem Boxing Championships where contestants fight it out with words in three-minute rounds. The poets step into a boxing ring and read out verses on a wide range of subjects, hoping to secure a win. In the final round, the last two combatants still standing must improvise a poem incorporating a random word the judges tell them to use.

tiny bookw Hassan Abed Rabbo of Beirut, Lebanon, owns a handwritten, unabridged version of the Islamic holy book, the Quran, which is so tiny it can rest on the tip of his finger. The book, which dates back hundreds of years, contains 604 pages adorned in gold ink and measures just 0.95 x 0.75 in (2.4 x 1.9 cm).

young picasso A distinctive painting style of bold colors and disjointed Cubist forms led to ten-year-old Hamad Al Humaidhan from Bath, Somerset, England, being hailed as a young Picasso—even though he had never seen any of the Spanish master's work. The Kuwaiti-born youngster began painting at age seven, his first six pieces selling for $1,000 each. He closes his eyes, sees an image in his head and then transfers it to the canvas.

ardent fan Over a period of nearly 20 years, Ann Petty of Wiltshire, England, has traveled more than 60,000 mi (100,000 km) to see Irish singer Daniel O'Donnell perform—including trips to the U.S.A., New Zealand and Australia.

log pile Logger Ron Fahey began removing a stack of logs from the grounds of Mount Allison University, Sackville, Canada, only to be stopped by an official who told him he was dismantling a work of art. The woodpile sculpture, called *Deadwood Sleep* by Paul Griffin, had been in the grounds for three years.

one-armed d.j. In Johannesburg, South Africa, in 2010, dance D.J. Nkosinathi Maphumulo, who lost his left hand in an accident at age 13, spun records for 60 hours straight with just a short comfort break every four hours.

clogged streets More than 2,500 people gathered in Pella, Iowa, on May 8, 2010, to dance together in wooden shoes.

phone-book furniture Daniel Tosches of Pasco, Florida, creates furniture and sculptures from pages of the phone book.

APPLE KILLER

Together with photographer Paul Fairchild, San Francisco artist Michael Tompert staged an exhibition of butchered and mangled Apple products. Tompert has shot, burned, hammered and sawed his way through a range of merchandise and even ran over seven iPods with a diesel locomotive. His greatest challenge was an iPad, which survived a series of blows from a sledgehammer, before finally exploding after its insides were heated with a soldering torch. He says he's trying to make people think about their relationship with these highly popular items.

chocolate train In October 2010, London, England, food artist Carl Warner unveiled the *Chocolate Express*, a 6-ft (1.8-m) train sculpture made from chocolate, and running on chocolate tracks. It took ten days to build and also incorporated chocolate rolls, Wagon Wheels, Crunchie bars and Dime bars.

lord of the sticks Patrick Acton of Gladbrook, Iowa, spent three years building a replica of the *Lord of the Rings* city Minas Tirith from 420,000 matchsticks.

photographic memories Munish Bansal of Kent, England, has taken pictures of his children every day for 13 years. He has filled more than 600 albums with over 8,500 digital images of his daughter Suman, 12, and her 10-year-old brother, Jay, since the day they were born.

part art Artist Franco Recchia from Florence, Italy, constructs models of cityscapes from the discarded parts of old computers. He uses circuit boards, casings, processing chips and other computer components as his building blocks.

golden monopoly San Francisco jewelry designer Sidney Mobell has created a Monopoly set made with solid gold and jewels. The dice are encrusted with diamonds and these alone cost $10,000.

girl gucci At just ten years old, Cecilia Cassini of Encino, California, was already an accomplished fashion designer. After receiving a sewing machine for her sixth birthday, she has gone on to design children's clothes, and a number of celebrities have bought her designs for their kids.

toast portrait Laura Hadland from Leicester, England, created a portrait of her mother-in-law, Sandra Whitfield, from 9,852 slices of toast. Laura and 40 friends used nine toasters to brown the slices from 600 loaves of bread to varying degrees before arranging them to make a lifelike mosaic measuring 32 ft 8 in x 42 ft 3 in (10 x 13 m).

intrepid builder Using 250,000 pieces of LEGO®, Ed Diment took nine months to build a 22-ft-long (6.7-m) replica of the World-War-II aircraft carrier U.S.S. *Intrepid* in the conservatory of his home in Portsmouth, England. The finished model weighed more than 500 lb (227 kg).

porcelain seeds In 2010, London's Tate Modern gallery staged a work called *Sunflower Seeds* by Chinese artist Ai Weiwei. The piece consisted of more than 100 million individually handmade porcelain replicas of seeds.

party pooper With the help of local schoolchildren from Sichuan Province, China, sculptor Zhu Cheng made a replica of the famous *Venus de Milo* statue—from panda dung. The poop statue later sold for $45,000.

Plastic Fantastic

Sayaka Ganz creates amazing wildlife sculptures from items of discarded plastic found in garbage cans, charity shops or donated by friends—and her finished works sell for more than $12,000.

Sayaka, who was born in Japan but now lives in Fort Wayne, Indiana, has made models of a dog, an eagle, a horse, a cheetah and a fish, varying in length from 18 in (45 cm) to 8 ft (2.4 m) and incorporating plastic sunglasses, cutlery, baskets and cooking utensils. The biggest sculptures contain up to 500 pieces of junk and take nine months to make. She sorts all her plastic into 20 color groups in her basement and then ties the chosen items onto a wire frame to create each sculpture. Sayaka studies photographs showing her animal subjects from different angles so that she can perfect the lines of motion. She says, "I get great satisfaction from fitting these objects together to create a beautiful form that seems alive."

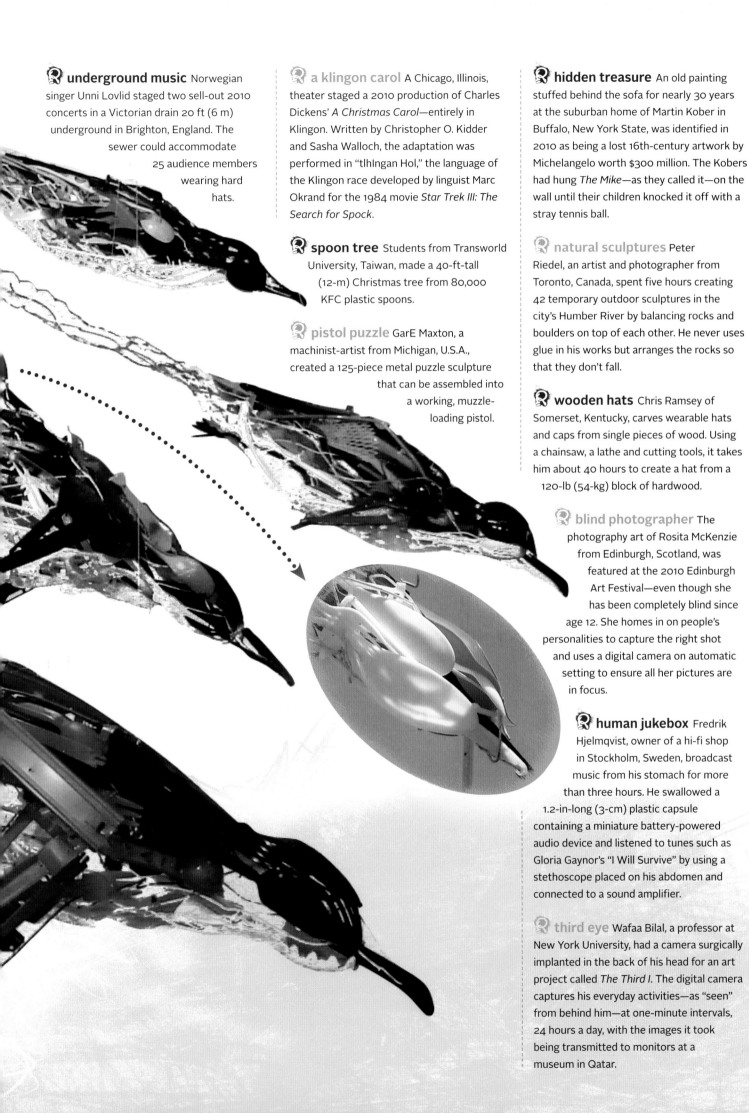

underground music Norwegian singer Unni Lovlid staged two sell-out 2010 concerts in a Victorian drain 20 ft (6 m) underground in Brighton, England. The sewer could accommodate 25 audience members wearing hard hats.

a klingon carol A Chicago, Illinois, theater staged a 2010 production of Charles Dickens' *A Christmas Carol*—entirely in Klingon. Written by Christopher O. Kidder and Sasha Walloch, the adaptation was performed in "tlhIngan Hol," the language of the Klingon race developed by linguist Marc Okrand for the 1984 movie *Star Trek III: The Search for Spock*.

spoon tree Students from Transworld University, Taiwan, made a 40-ft-tall (12-m) Christmas tree from 80,000 KFC plastic spoons.

pistol puzzle GarE Maxton, a machinist-artist from Michigan, U.S.A., created a 125-piece metal puzzle sculpture that can be assembled into a working, muzzle-loading pistol.

hidden treasure An old painting stuffed behind the sofa for nearly 30 years at the suburban home of Martin Kober in Buffalo, New York State, was identified in 2010 as being a lost 16th-century artwork by Michelangelo worth $300 million. The Kobers had hung *The Mike*—as they called it—on the wall until their children knocked it off with a stray tennis ball.

natural sculptures Peter Riedel, an artist and photographer from Toronto, Canada, spent five hours creating 42 temporary outdoor sculptures in the city's Humber River by balancing rocks and boulders on top of each other. He never uses glue in his works but arranges the rocks so that they don't fall.

wooden hats Chris Ramsey of Somerset, Kentucky, carves wearable hats and caps from single pieces of wood. Using a chainsaw, a lathe and cutting tools, it takes him about 40 hours to create a hat from a 120-lb (54-kg) block of hardwood.

blind photographer The photography art of Rosita McKenzie from Edinburgh, Scotland, was featured at the 2010 Edinburgh Art Festival—even though she has been completely blind since age 12. She homes in on people's personalities to capture the right shot and uses a digital camera on automatic setting to ensure all her pictures are in focus.

human jukebox Fredrik Hjelmqvist, owner of a hi-fi shop in Stockholm, Sweden, broadcast music from his stomach for more than three hours. He swallowed a 1.2-in-long (3-cm) plastic capsule containing a miniature battery-powered audio device and listened to tunes such as Gloria Gaynor's "I Will Survive" by using a stethoscope placed on his abdomen and connected to a sound amplifier.

third eye Wafaa Bilal, a professor at New York University, had a camera surgically implanted in the back of his head for an art project called *The Third I*. The digital camera captures his everyday activities—as "seen" from behind him—at one-minute intervals, 24 hours a day, with the images it took being transmitted to monitors at a museum in Qatar.

MAN-MADE MONSTERS

Using only manmade materials, Californian artist Doug Higley makes monsters for showmen to display at flea markets and fairs across the world. He has created fake mummified and petrified creatures, bogus mermaids, shrunken heads, chupacabras, freaky jungle pygmies and atomic death worms. His work has been exhibited in 34 countries and one of his mermaids appeared at Buckingham Palace, London. He also once created 42 mermaids for a car-dealer promotion in the U.S.A. and Canada, whereby potential customers were invited to see the "strange creature" found in the trunk of a trade-in vehicle and take a test drive. The gimmick sold thousands of cars!

Water Dog Mermaid

Chupacabra

🄡 **tentacle terror** In 2008, artists Filthy Luker and Pedro Estrellas positioned huge inflatable green octopus tentacles through the windows of an unnamed building in France.

🄡 **wooden chain** Markley Noel of Hickory Corners, Michigan, carved a 480-ft-long (146-m) wooden chain from a single 25-ft-long (7.6-m) maple plank. The chain, which has 1,993 links, each 4 in (10 cm) long, took him seven years to make.

🄡 **small portions** Using acrylic paints and a magnifying glass, French artist Stephanie Kilgast creates miniature clay models of food in 1:12 scale. She painstakingly molds the clay with scalpels, blades, art knives and toothpicks, and has made more than 600 cakes, pastries, fruit and full meals, including a full English breakfast with baked beans, bacon, sausages and fried eggs.

🄡 **phone dress** A London fashion company has introduced the M-Dress, a little black dress that also serves as a mobile phone. The dress, which has a tiny antenna in its hem, allows wearers to make and receive calls by putting their SIM card under the label. To take a call, they raise their hand to their ear; to end it they let it fall to their side.

🄡 **ancient shoe** Archeologists in Armenia have found a leather shoe more than 5,500 years old. The shoe, which was stuffed with grass, was discovered in a mountain cave where it had been kept in excellent condition thanks to a thick layer of sheep excrement, which acted as a protective seal.

🄡 **corn maze** Bob Connors cut images of Stewie and Brian, two of the characters from the animated TV comedy *Family Guy*, into a seven-acre cornfield maze at his farm in Danvers, Massachusetts.

🄡 **fashion ferrari** A full-size replica of a Ferrari Formula-1 car was made out of $60,000 worth of designer clothing. Eight people worked for five hours at a store in London's Carnaby Street to turn 1,999 items of clothing—including 1,682 red T-shirts, 88 pairs of jeans, 64 pairs of shoes and 31 belts—into a 14-ft-long (4.3-m) model car. The wheels were made from water bottles, the wing mirror from sunglasses and the tires from black jeans.

Deep Drawings

Chilean artist Fredo creates mind-boggling 3-D pencil drawings that appear to rise out of the page. Despite its 3-D appearance, all his work is pencil on flat paper. At only 17 years old, Fredo is already exhibiting his work in Chile.

strand of beads In October 2009, the city of Providence, Rhode Island, created a strand of red-and-white beads that measured 1,349 ft (411 m) long!

late returns In 2009, a former student at Camelback High School, Phoenix, Arizona, returned two library books that had been checked out half a century earlier, and enclosed a $1,000 money order for the fines. The books had been taken out in 1959, but the borrower's family moved to another state and the books were mistakenly packed away.

toothpick city Scott Weaver of Rohnert Park, California, spent thousands of hours during a 34-year period building a toothpick model of every major landmark in San Francisco, using a total of over 100,000 toothpicks. The construction, titled "Rolling Through the Bay," stands 9 ft (2.7 m) tall, 7 ft (2.1 m) wide and 2 ft (60 cm) deep. It has survived four house relocations, an earthquake, and Trooper—one of Weaver's four Great Danes—who once obliterated Fisherman's Wharf and about 100 hours' work with a careless wag of his tail.

human hoover Artist Paul Hazelton of Kent, England, has made a model of a complete bedroom—including a TV, armchairs and a wardrobe—out of dust! Known as the "Human Hoover," he collects dust from furniture, pictures and window sills, and then transforms the bunches of tiny particles into 3-D sculptures by wetting, shaping and drying them. Some of his dust models—which also include a briefcase, a moth and a humanoid—are 20 in (50 cm) high.

hot lips Makeup artist Rick DiCecca applied lipstick to over 300 women in one hour at Macy's Department Store, Chicago, Illinois.

lego ship For nearly a week, 3,500 children used 513,000 LEGO® bricks to build a 25-ft-long (7.6-m) model of a container ship in Wilhelmshaven, Germany.

DISK PORTRAITS

British artist Nick Gentry uses old 3.5-in computer floppy disks as a canvas for his imaginative portraits. The features of each face are mapped into a grid, with each section the size of one disk. The disks are then arranged to create a collage before the outline of the head is partly drawn and painted over it. He sometimes also incorporates obsolete cassettes and V.C.R. tapes into his facial images.

monster mona A giant version of the *Mona Lisa* went on display in a shopping mall in Wrexham, Wales, in 2009—50 times bigger than Leonardo da Vinci's 16th-century original. It covered 2,600 sq ft (240 sq m) and was big enough to fit 22 buses inside. A total of 245 people worked on the project under artist Katy Webster, and it took 987 hours to create, using 23 gal (86 l) of paint.

wicker men In Cluj, Romania, a team of 16 craftsmen created a huge wicker basket that was large enough to hold one million loaves of homemade bread. It took nine days to make and measured 59 x 33 ft (18 x 10 m), and was 31 ft (9.5 m) tall.

celebrity pumpkins Gardener David Finkle carves impressive portraits of famous people—including Barack Obama, Michael Jackson and Simon Cowell—out of pumpkins that grow on his small farm at Chelmsford in Essex, England.

concert for dogs Australia's Sydney Opera House staged a concert for dogs in 2010. More than a thousand dogs turned up for the 20-minute Music For Dogs event, which was organized by U.S. musician Laurie Anderson and her rock-star husband Lou Reed. It featured a concerto of high-pitch whistles, whale calls, synthesizers and strings—some inaudible to human ears.

couscous city French-Algerian artist Kader Attia built a scale model of the ancient city of Ghardaia, Algeria, entirely out of cooked couscous.

dental display To entertain and relax his patients, dentist Ian Davis from London, England, has created a series of sculptures featuring miniature men scrubbing, cleaning and repairing teeth. The men can be seen digging out fillings with tiny pickaxes and polishing and scaling teeth with the help of scaffolding—and all the teeth he uses are taken from the casts of real patients' mouths.

dollar mosaics A Latvian artist creates mosaics made entirely out of U.S. dollar bills. Irina Truhanova sketches an outline of her subject before filling it in with snippets of the bills. Her creations include the Statue of Liberty, a Bentley car and Russian Prime Minister Vladimir Putin.

urban dancers As part of its 2009 "Bodies in Urban Spaces" project, Dance Umbrella, choreographed by Willi Dorner, placed its performers in unlikely locations around the center of London, England. Passersby stumbled across dancers squeezed between pillars, wrapped around lampposts, folded into a bicycle rack and clinging to a wall like Spider-Man.

typewriter art Cerebral-palsy sufferer Paul Smith (1921–2007) of Roseburg, Oregon, became a world-famous artist by creating masterpieces using manual typewriters. He achieved his amazing images by pressing the symbols at the tops of the number keys, and as his mastery of the typewriter grew, he developed techniques to create shadings, colors and textures that made his work resemble pencil or charcoal drawings. Over the years, he created hundreds of artworks—each one taking him up to three months—including landscapes, animals and portraits.

underwater gallery Diving enthusiasts in Lithuania have opened the country's first underwater picture gallery. Twenty large-format photographs by local artists were put on display beneath the surface of Lake Plateliai, and the organizers hope to expand the project to include sculptures, stained glass and watercolor paintings. The idea originated after a couple from a diving club put their wedding picture underwater so that they could enjoy it every time they dived.

roadkill hats Fashion designer James Faulkner of Edinburgh, Scotland, has created a range of hats from roadkill. Inspired by the idea of using a dead magpie he found by the roadside to complement a friend's black-and-white dress, he has developed a range of 36 animal hats, using the wings, feathers and fur of squashed pigeons, rabbits, foxes, pheasants and crows.

27-hour concert Gonzales, a Canadian musician, played a 27-hour concert in Paris, France, in 2009. His 300-song set ranged from Britney Spears to Beethoven.

ant invasion Dutch artist Henk Hofstra painted some 500 giant red ants over the town of Drachten for his work "Invasion of the Ants." The ants—each 10 x 6½ ft (3 x 2 m) were created over three nights in May 2010 and were placed so that they appeared to be invading the De Lawei Theater, which was celebrating its 50th anniversary.

THE CANDY MAN
Mexico City artist Cristiam Ramos makes amazing candy portraits of celebrities. Instead of paint, he uses Gummi Bears, licorice, M&M's® and after-dinner mints as his artistic materials. His works include likenesses of Elvis and Michael Jackson from hundreds of M&M's®, and a portrait of Lady Gaga from gumdrops, M&M's® and yellow licorice.

Mini Me

Indonesian photographer Ari Mahardika has "cloned" himself dozens of times for a series of intricate montages. Using a self-timer to take photos of himself in different poses against a white background, he then shrinks the portraits into mini-me characters, positioning them so that it looks as though he is interacting with himself.

lost movie A lost Charlie Chaplin film valued at $60,000 was bought on eBay for $5.68 by a British collector in 2009. Morace Park of Essex, England, purchased the battered olive green film canister listed as "an old film" and was amazed to discover that the movie in question was *Zepped*, a 1916 Chaplin propaganda film poking fun at the zeppelin, the German instrument of terror during World War I. As recently as 2006, a movie expert stated that the seven-minute movie had almost certainly been lost forever.

junior drummer At just three years of age, Howard Wong's rock drumming has attracted nearly ten million hits on YouTube even though he can barely see over the top of his drum kit. Howard from Penang, Malaysia, first started playing at the age of 18 months and now performs regularly with his father's band.

bean mosaic A candy shop in Brighton, England, displayed a colorful mosaic of Queen Elizabeth II made from 10,000 jelly beans.

first exhibition When Leo Haines was born with cerebral palsy and a terminal condition affecting his lungs and heart, he was given only six months to live. However, in 2010 the five-year-old from Somerset, England, stunned doctors by opening his first art exhibition. He began painting alongside his grandmother and has since completed more than 40 works, which are said to be reminiscent of famous U.S. abstract artist Jackson Pollock.

feats

mysteries

food

arts

science

beyond belief

believe it!

world

animals

sports

body

transport

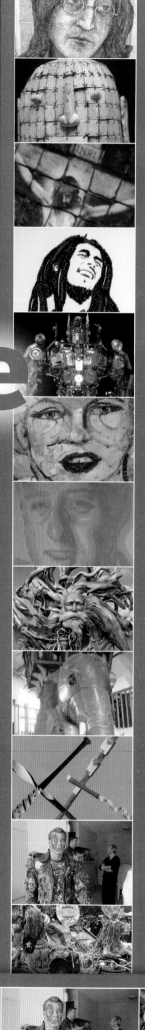

215
216
217
218
219
220
221
222
223
224
225
226
227
228
229
230
231
232
233
234
235
236
237
238
239
240
241
242

Life-size Transformers

Two 8-ft-tall (2.4-m) "Transformer" robot sculptures now stand in Ripley's museums in Orlando, Florida, and San Antonio, Texas. The heavy metal sculptures—each one weighing more than a ton—were built entirely from discarded car and bike parts in Bangkok, Thailand.

Ripley's
EXHIBITS

science

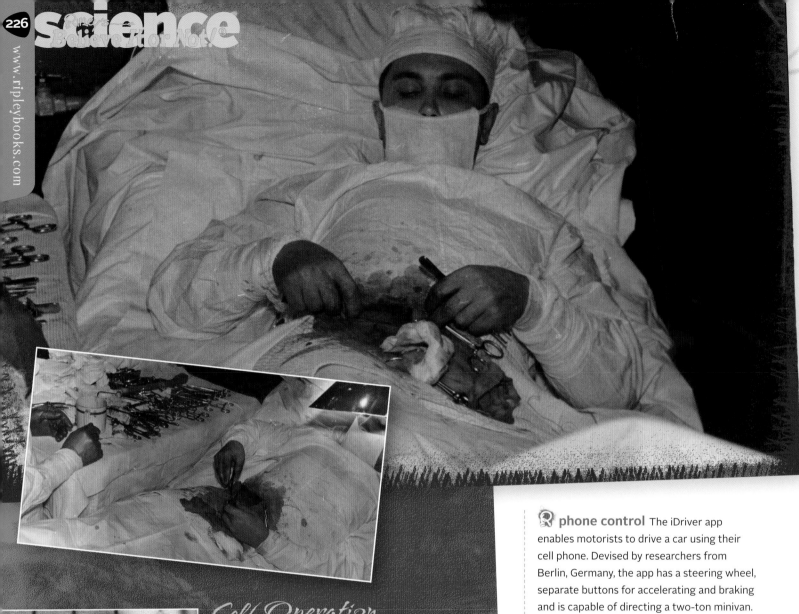

Self Operation

While on a 1961 expedition in the frozen Antarctic, 27-year-old Soviet doctor Leonid Rogozov saved his own life by performing an operation on himself to remove his dangerously inflamed appendix.

Suffering from fever and a pain in his right lower belly, he quickly diagnosed appendicitis. However, he knew that no aid plane would be able to cope with the blizzards or reach such a remote spot in time to evacuate him, so, as the only doctor at the station, he set about conducting an auto-appendectomy on the night of April 30. He was assisted by an engineer and the station's meteorologist, who handed him the medical instruments and held a small mirror at his belly to help him see what he was doing.

After administering a local anesthetic of novocaine solution, Rogozov made a 4¾-in (12-cm) incision in his lower abdomen with a scalpel. Working without gloves and guiding himself mainly by touch from a semi-reclining position, he proceeded to remove the appendix before injecting antibiotic into the abdominal cavity and closing the wound. The self-operation took 1 hour 45 minutes, and saved his life. If he had left it another day his appendix would have burst. His stitches were taken out a week later and he made a complete recovery.

phone control The iDriver app enables motorists to drive a car using their cell phone. Devised by researchers from Berlin, Germany, the app has a steering wheel, separate buttons for accelerating and braking and is capable of directing a two-ton minivan.

first computer Unveiled in 1946 at the University of Pennsylvania, ENIAC (short for Electronic Numerical Integrator and Computer) was the world's first general-purpose computer. It weighed 30 tons and occupied an entire room. Yet its computing ability can be re-created today on a silicon chip smaller than your thumbnail.

anti-flu suit A Japanese menswear company has developed a suit that it claims protects the wearer from the deadly H1N1 strain of influenza. The $550 suit, produced by the Haruyama Trading Company, is coated with the chemical titanium dioxide—an ingredient of toothpaste and cosmetics—that reacts to light to break down and kill the virus on contact.

oh, crumbs! The Swiss-based Large Hadron Collider, the world's most powerful particle accelerator and probably the most complex machine ever built, was shut down in 2009 after a bird passing overhead dropped a piece of bread on a section of machinery, causing parts of the accelerator to overheat.

skiing robot A skiing robot that can navigate slalom courses has been developed by researchers at the Jozef Stefan Institute in Slovenia. The robot, which is about the size of an eight-year-old child and uses regular skis, has a pair of computer systems. One of them is attached to cameras to help plot the robot's course down the slope, the other is attached to gyroscopes and force sensors to keep it stable.

beige world After examining the amounts of light emitted by galaxies, scientists at NASA have concluded that the Universe is not really black at all—more a dull beige. They say that the shade is constantly changing and has become much less blue over the past ten billion years because redder stars are now more dominant.

large dish The Large Zenith Telescope at the University of British Columbia in Canada uses a mirror made from a spinning dish of liquid mercury nearly 20 ft (6.1 m) in diameter.

bell tribute On August 4, 1922—the day of the funeral of Alexander Graham Bell—all telephone services in the U.S.A. and Canada were shut down for one minute as a tribute to the inventor, who, in the 1870s, had invented the first workable telephone.

plasma knife To help stem the loss of blood from serious wounds, the U.S. military has been testing a plasma knife, with a blade consisting of heated, ionized gas, which can cut through flesh just as easily as a steel scalpel. The plasma knife seals off the damaged flesh, stopping the bleeding and protecting against infection.

stone-age surgery When archeologists in France unearthed the 7,000-year-old skeleton of a man, they were amazed to see that he had an amputated arm. The Stone Age surgery was probably performed using a sharpened flint stone, with painkilling plants acting as an anesthetic and an antiseptic herb such as sage being used to clean the wound.

rotten eggs As part of a safety campaign in 2010, Puget Sound Energy, a utility company in Washington State, added the stench of rotten eggs to its gas bills. Natural gas is odorless, but providers add a chemical with a sulfurlike aroma to the gas so that leaks can be detected.

BODY ART

Hong Kong radiologist Kai-Hung Fung has created stunning images of the human body that look like works of art. Dr. Fung scans the patient using a conventional computer topography (CT) scan, generally used for diagnosing brain and cardiac problems, before feeding the information into a computer and adding vivid color.

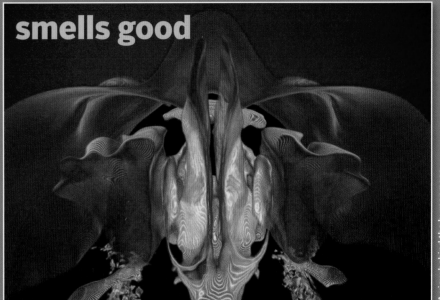

smells good

A view behind the human nose

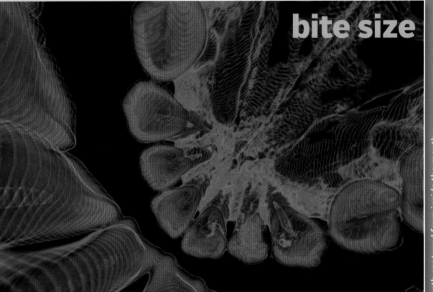

bite size

Teeth captured from inside the mouth

say what?

Curves inside an ear

bullet blocker Colombian tailor Miguel Caballero runs a boutique in Mexico City where jackets and shirts are not stacked by size but by how well they will stop a bullet. He uses secret materials, the most expensive of which, called Black, is so light that it can be scrunched up like paper but will protect the wearer from a bullet fired at point-blank range.

speed of sound Sound travels 4.3 times faster in water than it does in air. When something vibrates, it causes molecules to bump into each other. As water molecules are closer together, the vibrations transfer faster between themselves.

frozen with heat Water can be frozen solid—by applying heat! Supercooled water, which can stay liquid down to –40°F (–40°C), will freeze as it is being heated, as long as the temperature also changes the electrical charge of the surface with which the water is in contact.

black hole Scientists at the Southeast University in Nanjing, China, have created a pocket-size black hole—an 8½-in-wide (21.5-cm) disk that absorbs all the electromagnetic radiation thrown at it. The metal disk has 60 concentric rings that affect the magnetic properties of passing light, bending the beams into the center of the disk and trapping them in a maze of etched grooves.

shrinking coins A powerful electromagnetic field can shrink a coin to half its diameter. The technique is known as high-velocity metal forming, a process which creates an invisible, pulsed magnetic field that batters the coin with a strong shock wave, forcing it to change its physical shape in the blink of an eye.

robot olympics At the 2010 International Robot Olympics held in Harbin, China, humanoid robots from 19 countries competed in 17 disciplines, including running, walking, boxing, kung fu and dancing. All robots had to be less than 2 ft (60 cm) tall and be built in human form with a head, two arms and two legs. The opening event, the 5-m (5-yd) sprint, was won in a time of 20 seconds.

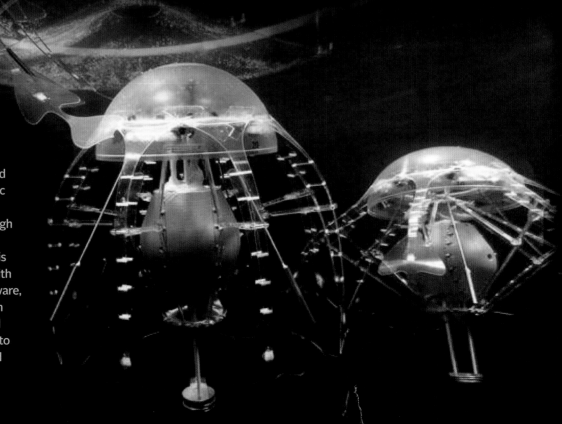

ROBOTIC JELLYFISH

Scientists in Germany have developed a range of biologically inspired robotic jellyfish that can swim. The battery-powered jellyfish are propelled through the water by eight electrically driven tentacles, the construction of which is based on the anatomy of fish fins. With the help of sensors and control software, the jellyfish steer themselves and can communicate by means of 11 infrared light-emitting diodes, enabling them to work together as a team and to avoid bumping into each other.

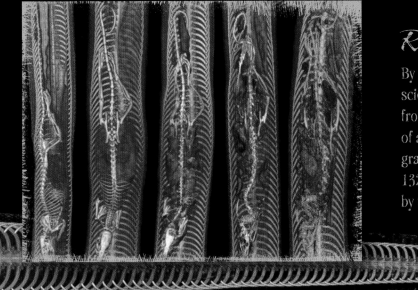

Rat Supper

By using a special scanning technique, scientists Henrik Lauridsen and Kasper Hansen from Aarhus, Denmark, were able to take X-rays of a python digesting a rat. The rat can be seen gradually disappearing during the course of 132 hours—5½ days—after being swallowed by the snake.

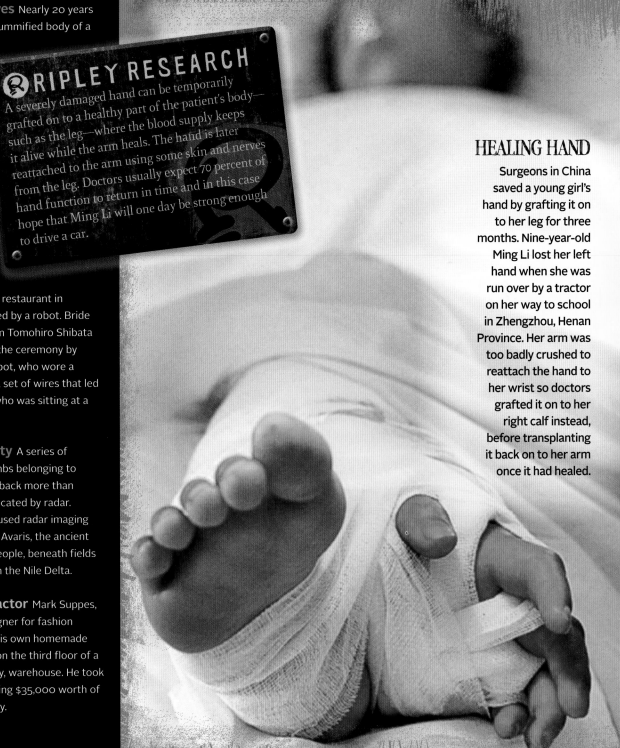

iceman's relatives Nearly 20 years after discovering the mummified body of a 5,300-year-old man—known as Oetzi the iceman—in a melting Alpine glacier, scientists have extracted DNA from a bone in his pelvis with a view to tracking down his living descendants.

robot wedding A wedding that took place in a Tokyo, Japan, restaurant in May 2010 was conducted by a robot. Bride Satoko Inoue and groom Tomohiro Shibata were directed through the ceremony by I-Fairy, a 4-ft (1.2-m) robot, who wore a wreath of flowers and a set of wires that led to a human controller who was sitting at a nearby computer.

underground city A series of streets, houses and tombs belonging to an Egyptian city dating back more than 3,500 years has been located by radar. Austrian archeologists used radar imaging to show the outlines of Avaris, the ancient capital of the Hyksos people, beneath fields and modern buildings in the Nile Delta.

homemade reactor Mark Suppes, a 32-year-old web designer for fashion house Gucci, has built his own homemade nuclear fusion reactor on the third floor of a Brooklyn, New York City, warehouse. He took two years to build it, using $35,000 worth of parts he bought on eBay.

RIPLEY RESEARCH

A severely damaged hand can be temporarily grafted on to a healthy part of the patient's body—such as the leg—where the blood supply keeps it alive while the arm heals. The hand is later reattached to the arm using some skin and nerves from the leg. Doctors usually expect 70 percent of hand function to return in time and in this case hope that Ming Li will one day be strong enough to drive a car.

HEALING HAND

Surgeons in China saved a young girl's hand by grafting it on to her leg for three months. Nine-year-old Ming Li lost her left hand when she was run over by a tractor on her way to school in Zhengzhou, Henan Province. Her arm was too badly crushed to reattach the hand to her wrist so doctors grafted it on to her right calf instead, before transplanting it back on to her arm once it had healed.

toy parts Dr. William H. Sewell invented an artificial heart pump prototype with parts from an Erector set toy while at Yale Medical School.

strad beaten In a sound test conducted in Germany before an audience of 180 people, a violin made of wood that had been treated with fungus for nine months was judged better than a $2-million 1711 Stradivarius. Scientists say a fungal attack changes the cell structure of the wood, giving it a warmer, more rounded sound.

lost army Twin brothers Angelo and Alfredo Castiglioni believe they have found the remains of a 50,000-strong Persian army, said to have been drowned in the sands of the Sahara Desert 2,500 years ago. The Italian archeologists have discovered bronze weapons, a silver bracelet, an earring and hundreds of human bones that are thought to have belonged to the lost army of Persian King Cambyses II, whose men were reportedly buried in a terrible sandstorm in 525 BC.

INVISIBLE MAN

Scientists at Tokyo University have developed camouflage technology that makes people disappear. A coat made of a high-tech reflective material has a video camera placed in it, which sends film to a projector. This, in turn, bounces the moving image off the front of the coat, making the wearer appear transparent, even when the fabric is creased.

stench busters The city of Beijing, China, has installed 100 high-pressure deodorant guns, which can spray dozens of liters of fragrance per minute, to combat the stench from one of the city's many overflowing landfill sites. Beijing's 17 million people generate nearly 20,000 tons of waste every day—7,700 tons more than the capacity of municipal disposal plants.

magnetic lift Scientists have successfully levitated fruit, insects, frogs and mice by applying a repelling effect on the water molecules in their bodies with powerful magnets.

quake-proof bed Wang Wenxi from Shijiazhuang, China, has invented an earthquake-proof bed. When an earthquake strikes, a strong board automatically slides into place, protecting the person from falling debris. His secure bed has cupboards at both ends with water, canned food, a hammer and a megaphone to help the occupant survive for several days beneath rubble.

solar slug *Elysia chlorotica*, a green sea slug that lives along the Atlantic seaboard of the U.S.A., runs on solar power. Scientists at the University of Maine have discovered that it photosynthesizes using genes "stolen" from the algae it eats.

MAGIC GEL

"Aerogel" was created in 1931 by U.S. scientist Samuel Stephens Kistler following a bet with a colleague over who could replace the liquid in gel with a gas without causing shrinkage. Even though it is 99.8 percent air, the unique substance aerogel can withstand temperatures of up to 2,550°F (1,400°C) and is strong enough to support 2,000 times its own weight.

® RIPLEY RESEARCH

Aerogel is derived from a silica gel, the liquid component of which is replaced with a gas to create an extremely low-density solid. It is 1,000 times less dense than glass, making it very lightweight. It has been used by NASA for thermal insulation of space suits and on the Mars Rover vehicle on its Stardust Mission to trap space dust. Whereas cosmic dust vaporizes on impact with solids and passes through gas, the nature of aerogel allows it to trap particles traveling at 1,350 mph (2,170 km/h) without damaging them.

Solar Detector

The Super-Kamiokande Detector is a gigantic cylindrical stainless steel tank, measuring 136 ft (41 m) high and 129 ft (39 m) in diameter, located more than half a mile underground in Japan. Holding 50,000 tons of water, it is lined with 11,146 ultra-sensitive light detectors and serves as a scientific observatory to monitor solar neutrinos—particles that are produced in the Sun by nuclear fusion. This will help us understand what goes on inside the Sun and how matter was created in the early Universe. The Detector is located underground to shield the experiments from cosmic rays and background radiation.

mysteries

food

arts

science

beyond belief

believe it!

world

animals

sports

body

transport

feats

225
226
227
228
229
230
231
232
233
234
235
236
237
238
239
240
241
242
243
244
245
246
247
248
249
250
251
252

Marilyn with wings

Mexican artist Enrique Ramos created this portrait of Hollywood icon Marilyn Monroe from hundreds of rainforest butterflies. Enrique has also created an image of United States' President John F. Kennedy in the same way. Both insect portraits are on display at the Ripley's Believe It or Not! museum in London, England.

Ripley's
EXHIBITS

Shocking Stories

ELEPHANT ELECTROCUTION

In an attempt to prove the dangers of Nikola Tesla's alternating current (AC) and the safety of his competing direct current (DC) for use in the home, Thomas Edison electrocuted an elephant in 1903. Topsy was an elephant with Forepaugh Circus at Coney Island's Luna Park, New York City, who had killed three men in three years, and her owners wanted her destroyed. Edison suggested electrocution, a method that had been used for human executions since 1890. Topsy was fed carrots containing potassium cyanide before a current of 6,600 volts was sent through her body, killing her in seconds. A crowd of 1,500 witnessed the event, which Edison also filmed.

MARY, THE HANGED ELEPHANT

Mary was a 5-ton Asian elephant who was hanged for her so-called crimes on September 12, 1916. Her story is a cautionary tale of circus abuse during the early 20th century. She had been prodded behind the ear by her trainer as she bent down to nibble on watermelon rind, so she grabbed him with her trunk and stamped on his head, killing him. Labeled a highly dangerous beast, the public demanded her death. She survived being shot with two dozen rounds, so it was decided to hang her. Mary was hanged by the neck the next day from an industrial crane in Erwin, Tennessee.

phone home A man has spent two years living in a cramped phone booth in Dalian City, Liaoning Province, China. He sleeps by curling up into a ball on top of cushions and hangs his spare clothes from the roof.

elephant collision Driving home from church in Enid, Oklahoma, a couple collided with an elephant that ran across the highway after escaping from a nearby circus. The elephant was unharmed apart from a broken tusk.

quiet companion Alan Derrick of Somerset, England, lived in a house with his friend's dead body hidden behind a sofa from 1998 to 2008.

paid piper Tourism bosses in Vienna, Austria, found a way to frighten off rats from the city's sewers—by playing the bagpipes. The Third Man tours, which walk the sewers made famous by Orson Welles' cult 1949 movie, were closed down when health chiefs ruled that the risk of rat bites was too great, but now they're back in business after hiring a bagpiper whose shrill sounds send the rodents running for cover.

dam coincidence J.G. Tierney drowned in 1922 while surveying the future site of the Hoover Dam. In 1935, his son Patrick became the last person to die in the dam's construction when he fell from an intake tower.

Ⓡ **political clown** A professional clown was elected to represent Sao Paulo in Congress after picking up 1.3 million votes in the 2010 Brazilian general elections. Tiririca (real name Francisco Oliveira) received the highest number of votes for any federal deputy across the country with his catchy TV slogans including: "What does a federal deputy do? I have no idea, but vote for me and I'll let you know."

Ⓡ **traffic calming** City transportation officials in Cambridge, Massachusetts, tried to calm drivers annoyed at receiving parking tickets by putting instructions on the reverse side about how to relax by bending the body into simple yoga positions.

Ⓡ **fast food** Perry Watkins of Buckinghamshire, England, has built a dining table that can travel at speeds of 130 mph (209 km/h). He took the chassis of a Reliant Scimitar sports car, fitted a 4-liter Land Rover Discovery engine boosted by nitrous oxide injection, and then added a table, six dining chairs and a fake meal. The driver sits under the roast chicken, the tax disc is stuck to a champagne bucket, the brake lights are built into rolled-up napkins and the exhaust fumes come out of two silver teapots.

Ⓡ **ambulance stolen** An Illinois man was arrested for stealing an ambulance in Mount Horeb, Wisconsin—with a patient and paramedics still inside it.

Ⓡ **bottleneck mystery** A 60-mi (96-km) traffic jam trapped thousands of vehicles on the Beijing–Tibet expressway for 11 days in August 2010—but then it completely disappeared overnight without any apparent explanation.

Ⓡ **lost letters** While on a 2010 field trip to the Alps, Freya Cowan, a geography student from the University of Dundee, Scotland, stumbled across a U.S.-bound mailbag from the *Malabar Princess*, an Air India plane that crashed near the summit of Mont Blanc while en route to London in 1950, killing all 40 passengers and eight crew on board. Some of the correspondence inside the mailbag was still in such good condition that she set about sending 75 letters and birthday cards on to their intended recipients 60 years late.

Ⓡ **super sub** Cyril Howarth from Lancashire, England, spent $75,000 on converting a 70-ft-long (21-m) canal narrow boat into a replica of a World-War-II German U-boat. Unlike other submarines, this vessel stays strictly on the surface.

Too Close for Comfort Two people found themselves in an unbelievable predicament after being thrown from their motorcycle in Hubei Province, China, in 2010. They flew headfirst into the mouth of a drainpipe just 1 ft 8 in (50 cm) wide and were stuck fast. Fortunately, passersby saw their feet protruding from the polluted water pipe and notified firefighters, who dug the couple free in just ten minutes.

blamed vampire A Fruita, Colorado, woman who drove her car into a canal in June 2010 blamed the accident on a vampire. She said she was driving on a dirt road late at night, when she spotted a vampire in the middle of the road and hastily put the car in reverse. When troopers arrived, they found the woman's car in the canal but there was no sign of the vampire.

upside down Wang Xiaoyu, a barber from Changsha, Hunan Province, China, gives haircuts while standing on his head. A trained martial artist, he performs his headstands on a table to achieve the right height for cutting customers' hair.

leisurely stroll Paul Railton was fined $100 in 2010 for taking his dog for a walk while driving alongside in his car. He was spotted driving at low speed along a country lane in County Durham, England, holding his Lurcher's leash through the car window as the dog trotted next to him.

sailing in circles A nautical novice who thought he was sailing around the coast of Britain in a counterclockwise direction ended up circling a small island off Kent instead. He was rescued by a lifeboat after running out of fuel off the 8-mi-wide (13-km) Isle of Sheppey, whose shore he had been hugging day and night on the principle of keeping the land to his right. He had not realized that Sheppey was an island.

mayo misery A consignment of mayonnaise fell off the back of a truck in Hyogo, Japan, causing an eight-vehicle pileup as cars and motorcycles skidded wildly on the crushed sauce. The highway had to be closed for five hours.

google alert A ten-year-old girl who decided to act dead while playing in the street with her friends sparked panic among neighbors when her image was captured by Google Street View cameras. Azura Beebeejaun was pictured lying face down on the pavement outside her home in Worcester, England, prompting residents browsing their neighborhood online to fear they had stumbled across a murder scene.

wake up! An Australian mining company has invented a hat that wakes up sleepy truck drivers. The hi-tech SmartCap is fitted with brain monitoring sensors, and if the driver seems to be drifting off, the cap sends a message to a computer screen in the truck cab, which then flashes a warning.

facebook phenomenon People across the world spend more than 700 billion minutes a month surfing through the website of Facebook, the Palo Alto, California-based social networking site. Since it was launched in 2004, more than 500 million people have joined Facebook—that's around eight percent of the world's population.

Head Stand

Kris Sleeman of the Dallas extreme performance group Traumatic Stress Discipline appears to feel no pain. At the 2007 grand opening of the Ripley's Believe It or Not! Odditorium in San Antonio, Texas, he lay face down in a pile of freshly broken glass bottles, and then invited Ripley employee Viviana Ray to stand on his head. Kris's pain-defying feats also included having a concrete block on his chest shattered by a sledgehammer while lying on a bed of nails.

GUARDIAN ANGEL

Police in Fribourg, Switzerland, hired a roadside angel to stop motorists driving too fast. Dressed all in white, the angel, played by a bearded actor, stood at different locations and flapped his wings at speeding drivers.

concrete breaker Kung fu champion Chris Roper from Suffolk, England, can break a 26-in-thick (66-cm) block of concrete with his foot, 20 in (51 cm) with his elbow and 12 in (30 cm) with his bare hand.

strong hair In November 2009, Manjit Singh from Leicester, England, pulled a double-decker London bus 70 ft (21 m)—using only his hair. By attaching a clamp to his thick ponytail, he managed to pull the seven-ton bus through Battersea Park. The feat made up for his disappointment in 2007, when he had been unable to pull a similar bus with his ears.

versatile performer Yang Guanghe, from China's Guizhou Province, can perform more than 30 different stunts—including standing on lit lightbulbs, lifting buckets of water with his eyelids, using an electric drill on his nose, standing on upturned knives, pulling a car with his eyelids and inserting a live snake into one of his nostrils then pulling it out from his mouth.

subway pushers Human "pushers" are hired to work on Tokyo's subway system to help cram more people into the overcrowded train cars.

road hogs A section of road near Eureka, Missouri, is covered with asphalt made from recycled pig manure, courtesy of a nearby hog farm.

junior matador At age 12 and standing only 4 ft 10 in (1.5 m) tall, seventh-grader Michel Lagravere from Mérida, Mexico, is a seasoned bullfighter who has challenged more than 50 snorting, charging 500-lb (227-kg) beasts in Colombia, Peru and France, as well as in his native country. Known as "Michelito," he first stepped into the ring with a young bull when he was just four and a half years old.

strong stomach Julika Faciu from Piatra Neamt, Romania, allowed 50 motorbikes and a 3-ton jeep to ride over his stomach, one by one.

· · · · · · · · · · ➤

STRONG MAN

George Lavasseur, a strong man with Ringling Bros. Circus in the early 20th century, was able to bear a 17-man human pyramid on his back that weighed a total of 3,257 lb (1,477 kg). The Detroit-born performer could also carry the weight of a fully grown elephant.

hoover fan As a teenager, James Brown from Nottinghamshire, England, had a collection of 50 vacuum cleaners—and his love for them has led to him opening Britain's first vacuum cleaner museum. He can identify different brands of vacuum cleaners in his collection simply by their sound.

3257 LBS

beyond belief

royal residence Janet and Philip Williams have turned their four-bedroom home in Woonona, New South Wales, Australia, into a royal museum, attracting thousands of visitors each year. They have more than 12,000 items of House of Windsor memorabilia, ranging from a life-size model of Queen Elizabeth II to a pair of Prince Charles and Princess Diana slippers. Even the toilet is decorated like a royal throne, complete with purple velvet trim.

$9,000 toothpick In December 2009, a toothpick that once belonged to British author Charles Dickens sold for $9,150 at an auction in New York City.

unwanted coins A stockpile of dollar coins worth more than $1.1 billion is languishing in storage because Americans prefer dollar bills. If stacked, the pile of coins would reach seven times higher than the altitude of the International Space Station.

cow suit Milkman Tony Fowler from Leicestershire, England, wore a black-and-white cow suit to receive his M.B.E. from Queen Elizabeth II at Buckingham Palace in June 2010. The Friesian outfit should have had a tail at the back, but Fowler's dog chewed it off.

same sneakers As part of a bet he made with his Spanish teacher, high-school freshman Ben Hedblom of Tampa, Florida, wore the same pair of sneakers every day for four years until he graduated—even though his toes eventually stuck out the front and he had to encase the shoes in plastic bags on rainy days.

pink lady Los Angeles actress Kitten Kay Sera has worn nothing but pink for over 25 years. "The Pink Lady," as she is known, even wears pink to funerals and once dumped a boyfriend because he was colorblind and therefore unable to appreciate the joy of pink. She dyes her Maltese dog, Kisses, in her favorite color using beetroot juice baths.

manure message To celebrate his wife Carole's 67th birthday, farmer Dick Kleis used a manure spreader to spell out HAP B DAY LUV U in a field visible from the living room of the couple's home in Zwingle, Iowa. It took him three hours and four loads of liquid manure to create the message—he was going to add a heart, too, but he ran out of manure.

bogus tycoon Echoing the real-life escapades of Frank Abagnale Jr. in the movie *Catch Me If You Can*, a 17-year-old boy from Yorkshire, England, posed as an aviation tycoon for six months. He tricked British companies into believing he was about to launch his own airline and that he had a fleet of jets. When the ruse was uncovered, the boy was found to be suffering from a form of autism, which enabled him to recall the exact detail of every airline's flight schedule.

renewed vows Margaret and John Beauvoisin of Hampshire, England, celebrated their diamond wedding anniversary in December 2008 by renewing their vows for the 60th time. The couple got married in 1948 and have renewed their vows every year since 1950, only missing out in 1949 because John was stationed in Bermuda with the Royal Navy.

doll house Bettina Dorfmann from Dusseldorf, Germany, owns more than 6,000 Barbie dolls—and some are worth up to $10,000. An entire room of her house is devoted to displaying 1,500 of them while another 3,000 Barbies from her collection are on show at exhibitions and museums around the world.

just the job Jason Sadler of Ponte Vedra Beach, Florida, earned more than $85,000 in 2009, promoting different businesses by wearing their T-shirts.

reptilian row A row over loud music between two South Carolina motel guests ended with one being accused of slapping the other in the face with the head of a 4-ft (1.2-m) python. The suspect was charged with assault and the weapon—the python—was handed over to his family for safe keeping.

jesus lives When a 50-year-old man was taken to a hospital with minor facial injuries after being hit by a car in Northampton, Massachusetts, in May 2010, he gave his name as Lord Jesus Christ. Police officers checked his I.D. and confirmed that it was indeed his legal name.

family success Father and son Brian and Jared Johnsrud of Marshfield, Wisconsin, both won cricket-spitting contests at the 2009 Central Wisconsin State Fair. Brian spat a thawed cricket 22 ft 8 in (6.9 m) to win the senior title and, minutes later, Jared spat his cricket 10 ft 5 in (3.2 m) to win the 9–11 age division.

DUST BUNNIES

These cuddly looking bunnies are actually composed of household detritus, including Christmas tree needles, discarded toddler toy parts, dryer lint, toenail clippings and human hair. Suzanne Proulx, from Erie, Pennsylvania, took 2½ years to collect enough dirt and dust to make 16 of her *Dust Bunnies*. Suzanne's first bunnies were a humorous comment on the dust and dirt that seemed to invade her house and multiply like wild rabbits. They are also about rebirth and renewal, taking what has been thrown away and creating something new.

sneaker line Collecting more than 10,500 sneakers sent in by readers, *National Geographic Kids* magazine unveiled a 1.65-mi (2.65-km) line of shoes, tied together by their laces, at Washington, D.C.

house of cards Without using glue or tape, Bryan Berg of Santa Fe, New Mexico, built a model of the Venetian Macao Resort-Hotel in Las Vegas from 218,792 playing cards. It took him 44 days and 4,051 decks of cards to complete the model that measured 33 x 10 ft (10 x 3 m) and weighed 600 lb (272 kg).

great shakes Dorena Young of Wallsburg, Utah, has a collection of more than 3,600 salt-and-pepper shakers. She has been collecting them for more than 60 years and has ones shaped like boats, cats, dogs, deer, vegetables, hats, lighthouses and sea horses. She even has a pair of J.F.K. and Jackie Onassis salt-and-pepper shakers.

packed court A total of 1,745 students played a single game of dodgeball on the University of California, Irvine, campus in September 2010.

daring plunge Amateur kayaker Christie Glissmeyer from Hood River, Oregon, paddled down the 82-ft-high (25.2-m) Metlako Falls at Eagle Creek, Oregon, in May 2010—a plunge that was nearly twice the height of any waterfall she had previously run.

hairy journey In 2007–08, German adventurer Christoph Rehage walked nearly 2,887 mi (4,646 km) across China from Beijing to Urumqi and took a picture of himself every day to document the growth of his beard.

Lint Leonardo

Laura Bell of Roscommon, Michigan, has made a replica of Leonardo da Vinci's painting *The Last Supper* out of laundry lint that measures 13 ft 8 in x 4 ft 4 in (4 x 1.3 m). She bought towels in the colors she wanted, laundering them separately to achieve the right shades. To obtain the amount of lint she needed to make the picture, she had to do about 800 hours of laundry and it then took her another 200 hours to re-create the famous Renaissance masterpiece.

king charles Charles Wesley Mumbere worked as a nurses' aide for years in the U.S.A., but on October 19, 2009, he reclaimed his crown as head of the mountainous kingdom of Rwenzururu in Uganda, ruling over about 300,000 people.

skateboarding priest Reverend Zoltan Lendvai, a Hungarian Catholic priest, spreads the word of God from his skateboard. Father Lendvai, whose first skateboard incorporated the papal coat of arms, has become a YouTube hit with a video showing the 45-year-old, in full clerical dress, demonstrating his moves for youngsters outside his church in Redics. He believes his skateboarding prowess will encourage more young people to attend church.

rolling, rolling, rolling... Lotan Baba, the "Rolling Saint" of India, spreads his message of peace by rolling on the ground from town to town across the country. He rolls 6–8 mi (10–12 km) a day and estimates that over the years he has rolled about 18,650 mi (30,000 km). His enthusiasm for rolling may be partly explained by the fact that as penance he once spent seven years standing upright, in the same place.

vertical burials An Australian funeral home is saving space by burying people vertically. Melbourne company Upright Burials places each corpse in a biodegradable bag and then lowers the body feet first into a cylindrical hole about 30 in (75 cm) in diameter and 9½ ft (3 m) deep. Using this method, the company hopes to bury up to 40,000 bodies in a field outside the city.

debt unpaid Former British Prime Minister Winston Churchill (1874–1965) died owing 13 rupees to the Bangalore Club of Bangalore, India. The club has maintained the ledger showing that debt and displays it—but refuses to allow anyone to pay his tab.

idaho caveman Richard "Dugout Dick" Zimmerman (1916–2010) left his old life as a farmhand behind in 1947 and began digging out a series of caves near Salmon, Idaho. He cultivated a garden and lived without modern amenities for more than 60 years. Some of his caves were up to 60 ft (18.5 m) deep and were furnished with cast-off doors, car windows, old tires and other discarded items.

homemade plane In July 2010, 82-year-old Arnold Ebneter of Woodinville, Washington State, flew his homemade lightweight airplane, the E-1, nonstop from Everett, Washington State, to Fredericksburg, Virginia—a journey of 2,327 mi (3,746 km)—in 18 hours 27 minutes.

in a flap When Darren Cubberly's racing pigeon, Houdini, failed to arrive at the end of a 224-mi (360-km), six-hour race from the island of Guernsey to the West Midlands, England, he gave up hope of seeing the bird again. Then, five weeks later he received a call from Panama City—5,200 mi (8,370 km) away—to say that Houdini was there. It is thought she landed on a ship traveling to the area.

fire trim Italian-American hairdresser Pietro Santoro cuts hair using a naked flame at his barber shop in Washington, D.C. He says that cutting hair with fire gives it more body.

Dried Shark

A seafront store in Taiwan offers whole dried sharks for sale at a price of 6,500 Hong Kong dollars (U.S.$844) per 1 lb 5 oz (600 g). Shark fins are a popular delicacy in Chinese soup, while other parts of the shark are considered to have beneficial medicinal properties.

SKELETON STAFF

When the Post-Mortem Club held its annual breakfast in Chicago in 1934, the guest of honor was the skeleton of its late founder, Mr. J. M. McAdou of Florida, who had died the previous year. The club was an organization of naprapaths (practitioners of a manual medical technique similar to osteopathy) and had a rule that stated each member should leave them his skeleton so that it could attend future meetings… although probably not vote.

polar riddle When video footage showed a large, white beast lying on the shore, British TV presenter Naomi Lloyd excitedly told viewers that a polar bear from the Arctic had been washed up in Bude, Cornwall. It subsequently emerged that the animal was actually a cow that had been bleached white by seawater.

game proposal A New York City video-game fan proposed to his girlfriend with gold coins in a specially designed level of Super Mario World. Having persuaded her to play the game, he used a level-editing program called Lunar Magic to spell out "Lisa will you marry me?" on screen. He then recorded her delighted reaction in a video posted on YouTube.

resuscitating roadkill A 55-year-old man was arrested on a remote highway northeast of Pittsburgh, Pennsylvania, after he was seen performing mouth-to-mouth resuscitation on roadkill. Witnesses said the possum in question was not just playing dead, it had been deceased for some time.

slimy cure According to the African religion of *Ifa Orisha*, drinking the juices and mucus of Giant African snails can cure the sick.

dog driver A man was run over by his own dog in 2010 after it jumped into his pickup truck and accidentally knocked it into gear. Christopher Bishop of Webster, Florida, was lying under his truck checking for oil leaks and had the vehicle in neutral, the engine running and the driver's door open, when his bulldog, Tassey, leaped in and hit the gear stick into reverse, sending the vehicle rolling over his owner's body. Luckily, Christopher survived the incident without major injury.

Ripley's
REVISITED

RIPLEY'S HERO

Daring Thai snake charmer Khum Chaibuddee, also known as the "King of Cobras," was honored as a Ripley's Ambassador by the *Ripley's Believe It or Not* museum in Pattaya, Thailand, in 2010. He celebrated by performing with his deadly cobras and even kissing them, his signature trick. In *Ripley's Believe It or Not! The Remarkable Revealed*, we reported that a fearless Khum had kissed 19 highly poisonous cobras one by one on the head without being bitten.

beyond belief

CAR COFFINS

Automobile fan Danny Mendez of Winchester, California, has designed a range of $1,500 fiberglass coffins in the shapes of classic cars. Each Cruisin' Casket features motorcycle headlights, alloy wheels from golf carts and extending side exhausts that serve as handles for pallbearers. In the absence of a death in the family, the coffins can also double as ice coolers.

flamboyant funeral Flamboyant Hong-Kong lawyer Kai-bong Chau, 75, was buried in March 2010 with paper replicas of his gold and pink Rolls-Royce cars and a selection of his most colorful outfits. Paper models of cars, homes and money are traditionally burned at Chinese funerals to provide the dead with comfort and luxuries in the afterlife.

strange venue Jason and Rachael Storm decided to start their life together in 2008 by getting married at a place where it usually comes to an end—a funeral home in St. Joseph Township, Michigan, where the groom was a director.

blessed computers To attract bankers and financiers from the City of London to his church, the Rev. Canon David Parrott performed a service in which he blessed their cell phones and laptop computers.

wrong funeral After reading a death notice in her local paper in Merthyr Tydfil, Wales, stating that upholsterer Ron Jones had passed away, Margaret Griffiths sat through the funeral service for her old friend—only to discover later that she had got the wrong Ron Jones. The confusion arose because there were two men named Ron Jones of similar age in the town and both had worked as upholsterers.

young undertaker In September 2010, George Simnett set up his own funeral business in Leicestershire, England—at age 17.

snow palace To create a fairy-tale setting for his ultimately successful marriage proposal to Christi Lombardo in February 2010, Ryan Knotek built a snow castle near his home in Parma, Ohio. Using blocks of snow, he constructed a one-room, one-story palace topped with roof spires and furnished inside with a portable heater to keep the winter chill away.

favorite ride Vic Kleman of Knoxville, Pennsylvania, has ridden the Jack Rabbit roller coaster at Kennywood Park in West Mifflin near Pittsburgh more than 4,000 times since 1959. To celebrate the 90th birthday of the wooden ride, which has an 85-ft (26-m) double-dip drop, 78-year-old Vic went on it 90 times in one day in August 2010.

CRAB DISPENSER

A food vending machine in Nanjing, China, sells live crabs. Designed by Shi Tuanjie, the machine offers live hairy crabs and accompanying bottles of vinegar. The crustaceans vary in price from $2 to $7, according to size. The crabs, a tasty delicacy in the region, are packed into plastic boxes and chilled to 40°F (5°C), leaving them sedated but still alive. An average of 200 crabs a day are sold, and customers are promised compensation of three live crabs should their purchase happen to be dead.

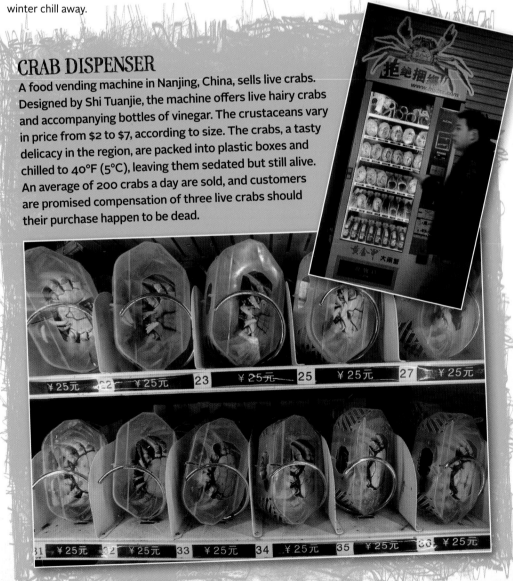

mobile chapel A 1942 firetruck owned by Rev. Darrell Best, of Shelbyville, Illinois, has been converted into a mobile wedding chapel called "Best Man." It has stained glass windows, an altar, two wooden pews and a fully working pipe organ.

bmw tomb Following his death at age 51, the family of motoring fanatic Steve Marsh of London, England, built him a tomb in the shape of a shiny black BMW, complete with personalized number plate "STEVE 1" and a parking ticket.

boxed art Vending machines in Germany sell miniature works of art in boxes for less than $3. About 100 refurbished machines, which once sold cigarettes or chewing gum, now sell tiny one-off sculptures, collages and paintings by professional artists.

saddle sore Riding 49cc mini-bikes that averaged just 20 mph (32 km/h), Ryan Galbraith and Chris Stinson traveled the 445 mi (716 km) from Denver, Colorado, to Sturgis, South Dakota, in 25 hours 29 minutes in 2009.

high fives Paralympic Alpine skiing silver medallist Josh Dueck of Vernon, Canada, high-fived 9,307 people in 24 hours in Vancouver in September 2010.

pole balance David Cain of Liberty Township, Ohio, can balance a 58-ft-long (17.7-m) fiberglass pole on his chin for more than 21 seconds. It took him two years to master the skill.

filthy rich Sixty-year-old Curt Degerman of Skellefteå, Sweden, ate from trash bins and collected cans for recycling for 40 years, but when he died it was discovered he was worth more than $1.4 million.

loop the loops Setting off at an altitude of 5,900 ft (1,800 m), Hungarian tandem paraglider Pál Takáts and his co-pilot Gábor Kézi performed 45 consecutive loop the loops on their descent over Lake Walenstadt, Switzerland.

wayward gps In 2009, a driver was fined after following the directions of his GPS up a narrow dirt track, unsuitable for cars, to the very edge of a 100-ft (30-m) cliff drop in West Yorkshire, England.

welded to flagpole On April 29, 2009, Alex Almy and Jesse Poe of Fruita Monument High School in Fruita, Colorado, spent 75 minutes welding a car around their school's flagpole as a year-end prank. They took off the passenger door and part of the roof to slide the Eagle hatchback into place before getting busy with welding tools. However, because the flagpole itself was undamaged and the boys agreed to remove the car, no one was punished.

Huge Hole

A 66-ft-wide (20-m) sinkhole opened up overnight in the yard of the Zhang family home in Leshan, China. Several fruit trees disappeared down the hole, which was more than 130 ft (40 m) deep and stopped less than 3 ft (1 m) from the house.

Ripley's Believe It or Not!

beyond belief

human punchbag Xiao Lin, a fitness coach from Shenyang, China, rents himself out as a punchbag for stressed women who want to let off steam. The women pay $15 for a 30-minute session during which they can hit him as hard and as often as they like.

mother cat Peter Keonig, a Buddhist bank robber serving five years for armed robberies in Germany, had his request for his cat to be granted visiting rights to him in jail rejected by a court—despite his plea that the animal is the reincarnation of his mother.

bearly believable! A 2010 survey showed that more than one-third of British adults still take a childhood teddy bear to bed with them at night.

cool customer A man walked into a restaurant in Warren, Michigan, with a 5-in (12.5-cm) knife sticking in his chest and calmly ordered a coffee. The 52-year-old, who had walked a mile to the restaurant after having been stabbed, did not complain of any pain and simply told staff that he was waiting for an ambulance to come to care for him. Following treatment in a hospital, the man was expected to make a full recovery.

Upside-down House A totally upside-down house opened as a tourist attraction in the grounds of a zoo in Gettorf, Germany, in 2010. Standing on a pointed roof and supported by steel beams in the attic, the 23-ft (7-m) house boasts an upside-down kitchen, as well as a completely inverted bathroom, living room and bedroom. Workers screwed 50 separate pieces into the "floor" (actually the ceiling), including beds, tables and a microwave oven. Needle and thread were used to keep bed linen in place.

dancing cop Dressed in police blues, white gloves and an officer's cap, Tony Lepore dances while directing the traffic at an intersection in Providence, Rhode Island. He began his dance routine in the 1980s through boredom and although he retired from the police department in 1988, he returns each year for two weeks to entertain passersby.

own juror William Woods was about to stand trial in Ottawa, Ontario, Canada, in 1999 on charges of dangerous driving, but the trial had to be postponed because Woods was summoned for jury duty—for his own case.

snake smuggler After customs officers in Kristiansand, Norway, discovered a tarantula in the bag of a ferry passenger who had traveled from Denmark, they decided to conduct a full body search. On investigation, they also found 14 royal pythons and ten albino leopard geckos taped to the man's torso and legs.

cash flow A 47-year-old Ukrainian man got his arm stuck in a public toilet in Chernigov for three hours after trying to retrieve $24 that he had dropped. With the man trapped up to his elbow, rescuers had to use hydraulic shears to cut him free. He emerged unharmed but $24 poorer, while the toilet itself was completely destroyed.

great survivor Frano Selak, a music teacher from Petrinja, Croatia, cheated death seven times, surviving three car accidents, two bus crashes, a train crash and even a plane crash—accidents that otherwise left 40 people dead. His run of good luck continued when he won $1,000,000 in a lottery. To give thanks for being the luckiest man alive, he gave away his winnings to family and friends.

subway hideaway A 13-year-old boy who thought he was in trouble at school spent 11 days hiding on the New York City subway in 2009. Francisco Hernandez Jr. hid on the D train he normally rides during his short commute from his Brooklyn home to school. He slept on trains and survived on junk food he bought from newsstands along the route.

HEAD FOR HEIGHTS

A six-year-old boy slipped through window bars of an eighth-floor apartment in Hubei Province, China, but ended up dangling by his ears 60 ft (18 m) above the ground after they got trapped in the bars because the rest of his head was too wide to pass through.

surrounded city Although the city of Carter Lake is in Iowa, it is surrounded on three sides by the city of Omaha, Nebraska, and on the fourth by the Missouri River. It was formed by a flood that straightened the course of the Missouri and is the only city in Iowa that lies west of the river. It even gets its utility services from Nebraska.

pillow talk In a special ceremony in March 2010, Korean Lee Jin-gyu married a large pillow adorned with a picture of female Japanese animated character, Fate Testarossa. He put the pillow in a wedding dress for the service, which was conducted before a priest. He takes the pillow everywhere—and when he and his pillow bride go to a restaurant, the pillow gets its own seat and its own meal.

cesspit hell A Chinese man was rescued in 2010 after spending two days stuck up to his neck in a toilet cesspit. The man had slipped while using an outhouse toilet in Wuyuan, Inner Mongolia, and had fallen into the pit below. Unsurprisingly, as soon as he was freed, he ran to a nearby pond to have a wash!

wonder well Chand Baori, a 100-ft-deep (30-m) stepped well in the village of Abhaneri, Rajasthan, India, was built more than a thousand years ago with 13 stories and 3,500 steps.

bike burial When Harry "The Horse" Flamburis, a Hells' Angels motorcycle club leader from Daly City, California, died, he was buried with his motorbike.

LIVELY LANDINGS......

Is it a Bird?

Giant 300-ton Boeing 747s coming in to land at Princess Juliana Airport on the Caribbean island of Saint Martin fly just 60 ft (18.4 m) above the heads of vacationers on Maho Beach. They fly so low that they blow sand into the faces of plane spotters gathered below. The beach is right next to the runway, which, at 7,054 ft (2,170 m), is the shortest in the world to regularly accommodate 747s.

Over the autobahn
Leipzig Hall Airport, Germany

Low tide
Barra Airport, Scotland

Crossing the highway
Gibraltar Airport

Smoothed ice and snow
Ice runway in Antarctica

Page numbers in *italic* refer to illustrations

abdomen, breathing in a long way 124, *124*, *163*, *163*
Abdulleh, Safia (Som) 32
Abraham, Franz (Ger) 200
Abramović, Marina (Ser) 210
Abramovich, Roman (Rus) 134
accents
  bats with regional 67
  Foreign Accent Syndrome 110
Acton, Patrick (U.S.A.) 218
Adams, Ansel (U.S.A.) 207
adhesive tape, sculpture made of 202, *202*
Adili Wuxor (Chn) 160
aerogel 230, *230*
Afanasiev, Nick (U.S.A.) 105, *105*
Ahlgren, Anders (Swe) 89
Ai Weiwei (Chn) 218
airbeds, racing over waterfalls on 94, *94*
aircraft carrier, LEGO® replica of 218
airplanes
  babies born in 119, 124
  basketball shot made from 96
  boy pretends to be tycoon 238
  car converts to 136
  converted to boat 140, *140–1*
  crossing roads 245, *245*
  escapologist 153
  fly low over beach 245, *245*
  flying to school 140
  found under ice 132–3, *133*
  hits warthog on runway 140
  homemade 143, 240
  huge model 142
  hypersonic 137
  ice runway 245, *245*
  inflatable fighter planes 143, *143*
  land on beach 245, *245*
  lands on highway 136
  LEGO® replica of 208
  monkeys smuggled onto 60
  passenger accidentally ejects himself 136
  pilot saved by ejector seat 138, *138–9*
  pulling with eyelids 170
  tailcone falls off 140
  wing falls off 138, *138*
  wingwalking 160
airports
  size of Heathrow 136
  unusual runways 245, *245*
airship, at Chicago World's Fair 168
Al Humaidhan, Hamad (U.K.) 217
Albanese, Matthew (U.S.A.) 216, *216*
Alex, Vicki (U.K.) 108
Ali, Hadji (Egy) 165, *165*
Ali, Kalim (Ind) 128
Ali, Muhammad (U.S.A.) 203
aliens
  April Fool's hoax 181
  driver forced to drive in bus lane by 141
  landing port built for 181
  Roswell Incident 181, *181*
Allen, Claire (U.K.) 127
allergies 73, 126
alligators
  live in house 78
  lost at sea 63
  made into motorbike 134, *134–5*
Allison, Brenda (U.K.) 119
Almy, Alex (U.S.A.) 243
alphabet, very small 53
Alvarado, Requelme Abanto (Per) 108
Alvarez, Angel (U.S.A.) 121
Alvarez, Felipe (Col) 96, *96*
ambulance, stolen 235
Amorim, M. de (Bra) 94
Anderson, Laurie (U.S.A.) 222
Anderson, Marvadene (U.S.A.) 128
Andes, Nick (U.S.A.) 149
angel, to stop speeding 237, *237*
animal skins
  inflated 198, *198–9*
  beer bottles in 193, *193*
Aniston, Jennifer (U.S.A.) 215
Anne, Princess (U.K.) 91
Annie K. (U.S.A.) 202, *202*
Antarctic, very old butter found in 190

ants
  destroy electrical equipment 78
  exploding 63, *63*
  as living larders 62
  painful ritual 62
  paintings of 222
  portrait made with dead 58–9, *58–9*
  start fire 25
  Velcro-like claws 78
anvils, shot into air 94
Aparicio, Julio (Spa) 100, *100*
apartments
  security measures 42
  underground 44
ape, discovered in Venezuela 180, *180*
Apple products, exhibition of destroyed 217, *217*
Appleton, Paul (U.S.A.) 81
appliances, tree sculpture from 210
aquarium, octopus floods 79
Aretz, Achim (Ger) 153
Aristizábal, Victor (Col) 96, *96*
Armour, Andrew (Dom) 63, *63*
arms
  arm wrestling 123
  armless and legless woman 164, *164*
  armless cyclist 106, *106*
  contortionist 165, *165*
  holding aloft continuously 158, *158*
  one-armed D.J. 217
  parasitic twin 108
  self-amputation 121
  stuck in toilet 244
  very long hair on 25
armies
  lost army found 230
  war-time deceptions 17, 143, *143*
Arscott, Ann (U.K.) 113
Ashby, Stuart (U.K.) 193
Aspairt, Philibert 51, *51*
asphalt
  lake of 50
  pig manure recycled into 237
Aspland, Jamie (U.K.) 122
asteroid, explodes in atmosphere 41
astronauts
  tears 50
  urine jettisoned from Space Shuttle 49
astronomy, giant neutrino detector 231, *231*
Atlantic Ocean, rowing across 94, 96
Attia, Kader (Alg) 222
audio tapes, large collection of 215
Audubon, John James (U.S.A.) 201
Awasthi, Akash 146–7, *146–7*
Aziere, Dan (U.S.A.) 126

Baba, Lotan (Ind) 240
babies
  bigger than mother 119, *119*
  born in airplane 119, 124
  enormous 107
  "frozen" after surgery 118
  kept warm with sandwich bag 124
  mummified 22, *22*
  premature baby survives after cuddling 118
  prenatal surgery 109
  significant numbers for 29
  sisters give birth at same time 16
  very big 118
  very tiny 119
  with tail 109
baboons
  in circus 70
  eat vineyard's grapes 66
  sells tickets for zoo 61
bacon
  bacon-flavored envelopes 186
  enormous sandwich wrap 195
  sculpted head 191, *191*
Bacon, Kevin (U.S.A.) 191, *191*
Bacon, Phyllis (U.K.) 174, *174*
Bacon, Tad and Karen (U.S.A.) 85
bacteria
  on dental floss 118, *118*
  in human body 113
  large colonies of 38
  microbial art 202
  music helps work faster 50
  in rain 177

bacteria (*cont.*)
  in toxic lake 52
bagpipes, frighten rats 234
Bai, Chouthi (Ind) 74
Bai Deng (Chn) 171, *171*
Baines, Kelvin (U.K.) 157
Bajpai, Radhakant (Ind) 25, *25*
baked beans, rat found in tin of 189
Baker, Sally (U.K.) 134
Baliker, Paul (U.S.A.) 35, *35*
Balka, Miroslaw (Pol) 208
balloons
  crossing English Channel under 149, *149*
  dinner party under hot-air balloon 194
  hydrogen hot-air balloons 17
balls
  ancient metal spheres found 180
  ancient stone balls found 178
  baseball mementos 200
  dog swallows 72, 79
  holding multiple tennis balls 169
  mosaic made of 212, *212*
bananas
  banana ketchup 195
  double banana in one skin 190
  peels found on mountain 188
  underwear made from 190
bananas ketchup 195
banknote mosaic, made from screws 216
Bansal, Munish (U.K.) 218
bar, bartering for drinks in 190
barbecue, giant 191
Barbie dolls, large collection of 238
Barnum & Bailey Circus 30, 31, 116
Barraza, Hansy Better (U.S.A.) 206
Barrett, Jasper (U.S.A.) 178
Bartek, Jim (U.S.A.) 214
Bartholomew, Pamela (U.S.A.) 140, *140*
base jumpers, leap from tallest building 46
baseball
  armless pitcher 110
  bat hits fan 98, *98*
  breaking bats over leg 149
  carved bats 87, *87*
  decorated balls as mementos 200
  foul balls 94
  injuries 99
  successful pitcher 93
  switch-hitting homers 96
Bass, Rebecca (U.S.A.) 131, *131*
bathroom, image of Satan appears in 16
bathtub, motorized bathtub on Amazon 160
bats
  giant colony in cave 72
  orphans rescued 74, *74–5*
  regional accents 67
battery, very ancient found 180
Battles, Ashley (U.S.A.) 160
Bauer, Kirk (U.S.A.) 112
Baze, Russell (Can) 93
Beach Boys (U.S.A.) 214
beaches
  enormous beach towel 153
  giant artwork on 214
  mass burial on 171
beads, very long strand of 221
beards
  bearded women 29, *29*, 126, *126*
  documenting growth of 239
  multiple styles 128
  as sculpture 21, *21*
  very long 25
  woven to resemble snowshoe 113
bears
  abandoned cub adopted 82
  deterred by zucchini 75
  drives car 61
  lives with tiger and lion 66, *66*
  milk can stuck on head 66
  steals teddy bear 83
  walks into grocery store 60
  yoga routine 76
The Beatles (U.K.) 110
beauty contest, after cosmetic surgery 114
Beauvoisin, Margaret and John (U.K.) 238

beavers
  attacks fisherman 73
  huge dam 84
Beckham, David (U.K.) 128
bed, earthquake-proof 230
bedroom, dust model of 221
Beebeejaun, Azura (U.K.) 236
beer
  bottles in animal skins 193, *193*
  deep-fried 195
  drinking in many different pubs 193
  made by light of full moon 188
beer crates
  building made of 47, *47*
  motorized 142
beer mats, apartment made of 170
bees
  bee beard competition 72, *72*
  cure multiple sclerosis 110
  dog eats beehive 72
  drink human tears 85
  swarm on clothes line 84
beetles
  bifocal eyes 63
  infestation of stinkbugs 79
  very strong 66
Bell, Alexander Graham (U.K.) 227
Bell, Charlie (U.K.) 156
Bell, Laura (U.S.A.) 238–9, *239*
Bellard, Fabrice (Fra) 170
Belluso, Rose Ann (U.S.A.) 110
belly button fluff, teddy bears made of 108, *108*
Benbenek, John (U.S.A.) 186
Bentley, Dr. John Irving 179, *179*
Berendes, Henry Michael (U.S.A.) 29
Berg, Bryan (U.S.A.) 214
Berkowitz, Valerie (U.K.) 32
Berlin Wall, chocolate replica of 187
Bertoletti, Patrick "Deep Dish" 184–5, *184–5*
Best, Rev. Darrell (U.S.A.) 243
Betra, Millie (U.S.A.) 156, *156*
Bews, Captain Brian 138, *138–9*
Bible, world tour for 200
bicycles
  amphibious bicycle 135
  armless rider 106, *106*
  bicycle-powered Porsche 142, *142*, 207
  coal-powered 136
  cycling across U.S.A. 94
  cycling round world 92
  cycling up steps 93, *93*
  injuries on 99
  legless rider 106, *106*
  long journey on mini-bikes 243
  owner rides for 60 years 143
  prisoners' Tour de France 92
  riding on tightrope 169, *169*
  wooden 141
Bihain, Jörn (Bel) 47, *47*
Bikila, Adebe (Eth) 89
bikini, made of raw meat 206
Bilal, Wafaa (U.S.A.) 219
Bindra, Abhinav (Ind) 89
birds
  chicken/guinea fowl hybrid 72
  chicken kill fox 70
  chicken lays huge egg 80
  cockerel changes sex 64
  crane wears slippers 66
  crossbow bolt in head 77, *77*
  dead birds fall from sky 174
  dive through ice 74
  hawk attacks postman 76
  huge flock of starlings 41, *41*
  long migration 62
  mark on car 7, *7*
  mystery illness 62
  owl chick escapes lion 76
  parrot arrested 76
  pigeon arrested for spying 82
  pigeon droppings halt concert 208
  pigeon faster than broadband 77
  pigeon races to wrong destination 240
  rooster arrested 74
  stork's romantic attachment 83
  swans' fidelity to partners 62
  very old chicken 85
  very smelly 63
  very valuable book 201

Bishop, Christopher (U.S.A.) 241
Björk (Ice) 210
black holes
  gigantic 52
  man-made 228
bladder, fish found in 112
Blaine, David (U.S.A.) 147
Blanchard, Jean-Pierre (Fra) 17
Blayze, Sue (U.K.) 149
blind people
  abseiler 97
  catches huge fish 93
  drives car at speed 157
  photographer 219
  "seeing" with echolocation 122
  sprinter 97
  writes book in Morse Code 110
blindfolded, typing books 208
blood
  large number of donations 120
  painting with 211, *211*
  sweating 105, *105*
blowtorch, fire-eating with 19, *19*
Boa Sr. (Ind) 40
board game, with real people as pieces 203
boats and ships
  billionaire's yacht 134
  built in back garden 141
  canal boat converted into submarine 235
  catamaran built of plastic bottles 142
  crews disappear 174, 181
  giant liner 142
  human-powered Viking longboat road vehicle 141
  kite-powered cargo ship 141
  LEGO® replicas 218, 221
  long time at sea 134
  looks like zipper 142, *142*
  lost sailor circles island 236
  model of warship 216
  plane converted to 140, *140–1*
  ship found under World Trade Center 135
  shipwreck still leaking oil 142
  whale jumps onto yacht 80, *80–1*
  young round-the-world sailor 92
Bocabeille, Jean (Fra) 186
body painting 8, *8*, *12*, *12–13*, 201, *201*, 213
body piercings, multiple 128
Böhling, Ivar (Fin) 89
Bolt, Usain (Jam) 67
Bond, Josh (U.S.A.) 39
bones
  chapel decorated with 50
  growing extra 126
  made into artworks 212
  muscles turn to 115
  stretching 127
  stuck in lung 121
  under Paris 51, *51*
bonobos, share food 75
Boo, Jinxi (U.S.A.) 125, *125*
books
  author writes ten pages a day 209
  huge number of library books borrowed 206
  large collection of paperbacks 214
  quantities of paper used for 213
  smallpox scabs found in 114
  tiny copy of Quran 217
  typing blindfolded 208
  very long title 214
  very overdue library books 203, 221
  very valuable 201
  written using Morse Code 110
Booth, David (U.K.) 20
boots, welly wanging contest 94
Borbon, Spencer (U.S.A.) 215
Botox, cures stroke victim 122
bottles
  beer bottles in dead animals 193, *193*
  car on track of upright bottles 135
  catamaran built of plastic bottles 142
  diamonds on liqueur bottle 188
  message in 20
  walking with milk bottle on head 153, *153*
bottom, bionic 114
Bottoni, Stefano (Ita) 169
bouncy castle, crossing lake on 15, *15*

Bowen, Eli (U.S.A.) 106, *106*
bowling
　centenarian player 94
　woman champion 93
boxing, poem boxing contest 217
Boy Scouts, elderly Scout retires 152
Boyle, Iain and Rachel (U.K.) 53
Bradac, Zdenek (Cze) 147, 160
Bradford, Robert (U.K.) 216
brain
　medicinal uses for vulture brains 118
　needle removed from 126
　number of neurons in 115
Brandt, Francois Antoine (Nld) 88
bread
　dead mouse found in 189, *189*
　shuts down particle accelerator 226
　very expensive loaves 188
breast implants, stop bullets 120
breathing in a long way 124, *124*, 163, *163*
Brennan, Ian (U.S.A.) 216
Brewer, Carl (U.S.A.) 135
Brick, Jacqueline (U.K.) 32
bridge, mass breakfast on 186
Broadbent, Betty (U.S.A.) *26–7, 27*
Broom, Richard (U.K.) 208
brothers, long-lost 14
Brown, Chris (U.K.) 121
Brown, James (U.K.) 237
Brown, Jeremy (U.S.A.) 110
Brown, Leven (U.K.) 96
Brown, Louise (U.S.A.) 206
Brown, Rupert and Emma (U.K.) 80
Bruin, Dick de (Nld) 24
Bruns, Ed (U.S.A.) 128
Budiselic, Kruno (Cro) 152
Buenrostro, Adrian Rodrigues (Mex) 152
bug-eating parties 187, *187*
Bulatovic, Zoran (Ser) 107
Bulled, Roger and Leslie (U.K.) 137
bullets
　breast implants stop 120
　bulletproof clothes 228
　found in body 108, 110
　in head 128
　in lung 114
　man survives multiple 121
　sneezed out of nose 126
bullfighting
　bullfighter quits job mid-fight 97
　matador gored 100, *100*
　very young matador 237
bulls, fire festival 94, *94*
burgers
　burger-scented candles 190
　enormous 190
　giant barbecue 191
　lion meat 195
　very old 195
burglars
　caught by webcam 24
　parrot scares off 72
　woman pretends to be dog 29
burial suit, jade 173, *173*
Burkhart, Melvin (U.S.A.) 19
Burrard-Lucas, Will and Matt (U.K.) 82
Burrows, Terry (U.K.) 171
Burton, Finley (U.K.) 118
buses
　covered with knitting 201
　jet-powered school bus 136, *136*
　pulling with hair 237
　very long distance traveled 137
business card, giant 200
Buss, Mike (U.K.) 121
Butera family (U.S.A.) 64
Butler, Lareece (S.A.) 107
butter, very old 190
Byrd, Richard (U.S.A.) 168

Caballero, Miguel (Col) 228
Cadogan, Merlin (U.K.) 148, *148*
café, in underground cistern 194
Cain, David (U.S.A.) 243
cakes
　realistic model of dog 187, *187*
　very tall 186
Caliro, Aldo (Ita) 209
Calloway, Denny (U.S.A.) 7, *7*
Calman, Bette (Aus) 156
Calvo, David (Spa) 160
camel, falls into sinkhole 73
cameras
　diver loses 24

cameras (*cont.*)
　found in fishing net 29
　implanted in back of head 219
　octopus steals 85
camouflage, zebras 81
Campbell, Sir Malcolm (U.K.) 160
Campbell, Naomi (U.K.) 203
candles, burger-scented 190
candy portraits 222, *222*
Cañizares, Santiago (Spa) 92
Cannon, Peter (Aus) 24
canoe, chicken feast in 186
cans
　mouse found in cola 189
　rat found in baked beans 189
　stuck on cat's head 64
Capes, Ryan (U.S.A.) 156
Carbone, Giorgio (Ita) 38
cargo cult 39
Carny, Ses (U.S.A.) 157, *157*
Caro, Susanne (U.S.A.) 114
Carranza, Lydia (U.S.A.) 120
Carrazza, Joe (Aus) 186
Carrier, Steve (U.S.A.) 149
Carrière, Eva (Fra) 176, *176*
cars
　abandoned in sea 29, *29*
　amphibious supercar 142
　assembly line at Chicago World's Fair 168
　bear drives 61
　Beatles tribute 131, *131*
　bicycle-powered Porsche 142, *142*, 207
　blind man drives fast car 157
　BMW-shaped tomb 243
　burial with paper replicas of 242
　car-shaped coffins 242, *242*
　chocolate-powered 190
　collides with elephant 234
　converts to airplane 136
　dead man found in car in river 29
　dog sounds horn for help 74
　dog taken for walk by 236
　driver claims aliens forced him to drive in
　　bus lane 141
　drives through garage wall 135, *135*
　driving with cell phone app 226
　drunk driver in toy car 137
　elephants wash 64
　expensive toy car 135, *135*
　guardian angel to stop speeding 237, *237*
　homemade supercar 134
　huge mileage 141
　Hummer converted to horse-drawn
　　carriage 140
　kitten survives in engine 72
　knitted cover for 214
　learner crashes into apartment 142
　lion opens door 82, *82*
　loses all four wheels at once 137
　marathon car-wash 152
　mayonnaise causes highway crash 236
　no-parking lines painted under 134
　painting with remote-control cars 215
　pulling with eyelids 237
　replica made from clothes 220
　rolling over abdomen 123
　sculpture from old car parts 214
　speed record 160
　spontaneous human combustion in 179
　starts first time after long disuse 137
　on track of upright bottles 135
　Transformer made from 206
　vampire blamed for accident 236
　very fast electric car 141
　very valuable parking space 141
　Wall of Death 150–1, *150–1*
　welded around flagpole 243
carvings, whittling 164, *164*
Casagrange, Andy Brandy IV (U.S.A.) 203
Case, Rachel Betty (U.S.A.) 108, *108*
Cassini, Cecilia (U.S.A.) 218
Castiglioni, Angelo and Alfredo (Ita) 230
castles
　built of hay 210
　built of snow 242
　ghost photographed in 178, *178*
　new medieval castle built 54
catacombs, under Paris 51, *51*
caterpillars, invisible 70, *70*
cats
　bionic legs 77
　can stuck on head 64
　"cat" spelled out in fur 70
　dyed pink 77

cats (*cont.*)
　extra digits on paws 64, *64*
　four-eared kitten 74
　huge number in house 74
　kitten survives in car engine 72
　kitten survives in washing machine 75
　large collection of statues of 169
　long journey by 79
　marriage to 80
　mummified 23, *23*
　not allowed to visit prisoner 244
　predicts patients' deaths 176, *176*
　saves man from fire 62
　survives burial in rubble 60
　survives fall 70
　washing machines for 82
caves
　blind fish in 70
　huge number of bats in 72
　large colonies of bacteria 38
　living in 24, 50
　man digs 240
　under Paris 51, *51*
CDs, cremation ashes in 235
cell phones
　dress used as 220
　driving car with cell phone app 226
　in India 53
　iPhone first-aid app used in earthquake
　　123
　stolen one bought back by owner 17
　thief photographs himself with stolen
　　cell phone 14
　unlucky number 28
　vicar blesses 242
centenarians
　non-existent 32
　plays bowling 94
　school pupil 24
centipedes, eating 192, *192*
cesspit, man rescued from 244
Chaibuddee, Khum (Tha) 241, *241*
chain, carved from wood 220
chair, enormous 203
Chalk, Dale (Aus) 108
Challis, Paul and Maria (U.K.) 32, *32*
chameleons
　new species found in snake's mouth 78
　very long tongues 67
champagne, found in shipwreck 195
Chang Du (Chn) 112, *112*
Chao Muhe (Chn) 20
chapels
　decorated with bones 50
　executive box decorated like Gothic
　　chapel 97
　mobile wedding chapel 243
Chaplin, Charlie (U.S.A.) 223
Chapman, Sail (U.K.) 148
Charles, Prince of Wales 149, 238
Charles, Shemika (U.S.A.) 157
Chau, Kai-bong (Chn) 242
Chavez, Hugo (Ven) 20
cheetah, speed 67
Chen Forng-shean (Twn) 208
Chen Jinmiao (Chn) 134
Chen Kecai (Chn) 160, *160*
Chen Xinnian (Chn) 44
cherry stems, knotted with tongue 7, *7*
chewing gum
　nonstick 190
　sculpture from 210, *210*
Chicago World's Fair 161–8, *161–8*
chicken
　chicken/guinea fowl hybrid 72
　cockerel changes sex 64
　feast in canoe 186
　kill fox 70
　lays huge egg 80
　rooster arrested 74
　very old 85
Childers, Michelle (U.S.A.) 120
chili sauce, extremely hot 186
chimpanzees
　make cutlery 61
　paintings by 67
　smoking and drinking problem 66
chin
　advertising space on 112, *112*
　balancing long pole on 243
chocolate
　chocolate-powered racing car 190
　clothes made of 189
　giant coin made of 188

chocolate (*cont.*)
　giant cupcake 193
　replica of Berlin Wall 187
　replica of Great Wall of China 187
　shoes and handbags 190
　skulls 190, *190*
　train sculpture 218
Chopra, Priyanka (Ind) 203
chopstick, in stomach 122
Chouinard, Jim and Maribel (U.S.A.) 24
christening gown, used by large family 29
Christmas-themed funeral 32
Christmas tree, made of plastic spoons
　219
Chugg, Sami (U.K.) 110
church, family all marry in same 32
Churchill, Lady Randolph (U.S.A.) 27
Churchill, Sir Winston (U.K.)
　false teeth 119
　leather portrait of 203
　unpaid debt 240
Ciaglia, Joe (U.S.A.) 156, *156*
cigarette, exploding 110
cigarette packets, house decorated with
　43, *43*
Clark, Tony (U.S.A.) 96
Clay, Alex (U.S.A.) 123
cliffs
　coffins hung over 44
　dog survives fall 80
　GPS takes driver to edge of 243
climbing
　frozen waterfall 95, *95*
　Olympic Games 90
　one-handed climber 108
　with vacuum cleaner suction 171
　young climber 148
Clinton, Bill (U.S.A.) 11, *11*
Clinton, Hillary (U.S.A.) 11
clocks
　enormous 43, 157
　large number in Pentagon 47
　wound by hand for 600 years 47
clog dance, mass 157, 217
clothes
　always wearing pink 238
　bulletproof 228
　cell-phone dress 220
　enormous T-shirt 209
　gum-wrapper prom dress 208
　invisibility coat 230, *230*
　made of chocolate 189
　manure-covered T-shirts 213
　promoting businesses with T-shirts 238
　replica car made from 220
　sculpture from discarded clothing 213,
　　213
　very valuable sari 212
　wearing multiple T-shirts 152
　young designer 218
clouds
　Brocken Specter 54, *54*
　graffiti 208
　new type found 52
　snow prevented from falling on Moscow
　　48
　very high 49
clown, elected 235
Coach, Allison (U.S.A.) 157
coal-powered bike 136
cobras, kissing 241, *241*
Cockerill, Tim (U.K.) 18–19, *18–19*
cockroaches, population growth 62
coconuts
　octopuses live in 79
　piercing with finger 124
Coe, Robert and Sandra (U.S.A.) 72
coffins
　car-shaped 242, *242*
　escapologist gets out of 153
　glass window in 177, *177*
　groom goes to wedding in 32
　hung over cliffs 44
　JCB carries 32, *32*
　man comes back from dead in 32
　unidentified occupants 176
Cognac, very old bottle of 188
coins
　country's name mis-spelt on 14
　giant coin made of chocolate 188
　huge gold coin 24
　in stomach 121
　unwanted 238
Colón, David Morales (Pue) 28, *28*

Colón de Carbajal, Cristóbal (Spa) 91
colorblindness, zebra camouflage 81
Columbus, Christopher (Ita) 91
Colwill, Sarah (U.K.) 110
comas
　long-lasting 110
　waking from 108
combustion, spontaneous human 179, *179*
comedy gig, very long 214
comic, very valuable 203
computers
　ancient computer found 178
　first 226
　models of cities made from 218
　portraits on floppy disks 221, *221*
　vicar blesses 242
concrete, breaking with elbow 237
Conley, Jamison (U.S.A.) 60
Connery, Sean (U.K.) 42
Connolly, James B. (U.S.A.) 89
Connors, Bob (U.S.A.) 220
Constantine, King of Greece 91
contortionists 115, *115*, 122, 158, *158*,
　165, *165*
Conway, Matt (U.S.A.) 136
Cook, Ian (U.K.) 215
cookies, professional tester 186
Cool, Les (U.S.A.) 20, *20*
Cooley, Frances (U.K.) 190
Corbett, James (Aus) 214
cosmetic surgery
　beauty contest for 114
　to look like Jessica Rabbit 110
Coubertin, Baron de (Fra) 88
cougar, dog saves owner from 61
couscous, model of city 222
Cowan, Freya (U.K.) 235
Cowell, Simon (U.K.) 222
cows
　jumps onto roof 60
　maze in shape of 216
　milkman receives honor wearing cow
　　suit 238
　mistaken for polar bear 241
　prosthetic legs for 63
　rescued from apartment block 64
　Shakespeare plays to improve milk
　　yields 215
　six-legged calf 79
　survives lightning strike 81, *81*
　woman breast-feeds calf 74
Cox, Vin (U.K.) 92
Crabbe, Buster (U.S.A.) 91
crabs
　long walk 75
　sold in dispenser 242, *242*
Craig, Gary (U.K.) 170, *170*
Craig, Rita (Can) 188
crane, dinner parties hanging from 194
crater, found in satellite picture 52
Crawford, K. Michael (U.S.A.) 213
cremation ashes
　in CDs 235
　sculpture from 206
　turned into works of art 33, *33*
cricket-spitting contest 238
crochet
　lions 200, *200*
　water tower cozy 210
crocodiles
　grabs elephant's trunk 82, *82*
　live in house 78
　piece of wood mistaken for 16
　in prison 79
　recognize own names 67
　rubbery fat 83
　tries to take fisherman's catch 97
Cromar, Angie (U.S.A.) 108
Crum, Cookie (U.S.A.) 150–1, *150*
Crucifixion, image made from toast 183,
　183
crystals, weeping 177
Csrefko, Andrea and Laszlo (Hun) 16
CT scans, as art 227, *227*
Cubberly, Darren (U.K.) 240
cucumbers
　cutting with playing card 171, *171*
　giant 157
Cui Jinxin (Chn) 60
cupcake, giant 193
curry
　boom in curry houses 191
　feeding to sheep 187

curry (cont.)
  gold and silver in 193
Curry, Raymond (U.K.) 110
curses, festival of 39
cutlery
  chimpanzees make 61
  swallowed 191, *191*
cyclone, wind speed in 49
Cyparis, Louis Auguste (Mtq) 37

Daalmans, Margaret (Nld) 191, *191*
Daisher, Miles (U.S.A.) 94
Dali, Salvador (Spa) 206
dams
  coincidental deaths 234
  giant beaver dam 84
  ibexes climb on face of 71, *71*
  police guard 38
Dannecker, Alex (U.S.A.) 7, *7*
darkness, as art installation 208
Das, Ramchandra (Ind) 54
Davis, Chelsea (U.S.A.) 101, *101*
Davis, Geena (U.S.A.) 91
Davis, Ian (U.K.) 222
Davis, Ron (U.S.A.) 76
de Burgh, Frank and Emma (U.S.A.) 27, *27*
de la Paz, Neralda (U.S.A.) 213, *213*
Deacon, Elly (U.K.) 171
Dean, Jeremy (U.S.A.) 140
death
  body hidden behind sofa 234
  Brocken Specter 54, *54*
  cat predicts patients' deaths 176, *176*
  coincidental deaths on dam 234
  coming back from dead in coffin 32
  "Day of the Dead" festivals 39, *39*
  dead man found in car in river 29
  dead man mistaken for Halloween dummy 14
  dead men elected 15, 25
  embalmed bodies kept in house 29
  embalmed body on motorcycle 28, *28*
  image of child's face on oven door 178
  life-size cardboard cutout of dead man 32, *32*
  man goes to own funeral 14
  man keeps "dying" 114
  man killed by receiving cremation bill 28
  mediums communicate with 176–7, *176–7*
  mysterious jars 177
  painting with corpse's hand 213, *213*
  vertical burials 240
  woman comforts dead daughter 177, *177*
  woman starts breathing in funeral home 128
deer, lives in house 64
Degerman, Curt (Swe) 243
Delap, Beatrice (U.K.) 28
Delvoye, Wim (Bel) 201
DeNigris, Paul (U.S.A.) 32
dental floss, magnified appearance 118, *118*
dentures
  Churchill's 119
  in lungs 121
Depp, Johnny (U.S.A.) 28
Derrick, Alan (U.K.) 234
Dev, Harpreet (Ind) 142
Dew, Tony (U.K.) 212
Di Furia, Gaetano (U.K.) 32, *32*
diamonds
  dog swallows 64
  expensive toy car 135, *135*
  on liqueur bottle 188
  in tattoo 128
  vuvuzela horn 214
Diana, Princess of Wales 149, 238
dice, mosaics made of 208
DiCecca, Rick (U.S.A.) 221
Dickens, Charles (U.K.) 219, 238
Dickinson, Leo (U.K.) 152
Dietrich, Dorothy (U.S.A.) 147
Diment, Ed (U.K.) 218
Dimmock, Frank (U.K.) 157
dining table, very fast 235
Diogo, Paulo (Por) 99, 99
dissection, of father's body 127, *127*
Dissmore, Perry (U.S.A.) 97
diving
  by horses 14, *14*

diving (cont.)
  diver hits board 101, *101*
  injuries 99
  scuba diving dog 64
D.J., one-armed 217
DNA, extracted from mummy 229
document, very old found 14
dodgeball, giant tournament 92
dogs
  allergies 73
  barbecue fork in head 64, *64*
  bravery medal for 67
  burglar scared off by woman pretending to be 29
  chihuahuas attack police 74
  concert for 222
  disguised as wild animals 73, *73*
  drives truck over owner 241
  dyed pink 238
  eats beehive 72
  eats golf balls 79
  eats owner's toe 77
  found on ice floe 64
  goes fishing 84
  ice-cream van for 190
  knows taxi routes 78
  large muscles 67, *67*
  large vocabulary 78
  lights powered by poop 43
  long journey 62
  long-lost 66, 82
  magnets in stomach 79
  Mickey Mouse on fur 7, *7*
  overgrown coat 76, *76–7*
  paintings by 61
  parachute jumps 60
  pushes baby stroller 70
  Queen's corgis 80
  realistic cake model 187, *187*
  rescued from storm drain 70
  saves owner from cougar 61
  saves owner from fire 84
  scuba diving 64
  shoots owner 64
  skateboarding 76
  sounds car horn for help 74
  survives being hit by train twice 64
  survives fall over cliff 80
  swallows ball 64
  swallows diamond 64
  swallows glass 75
  swollen tongue 77
  taken for walk by car 236
  two rows of teeth 67
  very tall 66
  very ugly 75, *75*
  walks on back legs 80, *80*
  washing machines for 82
  wedding for 72
  wind blows kennel away 79
  world tour 77
doll house, very valuable 208
dolls
  large collection of Barbie dolls 238
  very expensive 210
domino chain, human 169
Dong Changsheng (Chn) 170
Dore, Ahmed Muhamed (Som) 32
Dorfmann, Bettina (Ger) 238
Dorner, Willi (U.K.) 222
Dornon, Sylvain (Fra) 148, *148*
Douglas, Eric Gordon (U.K.) 32
Douthett, Jerry (U.S.A.) 77
Dowling, Rob (Irl) 160
Doyle, Sir Arthur Conan (U.K.) 175, 177
Dreher, Peter (Ger) 210
dress, made from aluminum cans 7, *7*
driftwood, sculptures made from 35, *35*
Drimmer, Dave (U.S.A.) 140, *140–1*
drummer, very young 223
Dueck, Josh (Can) 243
Duff, Owen (U.S.A.) 153
Duke, Charlie (U.S.A.) 216
Dumont, Etienne (Swi) 111, *111*
Dunbar, Dean (U.S.A.) 97
Duncan, Neil (U.S.A.) 112
Dunkley, Kez (U.K.) 93
Duschl, Gary (U.S.A.) 6, *6*
Dwivedi, Twinkle (Ind) 105, *105*
Dyrdek, Rob (U.S.A.) 156, *156*

Earle, Jack (U.S.A.) 117, *117*
Earnshaw, Charles (U.S.A.) 21, *21*
ears
  four-eared kitten 74
  one-eared rabbit 74, *74*
  save child from fall 244, *244*
  very long earlobes 108
  very long hair in 25, *25*
earthquakes
  earthquake-proof bed 230
  iPhone first-aid app used in 123
  makes river flow backwards 44
  moves city 40
  twists rail tracks 52, *52*
Eastlack, Harry (U.S.A.) 115
eating strange objects 192
eBay, grandmother sold on 25
Ebneter, Arnold (U.S.A.) 240
echolocation, boy "sees" with 122
eclipses, solar 52
ectoplasm 176–7, *176–7*
Eddy, Matt (U.S.A.) 153
Edge, Donald (U.K.) 188
Edison, Thomas (U.S.A.) 234
Edwards, Annette (U.K.) 110
eggs
  chicken lays huge 80
  eating eggshells 192, *192*
  multiple double yolks 186
  smell of rotten eggs on gas bills 227
  tortoise eggs delivered by cesarean 80
  triple yolk 80
  in turtle fossil 80
Eiffel Tower, Paris
  rollerblader leaps from 157
  weight of 42
Einstein, Albert (Ger/U.S.A.) 122
Eiriksson, Fridgeir (Ice) 194, *194*
El-Ajouz, Joe (Aus) 190
Eland, Karen (U.S.A.) 200
electricity
  at Chicago World's Fair 168
  long power outage 48
  shot through body 152, *152*
elephants
  armor 57, *57*
  car collides with 234
  crocodile grabs trunk 82, *82*
  electrocuted 234, *234*
  elephant-dung platform shoes 207, *207*
  enormous 30–1, *31*
  glass 44
  hanged 9, 234, *234*
  plays with monitor lizard 21, *21*
  secret language 82
  wash cars 64
Elizabeth II, Queen 238
  corgis 80
  jelly bean mosaic of 223
Elrington, Ptolemy (U.K.) 212, *212*
embroidery, map of London Underground 214
emeralds, large number dug up 170
Engel, Howard (Can) 121
English, Ron (U.S.A.) 208
Enslow, Seth (U.S.A.) 169
envelopes, bacon-flavored 186
escapologists 146–7, *146–7*, 153, 154–5, *154–5*
Escobar, Andrés (Col) 96
Escobar, Pablo (Col) 16
Espin, Fernando (Ecu) 85
Esquivel, Martin (Mex) 67
Estrellas, Pedro (U.K.) 220
Etchells, Joseph (U.K.) 136
Eugenio, Michelle (U.S.A.) 14
Evans, Mark (U.K.) 203
Evans, Zach (U.K.) 50
Evaristti, Marco (Chl) 192
Everest, Mount
  parachuting onto 152
  young climber 157
Everingham, Luke (Aus) 43
Exon, Fiona (U.K.) 186
explosion, very powerful over Siberia 174
explosives, removed from scalp 105
eyebrows, very long hair 25
eyelids
  glued shut 120
  lifting weights with 237
  pulling airplane with 170

eyes
  beetle with bifocal eyes 63
  constant winking 126
  fishing hooks hanging under 157, *157*
  frogs 78, *78*
  popping out of head 163, *163*
  reading in complete darkness 113
  sea urchins 72
  worm in 127
Eyser, George (U.S.A.) 89

face
  baby with two faces 124
  covered in hair 128–9, *129*
  crying face in glacier 50, *50*
  dislocating jaw 97, 165, *165–6*
  hammering nails into 166, *166*
  image of child on oven door 178
  image of Jesus Christ in satellite picture 50
  image of woman's face found on rabbit 178
  transplant 123
  very ugly 164, *164–5*
Facebook, time spent on 236
Faciu, Julika (Rom) 237
Fahey, Ron (Can) 217
Fairburn, Simeon (Aus) 127
Fairchild, Paul (U.S.A.) 217, *217*
fairies
  photographs of 174, *174*, 175, *175*
  tree pods 178, *178*
Falquerho, Yann (Fra) 50
Fan Qianrong (Chn) 192, *192*
Fan Sijia (Chn) 114, *114*
Fard, Arash (U.K.) 195
Farrell, Colin (Irl) 128
Faulkner, James (U.K.) 222
Fear, Liz (Aus) 75
feces, eating 192
feet
  armless people use 108, 123
  dog eats owner's toe 77
  extra toes 109, *109*, 128
  footprints worn into floor 16, *16*
  fork stuck in 122
  rotating 7, *7*, 109
fence post, man speared with 110
Ferring, Winnie (U.S.A.) 169
festival, huge number of people at 44
Ficca, Claudia (Can) 212
Fichte, Ludwig (Ger) 156
Filthy Luker (U.K.) 220
Fine, Jay (U.S.A.) 40, *40*
fingers
  amputated tip on keychain 122
  extra 128
  kept in freezer 110
  magnetic implants 107, *107*
  man eats 107
  piercing coconuts with 124
  soccer player loses 99, *99*
  very strong 110
Finkle, David (U.K.) 222
Finney, Clint (U.S.A.) 162
fire
  ants start 25
  blowtorch on face 163, *163*
  bull with fiery horns 94, *94*
  cat saves man 62
  cutting hair with 240
  dog saves owner 84
  enormous fireball 178
  escapologists 146, *146–7*
  fiery crater in desert 45, *45*
  fire-eating 18, *18*
  firefighters' water freezes 55, *55*
  ghost photographed in 181, *181*
  man sleeps through house fire 16
  money burnt to keep child warm 16
  Olympic flame 91
  oxygen masks save tortoises 82
  river catches fire 40
  spontaneous human combustion 179, *179*
  stuntmen contest 170, *170*
fireworks
  extreme festival 44, *44*
  firecrackers thrown at man 44, *44*
fish
  blind fish lives underground 70

fish (cont.)
  changes color 72
  climbing abilities 85
  eats turtle 70
  fall from sky 48
  found in bladder 112
  goldfish plays musical instruments 85
  hits kayaker 97
  hospital for 74
  huge number found dead 176
  long-lived goldfish 70
  look after manatees 70, *70*
  regurgitating live fish 81
  thumb found inside 20
  in tunnels under Paris 51
fishing hooks, hanging under eyes 157, *157*
Fitzpatrick, Noel (U.K.) 77
flagpole, car welded around 243
Flamburis, Harry "The Horse" (U.S.A.) 244
flies, dead flies as artwork 202, *202–3*
floating, for long time 152, *152*
floods, make gigantic lake 53
fog, catching in nets 41
Foggett, Shaun (U.K.) 78
Followill, Jared (U.S.A.) 208
Folse, John (U.S.A.) 193
food
  alien material in 189
  miniature clay models of 220
  prisoners' final meals re-created 213
  speed-eating 184–5, *184–5*, 188
football
  injuries 99
  player insures hair 112
footprints, scorched 105
Ford, Florence Irene (U.S.A.) 177, *177*
forest, haunted 181
fork, in foot 122
Forman, Austin (Can) 61
Forse, Stephen (U.K.) 189, *189*
Fortune, Lt. Ian (U.K.) 112
fossils
  of ancient spider 61
  eggs in fossil turtle 80
  giant limestone spikes 38
  squid ink 83
Foster, Mary Ann (U.S.A.) 44
Fowler, Tony (U.K.) 238
Franco, Dr. Vito (Ita) 201
Fredo (Chl) 221, *221*
Freeman, Brian (Aus) 17
French fries
  speed-eating contest 188
  very long 186
frogs
  close road 78
  eaten by other creatures 85, *85*
  eating still-beating hearts 189, *189*
  eyes 78, *78*
  long nose 73
  tadpoles with extra legs 79
  very tiny 77
Froman, Sonny (U.S.A.) 213
funeral home, wedding in 242
funerals
  ashes burnt in Viking ship 32
  Christmas-themed 32
  ice-cream van cortege 32
  JCB carries coffin 32, *32*
  man goes to own 14
  motorbike hearses 32
  police tow body away 32
  telephone services shut down for 227
  tractors at 32
  very young undertaker 242
  for whale 79
  wives commit *suttee* 44
  of wrong person 242
Fung, Kai-Hung (Chn) 227, *227*
fungi
  in dung 52
  microbial art 202
Furman, Ashrita (U.S.A.) 153, *153*
furniture, phone book 217
Furze, Colin (U.K.) 136

Gabenhart, Darlene (U.S.A.) 7
Gadd, Will (Can) 95, *95*
Gaga, Lady (U.S.A.) 206, 212, *212*
Gage, Phineas (U.S.A.) 112, *112*
Galbraith, Ryan (U.S.A.) 243

gall stones, multiple 108, *108*
gambler, mummified hand 15
Ganz, Sayaka (U.S.A.) 218, *218–19*
Gao, Mr. (Chn) 120, *120*
Gao Yang (Chn) 124
Gardner, Rulon (U.S.A.) 97
Garr, Susan (U.S.A.) 70
Gaynor, Gloria (U.S.A.) 219
Geary, Carl Robin Sr. (U.S.A.) 25
Geddes, Doyle (U.S.A.) 203
Gentry, Nick (U.K.) 221, *221*
Gettmann, Wolfgang (Ger) 63
Ghetti, Dalton (U.S.A.) 209
ghosts
 ectoplasm 176–7, *176–7*
 in forest 181
 green glow 177
 haunted house for sale 39
 photographs of 178, *178*, 181, *181*
 serves in pub 193
 of slaves 178
 spirits sold 28
 very haunted house 180
Gifford, Brad (U.K.) 107
Gilpin, James (U.K.) 193
Ginther, Joan (U.S.A.) 14
giraffes, collecting pictures of 213
glaciers
 crying face in 50, *50*
 man-made 54
gladiators, school for 47
Glazebrook, Peter (U.K.) 188
glider pilot, survives crash 139, *139*
Gliniecki, Al (U.S.A.) 7, *7*
Glissmeyer, Christie (U.S.A.) 239
gnome, giant 152
Gnuse, Julia (U.S.A.) 107, *107*
Goard, Debbie (U.S.A.) 187, *187*
goats
 clear weeds 78
 walks tightrope 81
Goebel, Sven (Ger) 170
gold
 in curry 193
 expensive toy car 135, *135*
 huge coin 24
 metal detector finds on first outing 20
 Monopoly set 218
 painting with 213
 tattoos 124
 vending machine for 47
 vuvuzela horn 214
goldfish
 longevity 70
 plays musical instruments 85
golf
 dog eats balls 79
 elderly player hits hole-in-one 92
 extreme golf 94
 insect loses match 93
 right-handed man plays with left hand 96
Goncalves, Ademir Jorge (Bra) 14
Gonzales (Can) 222
Goodall, Marion (U.K.) 25
Goosney, Stephen (Can) 14
Gorbunov, Sergei (Rus) 64
Gough, Fred (U.K.) 110
Gowen, Zach (U.S.A.) 93
graduate, elderly 149
graffiti, cloud 208
grandmothers
 huge number of descendants 16
 sold on eBay 25
Grant, John (U.K.) 72
Grant, Pauline (U.K.) 61
grapes, baboons eat vineyard's 66
grasshopper, pink 76, *76*
Great Wall of China, chocolate replica
 of 187
Greenberg, Brooke (U.S.A.) 115
Greenwood, Derek (U.K.) 32
Gregory, Barbara and Dennis (S.A.) 29
Gregory, Natasha (U.K.) 77
Gregory, Dr T. Ryan (Can) 202
Grendol, Joseph (U.S.A.) 165, *166*
Grey, Jimmy (U.S.A.) 42
Griffin, Paul (Can) 110
Griffiths, Frances (U.K.) 175, *175*
Griffiths, Margaret (U.K.) 242
Grylls, Bear (U.K.) 194
Grzebski, Jan (Pol) 110
Gschmeissner, Steve (U.K.) 118, *118*
guacamole, enormous bucket of 188
Guerra, Alain (U.S.A.) 213, *213*

Guevara, Che (Arg) 208
guinea fowl/chicken hybrid 72
guinea pigs, overrun apartment 84
guitarists
 multiple concerts in one day 207
 play to sharks 203
 whirling arm 215
Gulpen, Robert (Swi) 135
gum-boots, welly wanging contest 94
gum-wrappers, prom dress made of 208
Gunnarson, Dean (Can) 147
Gurjar, Badamsinh Juwansinh (Ind) 25
Guyot, Michel (Fra) 54
Guzy, Jozef (Pol) 32

Haase, Anna (Ger) 50
Hadland, Laura (U.K.) 218
Hagens, Gunther von (Ger) 114
hailstones, giant 40, 53
Haines, Leo (U.K.) 223
hair
 cutting with flame 240
 eating 192
 face covered in 128–9, *129*
 football player insures 112
 free haircuts 152
 long arm hair 25
 long eyebrow hair 25
 portraits on 104, *104*
 pulling bus with 237
 sculpture from 210, *210*
 upsidedown barber 236
 very long 25, 105, 113, *113*, 166, *166*
 very long ear hair 25, *25*
 very long leg hair 25
 very long mustache 25
 woman survives by sucking water
  from 113
Hairova, Ravila (Uzb) 79
Halder, Patit Paban (Ind) 74
Hallowes, Harry (U.K.) 47
Hallquist, Wayne and Laurie (U.S.A.) 126
hammock, enormous 206
hamsters, living in hotel as 50
handbags, chocolate 190
hands
 amputated fingertip on keychain 122
 breaking concrete with 237
 extra fingers 128
 finger kept in freezer 110
 grafted onto leg 229, *229*
 hairy transplants 108
 holding multiple tennis balls 169
 magnetic implants in fingers 107, *107*
 man eats finger 107
 mummified 15
 nail in 123
 one-handed basketball player 96
 one-handed climber 108
 painting with corpse's hand 213, *213*
 piercing coconuts with finger 124
 pulled off in tug-of-war 109
 soccer player loses finger 99, *99*
 very strong 110
handsprings, multiple back 169
Hanrahan, Karen (U.S.A.) 195
Hansen, Kasper (Den) 228–9, *229*
Hansen, Phil (U.S.A.) 11, *11*
Hare, Steve (U.K.) 214
hares, permanent pregnancy 75
Haridas (Ind) 158
Harp, Christy (U.S.A.) 187
Harrington, Les (U.K.) 42
Harrington, Padraig (Irl) 94
Harris, Joshua Allen (U.S.A.) 200
Harrop, Bob (U.K.) 188
Harsh, Navratan (Ind) 66, *66*
Hart, Colin (U.K.) 24
Hartel, Lisa (Den) 89
Haruf, Kent (U.S.A.) 208
harvestmen 68, *68–9*
Hastings, David (U.K.) 181
Havel, Dan (U.S.A.) 43, *43*
hay, castle built of 210
Hay, Tran Van (Vnm) 25, 105
Hayes, Anato (U.S.A.) 163, *163*
Hayes, Chris (U.K.) 15, *15*
Hayes, Reg (U.K.) 152
Hazelton, Paul (U.K.) 221
head
 boy survives hook penetrating 126
 bullets in 108, 128
 burying in sand 158, *158*
 camera implanted in back of 219

head (cont.)
 hammering nail into 19, *19*
 horn implanted in 111, *111*, 122
 horns on forehead 115
 human heads found in air freight 112
 iron rod through 112, *112*
 knife stabbed right through 118
 live explosive removed from 105
 looking backwards 164, *164*
 missing from hanged man 110
 nail found in 113
 painting on 213
 preserved cryogenically 24
 two-headed snake 67
 walking with milk bottle on 153, *153*
heart
 artificial heart made with toys 230
 baby "frozen" after surgery 118
 man survives long time after stops
  beating 124
Hedblom, Ben (U.S.A.) 238
hedge, very long 50
hedgehog, no-parking lines painted over
 dead 16, *16*
Heinrichs, Ben (U.S.A.) 84
helicopters
 backflipping dirt bike over 152
 pilot survives shooting 112
 rescues van stranded by GPS 137
 static electricity 136, *136*
 vulture flies into 81
Helland, Ola (Nor) 213
Hempleman-Adams, David (U.K.) 194
Hendrix, Jimi (U.S.A.)
 leather portrait of 203
Henriques, Jack (U.K.) 191
Herbert, Tom (U.K.) 188
Hernandez, Christian (Mex) 97
Hernandez, Francisco Jr. (U.S.A.) 244
Hersch, Dave (U.S.A.) 134
hiccups, surgery to stop 128
Hiemenz, Bob "Tracker Bob" (U.S.A.) 215
Higley, Doug (U.S.A.) 220, *220*
Hildebrandt, Norah (U.S.A.) 26, 27, *27*
Hill, Jamie (U.S.A.) 170
Hinds, Lt. Sidney (U.S.A.) 90
Hindu sadhus 158–9, *158–9*
hippopotamus, pink 82
Hitchcock, Alfred (U.K.), image projected
 onto trees 174, *174*
Hitler, Adolf (Ger) 16, 91
Hjelmqvist, Fredrik (Swe) 219
Ho, Dr. Thienna (U.S.A.) 110
Ho Eng Hui (Mal) 124
Hodges, Casey (Aus) 160
Hodgson, Alistair (U.K.) 123
Hofstra, Henk (Nld) 222
Hoketsu, Hiroshi (Jap) 89
Holm, Irmgard (U.S.A.) 120
holograms 207, *207*
Hong Kong (Chn) 109
Hook, Owen (U.K.) 143
Hooper, Cedric (U.K.) 190
Hoover, Cynthia (U.S.A.) 113
Horkin, Kevin (U.K.) 178, *178*
horns
 on forehead 115
 implanted in head 111, *111*, 122
horses
 antivenom production 124
 enormous rocking horse 212
 high dives by 14, *14*
 Hummer converted to horse-drawn
  carriage 140
 Olympic Games 90
 riding injuries 99
 very intelligent 84
 very small 77
 veterinarian trapped under 83
hospital, for pet fish 74
Hostetler, Keri (U.S.A.) 70
Hot, Les (U.S.A.) 20, *20*
hot cross bun, very old 187
hot dog, very expensive 186
hot-water bottle, being blown up 7, *7*
Houghton, Jane (U.K.) 115
houses
 bulldozed to prevent bank repossessing
  43
 converted into 007 movie set 42
 covered in greenish goo 174
 cow jumps onto roof 60
 decorated with cigarette packets 43, *43*
 haunted 39, 178, 180

houses (cont.)
 hit by meteorites 48
 lava engulfs 37
 living in trees 39
 made of steel 168
 ram runs amok in 72
 rotating house 43
 as sculpture 43, *43*
 upside-down 244
 very narrow 53
 very small 47, *47*
Howard, Brierley (U.K.) 66
Howarth, Cyril (U.K.) 235
Howell, Gwen (U.K.) 76
Howerton, Clarence C. "Major Mite"
 (U.S.A.) 116–17, *116–17*
Hu Gua (Chn) 186
Hua Chi (Chn) 16, *16*
Huang, Victor (Nzl) 85
Huang Jianjun (Chn) 143
Huang Lijie (Chn) 82
Huang Yuyen (Twn) 80
Huckvale, David (U.K.) 128
Hughes, Howard (U.S.A.) 140, *140–1*
Hughes, Stuart (U.K.) 135
hugs, multiple 149
Hui Chung (Chn) 105
hummus, enormous plate of 190
hurricanes, tree survives 50
Hutton, Paul (U.K.) 137
hypnotizing rabbits 80

ibexes, climb dam face 71, *71*
ice
 birds dive through 74
 falls from sky 44
 firefighters' water freezes 55, *55*
 frozen waterfall 95, *95*
 giant hailstones 40, 53
 icicles kill people 49
 immersion in 160, *160*
 lake under 41
 lighthouse covered in 53, *53*
 man-made glaciers 54
 musical instruments made of 210
 planes land on 245, *245*
ice cream
 for dogs 190
 ice-cream vans at funeral 32
 whole meal of 188
ice hockey
 lucky escape for player 98, *98*
 match delayed for long time 92
igloo, built in yard 42
influenza, anti-flu suit 226
Ingram, Ted (U.K.) 152
Inoue, Satoko (Jap) 229
INSA (U.K.) 207
insects
 bug-eating parties 187, *187*
 eating 195, *195*
 mosquito-killing contest 80
Internet
 anti-leak document leaks 16
 pigeon faster than broadband 77
 time spent on Facebook 236
invisibility coat 230, *230*
iPad, portraits made on 215
Irwin, Steve (Aus) 64
Isner, John (U.S.A.) 96
isopods, giant 83, *83*
Isungset, Terje (Nor) 210
Ivanisevic, Goran (Cro) 92
Ivanov, Vyacheslav (Rus) 90

Jablon, Jim (U.S.A.) 134, *134–5*
Jackson, Brian (U.S.A.) 7, *7*
Jackson, Jessiah (U.S.A.) 126
Jackson, Michael (U.S.A.)
 candy portrait of 222, *222*
 income after death 217
 pumpkin portrait of 222
James, Cathy (Aus) 79
jaw, dislocating 97, 165, *165–6*
Jefferson, Thomas (U.S.A.), portrait on
 hair 104, *104*
Jeffries, John (U.S.A.) 17
jelly bean mosaic 223
jellyfish
 adhesive tape sculpture 202, *202*
 fisherman stung by 63
 robot 228
 turned into caramel candies 195
Jennings, Desiree (U.S.A.) 110

Jesus Christ
 face in satellite picture 50
 man named Lord Jesus Christ 238
 toast art 183, *183*
Ji Yong-Ho (Kor) 214, *214*
Jian Tianjin (Chn) 108
Jiang Juxiang (Chn) 28
Jin Songhao (Chn) 160, *160*
Jin Y. Hua (Chn) 104, *104*
Johnson, Larry (U.S.A.) 112
Johnson, Lyndon B. (U.S.A.), portrait on
 hair 104, *104*
Johnsrud, Brian and Jared (U.S.A.) 238
jokes, very long comedy gig 214
Jolie, Angeline (U.S.A.) 128
Jones, Rhiannon Elizabeth (U.K.) 29
Jones, Robert (U.K.) 47
Jones, Ron (U.K.) 242
Jones, Ron (U.S.A.) 110
Jordan, Bethany (U.K.) 128
judges, numbers of 53
juggling
 underwater 148, *148*
 upside down 160
Juliff, Laura (Aus) 160
Jupiter
 Great Red Spot shrinks 49
 loses belts 180

Kanaguri, Shizo (Jap) 90
Kane, Kyle (U.K.) 114
Kang Mengru (Chn) 118
Kangkang (Chn) 124
Kanichka 66, *166*
karaoke, nonstop 215
karate, young champion 169
Kato, Sogen (Jap) 32
Kautza, Andy and Connie (U.S.A.) 152
Kaye, Luke (U.K.) 119
Kazemi, Ali (Iran) 90
Keats, Jonathan (U.S.A.) 209
Kellas, John (U.K.) 72
Kelly, Lisa (U.K.) 118
Kendik, Alex (Can) 7, *7*
Kennedy, John F. (U.S.A.)
 portrait on hair 104, *104*
 salt-and-pepper shaker 239
Kenny, Gene (U.S.A.) 171
Keonig, Peter (Ger) 244
Kepner, Jeff (U.S.A.) 108
Kerr, Henry (U.K.) 32
ketchup, banana 195
Key lime pie, giant 186
Keysaw, Chelsea (U.S.A.) 124
Kézi, Gábor (Hun) 243
Khanapiyeva, Sakinat (Rus) 148
Khris, Taig (Alg) 157
Kidder, Christopher O. (U.S.A.) 219
kidneys
 giant stone removed from 120, *120*
 large number of stones removed from
  120, *120*
 nail removed from 120, *120*
Kilgast, Stephanie 220
killer whales, penguin escapes 62, *62*
King, Stephen (U.S.A.) 209
Kings of Leon (U.S.A.) 208
Kipping, Chelsey (U.S.A.) 169
Kirby, Dr. Richard (U.K.) 70, *70*
Kirchen, Derek (U.K.) 121
kissing cobras 241, *241*
Kistler, Samuel Stephens (U.S.A.) 230, *230*
kite-powered cargo ship 141
Klein, Roelof (Nld) 88
Kleis, Dick (U.S.A.) 238
Kleman, Vic (U.S.A.) 242
Klinger, Doug 149
Klingon, performance of *A Christmas
 Carol* in 219
knives
 man orders coffee with knife stuck in
  chest 244
 in neck 114
 plasma knife 227
 stabbed right through head 118
 standing on 237
Knotek, Ryan (U.S.A.) 242
Kober, Martin (U.S.A.) 219
Kocaman, Hatice (Tur) 126
Koller, Habu (Ger) 164, *164*
Kolodzinski, Jeff (U.S.A.) 92
Kongee, Leo (U.S.A.) 166, *166*
Kopp, Benjamin (U.S.A.) 110, 136
Kosen, Sultan (Tur) 114

Krankl, Matthias (Ger) 142
Krause, Fred (U.S.A.) 64
Krupnik, Ari (U.S.A.) 208
Kuksi, Kris (U.S.A.) 203, 203–5
Kulick, Kelly (U.S.A.) 93
Kulkarni, Deepa (U.S.A.) 110
Kumar, Anil (Ind) 121
Kumar, Santosh (Ind) 140
Kumthekar, Heramb Ashok (Ind) 128
Kurkul, Gennadi (U.K.) 72

LA Pop Art 215, 215
Laak, Phil (U.S.A.) 160
Lacey, Lexi (U.K.) 124
Lagravere, Michel (Mex) 237
Lahue, Mike (U.S.A.) 191
Laity, Bill (U.S.A.) 93, 93
Lajic, Radivoje (Bos) 48
Lambert, Kyle (U.K.) 215
landmines, rats hunt 28, 28
landscapes, model 216, 216
Langan, Mark (U.S.A.) 202
Langeder, Hannes (Aut) 142, 142, 207
Langseth, Hans (Nor) 25
lanterns, paper 171
Lapeyrouse, Tracy (U.K.) 76
LaPierre, Sandy (U.S.A.) 60
Larkin, Tommy (Can) 14
Larrieux, Vicki (U.K.) 193
Larson, Lief (U.S.A.) 200
LaRue, Josh (U.S.A.) 110
Latin tattoos 128
Laue, Kevin (U.S.A.) 96
laundry, Olympic Games 89
laundry lint, replica of The Last Supper 238–9, 239
Laurello, Martin (U.S.A.) 164, 164
Lauridsen, Henrik (Den) 228–9, 229
Lavasseur, George (U.S.A.) 237, 237
lawn mower, very fast 160
lead, gargling with molten 18, 19
Lee, Jin-gyu (Kor) 244
leeches
    found in girl's nose 128
    robber's blood found in 24
Lefson, Joanne (S.A.) 77
LeGendre, Robert (U.S.A.) 89
LEGO®
    mending monuments with 210
    replica of airplane 208
    ship replicas 218, 221
legs
    amputees climb mountain 112
    armless and legless woman 164, 164
    bent behind head 7, 7
    bionic legs for cat 77
    five-legged rat 60
    free bionic leg 128
    hand grafted onto 229, 229
    legless cyclist 106, 106
    man sews wound up himself 109
    one-legged wrestler 93
    prosthetic legs for cow 63
    self-amputation 108
    six-legged calf 79
    soccer player breaks 100, 100–1
    stretching bone 127
    tadpoles with extra legs 79
    two-legged lamb 60, 60
    two-legged pig 84, 84
    very long hair on 25
Lei Zhiqian (Chn) 135
lemurs, rub themselves with millipedes 78
Lendavi, Reverend Zoltan (Hun) 240
Lennon, John (U.K.),
    phone book portrait 145, 145
    toilet sold 25
Leonardo da Vinci (Ita)
    cholesterol levels of Mona Lisa 201
    coffee painting of Mona Lisa 200
    giant Mona Lisa 222
    laundry lint replica of The Last Supper 238–9, 239
    Rubik's cube version of The Last Supper 208
Leonardo, Jesus (U.S.A.) 93
Lepore, Tony (U.S.A.) 244
Levi, Kobi (Isr) 206
Levine, Philip (U.K.) 213
levitation, with magnets 230
Lewis, Jim (U.S.A.) 25

Lewis, Paul (U.K.) 115
Li Guiwen (Chn) 135
Li Liuqun (Chn) 187
Li Sanju (Chn) 195
Li Weiguo (Chn) 135
Libertiny, Tomas Gabzdil (Nld) 85, 85
libraries
    huge number of books borrowed 206
    very overdue books 203, 221
Liew Siaw Hsia (Mal) 124
Lighthart, Edward (U.S.A.) 123
lighthouses
    covered in ice 53, 53
    in lakes 53
lightning
    boy struck on Friday 13th 20
    cow survives 81, 81
    hits Hong Kong 41
    hotspot 49
    lucky escape 107
    patterns on skin 118, 118
    strikes Statue of Liberty 40, 40
lights
    at Chicago World's Fair 168
    luminous beams in sky 44
    Marfa Lights 174
    powered by dog poop 43
    produced from patient's chest 176
    rays from star switch on 168
limousine, tractor-trailer 140, 140
Lin, Mr (Chn) 84
Lin Su (Chn) 29, 29
Lin Yaohui (Chn) 126
Lincoln, Abraham (U.S.A.), assassination 110
lines, alignments on 181
Ling Wan (Chn) 42
lions
    burgers made from 195
    crochet 200, 200
    lives with tiger and bear 66, 66
    opens car door 82, 82
    owl chick escapes 76
    stolen from circus 14
    zebra camouflage and 81
liposuction, eating own fat 192
lipstick, mass application of 221
Liu, Victor (Chn) 200, 200
Liu Chengrui (Chn) 126
Liu Wei (Chn) 108
Lizardman 8, 8
lizards
    elephant plays with 21, 21
    lizard boy 66, 66
Lloyd, Naomi (U.K.) 241
Lobrano, Roberto (Ita) 188
lobster, blown up by World War II mine 20
locusts, as pizza topping 186
logs, sculpture mistaken for pile of 217
Lombardo, Christi (U.S.A.) 242
London, Ken (U.S.A.) 140, 140–1
London Underground, embroidered map of 214
Loos, Arthur (U.S.A.) 163, 163
Lopez, Felipe (U.S.A.) 96
Lopez, Heidi (U.S.A.) 16
Lorenc, Richard (U.S.A.) 29, 29
Lotito, Michel (Fra) 192
Love, Robyn (U.S.A.) 210
Lovlid, Unni (Nor) 219
Loys, François de (Swi) 180, 180
Luciano, Davide (Can) 212
luck, accident survivor wins lottery 244
lunch, on very long table 193
Lunden, Leon de (Bel) 90
lungs
    bone stuck in 121
    bullet in 114
    cashew nut in 121
    collapsible 62
    false teeth in 121
    grass found in 121
    pea plant growing in 110
    plastic eating utensil found in 121
    stolen 29
    twigs in 121, 121

Ma Xiuxian (Chn) 24
McAdou, J.M. (U.S.A.) 241, 241
macaroni, enormous meal of 193
McCarthy, Ellen (Irl) 107

McCartney, Macie (U.S.A.) 109
McCartney, Paul (U.K.) 110
McClure, Daryl (U.S.A.) 32
McCormack, Janice (U.K.) 193
McDaniels, Grace (U.S.A.) 164, 164–5
McFarlane, Steve (U.S.A.) 124, 124
McGlone, Brittney (Aus) 160
MacGregor, Helen (U.K.) 14
McHargue, Ozella (U.S.A.) 32
Machida, Lyoto (Bra) 192
Mack, Captain Ringman (U.S.A.) 163, 163
McKenzie, Rosita (U.K.) 219
McNaught, Ryan (Aus) 208
McPhee, Ben (Aus) 148
McPhee, Russell (Aus) 122
McPherson, Lydia (U.S.A.) 166, 166
McTindal, Russ (U.S.A.) 73
maggots, in mouth 156
Mahardika, Ari (Idn) 223, 223
Mahut, Nicolas (Fra) 96
mail
    hawk attacks postman 76
    lake deliveries 40
    long-lost 235
    very late delivery 17, 20
Maimaiti Hali (Chn) 124
Maine, Patti Froman (U.S.A.) 213
"Major Mite" (U.S.A.) 9, 9, 116–17, 116–17
Malarchuk, Clint (U.S.A.) 98, 98
Malindzi, Thuli (S.A.) 187
Malvada, Marina (Can) 190, 190
manatee, fish look after 70, 70
Mandela, Asha (U.S.A.) 113, 113
Mangrum, Lloyd (U.S.A.) 93
manholes, large collection of 169
Manley, John (U.S.A.) 121
Manorama, Aachi (Ind) 210
manure
    elephant-dung platform shoes 207, 207
    fungi in 52
    message spelt out in 238
    recycled into asphalt 237
    replica of Venus de Milo 218
    T-shirts covered in 213
map, embroidered 214
Maphumulo, Nkosinathi (S.A.) 217
marathons
    Olympic Games 88
    running with tumble-drier on back 93
March, Dave (U.S.A.) 142
Marfa Lights 174
margarine sculpture 186, 188, 188
Marley, Bob (Jam) 197, 197
Marque, Albert (Fra) 210
Mars, methane on 41
Marsh, Garry and Joan (U.K.) 70
Marsh, Steve (U.K.) 243
Marshall, Mary (U.K.) 177, 177
Marshall, Rob (Aus) 210
Martin, Anna (U.S.A.) 179
Martin, Anthony (U.S.A.) 153, 154–5, 154–5
Masala, Daniele (Ita) 90
Masher, Eddie (U.S.A.) 114, 114
Maso da San Friano (Ita) 210
Mason, Paul (U.K.) 115
matchsticks
    replica of Lord of the Rings city 218
Mathew, Joby (Ind) 123
Matt the Knife (U.S.A.) 147
Matthews, John (U.S.A.) 127
mattress, money hidden in 17
Maxton, GarE (U.S.A.) 219
May, Henrik (Ger) 96, 96
May, Sydney (U.S.A.) 60
Mayers, Rev (Aus) 211, 211
mayonnaise, causes highway crash 236
mazes
    cartoon characters in 220
    cow-shaped 216
Mazzotta, Matthew (U.S.A.) 43
meat, bikini made of raw 206
meatballs
    giant 190
    made with own fat 192
Medici, Cosimo I de' (Ita) 210
Mehta, Sameer (Ind) 128
melons
    close motorway 137
    slicing on woman's stomach 186
Mendez, Danny (U.S.A.) 242, 242
mercury, telescope mirror 227

Merlini, David (Hun) 147
mermaids, fake 220, 220
Meselmani, Hasnah Mohamed (Leb) 177
metal
    removed from stomach 108
    shrinking with magnets 228
metal detector, finds treasure on first outing 20
meteorites
    crater found in satellite picture 52
    explosion over Siberia 174
    hits truck 49
    multiple strikes on house 48
methane
    lake on moon 38
    lights powered by dog poop 43
    on Mars 41
Metz, Jonathan (U.S.A.) 121
Meyer, Allen (Can) 94
Meyer, Edward (Can) 9
Miao, Mrs (Chn) 108, 108
mice
    found in can of cola 189
    found in loaf of bread 189, 189
    found in milk container 189
Michelangelo (Ita), long-lost painting by 219
Mickelson, Phil (U.S.A.) 96
microbial art 202
migraine
    Chinese accent after 110
    unusual cure for 110
migration, by Arctic terns 62
Milhiser, John (U.S.A.) 148, 148
milk
    dead mouse found in 189
    milkman receives honor wearing cow suit 238
    Shakespeare plays to improve yields 215
    statues drink 178
millepedes, lemurs rub themselves with 78
mine, lobster blown up by 20
Ming Li (Chn) 229, 229
Mitchell, Gary (Can) 188
Mitchell, Ralph (U.K.) 152
Mitzscherlich, Uwe (Ger) 80
Mobell, Sidney (U.S.A.) 218
Mohammed, Hassani 115, 115
Moline, Dino (Arg) 138, 138
Monaro, Anna (Ita) 176
Monet, Claude (Fra), giant replica of painting 212
money
    burnt to alert rescuers 14
    burnt to keep child warm 16
    children find stolen 29
    coins in stomach 121
    dollar bill mosaics 222
    hidden in mattress 17
    hidden in shoe 15
Monforto, Steve (U.S.A.) 94
monk, mummified 22, 22
monkeys
    as guards 96
    smuggled onto plane 60
Monopoly set, gold 218
Monroe, Marilyn (U.S.A.)
    coffee mosaic of 209
    made from butterfly wings 233, 233
    portrait on leaf 200
    typed portrait of 201
Moon
    beer made by light of full moon 188
    giant pit on 44
    scratch 'n' sniff artwork 216
moons
    changing places 49
    methane lake on 38
Moore, Amanda (U.K.) 119, 119
Moore, Caroline (U.S.A.) 52
Moore, Hilmar (U.S.A.) 149
moped, with flamethrower 136
Morrell, Professor A.L. (U.S.A.) 164, 164
Morrison, Chris (U.K.) 79
Morse Code, blind man writes book in 110
mosaics
    coffee 209
    dice 208
    dollar bills 222
    huge mural 207

mosaics (cont.)
    jelly bean 223
    plastic balls 212, 212
    screws 216
mosquito-killing contest 80
Moss, Channing (U.S.A.) 121
Moss, Kate (U.K.) 201
motorcycles
    alligator made into 134, 134–5
    backflipping dirt bike over helicopter 152
    embalmed body on 28, 28
    as hearses 32
    long jump on 156, 169
    man buried with 244
    miniature 140
    ridden over stomach 237
    rider leaps to safety on truck 135
    riders trapped in drain 235, 235
    swan knocks rider off 81
    Wall of Death 150–1, 150–1
    without front wheel 141, 141
mountains
    amputees climb 112
    banana peels found on 188
    extreme golf 94
    highest unclimbed 49
    man digs tunnel through 54
    painted white 48
    school built on side of 52
    young climbers 148, 157
mouth
    lifting weights with 92, 92
    maggots in 156
movies
    house converted into 007 movie set 42
    lost Chaplin film 223
    stage version of Ben Hur 200
    12 parts for one actress 203
    veteran actor 210
Mozart, Wolfgang Amadeus (Aut) 50
Muhr, Magnus (Swe) 202
Mullane, Simon and Angie (U.K.) 42
Mullen, Dermot (U.K.) 77
Mullikin, Garret (U.S.A.) 127
Mumbere, Charles Wesley (Uga) 240
mummies 22–3, 22–3
    DNA extracted from 229
    European mummies found in China 174
    fake 220, 220
    mummified hand 15
Munch, Edvard (Nor) 202
Murchison, Lauren (U.S.A.) 90
Murdock, Karen 84
music
    broadcast from stomach 219
    concert for dogs 222
    concert in catacombs 51
    concerts in sewer 219
    fan travels long distance to concerts 217
    helps bacteria work faster 50
    listening to one album constantly 214
    pigeon droppings halt concert 208
    very long concert 222
musical instruments
    fungal treatment for violin 230
    goldfish plays 85
    made of ice 210
    played without touching 202
mustache, very long 25
Mwangi, Lazarus 115, 115

nachos, giant tray of 190
Nadiri, Sikeli (Fij) 105
Naganandaswamy, S.C. (Ind) 152, 152
nails
    hammering into face 166, 166
    in hand 123
    in head 19, 19, 113
    lying on bed of 159, 159
    removed from kidney 120, 120
Nasheed, President (Mdv) 54
nativity scene, on head of a pin 209
neck, impaled on stick 127
needles
    in body 122
    removed from brain 126
Nelson, Admiral Horatio (U.K.) 216
Nero, Emperor 88
Netherland, Dan (U.S.A.) 110
Nevins, Dan (U.S.A.) 112
Newman, Lyn (U.K.) 72

Newman, Mike (U.K.) 139, *139*
Niagara Falls, stopped 52, *52*
Nijhuis, Tony (U.K.) 142
Nikulin, Ivan (Rus) 128
Nintendo, as collector's item 200
nipples, pulling weights with 163, *163*
Nixon, Richard (U.S.A.), portrait on hair 104, *104*
Nixon, Steven (U.K.) 114
Noel, Markley (U.S.A.) 220
Noel-Baker, Philip (U.K.) 91
Noemmer, Franz-Xaver 74, *74*
Nolasco, Jess (Can) 188
Nong Youhui (Chn) 113
Norphel, Chewang (Ind) 54
Norris, Matt (U.S.A.) 141
Norsigian, Rick (U.S.A.) 207
nose
  bullet sneezed out of 126
  leech found in 128
  nosebleed causes death 122
  snakes in 237
  touching for long time 148, *148*
  using electric drill on 237
nuclear reactor, homemade 229
nude people, mass hug 201
numbers
  baby's significant birthday 29
  lucky number in lottery 28
  memorizing 171
  unlucky cell phone number 28
Nurmi, Paavo (Fin) 89
nut, in lung 121
Nuwame, Luanga (Can) 203

Oatman, Olive (U.S.A.) 26, *26*
Obama, Barack (U.S.A.)
  portrait of on leaf 200
  pumpkin portrait of 222
  typed portrait of 201
O'Connor, John (Irl) 179
octopuses
  floods aquarium 79
  huge tentacles through window 220
  live in coconut shells 79
  psychic abilities 79, *79*
  steals camera 85
O'Donnell, Daniel (Irl) 217
Officer, Robert (U.S.A.) 148, *148*
Ofili, Chris (U.K.) 207
Ogg, Kate (Aus) 118
O'Hearn, John (U.S.A.) 212, *212*
oil wells, under school 48
Okrand, Marc (U.S.A.) 219
Oliver, Paul (Aus) 73
Olympic Games 88–91
Onac, Aydin (U.K.) 195
Onassis, Jackie (U.S.A.), salt-and-pepper shaker 239
Ondash, Jeff (U.S.A.) 149
orangutans
  takes photographs 60
  in tunnels under Paris 51
  zoo's animal escape drill 60, *60*
organs
  organ donor 110
  pierced by rod 128
  in wrong places 128
origami, tiny models 206
Ortega, Daniel Roberto (U.S.A.) 33, *33*
Orwell, George (U.K.) 208
otter, on kayaking trips 63
oven, image of child's face on door 178
owl chick, escapes lion 76

paintings
  of ants 222
  body painting 12, *12–13*, 201, *201*, 213
  by chimpanzee 67
  by dog 61
  by holidaymaker 210
  by whale 80
  coffee 200
  giant *Mona Lisa* 222
  giant replica of Monet painting 212
  on head 213
  help police improve powers of observation 203
  laundry lint replica of *The Last Supper* 238–9, *239*
  many artists for 213
  microbial art 202
  Munch's *The Scream* re-created with cardboard boxes 202

paintings (*cont.*)
  portrait on hair 104, *104*
  of same subject 210
  thrown away by mistake 206
  using blood 211, *211*
  using typewriter 222
  using words from *Alice in Wonderland* 215, *215*
  very early image of a watch 210
  very valuable painting found behind sofa 206
  very young artists 217, 223
  with corpse's hand 213, *213*
  with gold 213
  with remote-control cars 215
Palladino, Eusapia (Ita) 176
pandas
  dog disguised as 73, *73*
  dung replica of *Venus de Milo* 218
  genetic puzzle 72
paper
  eating 192
  quantities used for books 213
  tiny origami models 206
paragliding, looping the loop 243
Parfitt, George (U.K.) 29
Park, Morace (U.K.) 223
Parker, April (U.K.) 75
parking space, very valuable 141
parking tickets, relaxation instructions on 235
Parkinson family (U.S.A.) 83
parrots
  arrested 76
  mystery illness 62
  scares off burglars 72
Parrott, Rev. Canon David (U.K.) 242
Parsons, Ken (Can) 215
particle accelerator, bread shuts down 226
Pasquette, Didier (Fra) 169
pasta, enormous meal of 193
Pastrana, Travis (U.S.A.) 152
Paswaan, Deepak (Ind) 108
Pattison, Jim Jr. (Can) 6, *6*
Patiz, Vicente (Ger) 207
Patton, George S. (U.S.A.) 91
Pazos, Leslie (U.S.A.) 16
Pazos, Saby (U.S.A.) 16
Peabody, Harold (U.S.A.) 32
Peacock, Melissa (U.K.) 110
Pearce, Henry (Aus) 89
Peladi, Zsolt and Geza (Hun) 24
Pemberton, Wesley (U.S.A.) 25
Pemberton, Zoe (U.K.) 25
pen, enormous 156
pencils, carving tips 208–9, *209*
Penfold, Sheila (U.K.) 93
penguin, escapes killer whales 62, *62*
Pennington, Brad (U.S.A.) 97
Penny, Jessica (Aus) 160
Penrose, Cliff (U.K.) 80
performance art 210
Peric, Daniel (Ger) 123
Pericolo, Bridget and Angelo (U.S.A.) 14
Peterkin-Vertanesian, Brian (U.S.A.) 25
Petty, Ann (U.K.) 217
Pheidippides (Grc) 88
Philippoussis, Mark (Aus) 92
phone books
  furniture and sculpture from 217
  portraits from 145, *145*
photographs
  blind photographer 219
  children photographed every day 218
  clones of photographer in 223, *223*
  documenting growth of beard 239
  of fairies 174, *174*, 175, *175*
  of ghosts 178, *178*, 181, *181*
  of model landscapes 216, *216*
  orangutan takes 60
  of roadside litter 208
  taken every year 217
  underwater gallery 222
  very valuable 207
pi, calculating 170
pigs
  enormous tusks 72
  invited to vote in election 61
  real piggy bank 24
  tattooed with designer logos 201
  on trampoline 76
  two-legged 84, *84*
Pilâtre de Rozier, Jean-François (Fra) 17
pillow, marrying 244

pineapples, as status symbols 188
pistols, duelling at Olympic Games 90
pizza
  exotic meats 195
  giant 190
  huge chain of 188
  locust topping 186
placenta, in health drink 186
planets
  atmosphere of vaporized rock 49
  Jupiter loses belts 180
  Jupiter's Great Red Spot shrinks 49
  methane on Mars 41
  new ring found round Saturn 53
  solar eclipses 52
  very windy 48
plankton 70, *70*
plants, toilet for treeshrews 62, *62*
plasma knife 227
plastic bags, inflatable polar bears made from 200
plates, edible 189
playing cards
  cutting cucumber with 171, *171*
  memorizing 171
  model of hotel 239
  throwing long distance 171
plowing competition, teenager wins 171
Podolsky, Dominik (Aut) 14
Poe, Jesse (U.S.A.) 243
poem boxing contest 217
poison, antivenom production 124
poker, very long session 160
Polamalu, Troy (U.S.A.) 112
polar bears
  cow mistaken for 241
  made from plastic bags 200
Poleykett, Scott (U.K.) 96
police
  chihuahuas attack 74
  dancing traffic cop 244
  guard dam 38
  improving powers of observation 203
  use tractor 137
  win lottery 20
Pollock, Jackson (U.S.A.) 223
Pondella, Christian (U.S.A.) 95, *95*
Pontico, Ruth (U.S.A.) 117, *117*
Ponting, Herbert (U.K.) 159, *159*
Poole, Mitch (U.S.A.) 200
Pope, Simon (U.K.) 186
Popeyed Perry (U.S.A.) 163, *163*
Popova, Julia (Rus) 114
population, boy/girl imbalance 53
Pordaeng, Loung (Tha) 22, *22*
portraits
  burger grease 11, *11*
  candy 222, *222*
  carved pumpkins 222
  cassette tape 197, *197*
  on floppy disks 221, *221*
  on iPad 215
  leather 203
  made with dead ants 58–9, *58–9*
  mosaic 208, 212, *212*
  non-stop drawings 207
  portraits on hair 104, *104*
  three-dimensional illusion 206, *206*
  toast 183, *183*, 218
  typed 201
postage stamps
  large collection of 170
  very valuable 16
postcards
  recipient pictured in 14
  very late delivery 20
postman, hawk attacks 76
potato, enormous 188
potholes
  for sale 136
  turned into artworks 212
Potter, Dean (U.S.A.) 97, *97*
Poussin, Alexandre and Sonia (Fra) 169
Powell, Ivor (U.K.) 96
Powell, Lewis (U.S.A.) 110
Pras, Bernard (Bel) 206
Prasad, Padma (Ind) 193
Pratt, Don (U.K.) 141
pregnancy
  prenatal surgery 109
  woman with two uteruses 108
Presley, Elvis (U.S.A.), candy portrait of 222, *222*
Prichard, Richard (U.K.) 20

priest, skateboarding 240
prisoners
  cat not allowed to visit 244
  digs out of prison with spoon 20
  final meals re-created 213
  prisoners' Tour de France 92
  as school mascot 43
  typo keeps man behind bars 16
prisons
  dummy guard 24
  escapologist gets out of 153
  man caught in women's 29
  restaurant in 194
Proulx, Suzanne (U.S.A.) 239, *239*
pubs
  drinking beer in many different 193
  ghost serves in 193
  moved up hill 47
  rabbit visits 78
  very isolated 38
Pugh, Lewis (U.K.) 107
Pullen, Ernest (U.S.A.) 17
pumpkins
  giant 187
  portraits carved in 222
punchbag, human 244
Purbrick, Hilaire (U.K.) 50
Pushnik, Freda (U.S.A.) 164, *164*
Putin, Vladimir (Rus) 222
pythons
  as assault weapon 238
  fishermen catch 61
  lives in sewer 80
  moves into rabbit hutch 61
  "Serpent Queen" 156, *156*
  trapped in washing machine 61
  tries to catch marsupial 61, *61*
  X-rays of python digesting a rat 228–9, 229

Qin Yuan (Chn) 121
quadruplets 108, 118
Quran, tiny copy of 217

rabbits
  cleared from island 40
  dust bunnies 239, *239*
  hypnotizing 80
  image of woman's face found on 178
  jumping contests 94
  one-eared 74, *74*
  plays slot machines 78
Rabbo, Hassan Abed (Leb) 217
Railton, Paul (U.K.) 236
rain, bacteria in 177
Rains, Diane (U.S.A.) 85
Rak, Tomas (U.K.) 65, *65*
Ramannavar, Dr Mahantesh (Ind) 127, *127*
Ramlan (Idn) 108
Ramos, Cristiam (Mex) 222, *222*
Ramos, Enrique (Mex) 107, *107*, 233, *233*
Ramsey, Chris (U.S.A.) 219
Raphael (Ita), valuable drawing by 209
Rasmuson, Elizabeth (U.S.A.) 208
Rasmuson, Svante (Swe) 90
Rathbone, Keira (U.S.A.) 201
rats
  bagpipes frighten 234
  cleared from islands 40, 47
  five-legged 60
  found in tin of baked beans 189
  hunt landmines 28, 48
  X-rays of python digesting 228–9, 229
Rawlinson, Jim (U.S.A.) 63
Ray, Viviana (U.S.A.) 236, *236*
Reagan, Ronald (U.S.A.), portrait on hair 104, *104*
Recchia, Franco (Ita) 218
Reed, Lou (U.S.A.) 222
regurgitating objects 81, 165, *165*, 166, *166*
Rehage, Christoph (Ger) 239
Rellecke, Horst (Ger) 44
Ren Jiemei (Chn) 123
restaurants
  at high altitude 194
  boom in curry houses 191
  huge 168
  image of child's face on oven door 178
  in prison 194
  in underground bunker 194
  underwater 194
Reynolds, James (U.K.) 213
rice paddies, as art works 208
Rich, Lucky Diamond 15, *15*

Richardson, Orville (U.S.A.) 24
Richardson, Shauna (U.K.) 200, *200*
Riches, Peter (U.K.) 208
Richet, Charles (Fra) 176
Riedel, Peter (Can) 216, 219
Ringling Brothers Circus 116–17
rings
  found in city dump 14
  soccer player loses finger 99, *99*
Ripley, Robert (U.S.A.) 6, *6*, 162
Ripley's museums
  list of 255
  South Korea 6, *6*
Risuddin, Muhammad Akbar (Idn) 118
Ritson, Boo (U.K.) 201, *201*
rivers
  catches fire 40
  crossed by amphibious bicycle 135
  flows backward after earthquake 44
  motorized bathtub on Amazon 160
  natural logjam 41
  swimming down 94
  turns red 54, *54*
roadkill
  hats made of 222
  no-parking lines painted over 16, *16*
  trying to resuscitate 241
robbers
  blood found in leech 24
  dressed as Darth Vader 20
  photographs himself with stolen cell phone 14
Robbins, Todd (U.S.A.) 110
Robert, François (Swi) 212
Robinson, Blake (U.S.A.) 20
Robinson, Margaret Ann (U.S.A.) 168
robots
  conducts wedding 229
  jellyfish 228
  Olympic Games for 228
  skiing 227
Rocca, Max (Arg) 52
rocket, soldier impaled on 121
rocking horse, enormous 212
rocks
  ringing 176
  as sculpture 216, 219
Rodin, Auguste (Fra)
  coffee version of *The Thinker* 200
  electrical version of *The Thinker* 152, *152*
Rodriguez, Jamasen (U.S.A.) 169
Roentgen, Wilhelm (Ger) 122
Roger, Patrick (Fra) 187
Rogozov, Leonid (Rus) 226, *226*
roller coasters
  multiple rides on 242
  non-sick breakfast to eat before 193
rolling, traveling by 240
Romano, Charles (U.S.A.) 165, *165*
Romero, Jordan (U.S.A.) 157
rope, sleeping on 124
Roper, Chris (U.K.) 237
Roper, Sylvester H. (U.S.A.) 115, 136
Rossellini, Isabella (Ita) 210
Rouget de Lisle, Claude-Joseph (Fra) 203
rowing, across Atlantic Ocean 94, 96
Roy, Alan (U.K.) 170
royalty, house turned into museum of 238
rubber bands, very long chain of 157
Rubik's cube
  replica of *The Last Supper* 208
  skydiver solves 156
  solving in shark tank 160
Ruck, Dean (U.S.A.) 43, *43*
running
  across deserts 94
  backward 153
  blind sprinter 97
  in bomb suit 153
  long run on treadmill 121
  lunge running 169
  in stilettos 160
  with tumble-drier on back 93
Russev, Radoslav (Bul) 203
Ryan, Anna (U.S.A.) 112

sadhus, Hindu 158–9, *158–9*
Sadler, Jason (U.S.A.) 238
safety pin, in esophagus 122
Sakata, Harold (U.S.A.) 91
salamanders, giant 78
salami, enormous 194, *194*
salsa, enormous bowl of 187
Samuelson, Max (U.S.A.) 141

San Francisco, toothpick model of 221
Sanchez, Prax (U.S.A.) 113
sand
  enormous sandstorm 48–9, 49
  giant artwork on beach 214
  giant sculpture 215
  skiing on 96, 96
Sands, Chris (U.K.) 128
Sangermano, Darco (Ita) 126
Santoro, Pietro (U.S.A.) 240
sari, very valuable 212
Sarkadi, Sandor (Hun) 120, 120
Sasuphan, Supatra (Tha) 128–9, 129
Satan, image of appears on bathroom tile 16
Saturn, new ring found round 53
Saurin, Victor (Fra) 89
sausage machine, man sucked into 194
sausages, giant barbecue 191
Saxena, Bhagat (Ind) 193
Sayeg, Magda (U.S.A.) 201
Saylors, J.T. 165, 165–6
Schauerman, Chris 80
Schmidt, Agnes (Ger) 163, 163
schools
  actor in pirate costume 28
  built on mountainside 52
  elderly pupil 24
  flying to 140
  oil wells under 48
  prisoner mascot 43
Schrenk-Notzing, Baron Albert von (Ger) 177
Schuyff, Peter (Nld) 87, 87
Schwartz, Yitta (U.S.A.) 16
Schwarzenegger, Arnold (U.S.A.) 103, 103
scorpions, eating live 187
Scott, Matthew 31
Scott, Robert Falcon (U.K.) 190
screws, mosaic made from 216
sculpture
  adhesive tape jellyfish 202, 202
  bacon head 191, 191
  beard as 21, 21
  chocolate train 218
  cremation ashes 206
  discarded clothing 213, 213
  driftwood 35, 35
  enormous hammock 206
  giant sand sculpture 215
  hair clippings and chewing gum 210, 210
  houses as 43, 43
  inflated animal skins 198–9, 198–9
  junk plastic 218, 218–19
  margarine 186, 188, 188
  miniature clay models of food 220
  miniature tiger 208
  mistaken for log pile 217
  nativity scene on head of a pin 209
  old car parts 214
  old tires 214, 214
  pencil tips 208–9, 209
  phone book 217
  pistol puzzle 219
  rocks 216, 219
  shopping carts 212, 212
  teeth 222
  Terminator 103, 103
  Transformer made from cars 225, 225
  trash 203, 203–5
  tree sculpture from appliances 210
sea slug, uses solar power 230
sea urchins, vision 72
seals, collapsible lungs 62
seasickness, permanent 115
seeds, porcelain replicas 218
Selak, Frano (Cro) 244
Selogie, Cameron (S.A.) 195
Sena, Shiv (Ind) 120
Senturk, Metin (Tur) 157
Sepulveda, Lilian (U.S.A.) 16
Serra, Kitten Kay (U.S.A.) 238
sewage, music helps bacteria work faster 50
Sewell, Dr. William H. (U.S.A.) 230
sewers
  bagpipes frighten rats 234
  concerts in 219
  fat removed from 38
  python lives in 80

sharks
  beaten off with boogie board 107
  dried sharks for sale 240, 240
  guitar played to 203
  shark bites shark 79
  solving Rubik's cube in tank of 160
  surfer rides on 63
  swallows turtle 72
  woman escapes from 74
Sharma, Vijay (Ind) 122
Shaw, Justin (U.S.A.) 25
sheep
  burpless 75
  feeding curry to 187
  ram runs amok in house 72
  shrinking 60
  two-legged lamb 60, 60
Sheldon, Adam (U.K.) 183, 183
Shepard, Tyler (U.S.A.) 141, 141
Shepherd, Ernestine (U.S.A.) 124
Shi Tuanjie (Chn) 242, 242
Shibata, Tomohiro (Jap) 229
Shield, Arne (U.S.A.) 32
Shields, Kevin (U.K.) 108
Shimansky, Yair (S.A.) 128
shipwrecks
  ancient computer found in 178
  champagne found in 195
  still leaking oil 142
  watch found in 20
Sho Lau (Twn) 74
shoes
  bird wears slippers 66
  chocolate 190
  elephant-dung platforms 207, 207
  long line of sneakers 239
  money hidden in 15
  race in stilettos 160
  stolen 20
  unusual shapes 206
  very ancient 220
  wearing sneakers for four years 238
Shoffner, Roy (U.S.A.) 133
Shoppach, Kelly (U.S.A.) 98, 98
shopping carts, sculpture from 212, 212
Shoudt, "Humble" Bob (U.S.A.) 188
showers, singing in banned 20
Sibley, Dave (U.K.) 15, 15
sidewalks, heated 54
Sidorkin, Artyom (Rus) 121, 121
Silva, Elisany (Bra) 126, 126
Simmons, Erica (U.S.A.) 197, 197
Simnett, George (U.K.) 242
Simonov, Vasily (Rus) 114
Simpson, Sharon (U.K.) 54
Sinclair, Kat (U.K.) 213
Singapore, land reclamation 39
Singh, Frail Than (Ind) 28
Singh, Manjit (U.K.) 237
Singh, Sardar Pishora (Ind) 25
Singlee, the "Fireproof Man" 163, 163
sinkholes
  camel falls into 73
  opens up in yard 243, 243
  swallows factory 54
Sinnadurai, Nesan (U.S.A.) 97
Siwanowicz, Igor (Ger) 78, 78
skateboarding
  by dog 76
  by priest 240
  giant skateboard 156, 156
  injuries 99
skeletons
  chapel decorated with bones 50
  continuous growth 114
  guest of honor 241, 241
skiing
  robot 227
  on sand 96, 96
skin
  lightning patterns on 118, 118
  scaly growths on 119
  very stretchy 163, 163
Skinner, William (U.K.) 187
skulls
  chocolate 190, 190
  festival of 39, 39
  found in pond 40
  X-ray of Einstein's 122
skydiving
  by dogs 60

skydiving (cont.)
  escapologist 154–5, 154–5
  in kayak 94
  landing on Mount Everest 152
  legless champion 123
  parachute fails to open 115
  solving Rubik's cube 156
  surviving falls 107
Sleeman, Kris (U.S.A.) 236, 236
sleep
  hat to wake up sleepy drivers 236
  man sleeps through house fire 16
  narcolepsy 127
  sleeping on rope 124
  sleepwalker overeats 112
  standing man 158, 158
slot machines, rabbit plays 78
small people 124, 124, 126
  at Chicago World's Fair 168
  "Major Mite" 116–17, 116–17
  teenager 115
Smeathers, Gill (U.K.) 17
Smith, Paul (U.K.) 53
Smith, Paul (U.S.A.) 222
Smith, Reynolds Jr. (U.S.A.) 15
Smith, Rick Jr. (U.S.A.) 171
Smith, Simon (U.K.) 186
Smith, Tim (U.K.) 97
Smith family (U.K.) 157
smoking
  chimpanzee's problem 66
  exploding cigarette 110
  snake's habit 74
Smoltz, John (U.S.A.) 93
Smyth, Jason (Irl) 97
snails
  medicinal uses 241
  named after Steve Irwin 64
  speed 78
snakes
  antivenom 124
  fishermen catch python 61
  kissing cobras 241, 241
  new species of chameleon found in snake's mouth 78
  in nose 237
  python as assault weapon 238
  python lives in sewer 80
  python moves into rabbit hutch 61
  python trapped in washing machine 61
  python tries to catch marsupial 61, 61
  "Serpent Queen" 156, 156
  smoking habit 74
  smuggled onto ferry 244
  two-headed 67
  X-rays of python digesting a rat 228–9, 229
snow
  castle built of 242
  debt paid with snowball 50
  in desert for first time 44
  heated sidewalks 54
  over whole U.S.A. 41
  prevented from falling on Moscow 48
  purple snow 54
  snowball kept in freezer 54
snowshoe, beard woven to resemble 113
Soares, Hazel (U.S.A.) 149
soccer
  elderly coach retires 96
  executive box decorated like Gothic chapel 97
  fan flies long distances 97
  goalkeeper dislocates jaw 97
  goalkeeper drops aftershave on foot 92
  player breaks leg 100, 100–1
  player loses finger 99, 99
  soccer jersey tattoo 96, 96
  visiting every ground in England and Wales 96
softball, injuries 99
soil, eating 187, 192, 192
solar eclipses 52
solar power, sea slug uses 230
Somers, Wieki (Nld) 206
souls, sold online 28
sound, speed of 228
Space Shuttle, urine jettisoned from 49
Spak, Andres (Nor) 95, 95
Sparrow, Lucy (U.K.) 214

species, large number found in national park 49
speech, stroke damage 113
spiders
  as alien monsters 65, 65
  ancient fossil found 61
  barbed hairs 79
  eating 195
  enormous web 38, 38
  raid other spiders' webs 63
  smuggled onto ferry 244
  survival dance 63
  vegetarian 64
spitting, cricket-spitting contest 238
Spock, Dr Benjamin (U.S.A.) 91
spontaneous human combustion 179, 179
spoons
  Christmas tree made of 219
  prisoner digs out of prison with 20
sports
  most dangerous 99
  Olympic Games 88–91
  Olympic Games for robots 228
Spotz, Katie (U.S.A.) 94
Sprague, Erik (U.S.A.) 8, 8
Springer, Jim (U.S.A.) 25
spying, pigeon arrested for 82
squatter, awarded valuable piece of land 47
squid
  fossilized ink 83
  giant 70
  with human teeth 73, 73
Stadelbacher, Mary (U.S.A.) 61
Stanislawa P. (Pol) 177, 177
Stansfield, Jem (U.K.) 171
Star Wars
  bank robber dressed as Darth Vader 20
  tattoos 119
starfish, large numbers found on beach 49
stars
  huge star discovered 48
  rays from switch on fair lights 168
  supernova discovered 52
Stassart, Gilles (Fra) 186
statues
  drinking milk 178
  large collection of cat statues 169
  lightning strikes Statue of Liberty 40, 40
steak, huge 195
steam-powered bicycle 136
Steele, Tony (U.S.A.) 169
Stender, Paul (U.S.A.) 136, 136
Stephens, Olga Worth (U.S.A.) 179
Stepney, Alex (U.K.) 97
steps, cycling up 93, 93
Stevens, Jean (U.S.A.) 29
stilettos, race in 160
stilts, long walk on 148, 148
stinkbugs, infestation of 79
Stinson, Chris (U.S.A.) 243
stomach
  chopstick in 122
  coins swallowed 121
  cutlery removed from 191, 191
  hairball removed from 192
  magnets in dog's 79
  metal removed from 108
  music broadcast from 219
  parasitic twin removed from 118
  toothbrush removed from 121
stone, mysterious 180
store, bear walks into 60
stork, romantic attachment 83
Storm, Jason and Rachael (U.S.A.) 242
Stowe, Reid (U.S.A.) 134
Straitjacket, David (U.K.) 147
Strati, Saimir (U.S.A.) 216
stroke
  Botox cures 122
  singing after 113
  writing after 121
stroller, dog pushes 70
submarines
  canal boat converted into 235
  homemade 136
  loses torpedo 137
subway
  boy hides on 244
  pushing people onto 237
Sukegawa, Naoko (Jap) 188, 188

Sun
  eclipses 52
  giant neutrino detector 231, 231
  hydrogen content 52
Sun Fengqin (Mon) 122
sunbed, tanning artwork 201
Suppes, Mark (U.S.A.) 229
surfing
  Gaza Strip club 92
  marathon session 93, 93
surgery
  doctor operates on himself 226, 226
  plasma knife 227
  prenatal 109
  in Stone Age 227
Susanto, Andi (Idn) 110
sushi roll, giant 188
Sutcliffe, Dean (U.K.) 32
Suzuki, Yasuhiro (Jap) 142, 142
Sveden, Ron (U.S.A.) 110
swans
  fidelity to partners 62
  knocks rider off motorcycle 81
swimming
  across icy lake 107
  down river 94
  floating for long time 152, 152
  injuries 99
  obstacle race 90
  Olympic Games 88, 90
  underwater 90
swords, swallowing 165, 166
Szabo, Tibor (Can) 72, 72
Szymcakowi, Andrzej (Pol) 78

T-shirts
  covered in manure 213
  enormous 209
  promoting businesses 238
  wearing multiple 152
Tabary, Frederick (Fra) 50
tail, baby with 109
Takács, Károly (Hun) 89
Takáts, Pál (Hun) 243
tall people 114
  teenagers 126, 126, 128
  very tall thin man 114, 114
Tamas, Agnes (Hun) 79
tanks, inflatable 143, 143
tanning artwork 201
Tao Xiangli (Chn) 136
tape cassette art 197, 197
Tarasewicz, Leon (Pol) 206
Tarescu, Calin (Rom) 15
Tattersall, Mary (U.K.) 92
tattoos
  celebrity pictures 113
  celebrity signatures 110
  connect-the-dots 128, 128
  designer logos on pigs 201
  diamonds in 128
  entire body covered in 15, 15, 107, 107, 111, 111, 125, 125
  gold 124
  Latin inscriptions 128
  marriage proposal on leg 128
  on mummy 22, 22
  over long period 110
  Route 66 110
  soccer jersey tattoo 96, 96
  Star Wars 119
  tattooed ladies 26–7, 26–7
taxis
  dog knows routes 78
  driven backward 142
  driver left legacy by grateful passenger 141
Taylor, Kim (U.K.) 126
Taylor, Martin (U.K.) 100, 100–1
tea
  amount drunk in U.K. 190
  very expensive 190
teapots, large collection of 149
tears
  astronauts 50
  bees drink 85
  weeping crystals 177
Tebow, Tim (U.S.A.) 212
teddy bears
  adults take to bed 244
  bear steals 83

teddy bears (cont.)
made of belly button fluff 108, *108*
teeth
Churchill's false teeth 119
determining age from 115
dog with two rows of 67
false teeth in lung 121
filed to sharp points 119, *119*
mass extraction of 124
miniature sculptures made with 222
Teh, Mui-Ling (Can) 206
telephone booths
as entertainments center 208
living in 234
telephones
Alexander Graham Bell's funeral 227
cell phones in India 53
dress used as cell phone 220
driving car with cell phone app 226
iPhone first-aid app used in earthquake
123
large number in Pentagon 47
911 called after marriage refusal 29
stolen cell phone bought back by
owner 17
thief photographs himself with stolen
cell phone 14
unlucky cell phone number 28
vicar blesses cell phones 242
telescope, mercury mirror 227
temperature, salt water 41
tennis
multiple double faults 94
opponents bang heads 92
played on train 92
very long match 96
tents
giant 42
woman lives on traffic circle in 54
Terren, Dr. Peter (Aus) 152, *152*
testicles, cooking 190
text messages, huge number sent 149
Thavorn, Kamjai Khong (Tha) 16
Theodosius, Emperor 88
Theremin, Léon (Rus) 202
thermometer, giant 168, *168*
Thomas, Prena (U.S.A.) 54
Thompson, Don (U.K.) 90
Thornhill, Jesse (U.S.A.) 122
thumb, found inside fish 20
Thunberg, Nick (U.S.A.) 110
Thurman, Uma (U.S.A.) 208
Thuy, Nguyen Thu (Vnm) 207
tickets, models made from 216
Tierney, J.G. and Patrick (U.S.A.) 234
tigers
dog disguised as 73, *73*
lives with bear and lion 66, *66*
miniature sculpture of 208
tightrope walking over 169, *169*
tightrope walking
at great heights 97, *97*
by goat 81
over long period 160
over tiger enclosure 169, *169*
on top of skyscraper 169
time zones, multiple in Russia 54
Timilsina, Rohit (Nep) 169
Tipler, Matthew (U.S.A.) 122
Tiralosi, Joseph (U.S.A.) 124
tires, animal sculptures 214, *214*
Tiririca (Bra) 235
Titman, Nancy (U.K.) 187
Titterton, James (U.K.) 201
toads, leather from 78, *78*
toast, portrait made of 218
toddlers, very large 114, *114*, 121
toe, run over by forklift 7, *7*
Tohak, Bob (U.S.A.) 181
toilets
arm stuck in 244
bionic bottom 114
John Lennon's 25
motorized 134
plant toilet for treeshrews 62, *62*
tour of in Berlin 50
Tolaas, Sissel (Nor) 206
tomb, BMW-shaped 243
Tompert, Michael (U.S.A.) 217, *217*
tongue
blowtorch on 19, *19*
chameleons 67
dog with swollen tongue 77
lifting weights with 164, *164*

tongue (cont.)
very long 105, *105*
toothbrush, removed from stomach 121
toothpicks
model of San Francisco 221
very valuable 238
torpedo, submarine loses 137
tortoises
cesarean birth for eggs 80
extinct species re-created 80
long-lost 66
oxygen masks save 82
tortoise in love with plastic tortoise 85
Tosches, Daniel (U.S.A.) 217
towel, enormous 153
tower, weight of 42
Townshend, Pete (U.K.) 215
tractor-trailer limo 140, *140*
tractors
at funeral 32
police use 137
Tracy, Craig (U.S.A.) 12, *12–13*
traffic circle, woman lives in tent on 54
traffic jam, enormous 235
traffic violations, multiple fines for 135
trains
chocolate sculpture of 218
dog survives being hit twice 64
earthquake twists tracks 52, *52*
hotel room for train lovers 43
locomotive crashes out of station 137,
137
models made from tickets 216
tennis played on 92
toddler survives on track 105
trampolines
injuries 99
pig on 76
tramway, aerial 168, *168*
transplants
face 123
hand grafted onto leg 229, *229*
trapeze artist, elderly 169
Trappe, Jonathan R. (U.S.A.) 149, *149*
Traver, David (U.S.A.) 113
treadmill, long run on 121
trees
adorned with knitting 210
floating stump in lake 41
flowers only once 49
images projected onto 174, *174*
living in 39
quantities of paper used for books 213
survives hurricanes 50
tree pods 178, *178*
very dense wood 44
very smelly 41
woman impaled on 120
Tripathi, Ramesh (Ind) 152
Tripp, Charles B. (U.S.A.) 106, *106*
trucks
child drives long distance 141
dog drives over owner 241
hat to wake up sleepy drivers 236
meteorite hits 49
Trueman, Chris (U.S.A.) 58–9, *58–9*
Truhanova, Irina (Lat) 222
Tsonga, Jo-Wilfried (Fra) 92
tug-of-war
hand pulled off in 109
Olympic Games 90
tumors
on back 122, 124
enormous 120
tuna, very expensive 195
Tunick, Spencer (U.S.A.) 201
tunnels
man digs through mountain 54
man rescued from collapsed 15
network suddenly appears 174
under Paris 51, *51*
very long 50
turtles
eaten by fish 70
eggs in fossil 80
shark swallows 72
tusks, enormous 72
twins
huge family 108
identical twins in set of quadruplets 118
lead parallel lives 25
marry twins 28
parasitic 108, 118
"snake babies" 105

Twitter, help for round-the-world traveler
53
Twyman, Mrs Baker B. (U.S.A.) 126, *126*
tycoon, boy pretends to be 238
typewriters, pictures made with 201, 222

U.F.O.s
April Fool's hoax 181
landing port built for 181
pilot's close encounter with 181
Roswell Incident 181, *181*
ukelele players, mass gathering 214
umbrellas, mass dance with 171
underground apartment 44
underwear
made from bananas 190
wearing multiple pairs of underpants
170, *170*
unicycles, motorized 141
Universe, color of 227
urine
astronauts' 49
drinking 192
whisky made from 193
uteruses, woman with two 108

vacuum cleaners
climbing wall using 171
large collection of 237
Vaidya, Shripad (Ind) 214
vampire, blamed for car accident 236
van Dijk, Ria (Nld) 217
Van Gogh, Vincent (Nld) 203
Veal, Alan (U.K.) 194
vegetables, fear of 193
Veitch, Rachel (U.S.A.) 141
Venable, Colleen A.F. 128, *128*
vending machines
for gold bars 47
live crabs sold by 242, *242*
selling artworks 243
Venus de Milo, panda-dung replica 218
Verdasco, Fernando (Spa) 92
Vetrogonov, Sergiy (Ukr) 152
Vicentini, Tiziano (Ita) 189
Victoria, Queen 31
video game, marriage proposal in 241
Viking ship burial 32
Viljanen, Jouni (Fin) 94
Vincent, Pat (U.K.) 32
vineyard, baboons eat all grapes 66
Vinod, Varsha (Ind) 169
Viola, Lady (U.S.A.) 26, *26*
violins
enormous 208
fungal treatment for wood 230
Viskum, Morten (Nor) 213, *213*
volcanoes
constant eruptions 36, *36*, 37
cooking on 194, *194*
huge river of lava 37
living close to 37
mud volcano 44
opens rift in desert 39
power of 37
rapid growth of 37
Ring of Fire 52
sole survivor of 37
speed of lava 37
speed of pyroclastic flows 53
sunlight blocked by eruption 37
toxic gases from 48
underwater 37, 40
Vormann, Jan (Ger) 210
Voutsinas, Alex and Donna (U.S.A.) 20
vultures
flies into helicopter 81
medicinal uses for brains 118
vuvuzela horns
giant 201
gold and diamond 214

Wadile, Dhranraj (Ind) 120, *120*
Wainwright, Alfred (U.K.) 148
wakeboarding marathon 92
Wales, Don (U.K.) 160
walking
on all fours 159, *159*
hospitality for long-distance walkers 169
rotating feet 109
Wall of Death 150–1, *150–1*
Wallace, Amanda Kay (U.S.A.) 7, *7*
Walloch, Sasha (U.S.A.) 219
walls, ancient 181

Wang Liping (Chn) 89
Wang Wenxi (Chn) 230
Wang Xianjun (Chn) 120
Wang Xiaoyu (Chn) 236
Wang Xihai (Chn) 84, *84*
Wangenheim, Konrad von (Ger) 89
Warboys, Owen (U.K.) 141
Ward, Lydia (Nzl) 107
Warner, Carl (U.K.) 218
warthog, plane hits 140
washing machines
kitten survives in 75
for pets 82
python trapped in 61
Washington, George (U.S.A.), library
fines 203
wasps
giant nest 67
woman survives multiple stings 62
waterfalls
blind abseiler 97
frozen 95, *95*
Niagara Falls stopped 52, *52*
paddling kayak over 239
racing over on airbeds 94, *94*
Watkins, Barbara (U.K.) 126
Watkins, Jack (U.K.) 15, *15*
Watkins, Perry (U.K.) 235
Watson, Jessica (Aus) 92
Watson, Mary (U.K.) 141
Weaver, Jordan (U.S.A.) 208
Weaver, Scott (U.S.A.) 221
Webster, Katy (U.K.) 222
weddings
dogs get married 72
elderly couple 32
family all marry in same church 32
in funeral home 242
groom arrives in coffin 32
large age gap between couple 32
marriage to cat 80
marrying pillow 244
mobile chapel 243
robot conducts 229
twins marry twins 28
virtual bride 32
weights
elderly body-builder 124
lifting with eyelids 237
lifting human pyramid 237, *237*
lifting with mouth 92, *92*
lifting with tongue 164, *164*
pulling plane with eyelids 170
pulling with hair 237
pulling with nipples 163, *163*
running in bomb suit 153
running marathon with tumble-drier on
back 93
very small weightlifter 110
very strong grandmother 148
young weightlifter 114
Weissmuller, Johnny (U.S.A.) 91
well, very old 244
Welles, Orson (U.S.A.) 234
Werstler, Heidi Kay (U.S.A.) 20
whales
friendship with 63, *63*
funeral for 79
jumps onto yacht 80, *80–1*
paintings by 80
strange monster found on beach 180,
180
wheelbarrow, human 152
wheelchairs
crossing U.S. in 153
wheelies in 149
Wheeler, Vivian (U.S.A.) 29, *29*
whisky, made from urine 193
Whistler, J.A.M. (U.S.A.) 200
whistles, blown at litterbugs 43
White, Ron (U.S.A.) 171
Whitfield, Sandra (U.K.) 218
whittling 164, *164*
Williams, Andrew (U.K.) 62
Williams, Gareth (U.K.) 210
Williams, Janet and Philip (Aus) 238
Williamson, Mrs. Charles (U.S.A.) 179
Willis, Tom (U.S.A.) 110
Winchester, Jeanna (U.S.A.) 179
windows, speed cleaning 171
winds
blows dog and kennel away 79
speed in cyclone 49
very windy planet 48

Wiser, I.M. (U.S.A.) 20, *20*
Wiser, May B. (U.S.A.) 20, *20*
Wittenberg, Joe (U.S.A.) 128
wolverine, last in California 83
Wong, Howard (Mal) 223
wood
bicycle made of 141
chain carved from 220
eating 192
hats 219
Woodbury, Avie (Nzl) 28
Woods, William (Can) 244
Woodward, Irene (U.S.A.) 26, 27, *27*
Woolford, Geraint (U.K.) 20
Woolley, Dan (U.S.A.) 123
World War I, debt finally paid 16
World War II
deceptions 17, 143, *143*
lost battle site found 17
worms
in eye 127
very long intestinal 107
wrap, enormous sandwich 195
wrestling
Olympic Games 88, 89
one-legged wrestler 93
very successful school 96
Wright, Elsie (U.K.) 175, *175*
Wright, Everton (U.K.) 214
Wright, Hayley and Matthew (U.K.) 70
writing, after stroke 121
Wu Kang (Chn) 124, *124*

X-rays
of foreign bodies 122, *122–3*
python digesting a rat 228–9, *229*
Xia Xiao Wan (Chn) 207
Xiao Hao (Chn) 121
Xiao Lin (Chn) 244
Xiao Qiang (Chn) 80
Xiao Wei (Chn) 118
Xie Quiping (Chn) 25

Yang Guanghe (Chn) 237
Yang Jian (Chn) 28
Yang Kang (Chn) 28
Yang Maoyuan (Chn) 198, *198–9*
Yang Shaofu (Chn) 85
yo-yos, spinning multiple 148
yoga
bear's routine 76
elderly teacher 156
instructions on parking tickets 235
Yon, Michael (U.S.A.) 136, *136*
Young, Dorena (U.S.A.) 239
Yunusov, Muhammad (Kyr) 119

Zable, Mark (U.S.A.) 195
Zapata, Javier (Col) 93
zebras, camouflage 81
Zessin, Ellen (U.S.A.) 70
Zhang Lanxiang (Chn) 28
Zhang Ruifang (Chn) 115
Zhao Shuangzhan (Chn) 20
Zhou, Peter (Sgp) 207
Zhou Guanshun (Chn) 80
Zhou Yuqin (Chn) 192, *192*
Zhu, Mr. (Chn) 192, *192*
Zhu Cheng (Chn) 218
Zhu Xinping (Chn) 108
Ziegler, Robert (Swi) 137
Zimmerman, Richard "Dugout Dick"
(U.S.A.) 240
zipper, boat looks like 142, *142*
Zolotaya, Elena (Rus) 213
zoos
animal escape drill 60, *60*
baboon sells tickets 61

Page 9 (c) Getty Images; 12–13 Pictures courtesy of Craig Tracy; 14 (t) Getty Images; 15 (t) Honda Motor Europe Ltd, (l) Chin Boon Leng, (r) Reuters/Will Burgess; 16 (t/l, t/r) Reuters/Reinhard Krause, (b/l) Collect/PA Wire/Press Association Images; 17 Getty Images; 18-19 Alex Smith - www.as-images.com; 21 (t) Jagdeep Rajput/Solent, (b) Theo Stroomer/Demotix; 22 (l) EPA/Photoshot, (t/r) National Geographic/Getty Images; (b/r) Robyn Beck/AFP/Getty Images; 23 (t/l) SSPL via Getty Images, (t/r) Stephen L. Alvarez/National Geographic/Getty Images, (b) Jae C. Hong/AP/Press Association Images; 24 (t) The Cheeky/Rex Features, (b/l, b/r) wenn.com; 25 (b) Barcroft Media; 26 (t/r, t/l) Getty Images, (b) From the John and Mable Ringling Museum of Art Tibbals Digital Collection; 27 (c, t/r) Charles Eisenmann Collection/University of Syracuse, (b) Used with permission from Illinois State University's Special Collections, Milner Library; 28 (t) APOPO, (b/l) © EuroPics[CEN], (b/r) KeystoneUSA-ZUMA/Rex Features; 29 (t/l, t/r) © EuroPics[CEN]; 30 From the John and Mable Ringling Museum of Art Tibbals Digital Collection; 31 (b/r) Collection of the John and Mable Ringling Museum of Art Archives, (b/l, t/l, t/r) From the John and Mable Ringling Museum of Art Tibbals Digital Collection; 32 (l) Ross Parry Agency, (r) Caters News Agency; 33 Daniel Ortega; 36 (b) J.D. Griggs/US Geological Survey/Rex Features, (t) David Jordan/AP/Press Association Images; 37 (c/l) Ethel Davies/Robert Harding/Rex Features, (b/l, b/r) EPA/Photoshot; 38 (t) Donna Garde, TPWD, (b/r) John Terning, (b/l) Carl McCabe, 39 (t, b) LatinContent/Getty Images; 40–41 Massimo Brega, The Lighthouse/Science Photo Library, 40 (t, r) Jay Fine/Caters News; 41 (b) Apex; 42 www.Freitag.ch; 43 (t) Photo by Havel Ruck Projects, "Inversion". 2005, (demolished), Dan Havel & Dean Ruck, Site-specific sculptural installation, Art League Houston, Houston, Texas, (b) Imagine China; 44 (t) Tsuzuki Minako, (b) Reuters; 45 Dmitry Dudin; 46 Bloomberg via Getty Images; 47 (t/l) Alain Van de Maele, (b) Tom Mackie/Photolibrary; 48–49 ChinaFotoPress/Photocome/Press Association Images; 50 Specialist Stock/Barcroft Media ltd; 51 Will Hunt; 52 (t) © Russ Glasson/Barcroft USA, (c) © Vladone/istockphoto.com, (b) Malcolm Teasdale/KiwiRail; 53 (l) Mark Duncan/AP/Press Association Images, (r) U.S. Coast Guard photo by Petty Officer 2nd Class Lauren Jorgensen; 54 (t/l, t/r) Solent News/Rex Features, (b) EPA/Photoshot; 55 © Hulton-Deutsch Collection/Corbis; 58–59 Chris Trueman/Alexander Salazar Gallery; 60 (b) © Europics [CEN], (t/l, t/c, t/r) Reuters/Michael Caronna; 61 (r) Wenn.com; 62 (t) © Ch'ien C. Lee, (b) R. Roscoe (photovolcanica.com); 63 (t) © Barcroft Pacific, (b) Mark Moffett/Minden Pictures/FLPA; 64 (t/l, t/r) Caters News, (b) Nicole Kane; 65 (t/l) Caters News, (sp) Tomas Rak/Solent News/Rex Features; 66 (b/l) www.noahs-ark.org, (b) Barcroft Media ltd; 67 (t) © Stuart Isett/Anzenberger represented by: Eyevine; 68–69 Ingo Arndt/Nature Picture Library; 70 (t/l) Dr Richard Kirby/BNPS, (t/r) Conny Sandland/Rex Features, (b/l) Caters News; 71 Caters News; 72 (b/l) Tibo Szabo, Sue Lees, Photographer Michael Orescanin; 73 (b/l, b/r) China Foto Press/Barcroft Media ltd, (b/c) © Alex Potemkin/istockphoto.com, (t/r) Richard Young; 74 (t) Luke Marsden/Newspix/Rex Features, (b) Armin Weigel/DPA/Press Association Images; 75 Rossparry.co.uk/syndication/Doncaster Free Press; 76 (t) M & Y Agency Ltd/Rex Features; 77 (t) Jonathan Pow/Ross Parry Agency; 78 (t) www.toadfactory.com, (b/l) Igor Siwanowicz/Barcroft Media ltd; 79 Reuters/Wolfgang Rattay; 80 (t) Quirky China News/Rex Features, (b) James Dagmore/Polaris/Eyevine; 81 (b) James Dagmore/Polaris/Eyevine, (t) Chrissy Harris/APN; 82 (t) www.sell-my-photo.co.uk, (b) © Johann Opperman/solentnews.co.uk; 83 Image courtesy of Expedition to the Deep Slope 2006 Exploration, NOAA Vents Program; 84 Quirky China News/Rex Features; 85 (c) Luis Fernando Espin/Rex Features, (t) Karen Bacon/Solent News/Rex Features, (b) Michael Cenci/Solent News/Rex Features; 87 Peter Schuyff; 88–89 © dtimiraos/iStockphoto.com; 90–91 © -M-I-S-H-A- / iStockphoto.com; 92 © Akintunde Akinleye/Reuters/Corbis; 93 (t) AP Photo/Luis Benavides; (c/l, b/l, b/r) Swell.com; 94 (l) Iain Ferguson, The Write Image, (r) © Wifredo Garcia Alvaro/epa/Corbis; 95 Christian Pondella/Caters News; 96 (t) AFP/Getty Images, (b) Henrik May/ski-namibia.com; 97 (b) Jeffrey Cunningham; 98 (t) Harry Scull Jr./AP/Press Association Images, (b) Ron Jenkins/Fort Worth Star-Telegram/Polaris; 99 Eric Lafargue /www.LPS.ch/; 100 (b) Target Press/Barcroft Media ltd, (t) Stephen Pond/Empics Sport; 101 (t/l, t/r) Stephen Pond/Empics Sport, (b) Ryan Remiorz/AP/Press Association Images; 104 Sinopix/Rex Features; 105 (b/l, c) Nick Afanasiev, (t/r) Basit Umer/Barcroft Media ltd; 106 (t) Circus World Museum, Baraboo, Wisconsin; 107 (t) Dennis Van Tine/ABACA USA/Empics Entertainment, (b) Anders (The Piercing Guy) Allinger www.phatpiercings.com 108 (t) Chuck Nyce, (b) Quirky China News/Rex Features; 109 Reuters/China Daily China Daily Information Corp – CDIC; 110–111 Alan Humerose/Rezo.ch; 112 (t) Collection of Jack and Beverly Wilgus, (b) © Europics [CEN]; 113 Asha Mandela; 114 (t) Charles Eisenmann Collection/University of Syracuse, (b) Xinhua/Photoshot; 115 Christine Cornege/AP/Press Association Images; 117 (t/c) NY Daily News via Getty Images, (t/r) Getty Images; 118 (t) Image courtesy of the New England Journal of Medicine, (b) Steve Gschmeissner/Science Photo Library; 119 (t) Chad Grochowski (b) Bob Huberman; 120 (t) Quirky China News/Rex Features, (c/l, b/l) Tejnaksh Healthcare's Institute Of Urology, (b/r) EPA/Photoshot; 121 (b) Atlas Press/Eyevine; 122 (l) Science Photo Library, (r) Du Cane Medical Imaging ltd/Science Photo Library; 123 (l) Science Photo Library, (t/r) Scott Camazine/Science Photo Library, (b/r) Kaj R. Svensson/Science Photo Library; 124 (t) © Europics [CEN], (b/l, b/r) Pictures courtesy of Steve McFarlane; 125 Mario Rosenau/Bizarre archive/Dennis Publishing; 126 (t) Getty Images, (b) Reuters/Paulo Santos; 127 KPN India; 128 (t) Joey Miller; 132–133 Lou Sapienza/Polaris/Eyevine; 132 Philip Makanna/Polaris/Eyevine; 134 Barry Bland/Barcroft USA; 135 (b) Rex Features, (t) KPA/Zuma/Rex Features; 136 (t) Michael Yon, (b) Indy Boys Inc; 137 Roger Viollet/Getty Images; 138 (t) AP Photo, The Canadian Press, Lethbridge Herald, Ian Martens, (b) Gabriel Luque/Rex Features; 139 (t/l) AP Photo, The Canadian Press, Lethbridge Herald, Ian Martens, (t/r) Kurt Roy/Polaris/Eyevine, (b) Rob Yuill/Albanpix Ltd/Rex Features; 140 (t) David Drimmer, (b) www.themidnightrider.com; 141 (t) David Drimmer, (b) Pictures courtesy of Tyler Shepard sponsored by Dreyer Honda of Indianapolis, IN; 142 (t/l) Hannes Langeder/Rex Features, (t/r) Manfred Lang/Rex Features, (b) Wenn.com; 143 (t) East News/Rex Features, (b) Roger-Viollet/Rex Features; 146–147 Akash Awasthi; 148 (b) Edmond Hawkins, (t) Getty Images; 149 (r) Nick Obank/Barcroft Media ltd; 150 Courtesy of Cookie Crum; 151 (t) Reuters/Amit Gupta, (c) Reuters/Fayaz Kabli, (b) Getty Images; 152 (t) Nagananda Swamy, (b/l, b/r) www.tesladownunder.com; 153 (r) anthonyescapes.com, (b) Dan Callister/Rex Features; 154–155 anthonyescapes.com; 156 (t) Charles Eisenmann Collection/University of Syracuse, (b) Californiaskateparks.com; 157 Jayna Sullivan Photography; 158 (t/r) Raghu Rai/Rex Features, (b) Rajesh Kumar Singh/AP/Press Association Images; 159 Herbert Ponting; 160 Qiu xiaofeng/AP/Press Association Images; 161 © Swim Ink 2, LLC/Corbis; 163–166 (dp) Library of Congress; 168 (l) © Rykoff Collection/Corbis, (r) © Blue Lantern Studio/Corbis; 169 Quirky China News/Rex Features; 170 (t) The Shields Gazette, (b) EPA/Photoshot; 171 ChinaFotoPress/Photocome/Press Association Images; 174 (t) Ibon Mainar/Rex Features, (b) www.sell-my-photo.co.uk; 175 SSPL via Getty Images; 176 (t) Fortean Picture Library; 177 (t) Fortean Picture Library, (b) Courtesy of Donald Estes/Natchez Cemetery; 178 (t) Leon Shadeberg/Rex Features, (b) Courtesy of Caz Housey; 179 Fortean Picture Library; 180 (t) DeWitt Webb/www.cfz.org.uk, (b) Fortean Picture Library; 181 (t) Fortean Picture Library, (b) Tony O'Rahilly/Rex Features; 184–185 Zuma Press/Eyevine; 186 Paul Christoforou; 187 (t) Richard Jones/Sinopix/Rex Features, (b) Debbie Does Cakes/Rex Features; 188 Eddie Mitchell/Rex Features; 189(t) INS News Agency Ltd./Rex Features, (b) Kevin Le; 190 Marina Malvada/Rex Features; 191 (b) Annie B. Brady, (t) © EuroPics[CEN]; 192 ChinaFotoPress/Photocome/Press Association Images; 193 David Branfield www.davebranfield.com; 194 (t) Wenn.com, (b) Kristjan Logason/Demotix; 195 AFP/Getty Images; 198–199 Yang Maoyuan; 200 (t) Victor Liu/Solent News/Rex Features, (b) Images courtesy of Shauna Richardson; 201 Caters News; 202 Solent News/Rex Features; 203 (t/r) Kris Kuksi; 202–203 (b) Geoffrey Robinson/Rex Features; 204–205 Kris Kuksi; 206 Bernard Pras; 207 (t) Xia Xiao Wan, (b) Insaland.com; 208–209 Solent News/Rex features; 210 Getty Images; 211 (sp) Dr Rev Bloodpainter; (t) © Mafaldita/istockphoto.com; 212 Drew Gardner/Eyevine; 213 (t/r) Images courtesy of Morten Viskum and VEGAS gallery, London, (t/l) Guerra de la Paz; 214 Ji Yong-Ho/Solent/Rex Features; 215 LA Pop Art www.lapopart.com; 216 (l) Matthew Albanese, (t/l, r) matthewalbanese.com/Solent News/Rex Features; 217 Michael Tompert/Paul Fairchild/Rex Features; 218 Solent News/Rex Features; 219 Solent News/Rex Features; 220 www.grindshow.com; 221 (t) Fredo, (b) Nick Gentry/Barcroft Media ltd; 223 Ari Mahardhika/Solent News/Rex Features; 226 Pictures courtesy of Vladimir Rogozov; 227 Kai-Hung Fung/Barcroft Media ltd; 228–229 (t) Henrik Lauridsen, Kasper Hansen, Michael Pedersen and Tobias Wang; 228 (b) Focus/Eyevine; 229 (b) Quirky China News/Rex Features; 230 (t) Shizuo Kambayashi/AP/Press Association Images, (b) JPL/NASA; 231 Kamioka Observatory, ICRR (Institute for Cosmic Ray Research), The University of Tokyo; 234 © Illustrated London News Ltd/Mary Evans; 235 Quirky China News/Rex Features; 237 (t) © Europics [CEN], (b) Charles Eisenmann Collection/University of Syracuse; 239 (t) www.suzanneproulx.com; 240 Claire Carter; 241 © Bettmann/Corbis; 242 (t/l) Andy Willsheer/Rex Features, (c, b) Reuters/Sean Yong; 243 Quirky China News/Rex Features; 244 Quirky China News/Rex Features; 245 (t) Fabi Fliervoet/Solent News/Rex Features, (c/l) Flughafen Leipzig/Halle GmbH/DPA/Press Association Images, (b/l) Cover/Getty Images, (c/r) James D. Morgan/Rex Features, (b/r) Getty Images

Key: t = top, b = bottom, c = center, l = left, r = right, sp = single page, dp = double page.
All other photos are from Ripley Entertainment Inc. Every attempt has been made to acknowledge correctly and contact copyright holders and we apologize in advance for any unintentional errors or omissions, which will be corrected in future editions.

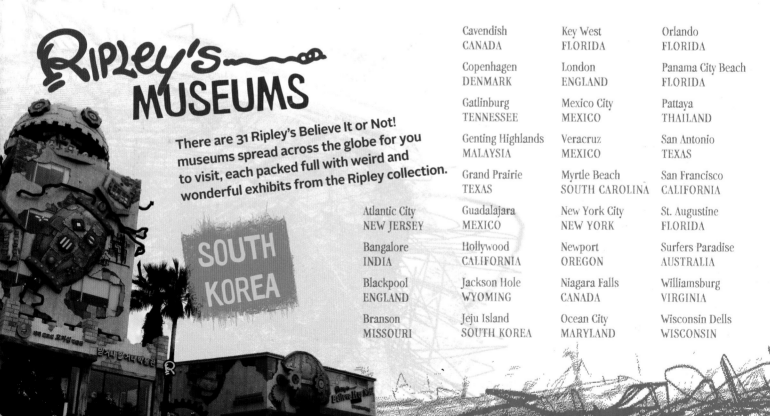

Ripley's MUSEUMS

There are 31 Ripley's Believe It or Not! museums spread across the globe for you to visit, each packed full with weird and wonderful exhibits from the Ripley collection.

Atlantic City NEW JERSEY

Bangalore INDIA

Blackpool ENGLAND

Branson MISSOURI

Cavendish CANADA

Copenhagen DENMARK

Gatlinburg TENNESSEE

Genting Highlands MALAYSIA

Grand Prairie TEXAS

Guadalajara MEXICO

Hollywood CALIFORNIA

Jackson Hole WYOMING

Jeju Island SOUTH KOREA

Key West FLORIDA

London ENGLAND

Mexico City MEXICO

Myrtle Beach SOUTH CAROLINA

New York City NEW YORK

Newport OREGON

Niagara Falls CANADA

Ocean City MARYLAND

Orlando FLORIDA

Panama City Beach FLORIDA

Pattaya THAILAND

San Antonio TEXAS

San Francisco CALIFORNIA

St. Augustine FLORIDA

Surfers Paradise AUSTRALIA

Veracruz MEXICO

Williamsburg VIRGINIA

Wisconsin Dells WISCONSIN

SOUTH KOREA

ANNUALS

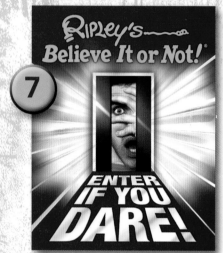

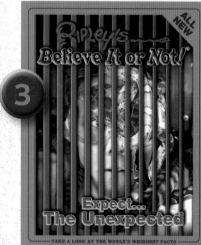